Published by BBC Worldwide Ltd
Series producers: Ray Butt and Gareth Gwenlan

First published 2000
Only Fools and Horses format and scripts © John Sullivan 2000
Additional material by Steve Clark
The moral right of the author has been asserted.

ISBN 0 563 55177 1

Published by BBC Worldwide Limited,
Woodlands, 80 Wood Lane, London W12 0TT

Commissioning Editor: Ben Dunn
Project Editor: Barnaby Harsent
Art Director: Linda Blakemore
Designed@Peacock

Photographs: © BBC

Set in Frutiger and Dom Casual by Keystroke, Jacaranda Lodge.

Printed and bound in Great Britain by Clays Ltd, St Ives plc

Also available:
The Only Fools and Horses Story ISBN: 0 563 38445 X
The Bible of Peckham Volume 1 ISBN: 0 563 55150 X

The Bible of Peckham

Volume 2

Written & Created by

★ ★ ★ JOHN ★ ★ ★

SULLIVAN

and ★NICHOLAS★ LYNDHURST

with
★ BUSTER ★
MERRYFIELD

8

 9

CONTENTS

SERIES SEVEN

SERIES SIX

Yuppy Love

INT. TROTTERS' LOUNGE. DAY

The Trotters' new dining suite is a bamboo and wickerwork affair with floral design cushions on the chairs (the kind of thing you'd expect to find in a conservatory).

Laying across the sofa and over the cocktail bar and hanging from the picture rail we have numerous beige trenchcoats.

Rodney, in his latest Jonathan Ross suit, is seated at the dining table working something out of the 'Rhaja' computer. He has a few note and reference books scattered over the table in amongst the salt and pepper pot, ketchup bottles and other dinner things.

Albert enters from kitchen carrying a plate of bread and butter.

Albert That's the way, Rodney. Don't bother helping me get the tea ready, you carry on poncing about with that computer.

Rodney I am not 'poncing about' with anything! In case it's slipped that senile, shrapnel-cluttered brain of yours, I happen to be studying for a computer diploma course.

Albert Oh I ain't forgotten, son. I remember you enrolling on a three-month course – two years ago!

Rodney It happens to be an extremely difficult exam!

Albert Well, you should know. You've failed it often enough.

Rodney I have not failed – well, not in the popular sense of the word. The other students have an advantage over me.

Albert: Yeah, they all pass.

Rodney I mean, they are sent to the evening college by their companies. All day long they are working with computers, knocking out data and programs, ain't they? Whereas all day long I am working with a suitcase, knocking out disposable lighters and Turkish raincoats!

Albert But even if you get your diploma, what difference will that make to Trotters Independent Traders?

Rodney I am not doing it for Trotters Independent Traders! I'm doing it for me! This diploma could be my passport to freedom, a decent job, a future! I mean, I can't go on for the rest of my life messing about with this sort of junk, can I? He wants me to stand in a market flogging raincoats with 'dry clean only' on the label! Puts the punters right off!

Rodney picks up one of the trenchcoats.

Albert Well, the way Del Boy was telling the other day, the future's never looked more promising.

Rodney Oh, Albert. That's all talk innit? Haven't you seen the change in him? He's gone all high-powered and trendy ain't he? He saw that film *Wall Street* about six bloody times! There's a character in that, right, called Gordon Gekko. Now he's a real tough, high-flying whiz-kid right, and Del wants to be just like him. He doesn't seem to realize that Gordon Gekko had brains. Del thinks all you need's a Filofax and a pair of red braces and you're a chairman of the board! Still, I will say one thing for him: he's been very encouraging with this course at the evening college.

Albert Yeah, how?

Rodney *(Has to think about it)* Well… well, he gives me a lift there each week!

Del enters from the bedroom area. He wears a shirt and tie and a pair of red braces. He carries a filofax and has now taken to smoking his cigars with the aid of a small, tortoiseshell cigar holder.

Del That's the way, Rodney. Don't bother about stocking up the van for the morning. You just carry on poncing about with that computer.

Rodney Derek, it is my college evening and I am trying to finish my homework!

Del *(Looks over Rod's shoulder at the work)* That's very good, Rodney. You'll get a star for that! *(Laughs)* I dunno why you bother, I really don't. I mean, you've always been the same, even when you was at school, it's always been books, learning, education. That's why you're no good at snooker.

Albert Fancy a bit of grub, Del?

Del *(Picking up some letters)* No thanks, Unc. Food is for wimps, and I've got me correspondence to catch up with.

Rodney it's tough at the top, eh Del?

Del We'll get to the top Rodney, no fear. This time next year we will be millionaires! *(Reading one of the letters)* Aha! Things are moving already. This is from the council. They've received my application to buy this flat and they're giving it consideration.

Rodney This flat? Why?

Del Well, we've been living in it since 1962. You were born in it. He was banned from it. I mean, we're all living in it, you know, the whole family. There's Mum and Grandad and, you know, everyone. This place holds many warm memories for me.

Rodney But why do we need to buy it?

Del So we can sell it!

Rodney Sell it? What for?

Albert A bloody good profit, with any luck!

Del Exactly. You see, Rodney, Peckham here is becoming a trendy area. I mean, it's full of wine bars and bistros, you know. Property prices are booming. So if we can flog this place to some chinless wonder at a vastly inflated price, well, that means that we can get a nice little drum out in the suburbs.

Rodney Del, council properties were built so the poorer classes would have somewhere to live! If they start selling them to hooray Henrys where are they gonna go?

Del Esher, Orpington – somewhere like that.

Rodney But they can't afford to buy houses!

Albert They can when they've sold their flats!

Del Yeah, yeah, 'course they can. It's money for old rope. *(Rubs hands together)* Lovely Jubbly!

Rodney It is immoral!

Del *(Reading letter)* Oh shut up, you tart!

Rodney Alright, think of it from our business point of view, eh? I mean this flat is in a wonderful position. It's 15 minutes from the West End, it's 15 minutes from the motorway.

Albert: And 15 minutes from the ground.

Del You're right, Rodders. I never thought of that! *(Starts writing in his filofax)* That's a very good selling point. I'm gonna make a note of that. That could put a few grand on, Albert. Yeah, don't worry. We'll make a nice little bit of bunce out of this old drum.

Rodney You have got no right to sell this place over my head!

Del You listen to me. I have lived here for 27 years, that gives me the right to decide its future!

Rodney And I was born here! That gives me more right than anyone.

Albert You might have been born here, but Del's the one who pays the rent arrears.

Del Yeah, that's right, and you take just how much I've paid in rent over the years.

Yuppy Love

I must have bought this place at least four or five times over and yet not one breeze block belongs to me – to us. But all that is gonna change!

Rodney You're just a snob, that's all you are!

Del I am not a snob, Rodney; I am a realist. I've grafted all my life to try to get us a nice little place out there in the fresh air and look at us – we're still here in this council-built Lego set! I used to watch you when you was a kid, you know, breathing in all the fumes from the motorway – you must have more lead inside you than a butcher's pencil, and I used to think, what is it doing to his little brain?

Albert Too late now, son.

Rodney Yeah, you see, that's right! I'm a fully gro… What d'you mean, it's too late now?

Albert I mean you're a full-grown man!

Rodney Oh… Yeah, that's what I was gonna say. Anyway, you've only paid the rent here since Mum died!

Del Oh leave it out, Rodney. I've been paying the rent here ever since I was old enough to 'op the wag! No-one else in this family ever worked. Mum tried her best, but her health let her down. And there was Dad, he would have loved a job but he had a sticky mattress and there was dear old Grandad, bless him. He was about as useful as a pair of sunglasses on a bloke with one ear! Everything we've got in life has come through my intelligence and my foresight.

Rodney Well, I'm glad somebody's owned up!

Del I don't know what you're moaning about. Your life's been a walk over. You never had to graft for it when you was a kid. I saw to it that you didn't have to! But what about me? When I was 11 years old, Rodney, Dad got me two – count 'em – two paper rounds. Every morning come rain, sleet or shine, there was Del Boy. 35 *Daily Sketches*, 40 *Heralds* and a *Spick 'n' Span* for the weirdo in Marley Road! And when I'd delivered them I went to another shop and started me second round! Dad always said he'd get me a bike!

Rodney I worked when I was a kid as well!

Del When?

Rodney When I was 11! When they were introducing North Sea gas to the area and you'd got hold of that consignment of do-it-yourself gas conversion kits, you remember? That Sunday you sent me down the Mountbatten Estate with a barrow-load of 'em. All day long I was down there knocking on doors. I missed me Sunday dinner and everything. And not one of the gits down there had the decency to tell me that the Mountbatten Estate was all-electric!

Del *(Obviously hiding a deep-felt guilt)* Oh yeah, I remember you coming back and telling me about that.

Rodney They just kept laughing at me! I thought it was that stupid flower-power shirt you used to make me wear.

Del That was a beautiful shirt, that, Rodney!

Rodney That was 'orrible! It was pink with little red poppies all over it.

Del That had been very fashionable, once.

Rodney But if you remember Derek, at the time I happened to be covered in chicken-pox! From a distance it looked like I was stripped to the waist! To this day I will never know what possessed you to send me to that estate. I mean, you had mates living there, so how come you didn't know it was all-electric.

Del It was a long time ago Rodders, I don't remember… Alright, so you grafted as well. He fought and died for his country many times! Which gives us the right to make a bit of profit out of this dump.

Rodney I wanna stay in this flat!

Albert You can buy it off Del then!

Del This is typical of you, Rodney, you don't move with the times. The world is changing out there; it's a financial jungle. It's a question of he who dares, wins, he who hesitates... don't!

Albert It's called the survival of the fittest.

Rodney No, Unc, it's called pull the ladder up, Jack, and sod the rest!

Albert There are times when you have to think of yourself, Rodney! I remember once when I was in the South Pacific.

Rodney Don't you dare give me another nautical nightmare! I've already been through the Adriatic with him once this afternoon. It's like the adventures of a Dover sole!

Del Alright, Rodney. Look, we won't move far away. There are some lovely areas round here. We'll buy a house that befits people like us.

Rodney What do you mean, people like us?

Del Well, yuppies.

Rodney I am not a yuppy!

Del No. But given time and a little help from me... *(He pats him reassuringly on the shoulder)*

EXT. QUIET SUBURBAN, TREE-LINED AVENUE. DAY. FILM.

The road contains magnificent houses with in and out drives.

The camera focuses on a street sign that reads "The Kings Avenue".
We pan up to show at least one of the houses before the three wheeled van comes into view driving towards us (Del driving in a trendy green coat, and Rod in the passenger seat wearing one of the common or garden beige trenchcoats as seen in the flat.

The van pulls to a halt.

Rodney What you stopping for?

Del *(Gesturing to houses)* Cop a load of this, bruv. I mean, this is what you call living. You know, I bet these gaffs have guest suites, swimming pools, jacuzzis! What have we got? A put-you-up, a damp patch and a jakarsey!

Rodney What do you reckon this sort of place goes for then?

Del Oh, I dunno, three-quarters of a million, maybe more. We'll be in one of these one day, bruv.

Rodney Oh yeah! What you got lined up, a decorating job?

Del No, listen to me. We just need an half-decent break and we'll be millionaires!

Rodney Del, I wouldn't live in this road if you paid me! It's poncy. It's... it's immoral!

Del Immoral? What you going on about, you dipstick?

Rodney You've got something like 18 acres of land here with about 12 families living on it.

Del These sort of people need a bit of space round 'em, don't they? I mean, down here you've got stockbrokers, private doctors... Porsches! This is the crème de la menthe of our community!

Rodney You could house thousands of people on this land!

Del What, more tower blocks? If you had your way, the only growth industry would be lift-repairing! Every time you go to these evening classes you end up talking like Ken Livingstone and Arthur Scargill. You wanna watch it or you'll end up with one of those funny hair cuts.

Rodney Are you gonna drive me to the adult education centre or are we gonna stand here admiring the privets all night?

Rodney climbs back into van and slams door.

Del Make sure the door's closed, Rodney.

Yuppy Love

Del climbs into driver's seat.
Look, Rodney. I wanna be successful, but not for the money. I want the power and the influence that success brings.
Rodney And what will you do with all this power and influence?
Del Spend it!

EXT. ADULT EDUCATION CENTRE/URBAN ROAD. DAY. FILM.

It is a grand, old, pre-war building that was once most probably civic offices. A sign outside reads: "Adult Education. Business and Commercial Studies".

We see the van pull up on opposite of road to building.

Del and Rod alight. Rod is carrying some paperwork in files.
Del Go on then, hurry up Rodney. They'll be calling the register in a minute!
Rod returns a sneer.
Del Mind the road! Remember what the Green Cross Code Man said?
Rodney You are getting on my bloody nerves!
Rod climbs the steps to entrance door. A small group of young people follow him up the steps.
Del *(Calls)* Rodney! Rodney! And if the big boys gang up on you again at playtime, you tell the teacher! *(Roaring with laughter).*
Rodney turns angrily.
Rodney Why don't you pi…
(Pleasantly to the group of young people) Evening.
We can hear Del roaring with laughter in background.
Now Cassandra ascends steps.
Rodney stares at her. Del's laughter now means nothing to him. He is smitten. He smiles at her and she returns a polite smile, passes him and exits to building.

Rodney watches her go.
Del And don't go losing your dinner money again!
Rod hasn't even heard him. He just stares into the building watching Cassandra. He now enters the building.

We cut across to Del who is still laughing to himself. As he turns back towards the van, his attention is drawn to something just a few yards away.

From Del's POV we see a rather trendy wine bar. Just pulled up at kerb is a porsche from which two attractive young ladies alight. They are yuppy slaves of fashion. They enter wine bar.
Del Now that's a bit of me!
Del pulls his stomach in and tightens the belt of his trendy green trenchcoat. From inside the van, he produces an Arnie Becker aluminium executive briefcase and, finally, the piece de resistance, the filofax. Holding the filofax prominently in front of him, he strides confidently towards wine bar.

INT. WINE BAR. DAY. STUDIO.
The interior is rather sparse and French. Marble-topped tables with wrought iron legs, etc. It should be quite crowded with early evening yuppies.

Marsha and Dale are standing at the counter, the barman pouring them their usual.

Incorporated within the wooden or marble counter there is a bar flap which at this moment is open.

We see Del enter in background. There is a slight nervous edge to him, he knows

he's in alien territory but feels they will soon recognise that he is one of them. He holds his filofax more prominently, like a masons' handshake. He spots the girls and makes his way to the counter area. A second barman enters, pulling the bar flap down behind him.

Dale notices Del and nudges Marsha. They both smirk and turn their heads away. They find Del a funny, odd person.

Del Oh – it's good to unwind, innit?

Marsha Sorry?

Del I say, after a hard day in the City, it's good to unwind.

Dale I imagine it must be very tiring.

Del Tiring? Tired, yeah, I'm cream crackered and that's no lie! Well, I've been up since six this morning trying to talk to a bloke in New York.

Marsha Why didn't you use a telephone?

The girls burst out in squeals of laughter. Del can't see the joke and can't see they are taking the rise out of him.

Del No, I've got a phone an' all that. No, I mean, it's just a long and stressful day in the old commodities market. It ain't all champagne and skittles. Oh no – buying, selling, making billion-pound decisions. It's a git of a journey home an 'all!

Dale What exactly do you buy and sell in the commodities market?

Del Oh, you know, this and that, whatever's going, you know. Iron ore, sugar beet. I made a killing today on olive oil. Gawd knows what Popeye'll say when he gets home!

(Laughs uproariously)

Barman Can I get you anything, Sir?

Del I'll have a bottle of Beaujolais Nouveau.

Barman Yes, sir.

Del A '79.

The girls burst out laughing. Del is at first confused by the laughter but then thinks

he understands.

Oh, Popeye? You got it, have yer? That was a good 'un, weren't it?

INT. ADULT EDUCATION CENTRE/URBAN ROAD. NIGHT. FILM.

There are cars parked at kerb outside of building, including a rather nice BMW. The doors burst open and a group of young people exit and descend the steps. (This is all to establish passage of time – night-classes have ended).

INT. FOYER OF EDUCATION CENTRE. NIGHT. FILM.

There are corridors, rooms and a flight of stairs. The foyer is quite crowded with students of various races, ages (although mostly young).

Along one wall runs a long coat rack from which people are collecting their belongings.

Rodney comes down stairs and then sits on a bench studying his paperwork. (We shall soon discover that Rod has in fact taken a women's beige trenchcoat. Smaller, and obviously more feminine than his own, but similar enough for no-one to notice.)

Rodney Oh bloody hell! How am I s'posed to do all this?

Cassandra approaches carrying a beige coat over her arm.

Cassandra Hello!

Rodney *(Looks up and reacts, surprised and delighted)* Oh! *(Realises this was too enthusiastic and cools it)* Hi!

Cassandra Sorry to interrupt you.

Rodney Oh what? No, it's alright, just some computer data I've to put into a program.

Cassandra It looks very complicated.

Rodney Well, yeah, it does look difficult,

Yuppy Love

but it's no problem… My name's Rodney.

Cassandra Cassandra.

Rodney and Cassandra shake hands

Rodney Oh Cassandra. That's a lovely name.

Cassandra Thank you. Um, I just wanted to say…

Rodney I'm glad we've bumped into each other 'cos I was trying to find a way of saying hello to you and I think it's really, you know, sort of liberated for you to make the first move.

Cassandra Move? No, you don't understand. You've taken my coat!

Rodney *(Looks at the coat he is holding, we now see it is a woman's coat)* Oh, I am so sorry.

Cassandra It's OK. They're very similar; it's an easy mistake to make. This one's yours.

Rodney Well, how'd you know it's mine?

Cassandra It's got your name written in it.

We see on the inside collar of his coat that someone has printed 'Rodney Trotter' in ballpoint pen.

Rodney *(horrified)* Look, I didn't write this. It's, it's most probably my brother you know – his idea of a joke!

Cassandra Well, whatever. We've sorted it out now.

Rodney Yeah.

Cassandra Well, nice meeting you.

Rodney And you.

Cassandra smiles a goodbye and moves towards exit.

EXT. ADULT EDUCATION CENTRE. NIGHT

Cassandra exits from building and starts to descend the steps.

Rodney exits the building and catches up with her.

She is holding car keys.

Rodney Cassandra! I was wondering whether you had time for a quick drink?

Cassandra Oh I'm sorry. I'm going out with a friend tonight.

Rodney Oh well, never mind! Um, can I walk you to your car?

Cassandra *(Considers his offer. Now, with a smile)* Oh thank you.

Rodney Pleasure.

They walk three steps to her car (the BMW) which is parked directly outside of building.

Cassandra Here we are!

Rodney I didn't realise you were parked so…

Cassandra Thank you for getting me here safely.

Rodney Oh think nothing of it. Nice car.

Cassandra It's my father's.

Rodney D'you live round this way?

Cassandra Blackheath. How about you?

Rodney Peckham.

Cassandra Where are you parked?

Rodney Me? Oh, I lent my car to my brother. Well I wish I hadn't now, after what's in my coat, the little rascal! Oh, I'll get a bus down the terminus.

Cassandra I'm going past the terminus – if you'd like a lift?

Rodney Oh thank you.

Rodney moves to passenger door wearing a look that tells he can't believe his luck. Now a voice in distance calls him.

Del Rodney! Rodders!

Rodney *(Freezes and mumbles almost silently)* Shit!!

Rodney pretends he hasn't heard Del. We now see Del standing outside of the wine bar.

Cassandra I think someone's calling you.

Rodney Really?

Del Hey, over here! I hung about for you. I'll give you a lift home.

Rodney Oh yeah. That's – someone I know. Well, thanks for the offer Cassandra.

Cassandra OK. Bye.

Rodney Yeah, bye.

Rodney starts walking across road to Del. Cassandra is still unlocking her car.

Del Who's the tart?

Rodney Shut up!

Rodney pushes Del in through the door of the wine bar.

INT. WINE BAR. NIGHT

Del What... what is the matter with you? They given you lines or something?

Rodney Why did you write my name inside that raincoat?

Del *(Can't hide his smirk)* Mum said to me on her deathbed...

Rodney Look, why did you write it, you git?

Del Alright, alright. She said to me, "Del Boy, make sure you always write Rodney's name in his clothes; that way no one'll nick 'em.' And I've kept my promise to her.

Rodney I was so embarrassed.

Del Yeah, but no one nicked yer coat, did they. Hey! Oh come on, come on, it was just a joke, you touchy sod. Come on, have a drink. I've got some wine and some mineral water. Right, I never liked Spitzers before, but now I'm right into 'em.

Rodney What are you still doing here?

Del Ah well, when I dropped you off I followed these two yuppy sorts, you know. Told 'em a few jokes, flashed me Filofax, knocked 'em bandy!

Rodney So where are they?

Del is now leaning on bar flap.

Del They went to the ladies a couple of hours ago and they ain't come back yet. Still, never mind, never mind eh? There's plenty more where they came from ain't there, eh? That's an idea, why don't we pull ourselves a couple of sorts and go on to a club?

Rodney sighs at Del's naivety and places his paperwork in Del's aluminium briefcase.

Rodney Nah, not me, Del. I'm off.

Del Oh come on. You're not going home already, are ya?

Rodney No, definitely not home. Not with Albert there. The last thing I need right now is another battle of the Baltic! Look, stick them in the van for me, would ya? I'll see you later Del.

Del: Yeah, yeah, alright, bruv. Yeah, I will, yeah.

As Del watches him leave he nibbles anxiously on the end of his pen.

Barman Excuse me, are you eating?

Del No, I'm just nibbling it.

Barman No, sir. Our bistro's just open and I wondered if you'd like a table for dinner?

Del Not me John. Dinner is for wimps.

INT. DISCO. NIGHT

This should look like a genuine disco rather than a pub which is turned into one at weekends. It should appear crowded with the 20–35-year-old set. Loud, recent and 'real' records are played. The place should be alive with movement, light and sound.

Lounging against the bar we see Rodney, who peers despondently into his pint of lager, Mickey Pearce, still wearing his trademark pork-pie hat, and Jevon. As we find the three at the bar Mickey is practising his hobby of lying, this time concerning his conquests with the girls at the disco.

Jevon is bored with Mickey's lies.

Rodney isn't really listening.

Mickey Jevon! Jevon!

Jevon What?

Mickey See the blonde bird? I've had her! And her mate. See that black sort at the back there? She's crazy about me! Phones me all the time.

Yuppy Love

Jevon You're a hell of a man, Mickey.

Rodney Mickey, are you doing this for charity?

Mickey What d' you mean?

Rodney Well, I just wondered whether it was sponsored bullshit.

Mickey I'm telling you the truth, Rodney!

Two attractive young girls pass by. They stop and smile at Jevon.

Girl in disco Hi, Jevon.

Jevon Wotcher, darling.

Girl in Disco Not dancing tonight?

Jevon Not at this precise moment in time. But being a creature of impulse, I am coiled like a spring, ready to move with sinuous grace when the music takes me. If either of you two should be in the vicinity when this occurs then – who knows – it could be your lucky night!

The girls both sneer at his flashness, but it's an enjoyable sneer (they like him and his style).

Jevon laughs out loudly at his own audacity as the girls move on.

Jevon OK – I've given you two losers an audience, and now it's time to do what I was put on this earth to do – to bring pleasure and excitement into the lives of attractive young women. And tonight's lucky winner is the chick sitting at the corner table.

We don't see her yet.

Rodney is too depressed to even look.

Mickey Nah, you've got no chance with her Jevon. I've seen five blokes ask her for a dance and she gave 'em all a blank.

Jevon Five ordinary mortals. She hasn't met me yet.

Mickey Just listen to it!

Rodney Well, you carry on, Jevon. Me and Mickey'll prepare the altar.

Jevon I'll wave to you as I leave.

Mickey *(Calls, sarcastically)* Don't forget, will yer? That Jevon, he does the business, though, don't he, Rodney eh? Still, I taught him everything he knows.

Rodney Oh turn it up, Mickey. Last time you went out with a bird you took her to a Bay City Rollers concert.

Mickey What's the matter with you anyway? You got a pimple on a boil or something?

Rodney Yeah sort of – it's called Del Boy.

Mickey Oh yeah. Yeah, he's getting a bit noncy, ain't he lately? I see him walking down the high street the other day with his Filofax held up in front of him. You know, a lot of people thought it was a protest march.

Rodney Yeah, well, he only uses it for business, don't he?

Mickey And what about that green coat of his, eh? He looks a right poultice, don't it?

Rodney Well, personally I think he looks very smart.

Mickey Oh leave it out, Rodney. He looks like the Incredible Hulk's little boy!

Rodney Oh I'll tell him next time I see him. I'm sure he'll find a way of showing his gratitude.

Mickey You don't have to tell him, do you? It's only a joke, that's all. *(Now quickly changing the subject)* I don't believe it. It looks like Jevon has fallen on stony ground!

We cut to Jevon chatting to the girl at the corner table – it is Cassandra. She is seated at table with her girlfriend (Emma) of the same age and class. Cassandra is smiling in a friendly and polite way but is obviously turning down Jevon's pleading overtures. We see Jevon finally admit defeat with a shrug and then make an embarrassed approach to bar.

As Jevon leaves corner table, Cassandra spots Rodney. She mouths the word 'Hi' and gives him a friendly wave. She then turns and begins talking to Emma.

Even though she is no longer looking at him and he is three seconds too late, Rodney returns the gestures as Jevon arrives back at bar.

Jevon She's a lesbian!

Mickey Quick, Rodney, phone the AA, tell them the sex machine's broken down!

Jevon D'you reckon you could do any better?

Mickey She probably likes the direct approach instead of all that old fanny you give 'em! Watch the master and learn!

Mickey makes his way towards the corner. We find Cassandra and Emma in mid-conversation, talking about one of Emma's boyfriends.

Emma I just never know whether to believe him.

Cassandra He always struck me as a pretty straightforward type.

Emma You don't know him like I do!

Mickey arrives. He slaps Cassandra gently on the arm with the back of his fingers.

Mickey Do you wanna dance?

Cassandra No!

Mickey Right!

Mickey makes his way through crowd to Rodney and Jevon.

Mickey Definitely a lesbian!

Rodney Oh don't be stupid they're all busy down the town hall! She'd dance with me!

Jevon and Mickey burst into laughter.

Jevon That's what we like about you Rodney, we're always guaranteed a laugh!

Mickey Look, I'm a first dan of lateral chatting and this is God's foster son! So what chance has a woll like you got?

Rodney I bet she'll dance with me!

Jevon You bet, do ya? Right, a tenner says she don't!

Mickey I'll have some of that! That's a score. Cover the bet.

Rodney Alright, I will! *(Produces a*

crumpled five and ten pound note. He now searches his pockets for more money)

Jevon Before you ask her to dance, why don't you see if she'll lend you a fiver?

Rodney A score!

Mickey You don't come to a disco expecting to make a profit, do ya?

Jevon That's very true, Michael!

Rodney I'll see you two later.

With a deep, apprehensive breath, Rodney sets off for corner table.

Emma He said he had a holiday home near Marbella. It turned out to be a caravan on the Isle of Sheppey!

Cassandra Well didn't you say something?

Emma Yes, but he said distance was relative.

Cassandra Well I suppose he's got a point. I mean compared to somewhere like Melbourne the Isle of Sheppey is near Marbella!

Rodney Hi!

Cassandra Hello – again! Em, was there something?

Rodney What? Oh, yes. Would you like to dance with me?

Cassandra Thank you.

She stands and walks onto the floor with Rodney.

We see Mickey's and Jevon's faces drop. They turn and look at each other in stunned silence as Cassandra and Rodney dance to a slow number. Rodney looks to his friends and give them an 'easy-peasy', 'no problem' look or gesture.

Jevon is devastated, and Mickey is stunned, they turn away and lean on the bar.

Mickey He's paid her, that's what he's done! He's offered her arf the winnings!

Jevon Mickey – shuddup!

Yuppy Love

INT. WINE BAR. NIGHT. STUDIO.

Del is leaning on counter writing something in his filofax.

He looks up and spots Trigger entering.

Del *(Calls)* Oh Trig! Trigger! Trig, over here!

Trigger Del Boy.

Del Hiya.

Trigger What you doing here?

Del I'm always here. This is my regular now. *(Calls Barman)* John, get my mate a pint of lager.

Barman I'm afraid we don't serve beer, Sir.

Del Oh. I remember now, yeah. It wasn't selling too well so they knocked it on the head. D'you fancy a Spitzer?

Trigger Er… yeah, I'll give it a try.

Del Yeah, anyway, what you doing down here, Trig? I thought you'd be in the Nag's Head.

Trigger Yeah, I was, but Mike's just barred me.

Del Barred you. What for?

Trigger He accused me of stealing one of his pork pies. What do I want his rotten pork pies for? I don't even like pork pies!

Del Oh, he's right out of order, that bloke.

Trigger Oh I'm thinking of suing him for defr… defn…

Del Slander.

Trigger Yeah.

Del I wouldn't worry about it, Trig, if I were you. He's done you a favour, actually. I mean, look around. This place is full of yuppy sorts. Yeah, we can't go wrong here. All we gotta do is learn to speak their language.

Trigger Why, they foreign then?

Del No, they're yuppies! They don't speak proper English like what we do. I mean, I've bin earholing 'em. It's all 'Ya', 'Sooper' and 'Fab'. And you've got to talk about money. It's their favourite subject. I mean, you chat about money and it really impresses them.

Trigger Yeah?

Del God's honest.

Trigger now spots the woman standing next to him.

Trigger I saw one of them old £5 notes the other day.

Del No, no, no, come here. I don't mean talk about your bloody coin collection, do I? I mean, you just gotta talk about your wealth.

Trigger But I ain't got none of that!

Del Nor have most of them. They're all living in sin with their flexible friends. You just gotta chat about it, you just gotta talk, that's all. Look, I'll show you how it's done.

Del and Trigger swap places. Standing next to Del is an attractive and well-spoken lady.

Look, watch me, watch this. It's all go when you're in a high-profile business, innit girls eh?

Girl Really?

Del Yes, 'cos I'm in stock and shares meself, yeah. I bought a few thousand shares in a little department store this afternoon. Now I've gotta phone me lawyer and me accountant. Gives you the 'ump, don't it? Excuse me, sorry, how do you spell 'Arrods?

Girl *(Taking her wine from barman)* Capital 'A'!

Del *(Offended, to barman)* Oh I say. *(Calls after her)* Beam me up, Snotty! Need all that don't ya?

Trigger Yeah. *(Passing Del a pork pie)* Want that? I don't like 'em.

Del Cheers Trig.

INT. DISCO. NIGHT. FILM.

People are leaving.

Jevon is dancing a smooch with an attractive girl. He stares deep into her eyes as if hypnotising her.

23

Mickey sits alone at bar. Rodney passes by with Cassandra and Emma.

Rodney See you around, Mickey.

Mickey Rodney, Rodney, hang on.

Rodney stops, Cassandra and Emma continue towards cloakroom.

What's happening, then eh? Come on, what's she all about?

Rodney Her name is Cassandra, she lives in Blackheath and she is giving me a lift home!

Mickey She got a car?

Rodney No she's giving me a crossbar! Of course she's got a car! We're dropping her friend off first, she lives next door to Cassandra.

Mickey You're going to Blackheath? You can give me a lift home, then eh?

Rodney No!

Mickey: Oh go on. I'm goin' a club over Blackheath. Just drop us off somewhere and I'll walk the rest of the way.

Rodney No, 'cos, um, well, she's only got a two-seater!

Mickey Yeah? Then how's she driving you and her mate home?

Rodney No, look, Mickey.

Mickey Jevon, we're off.

Jevon doesn't even look at them, he merely raises a hand in their direction, like a blessing.

Rodney You'd better not nause this up for me, Mickey.

Mickey Don't worry. I'll be on my double best behaviour – the complete gentleman.

Rodney You'd better be!

Mickey Promise! What's her friend's name?

Rodney Emma.

Mickey She do a turn? *(Rodney reacts)* Sorry, don't get the 'ump!

INT. WINE BAR. NIGHT. STUDIO

Del You see, nowadays these modern Eurobirds, they go for the mature men who've made it in life.

Trigger Yeah? Is that why we're having no luck?

Del I ain't tried yet! I'm just building meself up for the kill.

Trigger Yeah, well, you'd better hurry up. The first bell went just now.

Del Yeah, alright, alright. *(Now the girl at table catches eyes with Del.)* Could be on a winner here, Trig. Alright, play it nice and cool, son, nice and cool. You know what I mean?

Del smiles coolly and nods a greeting. The girl returns the merest of smiles and turns away.

Inspired by this tiny success, Del leans off counter and lights a cigar.

As he does so, the barman exits from counter area, leaving the bar flap up. Del now leans coolly on the non-existent flap and crashes straight through and onto the floor.

He then stands back up and tries to regain his composure unsuccessfully.

Del Drink up. We're going.

Trigger Ain't you gonna try for them birds?

Del No, no. You're cramping me style, Trig.

INT. CASSANDRA'S CAR. NIGHT. FILM.

Mickey Me and Rodney live near each other. Do you know the Nyerere Estate, Peckham?

Emma No, I can't say I've ever heard of it, no.

Mickey Well, it's a rather lively place, specially when the militants hold a Mardi Gras! Eh, Rodney? You two live in Blackheath?

Cassandra Yes.

Mickey Here, you heard of a drinker round there called the 'Down by the Riverside Club'?

Emma No, I can't say I've ever heard of

Yuppy Love

that either. Where is it?

Mickey Well, ooh, it's down by the riverside, innit?

Cassandra I've heard of it. It's got a terrible reputation, full of unsavoury characters.

Mickey *(Offended)* I'm a member!

Cassandra Whoops! Beg your pardon.

Mickey That's alright, darling, I didn't even hear it! Didn't even hear it!

Rodney Oh please, God!

Mickey Alright, fair enough. You get a few unsavoury characters in there, but we enjoy ourselves.

Emma So do lynch-mobs!

Mickey Ooh, bitchy! Just for that I'm not gonna let you give me a kiss good night.

Emma Euurgh, God!

Cassandra Here we are.

EXT. UPPER-MIDDLE-CLASS AVENUE. NIGHT. FILM

The houses are all detached and, although not in the class of 'The Kings Avenue', are obviously expensive.

We see Cassandra's car pull to a halt outside of a very nice-looking house with well-tended gardens.

Her BMW is a two-door model so she and Rodney have to alight to let Mickey and Emma out.

Emma Night, Rodney.

Rodney Good night, Emma.

Mickey Here, Rodney, clock the houses!

Rodney Yeah, nice eh?

Mickey Nice? You gotta be talking 300K! Gonna be a bit of a culture shock for Cassandra when she drops you off at Nelson Mandela House, innit? Anyway, I'd better walk it from here eh? I'll see you, Rodney. *(Calls)* Night, Cassandra. Good night Emma… love you!

Cassandra Good night.

Rodney Look, I'm sorry about Mickey.

Cassandra Don't be silly. We all have friends who are – over the top, shall we say?

Rodney Yeah. He's probably still upset about losing his money.

Cassandra How'd he do that?

Rodney Well you remember when I asked you to dance? Well, I did it for a bet. *(Cassandra reacts)* Well, no, I didn't mean it like that! Mickey said I wouldn't have the guts to ask you. But well, I did.

Cassandra I get the feeling that hidden in that statement somewhere there's a compliment.

Rodney Yeah, a big compliment.

Cassandra Alright, then, I suppose we'd better be getting you back to – what was it called? The Nyerere Estate?

Rodney I don't live in the Nyerere Estate!

Cassandra But I thought Mickey said…

Rodney *(Cuts in)* Mickey lives on the Nyerere Estate. I live near it. Well, past it. Well, quite a long way past it. I'll show you.

Cassandra *(Slightly bewildered)* OK.

They climb into car.

EXT. A QUIET SUBURBAN TREE-LINED AVENUE. NIGHT. FILM.

We see Cassandra's car driving towards us. Her car continues out of shot and we are left looking at a road sign which reads: 'The Kings Avenue'

Rodney is peering from window, desperately searching for the most impressive house.

Cassandra What a lovely road you live in.

Rodney Yes, it's quite nice. Ah, here we are. *From Rodney's POV we see a magnificent house with a Mercedes parked in the driveway.*

Cassandra You lucky thing, what a great house.

Rodney Oh well, I don't notice it really, you know. It's just a place to lay my head.

Ah, good, my brother got the car home safely. Well, thanks for the lift, Cassandra.

Cassandra Pleasure.

Rodney That's my number. Give me a ring sometime – if you want to.

Cassandra Thanks. Well, good night.

Rodney Night.

Rodney leans his face tentatively towards Cassandra's.

She leans forward and they kiss gently. Inspired by this small success Rodney moves his right arm as if to put it round her and get down to more serious stuff.

Cassandra *(Fending him off)* Good night, Rodney!

Rodney Yes, of course.

Rodney takes his trenchcoat from the back seat and gets out of the car.

He walks a few yards to the driveway of the house then waves back to Cassandra. The lights of the house are on. We see that Rodney's is scared of being discovered by the owners.

He takes a few steps onto driveway and calls back to Cassandra.

Rodney Byeee! *(Now to himself)* Please drive away!

We cut to the house where there is the silhouette of a woman staring out at Rodney from an upstairs window.

Rodney Oh my God!

He turns to the car.

Cassandra waves to him and then points to upstairs window as if telling him that his family are there.

Rodney looks to house. The woman has been joined by her husband at the window.

Rodney *(Nerves taut, eyes wide and unblinking, he waves to his 'family')* Hi, I'm home. Please, Cassandra, go!

Cassandra now drives away.

Rodney rushes for the protection of some bushes out on the public footpath.

He waits until he thinks the coast is clear. We now hear a clap of thunder. A few raindrops appear on the ground. Rodney puts his 'raincoat' on.

We now see he has taken Cassandra's coat again.

Rodney *(Looks up to heaven as the rain starts falling more heavily)* Cosmic. Cos-bloody-mic.

INT. TROTTERS' LOUNGE. NIGHT. STUDIO

Lightning flickers across window and rain gushes down the panes.

Del is seated in armchair. He is wearing a set of headphones and listening to a record which is playing on his stereo turntable.

By his expressions and hand movements, we would imagine he's listening to some great orchestral piece.

Albert enters from kitchen carrying a black rubbish sack.

Albert Del, Del Boy, Del!

He walks across and hits Del on the arm (the same arm he injured in the wine bar)

Del *(Leaps up in pain)* Aauughh! What'd you wanna do that for, you soppy old duffer?

Albert Bloody 'ell, I don't realise me own strength!

Del It has got nothing to do with your strength. I was having a few drinks earlier this evening in a very trendy wine bar with some of my yuppy friends when I happened to fall arse over head!

Albert You're gonna do yourself a lot of

Yuppy Love

damage if you ain't careful.

Del *(Referring to arm)* I've already done meself a lot of damage!

Albert I mean, you're not eating – eating's for wimps! And you're drinking so much you're falling over in boozers!

Del I wasn't drinking, in fact I was on some very trendy funny-tasting trendy water… oh forget it!

Albert I'm getting rid of that rubbish in the kitchen. Do you want me to chuck anything else down the chute?

Del Not unless you're feeling in a kamikaze mood!

Albert Look, why don't you let me do you some grub eh?

Del Yeah, alright Uncle. I am feeling a bit hungry. Do me a health-conscious fry-up will ya?

> *Albert exits to kitchen and Del takes the record from the turntable*

Del I don't care what they say, you can't whack The Who.

> *He places record in sleeve.*
>
> *The door from hall bursts open and Rodney fills the doorway. He is wet, drenched, soaked to the skin. He has Cassandra's coat over his head but his hair is still soaked. He is breathing heavily in anger and exhaustion.*
>
> *He stares at Del, daring him to make a funny remark.*

Del Alright?

Rodney What?

Del I said, alright?

Rodney Triffic!

Del What's it like out?

Rodney There's a few spots of rain in the air!

Del Yeah? It might help us shift some of those raincoats.

> *Del indicates the coats hanging round the room.*

> *He picks up Cassandra's coat and examines it.*

Del Blimey, that one shrunk. Come on, let's have it here. Did you have a good night?

Rodney Not too bad.

Del I stayed on at the wine bar a while, it's very nice, my sort of place. Then I went on for a drink – down by the riverside! Mickey Pearce called in at the last knockings and he told me that you'd met this posh tart and she'd given you a lift home in her flash car.

Rodney yeah, that's right.

Del What's she got, a convertible?

Rodney No! I asked her to drop me off half way. I fancied a walk.

Del What, in this weather?

Rodney Lots of people enjoy walking in the rain.

Del Yes I know, but they're usually recaptured pretty quickly.

> *Rodney goes to pour himself a brandy but finds the bottle is empty.*

Rodney Del, this bottle's empty.

Del Chuck it in the rubbish… It's alright, Rodney, you can't hide the truth from me. I know what happened tonight. I can read you like a book.

Rodney You know nothing, Del, so keep your nose out.

Del I've got 20 notes here – look, there they are – that says that I can guess what happened tonight. G'on then, you cover that.

Rodney Alright, go'n then, know-all, tell me!

Del Alright. That Mickey Pearce said that this Cassandra sort lived in a right nice drum.

Rodney Yeah, so?

Del So this is what I think happened. You've seen her house and the snob in you came racing to the surface and you thought: "Ooh, how can I take her back to Nelson Mandela House?" So on your way

home, you've made her drive up some right posh road – somewhere like The Kings Avenue – and then you stopped at some right nice little mansion and you pretended that's where you lived!

Rodney You don't half talk a load of rubbish!

Del Is that the truth?

Rodney Yes!

Del Thank you very much indeed. That's it, Rodney, you see, you're like an open book, my son – and it's thicker than my Filofax!

Del exits to bedroom area.

Rodney, his anger at boiling point, searches the room for something of Del's to damage.

Rodney I'll file your fax for you!

He find the filofax, dumps it in the rubbish sack.

Albert enters from kitchen.

Albert Still raining?

Rodney No, I took a short cut through a car wash!

Albert Alright, boy, don't have a go at me, I only asked! I'll chuck this stuff down the chute.

Del enters from bedroom area, carrying a towel. He throws it at Rodney.

Del Here y 'are, dry yourself off. You should never be ashamed of where you live, Rodney. Look, I want better than this but I'm not ashamed of it.

Rodney Oh but Del, you should have seen her road. There weren't one window boarded up, all the lamp posts worked. I mean what would she have thought if she'd have come back here eh? Well, just keep driving straight past the burnt-out panda car, Cassandra, and I live just before the next barricade.

Del I know how you feel, Rodney. I've been through the same emotions meself.

Rodney You?

Del Yes, me. Well it was about 15, 16 years ago. I met this bird. She was from Texas.

Rodney What, the do-it-yourself place?

Del No, no. Texas in America. She was some oil baron's daughter. She had one of these long double-barrelled funny names like Elly-May or something like that.

Rodney How would you meet an oil

Yuppy Love

baron's daughter?

Del I was working in the Tower of London at the time. I was doing the old Happy Snaps, you know? Second-hand Brownie, no film, pound a go – Lovely Jubbly! One day she asked me to take a picture of her and a Beefeater and one of them big crow things, right? So, anyway, we got chatting and I offered to show her round London. So, anyway, after a little while we fell deeply in love with each other... Cor, what was her name? Now, anyway, it doesn't matter, anyway. You know what she said to me one day?

Rodney Where's my picture?

Del No! She paid me a very great compliment. She said when she met me it reminded her of the day that President Kennedy was killed.

Rodney And that's one of the nicest compliments you've ever had?

Del Don't you see what she meant?

Rodney No.

Del Well, I like to think that she meant that everyone remembers where they were the day they met Del Trotter.

Rodney She might not have meant that!

Del Well what else could she have meant?

Rodney Well I don't know. Perhaps she meant you looked, yeah, you looked like Lee Harvey Oswald!

Del I don't look like Lee Harvey bleed'n' Oswald. Cor, who's Lee Harvey Oswald?

At this point Albert has entered from hall.

Albert He's the bloke what shot Kennedy. You look a bit like him, Del.

Del No, I don't.

Albert No, of course you don't. You look nothing like him. I'll get your grub.

Del Yeah.

Rodney So, anyway, what's you and Peggy-Sue gotta do with me and Cassandra?

Del 'Cos she wanted to see where I lived and I had the same struggle with my conscience as you've had. I was frightened if I brought her back here she might think less of me.

Rodney So you didn't?

Del No, I did.

Rodney When?

Del Well, it was one Sunday, years ago now.

Rodney Well, where was I?

Del You was down the Mountbatten Estate selling them gas conversion kits.

Rodney You bastard! You sent me down there on purpose with chickenpox. You just wanted to get rid of me so you and Annie bloody Oakley could have the flat to yourselves!

Del It wasn't like that, Rodney, wasn't like that. I was trying to present you with a challenge.

Rodney What, selling gas conversion kits on an all-electric estate? That's a challenge and an half that is!

Del No, it's alright, listen, I'll tell you the truth. Alright, so I wanted to get rid of you for a couple of hours. I mean, I was serious about her and wanted to make the best impression possible. I just thought, well, bringing her back to this tower block's bad enough but, I mean, if she saw you in that dopey shirt and your face covered in Randolph Scotts, well, that'd be good night Vienna, wouldn't it?

Rodney So she come back here?

Del Yeah. I gave her a pot of tea and a Lyons Victoria sponge. It was very nice.

Rodney And did she, you know, think anything less of you?

Del I dunno – I never saw her again. I mean she went home, you know, her holiday had finished.

Rodney Did she write to you?

Del Cor blimey, look at it, it's bucketing

down out there, innit?

Albert enters from kitchen with a plate of egg, bacon and beans.

Albert Here are, Del Boy. *(To Rodney)* Oi, some little bird phoned for you about 15 minutes ago. I think she'd been on drugs. She said you'd left your coat in the back of her car and she'd taken it back to your house in The Kings Avenue. The people there had never heard of you.

Rodney You conning git! You knew all along what had happened! Gimme that money back!

Del *(Now laughing)* No, no. You've learnt a very valuable lesson tonight, haven't you? Don't gamble. You never know when the cards have been stacked.

Albert I said, of course they'd never heard of him, he don't live in the The Kings Avenue, he lives on the Nyerere Estate!

Rodney You told her where I lived? Well, bang goes another dream.

Del Not necessarily, bruv. She phoned up, left her phone number and said that she'd wait up 'til midnight for you to call her.

Rodney You're kidding?

Albert She said she wants to hear from you tonight because she's going out tomorrow to buy a couple of tickets for some pop concert.

Del I bet it's Wet Wet Wet!

Rodney Yeah, I bet! Ah cheers, Del. Where's her number?

Del In my Filofax.

Rodney G-i-t!

Rodney rushes out through hall door as Del and Albert look at each other incredulously.

Yuppy Love

Danger UXD

INT. TROTTERS' LOUNGE/KITCHEN. DAY. STUDIO.

The table is laid for breakfast. Close to door which leads to the bedrooms area, we have two fridges which are standing next to each other. Laying on sofa is an empty cardboard box which has the words: "Matzuki. Video recorder" printed across it. We find Del and Albert over by the TVs studying the video recorder which is already plugged into TVs.

Del is trying to make it work. He presses various buttons and is obviously confused but is trying to put a brave face on things.

Lights and digital numbers are flashing on and off the machine.

Del This machine is gonna change our lives.

Albert Good.

Del This is top-of-the-range hi-tech.

Albert You can see that by all them lights.

Del Yeah, yeah. I don't know how we've managed so long without one.

Albert Nor do I... What is it?

Del What... what is it? It's a videotape recorder. It's got a little computer and everything. When you go on your holidays this thing will record all your favourite shows for you.

Albert Amazing.

Del Nothing but the best.

Albert How does it know you're on holiday?

Del You send it a postcard, don't ya? You programme its little computer, you daft old... *(presses more buttons).*

Albert No luck, eh?

Del It won't take me long. I'm a bit of a natural when it comes to technological things. I just got to get used to all its... er... its functions and its modes.

Albert I thought the bloke you bought it from said an idiot could work it.

Del Yes! *(Shouts)* Rodneeeey! Come on, shake a leg, it's gone six o'clock.

Rodney enters from the bedrooms area. He wears his working gear and moves in a half-asleep, zombie-like fashion. His hair is in a 'just got out of bed' style.

Rodney Yes, alright. Keep the noise down, will you?

Rodney shuffles to the breakfast table. Del watches him.

Del Cor blimey, look at the state of that. I've seen blokes crawl out of potholes looking better than that.

Albert You got in late last night, son. Out with that little bird of yours? What's her name – Cassandra?

Rodney That's right. Cassandra and I went to a concert at the Royal Albert Hall.

Albert Yeah? That takes me back. I used to go up there whenever I was on home leave. I saw some of the best there, Rodney. *(to Del)* Here, here, you ever heard of John Barbirolli?

Del Yes, course I have.

Albert Sir John was one of the greats.

Del Yeah, Barbra and Ollie were pretty good an' all.

Albert and Rodney look at each other in disbelief.

Albert I saw 'em all, Rodney. Adrian Boult, Sir Malcolm Sargent – wonderful times... Who'd you see?

Rodney Eric Clapton.

Albert Eric Clapton? He's a new one on me. Del Boy's got himself a video recorder.

Rodney Oh yeah? Yeah, there was an interesting article in the paper the other day. Did you know that Taiwan is the only country in the world that don't have any rubbish dumps, they just send it all to him.

Del Oi, oi, oi. That's enough of that. This is none of yer Taiwan junk. This was made in Formosa!

Rodney and Albert react.

Albert But Formosa is....

Rodney Albert, please don't confuse the issue!

Del Is what?

Rodney Is one of the world's leading man-ufacturers of audio/visual equipment.

Del And video recorders!

Rodney And video recorders.

Albert D' you want some breakfast, Del?

Del No thanks Albert. Breakfast is for wimps.

Albert Rodney?

Rodney Yeah, I'm starving.

Albert exits to kitchen, dum-dumming the 1812 overture.

Del Well, you know where I was last night while you was up at the Albert Hall, head-banging? I was having a drink with the managing director of the Advanced Elec-tronics Research and Development Centre!

Rodney Didn't that use to be Ron's Cash and Carry?

Del Yeah, yeah, that's right, but he changed the name. That bloke's come on a bundle in the last few years. That man is at the front of new technological frontiers. He's got a Queen's Award for industry plaque.

Rodney I know. I was there when you sold it to him.

Del Exactly! You and I, we both know it's a snide one but the punters don't! They're impressed by the image. And that's what today's modern business world is all about - image. You see, the right appearance can

fool the customer, right? Now, take me for instance. I'm a perfect example.

Rodney But you look exactly what you are.

Del Well, thank you very much. It's only 'cos I've got the right image. No, I mean, it's the little things, you know, it's like me aluminium briefcase there, me Mercedes key-ring, me Filofax. When people see these things they know exactly what I am.

Rodney It is a bit of a giveaway, innit?

Del Better than a Mason's handshake, bruv! It's like me jewellery. See, now a half-sovereign ring can say a lot about a man.

Rodney Combined with a medallion, it speaks volumes.

Del Exactly! Now we're talking the same language aren't we eh?

Albert opens door from kitchen. He is carrying a packet of cornflakes.

Hold it right there! Now look at Albert, Rodney. As you see him standing there, what is the first thing that comes to your mind?

Rodney Why have I got bloody cornflakes again?

Albert It's 'cos I can't get any food in that fridge. It's full up with tomatoes he bought last week!

Del Alright, alright, I'm gonna get rid of them today, aren't I? *(To Rodney)* No, I'm talking image-wise, aren't I? *(Referring to Albert)* That says to me, here is a man who has worked hard all his life for an honest crust. Here is a man of strong principles, here is a man you can trust. You see what I'm saying - you see how easy it is to fool people, eh? All you've got to do is have the right image. And that's what you've got to work on, Rodney.

Rodney Are you saying I've got to get an image?

Del No, what I'm saying is you've got to get rid of one! Look at me Rodders. You see, I wear a trendy trenchcoat, Gordon Gekko braces - you wear a lumberjack's

Danger UXD

coat and Gordon Bennett boots. My image says: 'I'm going right to the top, flat out!' Your image says: 'I'm going back to bed 'cos I'm shagged out!' You've got to be dynamic, Rodney.

Rodney Yeah, alright then.

Del exits to kitchen and opens the fridge which is filled to the top with boxes of tomatoes. He takes some of the boxes out as he talks.

Del I was being dynamic last night over at Ron's Cash… over the Advanced Electronics Research and Development Centre. I was where the big business opportunities occur and I was in a position to snap 'em up.

Cut to lounge

Rodney And what exactly did you snap up?

Albert That video recorder.

Rodney I bet the *Financial Times* index has gone through the roof!

Del enters carrying the boxes which he places on top of the other fridges.

Del No, I didn't just buy one – I bought 50 of 'em, rest of them are in the garage. I paid 50 quid each!

Albert But that's two and a half grand! Where'd you get two and a half grand from?

Del I didn't. I got 'em on the knock, you know, buy now, pay later. When I sell 'em Ronnie Nelson'll get his money.

Rodney But 50 quid each!

Del Mm.

Rodney Well, they've got to be hooky!

Del No, they are not hooky.

Del enters and takes some more boxes of tomatoes from the fridge.

No, the reason why they're so cheap is because they come from a consignment into which the manufacturers put the wrong instructions.

Cut to lounge

Rodney Oh great! So how are you gonna operate a video recorder with the instructions for a sandwich toaster?

Del enters from kitchen with more boxes.

Del I'm not – you are.

Rodney What?

Albert Well, you're the one who's taking a diploma course in computer science – again!

Del Yes, that's right, so programming a soppy little thing like that ought to be a doddle for someone of your talents.

Rodney Yes, alright, I'll do it for you.

Del Ah good boy, good boy. You know it makes sense. Listen, I want you to record a programme for me on ITV called *City News*. It's all about mega-powered business, Wall Street, big bangs and all that.

Rodney You on it?

Del You know, I think a surgical collar will suit you. Talking about suits, I want you to wear yours today. I want you to look really snappy for the punters, you know, with-it. We've got a high-profile image.

Rodney High profile? The only thing we've got that's high is this flat!

Del Look I've got an important phone call to make, so will you two take them tomatoes down to the van?

Rod and Albert sigh heavily and then pick up a couple of boxes each.

Del Oh, and don't forget the rest, alright? *He opens the two fridges and we see they are full of boxes of tomatoes. Del exits to the bedrooms area, carrying his cordless phone.*

INT. THE NAG'S HEAD. DAY. STUDIO.

The pub is fairly crowded with mainly market workers, but at the far end of the counter sits a yuppy estate agent, Adrian, and his girlfriend. She is eating a salad.

Also seated at the bar and some distance from the yuppies is Denzil, who is

*dressed in his lorry driving clothes.
We see Mike, who is standing towards
the back of the bar and out of the
yuppies' vision.*

*Standing on a heater plate we have a
large casserole pot, from which Mike is
spooning beef stew into two identical
bowls. He carries them carefully to front
of the bar, and places one down in front
of Denzil.*

Mike There's your stew Denzil. That's a
pound.

Denzil Cheers. I'll get you on the way back.
*Mike moves along bar to yuppy with
second bowl.*

Mike *(Calls to yuppy)* Boeuf
bourguignonne? That's £2.75.

Adrian Oh that's super.

Mike Bon appetite.
Mike moves back down bar to Denzil.

Mike So how's life treating you then, Denz?

Denzil The same as Paxo treats a turkey!

Mike Bad as that, eh?

Denzil Well, whatever happened to 'good
news' eh? Has it been privatised or
something?

Mike Here, I heard you'd started your own
haulage company – Transworld Express.
Any time, any load, anywhere.

Denzil That's right, but I've only got a
Transit.

Mike A Transit! So why all the big, world
wide slogans?

Denzil Well, I wanted to call it the Peckham
Courier Service. Parcels, small boxes, that
sort of thing. Then I bumped into Del.

Mike Oh don't tell me. Image, yeah?

Denzil Yes. He said, 'There is no place in
the modern business world for small
thinkers; you have gotta be big, brave and
brazen'.

Mike Why'd you listen to him?

Denzil Well, I keep telling myself I

shouldn't take no notice of him but Del
insists! Does he still drink in here?

Mike Yeah, occasionally. But since the
yuppies gentrified Peckham he's been
hanging round the wine bars and bistros. Of
course, one by one they're barring him.

Denzil Well, they're bound to, aren't they?

Mike *(Indicating towards the yuppies)* See
them over there? They only come in here to
avoid him.

Denzil I saw Rodney this morning. He was
wearing a suit.

Mike Someone must have died! There ain't
much good news around, is there?

Del Denzil, my ol' mate!

Denzil I was just going, Del!

Del No, not until I've bought you a drink,
you're not. Here pina colada for me, please,
Michael; same again for Denzil. You wanna
clean your pipes out more often. Listen
Michael, listen to me. I've just come back
from Folkestone. I've got 25, ten-kilo boxes
of fresh Jersey tomatoes, straight off the
ferry, still got the dew on 'em. £2.50 a
box, what do you say? Do your salads up a
treat.

Mike What, £2.50 a box?

Del Yup.

Mike Go on then, Del, I'll have one.

Del I put three boxes aside for you.
Rodney's on his way down with 'em. Let's
sit at the table Denzil. Tell me what you've
been up to.
*Denzil and Del move to table.
As they do so, Del spots the two yuppies.*

Del Ah Chloe, Adrian, how nice to see you
again.

Adrian *(Quietly to girlfriend)* Oh God, it's
him. *(Flatly to Del)* Hello.
Del and Denzil sit at table.

Del My sort of people.

Denzil You mean the bistro kids?

Del Ah yeah. Me and old Adrian were in
the wine bar the other night debating the

Danger UXD

Trust House Forte/Cunard merger. Oh yeah, that's the sort of thing I like these days, you know Denzil, the cut and thrust, to and fro of an honest, well-honed argument. I regret it now, but I ended up clumping him. But it's all forgotten about now eh?

Denzil Perrier water under the bridge eh?

Del Yeah. (*Mike hands over drinks*) Oh, cheers Mike.

> *Rodney enters. He is wearing a light grey, modern suit. We can only see his trousers as the three boxes of tomatoes he is carrying obscure his jacket from view.*

> *He glares angrily at Del as he thumps the boxes down on the counter. He turns and we see his suit jacket has numerous juicy, gooey tomato stains.*

Rodney Just look at me! I'm supposed to be going out in this tonight.

Del Well you've ruined it, haven't yer?

Rodney This is your fault! It's all so I could present an image. Well, I am presenting an image, I'm presenting the image of someone who's got tomato stains all over him!

Del That'll come off! Mike, give him something to wipe that up with, will ya?

Mike How about a slice of bread?

Rodney I need him, don't I? I bloody need him!

Denzil That was a nice suit this morning, Rodney.

Rodney Yeah, I know it was. Gawd knows how I'm gonna get it clean for tonight! I'll have to cancel my date with Cassandra and that'll ruin my evening and she might meet a geezer who isn't covered in tomato juice and that'll ruin my life and it's all your fault!

Del Oh shut up and sit down, you big old brass!

Mike (*To Denzil*) Here, Denzil, tell Rodney about your luck. That should cheer him up.

Del (*To Denzil*) 'Ere, what's that? No luck, me old mate?

Denzil Oh no, Del, lots of luck – and all bad! Last Friday was mine and Corinne's anniversary.

Del Oh my gawd!

Denzil No, Del, that's not the bad luck.

Del Oh sorry.

Denzil See a while back I got this contract with this plastics factory over Deptford. They make garden furniture, camping equipment, toys, the lot.

Del Oh yeah?

Denzil Yeah.

Del Carry on.

Denzil Yeah, well Friday afternoon I got this urgent call from the factory to go to a shop in High Wycombe and pick up 50 dolls. They were being returned, faulty stock. But it's my anniversary – isn't it? – and I've promised to take Corinne out for the evening. By the time I have got through all the rush-hour traffic it's half-past six and I've still got the dolls on board – so what do I do? Take 'em back to the factory like I'm supposed to and let Corinne down, or leave 'em on the truck until Monday and hope no one twigs?

Del Oh well, it's obvious, innit? You let Corinne down.

Rodney No. How can the return of faulty dolls be urgent? I'd have left 'em on me truck 'til Monday.

Denzil That's exactly what I did. And what happens? The factory went up in flames. Exploded, by all accounts. Normally I can carry on working for them because they've got other depots, but tomorrow morning I have got to hand in this unsigned docket which proves I collected the dolls but also proves that I didn't deliver them. When the governors find out they are either gonna think that I have become unreliable or, worse still, that I am on the thieve!

Rodney Yeah, it's a problem, innit Denzil?

Denzil Yeah.

Del It's no problem. Are you two gonna be plonkers for the rest of your lives? This is no stroke of bad luck, this is a gift from the gods! Give us that here.

Del grabs the docket from Denzil and writes on it.

Denzil What d'you think you're doing?

Del I'm getting you out of schtuck and in the money, right? Right now, listen. I've signed that docket and put on Friday's date. They'll be too busy to check this. Now, as far as anyone's concerned all them dolls went up in flames with the rest of the factory. Them dolls on the back of your truck no longer exist. This means that the owners will get more insurance money, you get an empty truck plus a hundred nicker bunce. Me and the Tomato Kid here get 50 dollies to flog down the market and the great British public have another bargain of a lifetime! Everyone's a winner! Petit déjeuner! *(Picks up Denzil's keys)* Alright? I am now gonna empty your van into ours. See you later, Denzil. Tata Mike. Ciao, Chloe, Adrian.

INT. TROTTERS' LOUNGE. DAY. STUDIO.

We have a large cardboard box which contains the dolls. The box has a con-signment number printed across it.

Albert has a knife or a pair of scissors and is cutting through the tape on top of the box.

Rodney is wiping the tomato stains from his suit with a damp cloth.

Del is replacing a few left-over boxes of tomatoes in fridges.

Albert How much d'you pay for 'em?

Del Two quid a piece. We might be able to knock 'em out for a tenner a go, that's four hundred smackers profit, eh? Lovely Jubbly!

Danger UXD

Rodney You've just bought 50 dolls that have got something wrong with 'em.

Del But you know what these quality-control geezers are like. One tiny little scratch on 'em and they stamp 'em 'Reject!'

Albert What about them dolls you were selling at Christmas?

Del There was nothing wrong with them dolls, was there? You laid 'em back like in your arms like that, they closed their little eyes and they looked exactly as if they was asleep.

Rodney Yeah, and we had to try 'n' keep 'em closed, didn't we? 'Cos when you opened 'em they was boss-eyed!

Del Yeah, well, they had put the eyes in the wrong way round, I grant ya, that's why they were such a bargain. Anyway the kids loved 'em. All except that little one who had nightmares and I think she was a bit funny to begin with. Anyway, these are probably Barbie or Sindy dolls, top of the range.

Rodney is reading delivery docket.

Rodney Del, these dolls ain't called Barbie or Sindy. These dolls are called Lusty Linda and Erotic Estelle.

Del You can't have dolls with names like that!

Rodney You can if you go to the right shops!

Albert now produces one of the dolls. It unfolds to its full height. It is one of those life-size, inflatable sex dolls. Del and Rodney look horrified at each other.

Del Bloody hell, what have we got ourselves into here?

Rodney Well, this is your fault, innit? You never stop to ask questions, do ya? You just go crashing in and to hell with the consequences!

Del That is because I've got a high profile.

Rodney Yeah, high profile and low forehead!

Albert They're big for little dolls, ain't they?

Rodney No, Unc. They ain't ordinary dolls. You get them advertised in… *(Winks at Albert)* magazines!

Albert Yeah? Where's that? *Radio Times*?

Rodney Oh for Gawd's sake, Albert, have a day off, will yer? I meant seedy magazines, for kinky, sleazy little men.

Albert You're pulling my leg.

Rodney Oh am I? *(Takes a rolled up girlie magazine from his inside pocket and finds the appropriate page)* Have a look at that then!

Albert He's right an' all, Del!

Del I know he is!

(Produces a second doll from box. This one should be a dusky colour.)

Blimey, look at this lot in here. We've got more colours in here than jelly babies!

Rodney We're gonna have to get rid of them a bit lively, Del.

Del Yeah you're right.

Albert *(Reading mag)* Look at the prices they sell for – £60 each.

Del On the other hand let's not be too hasty, eh Rodney?

Rodney Oi, come on, Del!

Del No, you were the one who was having a go at me just now for making quick decisions, weren't ya? Albert, let me just have a look at that magazine there.

Del hands his doll to Albert who now has both dolls.

Albert Don't give 'em to me!

He throws both dolls down behind the fridges. They are now out of sight.

Rodney Del, we can't sell these!

Del Rodney, Rodney, look at this. These things, they sell for 60 quid each, don't they? And these ones are self-inflating de luxe models, for the more discerning weirdo.

Rodney Or maybe they're specially made for bronchial perverts.

Del Rodney, if we could sell these for just 30 quid each, we'd make what? Fourteen hundred pounds profit.

Rodney is about to say something but the figure of £1,400 stops him.

Del That's fourteen hundred lovely pounds split right down the middle between you and me. That means by this time tomorrow you could have 600 quid of your own on your hip. And I know who'll buy 'em off us.

Rodney Who?

Del Dirty Barry.

Albert Who's Dirty Barry?

Del Well, he runs a little, um, 'personal' shop down the Walworth Road and he'll take the lot off us.

Rodney And what happens if Cassandra finds out?

Del Why, does she want one?

Rodney You know what I mean! She won't wanna see me again, will she?

Del Well, how is she gonna find out?

Albert You stand a fair chance of getting caught if you go walking round the streets in broad daylight with 'em!

Del Well we won't, will we? We'll go down there tonight with 'em, he stays open 'til about eight o'clock.

Albert Just get 'em out of here as quick as you can. I don't like the idea of sharing my home with these evil little things that'll bring nothing but bad luck.

Del Now you know how me and Rodney felt the day you moved in!

Rodney I don't want nothing to do with them, Del.

Del Look, we're supposed traders, aren't we? All we're doing is trading! This is just a one-off deal, that's all. I mean, people make a living out of this sorta thing, it's big business an' all, innit? I mean, you read about it in the Sunday papers, don't ya? All

those MPs and vicars all going off to them vice dens up in Soho to get whipped and beaten up and they pay 200 quid, you know, for the privilege an' all. And, blimey, they wanna walk round this estate one night, they'd get it done free and on the national health.

Albert Yeah, but them sort of people are sick!

Del Yes, I know! But they're still human beings! I mean, if some pervo wants to get it going with 'arf a pound of latex and a lump of oxygen, well that's his business. As far as I'm concerned he can have a meaningful relationship with a... with a barrage balloon.

Rodney As long as it's in the privacy of his own hangar?

Del Exactly. Now, listen, I'm gonna give Dirty Barry a bell and tell him to hang on for us tonight.

Albert Rodney, tell me the truth. You couldn't honestly go out and sell them horrible dolls, could ya?

Rodney To be honest with you, Unc, no I couldn't.

Del Barry – Del Boy.

Rodney But I know a man who can.

INT. A CHINESE TAKE-AWAY. NIGHT. STUDIO.

Like every Chinese take-away in the country, this one has a TV blaring in corner. Denzil is at the counter and there are a few other customers behind him.

From the TV, we hear the end theme music from the BBC Six O'Clock news, followed by the theme music from South East News.

The Chinese owner approaches Denzil.

Chinese owner That's £5.54.

Danger UXD

Denzil Cheers.

Chinese owner It's almost ready. I fetch for you.

The Chinese owner disappears to kitchen and Denzil turns to watch TV.

We now see the presenter of South East News on screen.

Presenter Good evening. Police in South London have warned the public to be on the lookout for 50 life-size inflatable dolls which went missing from a factory in Depford over the weekend. A police spokesman today said that, due to a technical error, the dolls have been loaded with gases which include the highly explosive and volatile gas, propane.

Denzil Dear God!

On TV screen we have news film of a burnt out factory.

Presenter *(over film)*... The factory which manufactures them was burnt to the ground on Saturday night and experts suspect the fire may have been caused by the presence of propane. The theft came to light when security men noticed a forged signature on a delivery docket. Police have warned that the dolls are potentially lethal, particularly when exposed to heat, and have appealed for their immediate return.

As the Chinese owner enters from kitchen with Denzil's takeaway, Denzil rushes out of the door.

Chinese owner *(Calls)* Your food is ready. *(To another customer)* Usually they take the food and run off without paying! This guy's got it all wrong!

INT. TROTTERS' LOUNGE. NIGHT. STUDIO.

The main light is off and only side lights show.

Rodney is in the process of getting ready to go out. He wears boxer shorts and socks. His shirt is unbuttoned and revealing a vest.

Del is over by the video recorder. He is jacketless but obviously dressed to go out and still wearing his red braces.

Albert is seated watching the TV which is showing a schools programme concerning St Paul's Cathedral.

Del I don't believe it! I knew I shouldn't have trusted you, Rodney!

Rodney Look, I've already told you. There is something wrong with that machine.

Del *(To Albert)* I asked him to set this to record a programme on ITV called *City News*. What have I got? Open University on BBC2! So instead of keeping my fingers on the ever-changing pulse of the stock market, I am watching Christopher dopey Wren on how he built St Paul's Cathedral!

Albert I think it's interesting.

Del Yeah, you would. You were most probably around when he applied for planning permission!

Rodney It's nippy in here, innit? Is it alright if I turn the thermostat up?

Del You sure it's not too technical for you? *Rodney gives him a sneer and switches the wall thermostat up. He returns to mirror.*

Del is now pressing various buttons on video recorder. He presses one and the screen goes blank.

Del Oh you dipstick, Rodney, now look what you've done?

Rodney Me?

Albert I thought Rodney knew about videos.

Del Yeah, *Emmanuelle In Bangkok* and that's about it.

Rodney I programmed that computer to record the programme you wanted. Now it's not my fault if it decided to record

something else, is it? That machine is...
(Tries to think of the correct technical term)
up the wall!

Del You're tryna blind me with science
now, ain't you?

Albert Personally I think these computers
are more trouble than they're worth.

Rodney How'd you figure that out?

Albert There was a film on earlier all
about computers.

Rodney You're joking? Oh I wish I'd
recorded it.

Del Oh hang around, Rodney, you most
probably did.

Albert It was called *War Games*. It was all
about this soppy kid who messes around
with computers. Then one day he broke
into the computer that controls the
American nuclear defence system. He
almost got us into World War Three!

Del No chance of that happening with
Rodney, is there? World War Three! This
plonker can't even get channel three!

Rodney *(Brandishing the instructions
pamphlet)* Have you read the instructions to
your video recorder?

Del No, I haven't actually read them.

Rodney Well, why don't you do that small
thing Derek? I think you'll find it very
interesting. Because we have instructions in
German, Spanish, French and Italian and
not one single word in English! And that's
why your machine don't work. It was made
strictly for sale in Europe!

Del But we're in Europe now, we joined
the Common Market.

Rodney Yes, I know that, but we've got a
different electrical system to the rest of
Europe and that's why your machine is on
the blink. Its components are burning out. It
is what's technically known as 'knackered!'
Ronnie Nelson's tucked you up.

Del *(Devastated. Flops down at table)* Oh
Bloody Hell! Well, that's all I need, innit?

Albert You won't be able to sell the others
now, Del.

Del Too late, Unc. I sold 'em all this
afternoon!

Rodney You sold 'em?

Del Mm, 70... er... 60 quid each, Rodney.

Rodney You'll have to give the money
back!

Del Why?

Rodney Because they don't work!

Del Well, what does he expect for 60 quid!
I mean, I've been tucked up. I'm just passing
it on, that's all. Don't worry about it, everything is gonna be cushty.

Rodney You are something else, you are!

Del You're too picky, Rodney, that's
your trouble.

*Del now reads the pamphlet while a
sulky Rodney continues getting ready.
Albert is reading a newspaper.*

*The silence is now broken by a six-
second-long sound-like air escaping from
a narrow gap in the valve of a balloon.*

*Del and Rodney look at each other and
then at Albert who reacts offended.*

Del What was that funny sound?

Albert I don't know. What you looking at
me for?

Rodney Well, most funny sounds in this
flat tend to emanate from your vicinity.

Albert Well I didn't do it!

*Del and Rodney shrug – it's a mystery but
anyone living on their estate is used to
odd noises.*

*We now hear the same sound only this
time it comes in short sharp bursts.*

Del What *is* that noise?

Rodney Oi, sshh!

*Now the three of them are listening
intently. Their eyes scour the room.
We can hear a hissing sound followed by
a sound similar to a large air bubble*

Danger UXD

rushing to the surface and then a loud plastic pop.

With the 'pop' the head and shoulders of the white doll appear above the top of the fridges. It happens suddenly so that the doll's appearance is frightening.

The Trotters react with cries of alarm and rush the the hall door and end up squashed against the door, looking in wide-eyed horror at the apparition.

Del What's happening, what's happening, Rodney?

Rodney How the hell should I know?
The Trotters re-enter the flat.

Del You're the one with the GCEs!

Albert It's come alive, that's what's happened!

Rodney Come alive! What'd you think this is. Pinocchio?

Albert I've seen this happen before! Years ago, I was in Jamaica and I saw a voodoo ceremony. This witch-doctor ran his hands over a dead cat and it come back to life!

Del Yeah? Pity he don't live round here; he could have a go at my video!
Now we hear the bubbling and hissing sounds again. Now, with a pop, the dusky doll appears above fridges.

Del That's you, that is, talking about Jamaica, look! *(Cautiously approaching dolls)* I don't understand it. I thought you were supposed to pull a string or press a button or something to inflate 'em!

Rodney So did I... They're right next to the hot-air duct. Well, that must have caused it. See, they must have a little canister of gas inside 'em and the heat set 'em off. *(To Albert)* Why d'you go and stick 'em next to the hot-air duct?

Albert I didn't know the heat would do that! Anyway, you're the one that switched the thermostat up!

Rodney Well, I didn't know the heat would do that either!

Del Yes, alright, alright you two, now just pack it in, for Gawd's sake, will ya? Whatever will our guests think? Ugly mares, ain't they?

Rodney Seen you with worse.

Del Rodney, you're gonna cop an unfortunate one in a minute.

Albert Listen, we can't stand here arguing. We've gotta do something before the black and white minstrels pop up!

Del Alright, don't panic, don't panic. We'll just deflate 'em.

Albert How?

Rodney Well, they're bound to have a little valve on 'em ain't they?

Del Yeah that's right.
They remain looking at the dolls, each of them afraid to make the first move.
Go then Rodney, have a look for it.

Rodney I'm not looking for it! It could be anywhere!
Del looks to Albert.

Albert And I ain't looking for it either. Could be illegal.

Del Well they ain't gonna call for the police are they? Cor blimey! *(To himself)* Do it yourself, Del Boy.
Del moves behind cocktail bar and examines the dolls without actually touching them.
There it is, right on the back there. Give us a matchstick Albert.
Albert produces his pipe and baccy from which he takes a box of matches.

Del Here y'are Rodney, have a go at that one.
Del is now pushing the matchstick into the dusky doll's valve.
Rodney is doing likewise to white doll.
Does Cassandra let you do this?

Rodney Shut up!

Del Nothing's happening.

43

Rodney Nah, same here.

Albert Maybe they're dodgy valves! We used to get it on the rubber dinghies in the navy.

Del Oh yeah, how can you tell?

Albert Well, once they're up they won't come down.

Rodney Well, you remember what Denzil said? They were faulty goods. He was taking them back to the factory. It must have been the valves that were faulty!

Del Well, how we gonna let 'em down?

Rodney How should I know?

Albert Can't you stick pins in 'em?

Del You're back to your voodoo again, aren't you? There's 60 quid in profit tied up in these two.

Rodney Oh look what's 60 notes eh? Come on, let's just burst 'em!

Rodney has picked up Del's smothered cigar from ashtray and is about to plunge it into one of the dolls.

Del *(Grabs Rodney's hand)* Rodney, Rodney, don't you dare do that. Give me that there. Cor, dear, your mother would turn somersaults in her grave if she could see you doing that. She did not bring us up to throw good money away, just 'cos we've got a little problem! We'll find a way in which we can get 'em down to Dirty Barry's.

Rodney And how are you gonna explain the fact that they are fully inflated?

Del Well, I'll just say they're samples. I'll say we blew 'em up so we could see 'em in all their natural beauty! We'll chuck 'em in the back of the van. They'll be out of sight then!

Albert But how you gonna get 'em out of this flat, down the stairs, through the main doors, right across the forecourt to where the van's parked without anyone seeing you?

Del I'll... I'll... *(To Rodney)* He always has to spoil everything, don't he?

Rodney He's got a point, though, ain't he? I mean, there's thousands of people on this estate. Someone's bound to notice you.

Del Alright, alright. Give me time. The first thing we've gotta do is to get these into another room. I mean, if that bloke from the council turns up to talk to us about buying this flat, Gawd knows what he'd think if he bumped into Pepsi and Shirley here... Albert, put these in Rodney's room.

Rodney What? No way! I've already got a wardrobeful of Mum's old clothes in my room. Them two would just about take the biscuit!

Del Who's gonna see 'em?

Rodney Well, in case I bring Cassandra back. Put 'em in your room.

Del No, case I bring a bird back. Put 'em in Albert's room.

Albert Case I bring... *(Realises his argument doesn't hold water)* Oh alright, put 'em in my room.

Albert moves round to cocktail bar and picks up one doll. Del picks up the other one.

Rodney I've gotta go and meet Cassandra. I'll see you later.

Del Alright, alright. Oi, Rodney, just make sure you don't do anything that might cause embarrassment to our family.

Rodney turns and looks in disbelief as Del and Albert stand there holding the dolls.

Rodney Del, I don't think I could do anything that would cause embarrassment to our family.

Del Good boy, good boy. Mum'd be proud of you. Mum! That's it Rodney, I think I've just worked out a way how we can get these down to Dirty Barry's!

Rodney Oh no!

INT. THE NAG'S HEAD PUB. NIGHT. STUDIO.
Boycie and Trigger are seated at bar. Boycie is wearing his wide awake

Danger UXD

business clothes. He sips a gin and tonic and puffs on a cheroot as he stares sternly into nowhere, obviously contemplating some deal that has not gone in his flavour. Trigger is wearing his council donkey-jacket and eats a cheese salad and sips a flat pint.

There is a pause as they both stare directly ahead, Boycie angrily and Trigger blankly.

They are the only people in the pub except for Mike.

Trigger These tomatoes are a bit manky, ain't they, Mike? Still, they make your beer taste better.

Mike I'll have you know they were fresh Jersey tomatoes!

Trigger Oh yeah, when?

Mike Why do you come in this pub, Trig?

Trigger *(Thinks about it)* For the company.

Boycie Trigger doesn't have many friends or opportunities for social outlet. Every weekend he goes down to the park and throws bread to the ducks. To him it's a dinner party. So during the week he has a straight choice between sitting in the cemetery or sitting in this pub. Unfortunately, the cemetery closes at six.

Mike What is the matter with everyone today? Trigger's done nothing but moan, you've got a face like a constipated rat – at least when Del Boy comes in he cracks a joke and has a laugh!

Boycie It is due to the activities of the aforementioned Del Boy that I have a face like a constipated rat! Derek popped in to see me this afternoon.

Trigger How is he?

Boycie A lot richer than before he popped in to see me this afternoon! He sold me some video recorders for £70 each. I snapped 'em up.

Mike For 70 nicker each! What they fall off, the back of a lorry?

Boycie If they did, they were going round a bend in Dusseldorf!

Mike How'd you mean?

Boycie I have just discovered that these machines only work on the continental current. To make them work on the British system would take a transformer the size of a suitcase and an electrician of such genius that I'd have to go head-hunting at Cape Canaveral!

Trigger Seventy nicker each?

Boycie Eh?

Trigger Those video recorders – seventy nicker each?

Boycie Yeah.

Trigger I'll have one.

Boycie No, no, Trig. See they only work on a continental… alright, I'll drop one round.

Trigger Cheers, Boycie.

Denzil enters in a mad rush.

Denzil Mike, Mike!

Even though the pub is virtually empty, Mike reacts in the time honoured way of all landlords.

Mike Hang on, hang on. I've only got one pair of hands.

Denzil Have you seen Del Boy?

Mike No, no. He ain't been in this evening.

Denzil Oh bloody hell! I've gotta do something really quick! Is your phone working?

Boycie laughs at this ridiculous question.

Boycie Is the phone working?

Mike Look, we had a spot of bother the other week. They tore the wires out. But what's all the panic?

Denzil I sold Del some dolls – inflatable dolls.

Boycie Inflatable dolls?

Denzil He didn't know they were inflatable! I never knew they were inflatable! I picked 'em up from a place called Playthings

– I thought it was a toy shop! Well, apparently the police are looking for them, they're dangerous! They've been fitted with the wrong gas cylinders. They're full of something called propane.

Mike Propane? Here, that's explosive innit?

Denzil Very! Del's got 50 little time-bombs on his hands. If them things get hot they are gonna have to re-do the A to Z! I'll drive round his flat. I'll see you later.

Trigger That's bad news, innit?

Boycie Terrible!

Mike That's tragic!

Now Mike and Boycie start laughing.

EXT. THE NYERERE ESTATE. NIGHT. FILM.

We are at the main doors to Nelson Mandela House. The three-wheeled van is parked 20 or so yards away.

The doors open and Albert, wearing his duffle coat and carrying the box containing the uninflated dolls, steps out and surveys the area.
Satisfied that no-one is looking, he calls back into building.

Albert Hurry up then. It's all clear.
Albert steps further out, still maintaining a watchful eye.

Now Del and Rodney exit from building. Del is wearing his trendy coat and carrying his filofax. Rodney is wearing the suit from previous scene.

They have their arms around the waists of the two inflatable dolls which are dressed in mum's old clothes.

Joan Mavis Trotter died in 1964 and the clothes reflect the era. She would have been a very fashion-conscious woman although her tastes would have leaned towards the gaudy. The dolls are both

wearing hats and one of them has been fitted with sun-glasses; the other wears calf-length boots which swim around her skinny vinyl legs.

As Del and Rodney exit from the building, the dolls' legs just drag behind them. They stop at the top of the steps, Del is trying to appear casual, as if he and his girl are simply taking the night air. Rod is dying a thousand deaths.

Del *(Breathes in the night air)* Well, what a lovely evening.

Rodney *(Can hardly talk as his facial muscles are paralysed in a death grin)* I'm gonna kill you!

Del *(To Albert)* Go and open the van. *(To Rodney)* It'll be alright as long as we don't draw attention to ourselves.

Rodney *(Gestures with his head, his eyes indicating upwards)* Look!
We see a woman on a third floor balcony of the tower block opposite.
She is taking her washing off a clothes horse. She spots the Trotters and gives them a friendly wave.
Del waves back royally with his filofax. The woman turns back to her clothes and then stops. She looks back to the Trotters with an incredulous expression.

Del Hurry up, Albert!
We see Albert at van trying to open the back door.

Albert It's locked!

Del Cor blimey! You got the keys, Rodney?

Rodney *(Fishes the keys from his pocket. To Albert)* Yeah, here y'are. Hurry up.
Albert rushes back for the keys.

Del Drive the van back over here, Unc.

Albert But I'm not insured.

Rodney Well, don't have a crash then! What if the police patrol sees us?

Del It's alright, these dolls ain't hooky.

Rodney I'm thinking more of a public

Danger UXD

indecency charge! How you gonna explain this in court?

Del I shall tell the truth, Rodney. I shall say, Yes, your honour, the other evening my brother and I decided to go out for a drink with two life-size inflatable dolls which were wearing my late mother's clothing. Can't put you in prison for that, Rodders.

Rodney No, they'd chuck us in Broadmoor. The Norman Bates wing, most probably.

Del Hold up.

> We see an elderly black man, Clayton, approaching. He wears a hat and a pair of quite thick glasses.

Clayton Good evening, Derek.

Del (*In a female voice and waving the hand of his doll partner as it to say hello*) Good evening, Clayton.

Clayton Good evening, Rodney.

Rodney Evening, Mr Cooper.

Clayton Good evening, ladies.

Del (*In a high-pitched voice*) Good evening.

> The van, Albert driving, pulls up next to Del and Rodney. Albert opens back door and the dolls are thrown in the back unceremoniously.

Rodney Right, that's me finished with 'em, OK?

Del Here, just a minute. Oi, ain't you coming down Dirty Barry's with us?

Rodney No, I ain't. I've got a date with Cassandra.

Del Look I had a date with that Simone sort from the cut-price butcher's and she had a bag of liver for us. I've knocked her on the head. Business comes first.

Rodney Well, I'm not knocking Cassandra on the head. Look, you bought 'em, he blew 'em up, so it's YP Derek!

Del YP?

Rodney Your problem!

Del (*Under his breath*) You dipstick! Come on, Albert, get in the van.

Albert Why have I gotta come in with ya?

Del I need you to help me carry 'em into Dirty Barry's.

> Del climbs into driver seat and a reluctant Albert gets into passenger seat.

Don't keep worrying. We're in the van now. No one can see 'em.

Albert I hope you're right.

Del Trust me. Have I ever put you wrong before?

> Albert pulls the hood of duffel coat over his head and the van pulls away from camera. As it does so we see the two dolls' faces peering out of back window. The van turns a corner and out of view.

> There is a tiny pause before Denzil's transit pulls into shot and screeches to a halt. Denzil alights from the van and rushes into building.

INT. UP-MARKET HAMBURGER RESTAURANT. NIGHT. FILM.

> This is not Wimpy, more Joe Allen. Rodney and Cassandra are seated at table.

> The restaurant is quite crowded with the 25- to 35-year-old set, all very casual. As we join Rodney and Cassandra they are involved in a light-hearted disagreement, lots of smiles and trying-not-to-laughs.

Cassandra You are a liar, Rodney!

Rodney (*Hand on heart, mockingly serious*) Oh Cassandra, that hurts me! I have never told an untruth in my life. I happen to come from an extremely honest family.

Cassandra You told me you lived in a great big house.

Rodney Well, I do live in a great big house! Nelson Mandela House – it's got about 70 flats in it. You can't get much

bigger than that!

Cassandra I drove you home to where you claimed to live and it most certainly was not a council estate! It was a mansion. I mean there was a brand-new Mercedes in the front and most probably an Olympic-sized swimming pool at the back. The people who owned the house came to the window and you had the gall to wave at them!

Rodney Yes, I remember. And I swore to myself that night that never again would I go out without my contact lenses!

Cassandra Oh shut up!

The waiter arrives with their meals. Hamburger and french fries for Rodney, hamburger and salad for Cassandra.

Waiter Enjoy your meal.

Rodney and Cassandra Thank you.

Rodney Well, you know when I saw your house, it looked so nice I decided to sprawns a bit.

Cassandra You must have known I'd find out.

Rodney No. I didn't think I'd ever see you again.

Cassandra Why?

Rodney Dunno, just didn't! I wanted to see you again but did you want to see me again?

Cassandra Yes, I did.

Rodney Why?

Cassandra Because I thought you lived in a great big house and had a Mercedes! *(Smiles at him)* Why did you want to see me again?

Rodney Well, I wanted to see what you looked like once I had my contact lenses in.

Cassandra And?

Rodney Well, it's come as a great disappointment, Cassandra. I'm sorry.

Cassandra Don't apologize. It happens to me all the time. I meet a guy, we get on well, he regains his sight – end of story.

Rodney It's a tough world.

Cassandra *(Nods in mock-sadness)* Mm! *They share a smile.*

Rodney is about to sip his beer.

I'd like to meet your brother.

Rodney *(Incredulous)* Why?

Cassandra It's just the things you've told me about him. He seems like an interesting kind of person.

Rodney Yes, Del can sometimes be interesting. But most of the time he's just baffling!

EXT. A YARD IN AN OLDER PART OF DOWNTOWN LONDON. NIGHT. FILM.

The yard is reached through an alley which is not wide enough to drive the van down.

The van parked at the top of this alley. Del is walking down through the alley carrying the two dolls horizontally under his arms.

Albert, still with hood of duffel coat pulled up, follows with the cardboard box containing the rest of the dolls.

They arrive at a grubby door, a sign above which reads: "Ecstasy. (Suppliers of adult requisites) Trade Entrance."

Del *(Referring to hood of Albert's duffel coat)* Take that thing off will you? You look like Little Red Riding Hood!

Albert I don't want anyone round here recognizing me!

Del Who the hell's gonna recognize you, eh?

Albert You might not believe it, but during the war I was quite a celebrity round these parts. It was 'cos of all the medals I won for bravery under fire.

Del The only acts of bravery you ever performed were under water!

Albert Say someone saw us holding these things. They might ring the press and they'd

Danger UXD

have a field day what with me being an old war hero! They'd call me one of those silly Fleet Street nicknames. They'd call me 'The Old Man of the PVC' or something like that!

Del Just stop moaning?

Del presses door buzzer.

Barry Who's there?

Del Barry, it's me, Del Boy.

Barry Hold on.

We now hear the sound of keys and chains.

Albert He's security-conscious, ain't he?

Del That's not security, he's just moving some of his stock.

INT. THE ECSTASY SHOP. NIGHT. STUDIO.

There are lots of boxes of non-specific stock, a couple of whips on wall, some chains and bondage stuff, maybe a leather studded bodice.

Dirty Barry is in his mid-30s, a seedy looking cockney. He is moving a box of chains away from the door, which he then opens.

Barry Come in.

Del enters with the two dolls.

Albert follows with the box (hood still up).

Who's the monk?

Del No, no, that's my Uncle Albert. He's alright, he's harmless.

Barry So what's occurring? You buying or selling?

Del Selling.

Barry Yeah? What?

Del What d'yer mean 'What?'! These things, of course! What d'yer think I'm doing, giving 'em a guided tour?

Barry Here, they're not the dolls the police are looking for, are they?

Albert Police?

Del No, of course not! I got these up north. There's a shop I know that's gone

out of business. And I thought I'll get these for my mate, Dir... er... Barry.

Barry Went out of business, did he? Yeah, it's happening everywhere, Del. The bottom's fallen out of this game. It's the government and their moral crusade – that and all the public information films on the telly.

Del Listen, Barry – now you're a business-man who knows a bargain when you see one. *(Referring to dolls)* Now these are the finest quality, top of the range. They normally retail around the 70 quid mark. I'm selling 'em for 30 nicker each.

Barry Yeah, you're right, Del. They are cheap. Someone's gonna get a bargain.

Del No, no, not someone, Barry, not someone: you!

Barry No can do, Del. See, I had a visit from the council yesterday. They've revoked me licence. Closed me down.

Del What?

Barry I'm out of business.

Del Twenty quid each, take 'em off me.

Barry I don't want 'em. Last night I had about 400 of them things. I sold 'em all this morning for 15 quid each..

Del So where can I sell 'em then? What about Soho?

Barry You won't have any joy there, mate. Their stockrooms are full. We sold 'em all our gear this morning. Nah I tell you, Maggie Thatcher's ruined this business.

Albert At last someone's got something good to say about her!

Del He's an old sailor. He's still got a bit of depth charge lodged in his brain. Come on, Brother Albert.

Del exits with the two dolls.

EXT. THE YARD AND ALLEY. NIGHT. FILM.

Del exits from the shop carrying the dolls. He makes his way down towards the van.

As he approaches the van, Albert has left the back door open and is just climbing into the passenger seat.

Del puts the dolls in back of van, closes back door and gets into driver's seat. We now have a shot looking directly into the windscreen of van.

Del and Albert are facing us and are unaware of the fact that behind them the two dolls are also facing the camera. The dolls' lightness is making them wobble with each movement of the van. It looks as if they are listening in on the conversation.

Del Just my luck, innit? If I could have bought them dolls a couple of days ago I could have outed 'em. Instead of that, Dirty Barry and his mates have flooded the market. And while they've got rid of their stock I'm lumbered here with Polythene Pam and Vinyl Vera. Get off, I've got an 'eadache!

Albert That's God's punishment, that is!
Del Will you stop going on about God and voodoo and all that? You'll be shaking bones and waving shrunken heads about next. Oh, I know, I know what to do. We'll hang on to 'em 'til the market picks up. I mean, it's only like the stock exchange, innit, you know, up and down, supply and demand, constantly fluctuating. We'll hang on to 'em and wait for the big bang!
Del smiles, satisfied with his plan.
He starts the engine and pulls away.

INT. UP-MARKET HAMBURGER RESTAURANT. NIGHT. FILM.
Rodney and Cassandra have finished their meal. They leave the table and walk to the coat rack.
Waiter Goodnight, sir, madam. Thank you.
Rodney Thank you.
Cassandra Can I give you a lift home?
Rodney Oh, no thank you. My mum warned me about girls like you. The lift home's all very well but you'll expect a lot

Danger UXD

more than a good night kiss, won't you? And I'm just not that sort of boy.

Cassandra And I thought you were a cert! Look, I promise I won't try and unbutton your shirt or take your string vest off.

Rodney Nah it's alright. If you give me a lift home you've got to go all round the one-way system, haven't ya? I'll take a short cut through the market.

Cassandra If you're sure. You be careful, though.

Rodney Oh, look, the baddies don't frighten me. I'm street-wise aren't I?

Cassandra Good! *(Kisses him gently)* And watch out for unexploded inflatable dolls. *(She smiles)*

Rodney *(The smile is wiped from his face and replaced with a look of horror)* What?

Cassandra Didn't you see it on the news tonight?

Rodney No, our telly's on the blink. Why, what did they say?

Cassandra You know like those creepy blow-up dolls you can buy?

Rodney Yeah, well I've heard about them.

Cassandra There's a factory in Deptford that makes them and apparently a whole batch of them has gone missing that were accidentally filled with an explosive gas.

> *Rodney is sick with worry but puts on a really false laugh.*

We shouldn't laugh!

Rodney No, we shouldn't!

Cassandra They could prove potentially dangerous!

Rodney Look, Cassandra, I've gotta go. I don't feel very well!

Cassandra What's wrong with you?

Waiter Anything the matter, sir?

Rodney I feel a bit sick, that's all. *(To Cassandra)* Look I'll phone you, OK?

Cassandra Yes!

> *Rod exits, quickly.*
> *A worried Cassandra follows.*

Waiter *(To second waiter)* That's the third complaint tonight. Where did we get those tomatoes from?

> *The second waiter shrugs.*

EXT. THE NYERERE ESTATE. NIGHT. FILM.

> *The doors burst open and Del and Rodney exit carrying the two dolls that are still in Mum's clothes.*

> *Rodney has one of those plastic bottles (plant spray) and he is spraying cold water over both dolls. They rush to the van.*

Del You better not be having me on, Rodney!

Rodney I'm not Del, honest!

Del I'll whack you straight in the mouth if you're pulling my leg!

> *They throw the dolls in back of van.*
> *They jump into the van, Del in passenger seat, Rod in driver seat.*

Explosive gas! I've never heard of anything so daft!

Rodney Shuddup and keep spraying!

EXT. AN AREA OF DERELICT GROUND. NIGHT. FILM.

> *Two winos are seated by an open fire sharing a bottle of sherry.*

> *The Trotters' van comes roaring and bumping its way across the ground. It pulls up close to the winos and Del and Rodney alight. They tear open the back door and drag the dolls out. Holding the dolls under the arms, so that their feet are dragging along the ground, Rodney and Del run away across the ground to a safe distance. They now throw the dolls down an embankment or ditch or lower ground and then move a few yards back to safety.*

Del *(To winos)* It's alright – just dropping them off.

The winos have witnessed all this and are wearing incredulous expressions.
Del and Rodney now wait, staring in the direction of the dolls.

Del shoots a couple of glances at Rodney.

Del Thought you said you heard a soosing sound?

Rodney They were Del. They were making a funny noise, like something was gonna happen!

Del Well, the only thing that's happened so far is poor old Mum's clothing's got all dirty! I shall have to take it all down the dry-cleaners now!

Rodney Del, them dolls are dangerous! They've been on the news, everywhere!

Del How d'you know it was those dolls that they were talking about?

Rodney I know, right, I just know!

Del Well, the only think that I know is I've got 60 quid laying out over there and us two are hanging about here like a couple of spare ones at a wedding. I've had enough of this, come on!

*Del starts walking towards the dolls as they explode. Del and Rodney dive for cover and the two winos look on incre-*duously, mud and brick-dust landing all around them.

Del and Rodney pick themselves up.
Rodney *(Childishly)* See!

Del I told 'em not to have the mutton vindaloo! Blimey, that could have gone off anytime, Rodders!

Del and Rodney make their way back to the van.

Rodney I know! We only just got rid of them in time! We was well lucky.

Del No, it's not luck, Rodney. It's Mum.

Rodney Mum?

Del Yeah, she's up there somewhere watching over us.

Rodney Oh – yeah.

We now hear the sound of an air-bubble coming to the surface.

Del *(Indicating Rodney's stomach)* The old April going is it?

The cardboard box containing the rest of the dolls is in the back of the van.
With a loud pop an oriental, female, plastic head pops up out of the box.

Del and Rodney cry out in alarm and start to get out of the van.

ALBERT TROTTER

MY DIARY

1940 - 1945

JUNE 17th 1941
Dartmouth, Devon: Got a letter today from my old pal
Ginger Hopkins. He wrote to tell me that our old
messmate, Sey Piggot has died of a sexually transmitted
disease. His girlfriend's husband shot him.

AUGUST 6th 1941
The Aegean Sea: I was called into to see my skipper
tonight and told he planned to recommend me for a
medal for my actions last night. We sailed into this
harbour on this Greek herring trawler. It was 23.00
and I was at the wheel heading into the unknown as
the night was blacker than a bailiff's heart. Suddenly
out of the darkness came this German torpedo boat.
Quick as a flash - and without giving a second thought
to me own safety or anyone else's - I swung the
wheel to port and sent the trawler right across the
German boat's bow. We were only slightly damaged but
Jerry sunk within a minute.

NOVEMBER 20th 1941
Aboard the USS Pittsburgh, The South China Sea: I'm
in big trouble. Last night was my big birthday celebration.
Me and some of the lads had a run ashore and got
completely larruped. We even sneaked a dancing girl
called Mimi back aboard for a few hours. I was still a
bit woozy when I went on watch at 6am. We on HMS
Pearless were supposed to be guarding the huge US
aircraft carrier USS Pittsburgh from Japanese subs.
Suddenly we smacked straight into her. I got the blame
because I was in the radar room watching the screen.
But I couldn't make head nor tail of it - it was all

blibs and blobs. It wasn't my fault though, the US vessel was at battle stations and wasn't showing any lights. They tried to get me on naval technicalities, like the fact that it was broad daylight. Anyway, the Pearless sank and we were picked up by the Pittsburgh. The skipper says I'm going to be court martialled and he'd already sent the papers on to Naval Headquarters at Singapore.

DECEMBER 4th 1941

HMS Finch, Somewhere on the Adriatic: Captain Kenworthy is up to his counter-worry idea again. He knows a lot of the blokes on the ship are feeling fearful and stressed so he thinks the best thing to do is create a counter worry to stop them thinking about U-boats and sharks. Yesterday he announced there was a cholera epidemic on the ship. It didn't really go to plan. Two blokes jumped overboard and were eaten by sharks. My throat is a bit sore... could I be going down with cholera?

JANUARY 2nd 1942

Valletta, Malta: Docked yesterday. All hell broke loose last night. The skipper found Chief Communications Officer Tubby Fox, always a bloke who liked to live it up given half a chance, in the radio room. Nothing unusual in that, but what got his goat was that Tubby had a bottle of gin in one hand and a Maltese girl in the other. He got put on a charge and the skipper started court-martial proceedings. He sorted it out to today, good and proper. He resigned his commission. There's a Navy rule that only commissioned officers

could control the radio room and he was the only com-
munications officer on board. That meant the ship
couldn't sail. The captain had no choice than to refuse
to accept Tubby's resignation. Once he'd done that he
couldn't proceed with the court martial.

APRIL 16th 1942
The Nile, Egypt: I nearly copped it yesterday. I was
throwing a mooring rope ashore when I tripped over a
coil of rope on the deck and tumbled over the side.
Everything they say about Nile water is true. It tasted
like washing water laced with some dodgy tobacco.
Luckily P.O. Speer saw me go over and chucked a line
to me. I was lucky not to get eaten by a crocodile.

JUNE 19th 1942
Aboard the HMAS Ashton, Somewhere in the Pacific:
It feels good to be back aboard a ship. Two days ago
we were attacked by a Kamikaze pilot. He came zoom-
ing towards us and I remember saying to our skipper
Captain Kenworthy that if he kept on carrying on like
that he was going to kill himself. I was right and in
the end he smashed right into us. There we were, nine
of us and the skipper all marooned at sea with all the
lifeboats smashed to pieces. After many hours we were
washed up on this island where the natives had never
seen a white man. At the start they were waggling
their spears and getting very angry. Captain Kenworthy
was very brave and told us to leave it to him. Now
Captain Kenworthy wore a wig, but you'd never have
known it, except in bad weather when it used to slide
to one side. Anyway he stepped forward towards these

angry natives and, brave as a lion, whipped his wig off. You should have seen their faces. The skipper knew they'd never seen a wig before. Unfortunately, though they didn't stay quiet for long and they didn't think he was a god. They killed him. They wanted the wig because they thought it must have magic powers. They all ran off and had a ceremony and while they were at it we had it away on our toes and got picked up by the ship I'm on now.

OCTOBER 8th 1942
Aboard the SS Gloncester, somewhere off Africa: Glad to be alive. We pursued a German battleship down the eastern coast of Africa right the way down to the Zanzibar Channel for three days and three nights. Finally caught it. Unfortunately she sunk us.

DECEMBER 3rd 1942
Off the coast of Africa: Just heard some sad news from one of the new lads. Old Tubby Fox has bought it. He'd become skipper of his own submarine-hunter. He died in Palermo harbour after dropping a depth charge in nine foot of water.

MAY 4th 1943
Jayapura, New Guinea: Blimey it's hot here. The guys are dropping like flies. My mate Bert Jones has got a mysterious tummy bug. The finest medical brains in Jayapura having been trying to find out what it is. Then this American Surgeon turned up on a yank destroyer. He twigged what it was straight away- Green Parrot Disease. Horrible it was.

JULY 18th 1943
Durban, South Africa: Glad to be alive. It's been a
scary day. A couple of black blokes came along today
and asked me, Jimmy Whitcroft and Jack Cook if we
wanted to go and see the jungle. We jumped at the
chance. We went off in this open lorry and after a
couple of hours the undergrowth started getting heavier
and heavier. We were deep in the heart of the jungle
and there was swamps, quicksand and everything. In the
end we had to get off the lorry and start walking. The
lads were mucking about making Tarzan noises. I got
cut off from the rest of them and suddenly found
meself in a clearing. I was trying to retrace my steps
and when I heard a noise behind me. I turned round
and standing there was the biggest lion I'd ever imagined. I looked at him and he looked at me. We just
stood there looking at each other and suddenly he went
Raaaagghhhvrrrr! I turned and legged it - and luckily
for me he just stood there. I'd come into Durban on a
hospital ship. We'd picked up some wounded from
Monty's North Africa campaign and dropped them off.
I helped carry some of the lads off the ship. It was
bloody tragic to see some of them and I cried for 'em.
Daft, I know but I couldn't help meself.

NOVEMBER 8th 1943
Aboard HMS Lock, Somewhere in the North Sea:
Cold...I've never been so bloomin' cold in my life. I
can't see myself ever thawing out and the ships only
run out of rum. Last night was so cold the flame of
my lighter froze.

FEBRUARY 10th 1944
Somewhere in the Barrant Sea: I feel like a sardine. I've been posted to a bloomin' submarine and we're dodging U-boats while trying to lay an underwater telephone line. If that wasn't bad enough, last night we were attacked by a whale. It thought we were a mate and it fancied us. It was shaking us all over the place. It went for about half an hour. The skipper told us to hang on for dear life and not to do anything to annoy it. He put the periscope up at one point and looked through the viewfinder. He went white as a sheet. God knows what he saw but he said he'd never eat halibut again.

APRIL 17th 1944
Portsmouth Harbour: Some of the blokes in the mess have heard how many times I've been on ships that have been torpedoed - five, so they've nicknamed me Boomerang Trotter.

MAY 3rd 1944
Ryde, Isle of Wight: Me, Chalkie Smith and Dennis Fowler have been selected train for a new Marine Parachute Unit, which has been specially formed for missions behind enemy lines. We've been undergoing parachute training and they've been showing us how to jump off things and land without breaking anything. Mind you, I think we might need more practice. Chalkie jumped off his bar stool tonight down the Dog and Duck while trying to impress a girl called Mavis and the silly fool broke his thumb. That's nothing. Our trainer, Sergeant-Major Walker will probably break his neck when he finds out.

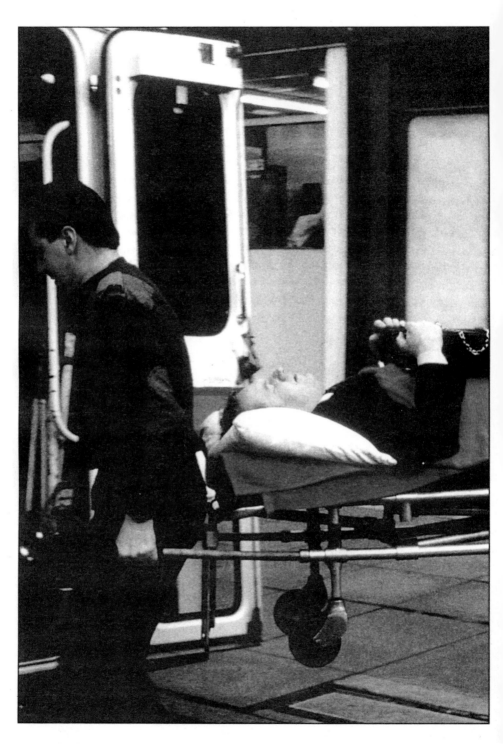

Chain Gang

EXT. THE ONE ELEVEN CLUB. NIGHT. FILM.

There is a sign which reads: "The One Eleven Club. Licensed Gaming Premises. Members Only."

In the car park between the Mercedes and Porsches, etc, we see Del's three-wheeled van.

INT. THE ONE ELEVEN CLUB. NIGHT. STUDIO.

All similarities to the Richardsons' 'Two Eleven Club' are purely coincidental. Unlike Monte Carlo the emphasis here is on card games and one-armed bandits as opposed to roulette. Also the only people wearing evening suits, save for Del, are the bouncers who all look as if they have just finished goverment training schemes to become jury-nobblers.

The clientele is varied. We have the obvious heavies in their two and three-piece traditional suits – the slightly younger set with their Glenn Hoddle haircuts and a strong contingent from the 'Greenpeace' section of the yardies. The women reflect their men's tastes which are usually hot and spicy and come in tin foil containers. There are more breasts and thighs on show than on Sainsbury's poultry counter.

The decor is chandeliers, crystal-effect table lamps, etc and the furnishings are similar, Georgian chairs, a chaise longue or two.
As with any licensed gaming premises the members play with plastic chips.
We have the large main 'playing area' (of which we will see little – just a glimpse of

a card game or whatever is necessary to give the atmosphere of a gaming club).

We come on card table where Del is sitting. He is wearing his evening suit and satin bow tie. During his converstion with Trigger, the croupier deals him two cards.

Trigger approaches. He wears his 'best clothes' (as per Christmas special). He sits next to Del.

Trigger Alright, Del Boy?

Del Wotcher, Trig.

Trigger No Dave?

Del Yeah, he's coming down later. He's bringing that bird of his – what's her name… Cassandra.

Trigger He's going a bit serious, ain't he?

Del No, birds always blow him out after a couple of weeks! That boy's been blown out more times than a windsock. Trig, don't look now, but you see the bloke at the bar? Don't look!

Arnie, who is in his late forties, is standing at bar laughing and joking with barman. He is smartly dressed and speaks with a middle-of-the-road accent – it's neither refined nor rough – it's the kind of accent the manager of your local B&Q would have. Arnie is a friendly and genuine kind of person, a 'solid bloke'. He has a gentle and generous nature and seems relaxed and at one with the world. He's the kind of bloke that anyone would get along with and trust.

Trigger Who, Arnie?

Del Yeah, Arnie. D'you know much about him?

Trigger No, not a lot. He only moved to the area a few weeks ago. He seems a nice

bloke though. He's a retired jewellery dealer, ain't he?

Del Yeah, that's what he told me. He's retired early, though, ain't he?

Trigger Perhaps he made enough, Del. Why, you lining something up, then?

Del I dunno, Trig. It's just that I've been having a few drinks and chats with him over the last couple of weeks and he let slip that even though he retired he still likes to do a bit of private business, all cash and confidentiality, to keep the old tax man off his back. So I thought I might give him a shove, see what I can pick up.

Trigger I heard your firm was broke.

Del I'm a businessman, Trigger. I've always got a little bit pugged away for emergencies. Anyway, who told you we was broke?

Trigger Dave.

Del Ah, you don't want to take any notice of him. He's only my financial adviser. What does he know about it? *(Referring to his two cards)* Cor, look at these cards, Trig. I'm not doing very well.

Trigger *(Produces two cards from top pocket)* D'you want these?

Del Trigger! *(Trigger exits)* That's me.

Arnie How're you doing?

Del Oh, hello, Arnie. Didn't spot you there.

Arnie I've only been here about five minutes.

Del Oh.

Arnie Most of that time spent talking to that doorman. Otto or whatever his name is.

Del Yeah? What's up with him then?

Arnie Ah, nothing. It's just, y'know, I'm not a member, so I usually drop him a few quid to get in. Tonight the price has suddenly gone up 30 per cent. Still, it's only money, isn't it?

Del That's right. Listen; if you get yourself a membership form I'll second you if you like.

Arnie Will you really?

Del Yeah.

Arnie That's very nice of you, Del.

Del That's alright.

Arnie I'd stick on that if I were you. If you pay nineteens you're laughing.

Del No, that's not my style, Arnie, not my style. 'He who dares, wins.'

Del places another chip. The croupier deals him another card.
Del looks at it then places his cards on table.

Del *(To Arnie)* Fancy a drink?

Del and Arnie move towards bar.
Holding the door open for guests is Otto.
Otto is a big, burly thug type dressed in an evening suit.

A couple are entering. The man is in his mid-fifties and looks like a crooked businessman rather than a heavy. The woman is 25 and brassy.

Man Evening, Otto.

Otto *(He takes their coats)* Evening, Mr Grayson. How's business?

Man Well, I've just gone into voluntary liquidation again.

Otto Oh congratulations, sir.

Man Thank you, Otto. *(Slips him a note)*

Otto Best of luck tonight, Mr Grayson.

He throws their coats on chair.

Now Rodney and Cassandra enter.
Rodney is wearing his best clothes.

Rodney Evening, Otto.

Rod and Cassandra pass Otto, who now reaches out and grabs Rodney by the back of his shirt collar and hauls him back.

Cassandra hasn't noticed this and walks on.

Rodney Cassandra, I'm just going to have a word with the doorman.

Cassandra turns and is horrified to see Rodney's predicament. Rodney eases himself gently free of Otto's grip.

Chain Gang

Is there a problem, Otto?

Otto Members only.

Rodney I am a member.

Otto Where's your membership card?

Rodney *(Pats his pockets)* Er… I appear to have left it at home.

Otto If you give me 20 quid, I'll let you in free!

Rodney Come on! I am a member. I've been a member for about five years or so.

We now see Trigger passing through the foyer.

Otto I'm afraid I shall have to ask you to leave, sir. *(Gestures to the outside pavement with a sweep of his hand)* Where would you like to land?

Rodney Come on, what's the prob…

Trigger Oh it's alright, Otto, he's Del Boy's brother.

Otto Is that right?

Rodney Yeah, honest.

Otto Oh in that case, have a nice evening, sir.

Rodney He's a laugh, old Otto! Always larking about.

Del and Arnie are seated at bar. Del drinks something exotic while Arnie drinks mineral water. Arnie is just telling Del the punchline to a joke.

Arnie So the gravedigger says to the vicar, 'Well, I've got to have somewhere to park me bike!'

They both roar with laughter.

Del now spots Rodney and Cassandra entering.

Del Listen, I'll see you in a minute, Arnie. *Del moves to join Rodney and Cassandra taking his drink with him.*

Rodney Oh Cassandra, this is my brother, Derek, and Del, this is Cassandra.

Del Hello, Cassandra, very pleased to meet you. Rodney's told me all about you – but don't worry, I'm not the type to shout it about.

Cassandra That's very kind of you, Derek. Rodney's told me all about you as well, although I must admit I didn't believe him – until now.

Del grins

Del *(To Rodney)* I like her!

Rodney Yeah. Well, shall we sit down, Cass?

Del Can I get you a drink, sweetheart?

Cassandra Just a coke and ice, please, I'm driving.

Del Right OK. Rodney you?

Rodney Non-alcoholic lager top, please.

Del I'll bring it to the table.

INT. THE ONE ELEVEN CLUB. NIGHT. STUDIO.

Arnie and Trigger are talking at a table. Del, Rodney and Cassandra are at another table.

Del Alright yeah, yeah. So what line of work you in, Cassandra?

Cassandra I work for a bank.

Del Oh really? Do they do loans?

Rodney Why don't you leave Cassandra alone?

Del I'm only being polite.

Cassandra They do arrange loans – according to status of course.

Rodney Well that leaves you out then, don't it?

Cassandra I don't actually work on that side of things. I'm in overseas investment.

Rodney Del does a bit of that. Albanian watches, Turkish raincoats, that sort of thing.

Del Would you like me to go and tell Otto what you called him just now? Rodney tells me your dad's in business.

Cassandra Yes, he's got his own printing workshop.

Del Oh yeah? What sort is that, family business, left to him sort of?

Cassandra No, there was no silver spoon involved. He used to live on a council estate

around this area.

Del Oh really? Perhaps I know him.

Rodney *(Dreading that being true)* Oh God!

Del What's his name?

Cassandra Parry. Alan Parry.

Del Parry... Alan Parry. Yes, little fella, one blue eye, one brown, talks with a squint, walks with a stutter.

Cassandra That's him!

Del and Cassandra laugh. Rodney doesn't want to laugh – he's frightened it might encourage Del – but he forces a polite smile.

Del That's him! Listen, I'm gonna leave you two lovebirds. And just remember, Cassandra, Rodney tells me everything!

Cassandra Thanks for the warning.

Del moves across to Trigger and Arnie.

Del Yeah.

Rodney I'm sorry about him, Cass.

Cassandra Why are you apologizing? I think he's lovely.

Rodney What – Del?

Cassandra Yes. He makes me laugh!

Rodney Well, yeah, I suppose he's alright. At times.

We cut away to Del, Trigger and Arnie.

Trigger Well, I'd better make a move. Gotta be up early for work in the morning. I'll be glad when I'm retired like you, Arnie.

Arnie Yeah, you can't beat it, Trigger. Drag yourself out of bed about 11 o'clock just in time to relax for the rest of the day.

Del You retired a bit early though, didn't you, Arnie? I thought you jewellery dealers were making so much bunce you carried on 'til you dropped.

Arnie Yeah, that's exactly what happened.

Del Eh?

Arnie Keeled over on the floor one day. Ticker trouble, stress of business. Doctors

gave me six months to live.

Del and Trigger look at each other. It's that awful moment we all dread – being confronted by someone else's illness. Neither of them can think of the right thing to say.

Del Oh yeah? Well, yeah.

Trigger Well, you don't wanna take too much notice of these doctors, Arnie. They'll say anything to get rid of you.

Arnie This was private.

Del No, you take that Georgie Collis. They only gave him six months to live. He was gutted, weren't he, Trig?

Trigger Well, upset.

Del Yeah, then they discovered, of course, that they'd only mixed up his records with another bloke's.

Trigger *(To Del)* Yeah, but the other bloke only had three months to live!

Del Yeah, I know, I know that Trig, that's not the point, though, is it? I was just trying to say to Arnie that these doctors can make mistakes.

Arnie No, you don't understand. The doctors said I didn't have long to go unless I changed my lifestyle. That's exactly what I did... gave up all the boozing and fags. Started doing all the little things I hadn't done for years, like walking, breathing some decent air. Have you any idea of the kind of damage that alcohol and nicotine does to your heart?

Del has the straw from his exotic cocktail to his lips. His cigar is in evidence. He reacts to Arnie's last words and places the glass on table and the cigar in the ashtray.

Rodney *(Calls)* Same again, Del?

Del No thanks, bruv, I'll just have a mineral water.

Rodney Arnie?

Arnie Mineral water for me too, son.

Chain Gang

Trigger No, nothing for me, Dave. I'm off. *(To Del and Arnie)* I'll see you around, then.
Del and Arnie say their goodbyes and Trigger exits.

Del Yeah, see you, Trig.

Arnie But the most important thing I ever did, Derek – the thing that changed my life was getting out of the business. Getting away from all that stress. I mean you might not believe this, I used to be taut!

Del Really? What was you learning then?

Arnie Tight, nervous tension!

Del Oh… taut. Oh you mean… right… oh yes.

Arnie Got away from all that now. Got me little house, got me wife Pat, lovely caring woman, got me boys, Gary and young Steven.

Croupier Thirty-three black.

Arnie What more could a man ask for? *(Now sending himself up, sings.)* 'And I think to myself, what a wonderful world.'
They both laugh at this. Del kills laugh half way through. Rodney delivers drinks.

Del Cheers, bruv. But you still do a bit, though, don't you?

Arnie Well, occasionally – with the right sort of person. Well, basically I'm just getting rid of stuff I've been left with.

Del Oh right, well just don't forget you know, I am a trader.

Arnie Interested in jewellery, are you?

Del I'm interested in anything, Arnie. So long as it's not cursed.

Arnie And you don't mind if it's arrived on the market via an unorthodox route?

Del No of course not. I do understand that some things have a tendency to, you know, float out of factory windows. I mean, that's just mother nature innit eh?

Arnie Are you in a hurry?

Del No, got all the time in the world, Arnie.

Arnie You meet me in the back of the car park in an hour's time.

Del Yeah, cushty!

Arnie Won't be long.

Del *(Delighted with this turn of events – rubs hands together)* Lovely Jubbly!

EXT. THE ONE ELEVEN CLUB CAR PARK. NIGHT. FILM.

We have a car park. In between the Mercedes and Porsches stands the three-wheeled van.

Del is standing outside smoking a cigar and checking his watch as he waits for Arnie to return.

Now Rodney and Cassandra exit.

Cassandra Well, good night, Del. Lovely meeting you.

Del And you too, sweetheart. And don't forget, I won't say a word.

Cassandra Thank you.

Rodney I'll see you in a little while.
Rodney and Cassandra walk across to her BMW. She opens door and climbs into driver's seat. Rodney is about to climb into passenger seat.

Del *(Calls)* Oi, Rodney, where do you think you're going?

Rodney *(Calls)* Cassandra's giving me a lift home.

Del *(Calls to Cassandra)* Ah, it's alright. Don't bother yourself, sweetheart. We've got the van here.

Rodney *(Reacts)* I don't believe him! *(Talks to Cassandra through open door)* Excuse me one moment, while I go and kill him.
Rodney storms back to Del.
What d'you think you're playing at, Derek?

Del I told you I've got a deal going down here in a little while.

Rodney Yeah, and I told you I don't want nothing to do with it.

Del I know you did, but I gotta meet that Arnie over the back of the car park there,

where it's nice and dark! Now I have only just recently met the geezer so I don't know what I'll be walking into, so I would appreciate a bit of back-up, alright?

Rodney Yeah, but I wanted to say good night to Cassandra.

Del Go on, then say good night, and get back here a bit lively!

Rodney (Frustrated) No, I meant... Oh bloody 'ell! Oh give me a minute.

Rodney walks back to the BMW and climbs into passenger seat.

Cassandra What's happening?

Rodney I'm gonna drive Del home. He's drunk.

Cassandra Drunk? He doesn't look drunk.

Rodney No, I know. It's a bad sign for him. He hides it well, you see. But I tell you, you could push him over with one little finger he'd fall flat on his face. I've lived with his problem since I was a little kid.

Cassandra How sad.

Rodney Yeah, I know, it's tragic. (now bright and breezy) Still, never mind, eh?

Rodney leans across and they kiss a long passionate kiss.

Del (Mumbles to himself) Blimey, let the poor girl up for air, Rodney.

The kiss continues. Now Cassandra's eyes open wide.

Cassandra Hands Rodney!

Rodney Sorry... D'you fancy coming out for a meal on Thursday?

Cassandra I thought I'd told you I'm on a week's training course.

Rodney Yeah, but you must be able to get a few hours off.

Cassandra Well, yes, if you fancy flying off to Guernsey I'd love to have dinner with you.

Rodney Guernsey? You gotta go all the way over to Guernsey?

Cassandra Yes. I did ask Guernsey if it would like to come to me, but it refused

point-blank!

Rodney Why do you have to go to Guernsey?

Cassandra Because – God! Watch my lips closely. Because that is where the training course is being held! Have you got some problem with this?

Rodney No, it's just that it's Guernsey.

Cassandra Is there something I should know Rodney? Did you and Guernsey have some kind of relationship once?

Rodney I've heard about these company training courses. They're just an excuse for loads of people to hold an orgy.

Cassandra Really?

Rodney Please be serious for one moment, Cassandra.

Cassandra Look, Rodney, if what you've heard is true and all these perfectly staid and boring people suddenly hurl themselves into a pit of carnal abandon, it doesn't mean I have to join in, does it?

Rodney No, I suppose not.

Cassandra There's no 'suppose' about it.

Rodney No, I'm sorry. You're right.

Cassandra 'Course I'm right. I mean, I'll take my whip, just in case!

They smile at each other. They are looking into each other's eyes.

Rodney I'll phone you.

Cassandra I'll phone you as well.

Rodney Better make sure we don't phone at the same time, otherwise we'll both be engaged... (Searches for the courage to say his next line) I love you.

Cassandra Do you?

Rodney just nods. We see a trace of smoke drift across his face.

Cassandra And I... (Coughs)

Rodney now coughs. Del is leaning on the car, his elbow on roof. The smoke is coming from his cigar which is close to the slightly open window.

Del Come on, Rodney, he's here.

Rodney sighs, annoyed and frustrated at

Chain Gang

his brother's intervention.

Rodney Don't have a nice time, will you?

Cassandra I'll try not to.

They kiss quickly and Rodney alights. Cassandra starts engine and with a toot of the horn drives off into the night.

Del and Rodney walk towards the Jaguar.

Del What were you doing with that girl?

Rodney I was saying good night.

Del Saying good night! She had her head in your mouth at one point!

Rodney You mean you was watching?

Del I couldn't help myself. Last time I saw anything like that it was at a circus.

Rodney goes to reply but starts coughing again.

Del What's up?

Rodney I've got a tickle in me throat.

Del You've most probably got her wig stuck in it!

They now hear the car, a late model Jaguar XJ6 and Arnie is in driver's seat. He presses the electric window down.

Del Alright?

Arnie Hop in the back.

Del Go on Rodney, get in the back.

Rodney climbs into the back, followed by Del.

Arnie Sorry I'm a bit late.

Del That's alright, Arnie. No problem.

On the passenger seat next to Arnie we see an executive style briefcase. Arnie hands it into the back to Del.

Arnie Open that.

Del opens case. Inside we see a large piece of folded felt. Del unfolds it to reveal 250 gold chains.

Del Jeez!

Rodney What'd you do, mug Mr T?

Arnie There's 250 chains there. Eighteen carat gold. Now if you was to go to some poncy Bond Street shop – you know the sort, with plenty of mark-up – they'd want

200 quid each for those. That's £50,000 sitting there.

Del Fifty grand! Here, wait a minute. This ain't the result of some raid, is it?

Arnie No, no. Nothing like that. No, no. Look, six months ago a client of mine asked me if I could get hold of these sort of things for him for the right price. Do you know Maxi Stavros?

Del No, I don't.

Arnie Oh you're lucky. Well, he's a nice enough guy, 'til it comes to money – then he gets nasty. Anyway, we agreed on a price and he was gonna pay me 25 grand.

Del Bloody hell!

Arnie He's got all these contacts in the States, you see; this sort of thing sells very well over there. It's the English hallmarks, the Yanks love all that. Anyway, I acquired the goods and I haven't heard from him since.

Rodney You could sue him for breach of contract.

Del Listen to it, will you?

Arnie No, son, there's no contract between friends. It's a man's word, handshake, a gentleman's agreement. Anyway, Mr Stavros is not the sort of man you'd want to sue. No, he's never let me down before so I suppose he's got troubles. But then, so have I. I can't wait any longer. I'm gonna have to let these go at half the wholesale price. That's 50 quid each.

Del So, what's the catch? I mean, you mentioned an unorthodox route.

Arnie I didn't pay the VAT. I assumed that they were for retail outside the European Union and therefore would not be liable for VAT. Now I'm lumbered with 'em. So what d'you reckon? You still interested?

Del Well, yeah, yeah, I'm interested, yeah. Well, yeah, I'll take two.

Arnie Two?

Del Oh alright, three.

Arnie No, I'm not running a corner shop, Del. I'm a dealer. I buy and sell jewellery in bulk. The whole lot or none at all.

Del *(Suddenly realising this is big time and embarrassed by his own small thinking)* Yeah, no, no, no, I know that, no, it's just that I meant I'll take two or three as samples to show my clients, you know?

Arnie Yeah, twelve and a half grand in cash and they're all yours.

Del Yeah, well, I don't think I've got that sort of money on me at the moment, Arnie.

Arnie I can wait. Look, you sell those round the pubs and clubs, the worst you do is double your money.

Del I'll take 'em.

Rodney *(Horrified)* Twelve and an 'arf thousand p...

Rodney reacts as he feels a sharp kick in the shin.

Del Subject to a surveyor's report, of course.

Arnie Oh, of course.

Del OK, then listen. D'you know the Nag's Head in Peckham?

Arnie I'll find it.

Del Right, well, I'll see you there tomorrow at one o'clock. *(Hands back the briefcase and chains)*

Arnie OK.

Del Take care of 'em won't you?

Del and Rodney alight from car, Rodney now has a slight limp. Arnie pulls away.

Rodney You kicked me!

Del Yes, that's because you've got a big mouth, Rodney. You nearly gave Arnie the impression that we were small time. If I can just pull this off, Rodney, I will double my investment. ·

Rodney Del, where you gonna get twelve and 'arf thousand pound?

Del Well, there's Boycie, he's got a lot of money, likes a gamble. Mike down the Nag's Head, he knows a bargain when he sees one.

I'll put together a little consortium!

Rodney What, you mean just hand the whole deal over to them?

Del No, no, no. I've got some money to put in.

Rodney No, Del. Don't you remember what I told you the other day? Our partnership is virtually broke.

Del No, Rodney, our partnership is potless. What I mean is *I've* got some money to put in.

Rodney You... How much?

Del *(Sheepishly)* Oh, it's only about four grand Rodders, that's all.

Rodney Four thousand pounds?

Del It's my nest egg.

Rodney That's more like a bleedin' ostrich egg! Where did you get that from?

Del It's just been money I've been saving up over the years. Little bit here, little bit there, y'know. It soon builds up.

Rodney You conning git!

Rodney walks away. Del follows.

Del Eh? No, no, you could have done the same thing.

Rodney Don't talk to me.

Del No, you could have done. No, you could. Mum said to me on her deathbed, she said, 'Del Boy...'

Rodney Shut up!

Del No, she did. She said, "You make sure that Rodney puts a shilling a week away and he'll never go wrong." But you wouldn't have none of it.

Rodney Not listening!

INT. TROTTERS' LOUNGE. DAY. STUDIO.

Albert is seated at table counting some money (a few fivers, tenners and coins).

Rodney, wearing his camouflage jacket, enters from hall. He is in a rather melancholy mood after seeing Cassandra off.

Albert You're back early. I thought you'd

Chain Gang

still be at the airport.

Rodney No, her plane got off on time. Where's Del?

Albert Well, him and Arnie and the rest of the consortium have gone down the jeweller's to have them chains examined.

Rodney The rest of the consortium! How many's in it?

Albert Well, there's Del, there's Trigger, there's... there's Mike, there's that feller Boycie and – there's me. Of course, there could be more by now.

Rodney What's he playing at? He's gone a bit public, ain't he?

Albert He's got to raise the money somehow. A chance to double your money doesn't come around too often. I've just been down the post office and got my savings out. Pity you weren't interested, Rodney. You could have made yourself a nice few bob.

Rodney Well, yeah, I suppose I could have, but the thing, is, you see, them chains are part of a VAT rip-off, ain't they?

Albert I know, that's why they're so cheap! Do you want a cuppa tea, son?

Rodney No, I don't want nothing.

Albert What's wrong?

Rodney Nothing. Everything's fine.

Albert Look, you got her hotel number, give her a call.

Rodney No way! She was supposed to call me at 12.30 and look, 12.37. No, she's probably having a drink and a laugh with all them yuppy sorts from the bank.

Albert She might be in bed, Rodney.

Rodney Eh?

Albert I mean, sleeping off the jet lag.

Rodney Jet lag? She's only gone to Guernsey!

Del enters. He is wearing his best-of-business clothes.

Albert So what the jeweller say?

Del They're pucca, Unc. They are the real McCoy! Solid gold, 18-carat. Top–class workmanship, just like Arnie said. Oh, we'll double our money on these, have no fear. Very shrewd move of yours, Rodney, you know, not to get involved in this deal.

Rodney Shut up!

Boycie enters. He is dressed in a particularly lairy way. He wears a three-piece cream suit, A brown shirt with some kind of pattern and a multi-coloured tie. He has a pair of sunglasses either hanging from his breast pocket or stuck on top of his head.

Boycie is followed by Arnie who has the briefcase chained to his wrist and Mike and Trigger.

Del Alright gentlemen? Would you like a celebration drink?

Boycie I think we should discuss the matter in private before we celebrate. I don't like being premature.

Trigger No, Marlene said something about that the other day.

Boycie reacts

Del I hope you don't mind, Arnie, but I and the consortium would like to have a little board meeting.

Arnie No, no, of course not.

Rodney Well, perhaps you'd like to wait in reception.

Del glares at Rodney's sarcasm.

Del Help yourself to some tea. There's plenty of egg mayonnaise and tomatoes in the fridge.

Arnie No, that's OK, thanks very much.
Arnie moves towards the kitchen with briefcase.

Boycie I think I would prefer it if the gold stayed in the room with us!

Del I don't believe him! I'm sorry about this Arnie.

Arnie I'm not blaming you, Derek. I'd like to keep an eye on it as well, Mr Boyce.

Arnie takes a key from pocket and unlocks wrist-cuff. He places the brief-case on the floor and leaning against door jamb so that half the case is in kitchen and the other half in lounge.

So if I leave it here, then we can both see it. Alright?

Boycie Perfect.

Arnie Thank you. *(Exits to kitchen)*

Del *(To Boycie.)* What is the matter with you? You're giving Arnie the impression you don't trust him!

Boycie And he wouldn't be far wrong, would he? I don't even know the man.

Trigger He seems a decent enough fella to me, Boycie.

Del That's right, that's right! He's a solid bloke, right, I can vouch for him.

Mike Well, he's played it straight down the line with us. He said those chains were worth 25K and we've just had it confirmed by an independent jeweller. So what more d'you want?

Boycie I want to know how he can afford to sell 'em at 50 per cent less than their wholesale price.

Mike 'Cos he bought 'em a long time ago when the price of gold was down.

Del Plus he didn't bother to tell those very nice people down at the VAT office.

Boycie Alright, here's my seven grand. *(Lays a large wad of £50 notes on table)*

Del *(Lays his bundle on top)* There's my four. Come on, then, Michael, let's see you.

Mike A thousand. *(Lays his notes on pile)*

Del That's it! Good, come on.

Trigger I've bin a bit strapped recently, Del. I could only get £274.50. My aunt Reen had to pawn her necklace for that.

Del Yes, alright, Trig, don't worry, don't worry, mate. We'll double your money for you. Come on, Albert, d'you go down the post office?

Albert I didn't get as much as I thought, son. I only got £189 and 26 new pee.

Del Oh I thought that you said that you had over 200-odd quid.

Albert I know. I miscalculated the interest. *Boycie has been working the figures out on a calculator.*

Boycie That means that we are £36.24 short of the target.

Rodney *(With the confident tone of the great decision-maker)* Not any more you're not! You can count me in! *(Places some notes and coins on table)*

Del Oh! Thank God for the Great Gatsby here! Oh Arnie, Arnie, come on, the board meeting's over.

Arnie And have you reached an executive decision?

Del Yes, yes, we have, the deal is on!

Arnie What a relief! Couldn't stand any more of that tea!

Del Yes.

Arnie picks up briefcase, places it on table and opens it.

Arnie This, gentlemen, is yours!

Del And here is the old doh ray me. *Arnie picks up the various bundles of notes. Scrapes the coins into his hand.*

Arnie Oh look at that, isn't that sweet? It reminds me of holidays in County Donegal.

Del Oh, is that a paddy tenpence piece? Oh, I'll change that for you.

Arnie Oh don't worry. I won't bother counting. I trust you.

Del That's right, good. Well, we've all got to learn to trust each other, Arnie. Don't worry about Boycie. He's just got his funny little ways. You ask his missus!

Arnie Oh that reminds me. Do you mind if I phone the wife?

Del Yeah, sure, no problem, no problem. Here, I'll get the phone for you. 'Ere, what about that drink, then, chaps? Celebration drink, eh? You're staying aren't you, Arnie?

Chain Gang

Arnie Yeah, a quick one, Del. Mineral water – something like that.

Del Leave it to me. Rodney, there's some beers in the fridge.

Rodney exits to kitchen.

Boycie Well, seeing as how it's a special occasion I think I'll have a drop of that port.

Mike Yeah, same here, Del.

Trigger I'll wait for Dave to come back with the beers.

Del hands drink to Boycie, then one to Mike.

Rodney enters with some cans of beer.

Arnie Pat? Yeah, it's me, love... yeah. No, I don't know what time I'll be back. Soon as I can drag meself away from this bunch of toerags.

It's now all light and jovial – the chaps, now including Arnie, having a drink and a laugh.

Del Don't wait up for him, Pat, he's probably on a ghoster.

Arnie *(Laughing, hand over mouthpiece)* Shut up! She'll think I'm back on the booze. So how's things at home love? *(Reacts. It's as if the blood has drained from his body)* What? When?...

The laughter slowly stops.

You mean he's here in London? No, I can't meet him, no! No, love, I haven't got them any more! Pat, I would not joke about a thing as serious as this. I've just this minute sold them to Del and his consortium. But I don't care how much money he's got... No, I am not getting excited! Alright, look, I will meet him... And I will explain the situation, alright? Alright, I'll talk to you soon love.

Trigger Everything alright, Arnie?

Arnie You know that client of mine I told you about?

Del Yeah, what, that Mr Stavros or whatever?

Arnie Yeah. He's in London, he's just phoned my house. He wants to meet me for lunch.

Rodney You mean he's come to pick up the chains?

Arnie Yes. Ironic innit? He's got 25 grand in cash to give me and I've just let 'em go for 12 and a half!

Boycie What's all this about, then?

Del Well, about six months ago Arnie made a deal on these chains with some international jeweller mush.

Mike So they weren't yours to sell in the first place?

Arnie No, no, they belonged to me... No, Mr Stavros never actually gave me any money for them, so in the eyes of the law they were still legally mine. But he's an odd sort of person. Once you've shaken hands on the deal, as far as he's concerned they're his property, and now he's come to collect.

Rodney And he is given to bouts of mindless violence, ain't he?

Arnie Very, very nasty.

Boycie Let him. If he wants a war, we'll give him one! Won't we?

Rodney Eh?

Albert I don't like the sound of that!

Mike Oh don't worry, Albert, there won't be many naval engagements in this one.

Rodney Well, look. Why don't we sell the chains back to Arnie – with a small profit, of course.

Boycie Are you off your trolley?

Trigger We'll still be making a bit each, Boycie.

Boycie We can double our money on these things!

Rodney Yeah, but Stavros is gonna give Arnie a bad time, ain't he?

Boycie I don't care if he redecorates Regent Street with Arnie! This is business! No, I have every sympathy for Arnie's predicament, but at the end of the day it's a bit like Mike's pub grub – tough!

Del I don't believe you sometimes. I just don't believe you. You call yourself a

businessman? You're missing the most important point of the whole situation! A man has arrived in London to buy 250 18-carat gold chains from Arnie here. He is willing to pay £25,000, with cash on the hip. But poor Arnie doesn't have them any more – we have!

Now a smile begins cracking across Boycie's face, followed by Mike and Rodney and then Albert. They all see the plan except for one.

Trigger So what you saying, Del?

Del Blimey! Give me a piece of chalk, somebody, will ya? What I'm trying to say is: why don't we ask Arnie to keep his lunch appointment with this man, and sell them chains for us? For which we will give Arnie a couple of grand for his trouble?

Rodney That way Stavros gets the goods at the agreed price.

Del Arnie gets a deuce in bunce, plus he keeps his kneecaps where nature intended.

Mike And our consortium gets ten and an 'arf grand profit for doing sod all!

Del Everyone's a winner! Après moi, le deluge.

Trigger I like the sound of that, Del Boy.

Arnie That is brilliant Derek, brilliant. Thank you!

Boycie *(Grudgingly)* Yeah, it's not a bad idea, Del.

Del *(Closing the lid on briefcase)* So, where is this, where is this restaurant of yours?

Arnie It's an Italian place off the King's Road. I'd better get my skates on.

Boycie I think it would be a good idea if we came with you, don't you, Arnie?

Del Yeah, he's right. I mean, you don't wanna go walking across the estate with a case full of gold, do you? Not on your own, anyway.

Arnie Fair enough. Well, let's get going. We haven't got long.

Boycie *(To Trigger)* 'Ere, Trig, don't let him

out of our sight.

Boycie, Mike and Trigger exit.

Del Go on, go on. Oi, come on, Albert, get that down ya and get in the van.

Del and Albert exit to hall.

Rodney holds back and looks appealingly at the telephone.

Rodney *(Quietly to himself)* Oh come on, Cassandra, ring! Well, I ain't phoning you, if that's what you think. I'm a man.

INT/EXT. ITALIAN RESTAURANT. DAY. FILM.

This is an up-market Chelsea restaurant. It is lunchtime and therefore quite crowded with smartly dressed couples, businessmen, etc. Arnie enters with the briefcase containing the gold chained to his wrist. The head waiter, Mario, approaches.

Mario May I help you, sir?

Arnie I'm expecting to meet Mr Stavros here. I wonder if he's booked a table?

Mario *(Checking reservation book)* Mr Stavros.

At this point we see Del and Boycie enter. Yes, he has booked a table. I'm afraid the gentleman hasn't arrived yet. Would you care to wait at the table?

Arnie Yes.

Mario, in italian, tells another waiter to take Arnie to his table.

Mario Portare il signore.

A look is shared between Arnie and Del and Boycie. Arnie follows the waiter towards his table.

Yes, gentlemen?

Del A table for two, please.

Mario Have you booked?

Boycie No, we haven't.

Mario I'm afraid we are very crowded at the moment.

Del This might make a bit of room. *(Del pushes a few notes in the waiter's top pocket.)*

Chain Gang

Mario Of course, grazie! Enrico…
In Italian, Mario tells another waiter to show Del and Boycie to a table. Arnie is arriving at his window table. At this point he is standing. He now sits out of frame and we see that he was masking the three-wheeled van which is parked opposite and to the right.

We pan to the left to see Mike and Trigger sitting in Mike's car.

We now see Del and Boycie at their table and both facing in Arnie's direction.

Del *(Quietly to Boycie)* Why didn't you sit that side?

Boycie 'Cos I wouldn't be able to see Arnie then. Why, what's the matter?

Del It's just we're both sitting on the same side. Sort of next to each other…

Boycie So?

Del So it might look a bit funny.

Boycie What d'you mean?

Del People might think that we're a bit funny.

Boycie Why don't you go and sit on the other side then?

Del 'Cos I wanna keep me eye on Arnie, don't I?

Boycie So do I!

Del Yes, I know. But it's my consortium!

Boycie I put most of the money in!

Del But it was my idea!

They now realise that because of the secret whispering, they have actually managed to draw attention to themselves.

Boycie gestures towards entrance door, where a burly Greek-looking man of about 50 enters.

Behind him is a younger and bigger Greek-looking man (as if he's a minder). Del reacts to the size of them.

Mario now leads the men towards Arnie's window table. As they approach Arnie looks up from his menu, but at the last second Mario directs them to the table next to Arnie where two business-type men are seated.

Del now becomes aware that Boycie has his hand on Del's hand.

Mario Nice to see you again, sir.

Del Get your hand off mine!

Boycie Eh?

Del I said, 'Get your hand off mine!' They'll think we're a couple of woofters or something!

Boycie They can think what they like! I've got seven grand sitting up there and that's all I'm concerned with!

Del But we musn't draw attention to ourselves! We've got to appear to be perfectly pukka people, right? So don't do anything that'll make us look different.

Boycie Alright.

Mario Would you care to order now gentlemen?.

Del and Boycie I'm not hungry.

We cut to Mike and Trigger seated in the escort.

Trigger Do you reckon it'll turn violent in there?

Mike I don't care if it does!

Trigger No?

Mike No, this is a fast car.

Albert What's he doing, Rodney?

Rodney What do you mean, what's he doing? You can see what he's doing! He's sitting in the window there reading a menu!

Albert It's a bit suspicious, innit?

Rodney What? A bloke sitting in a restaurant reading a menu – yeah, very iffy!

73

Albert I mean the other mush not turning up yet.

Rodney He's most probably got held up somewhere.

Albert Yeah? Where?

Rodney How the hell should I know where? Look, shuddup will you? Hold on, he's moving.

Arnie is beckoning to a waiter.

Arnie Could you get me a glass of water, please. I feel rather hot.

Waiter Yes, sir.

Arnie begins breathing more heavily – as if fighting for breath. He becomes consumed with panic. He holds his chest and sways unsteadily on his chair. Mario arrives.

Mario Would you care to order now, sir?

Arnie Yes, I'd like an ambulance.

Mario An ambulance, sir?

Arnie Yes, I'm not very well. An ambulance, quickly.

Mario Yes, sir! *(Calls to waiter in Italian)* Telefono per una ambulanza, presto! Are you alright, sir?

Del and Boycie are frozen to their seats as they look on helplessly.
Arnie now stands uneasily and he collapses slowly to floor.

Boycie What's happened?

Del It's Arnie! He's had a connery!

Boycie So, what are we gonna do?

Del I don't know! I think you are supposed to sort of pump their chests.

Boycie I'm talking about our bloody money and chains!

Del Well, there's nothing we can do at the moment, is there?

Boycie My money and my gold ain't going to no national health hospital! The entire kitchen staff'll be off to Miami if it does!

Del What you gonna do?

Boycie Watch! *(Moves towards the crowd)* Don't panic! I am a doctor.

Boycie is the most unlikely looking doctor imaginable, with his wide-awake suit, multi-coloured tie and sunglasses hanging from his breast pocket.
Boycie begins pushing through the crowd. Stand aside, stand aside. Let the dog see the rabbit. Oh yes, very nasty. He needs an operation!

Boycie now fiddles with handcuff device but cannot release it. He starts searching Arnie's pockets.

Woman He's not a doctor! He's mugging the poor man!

Boycie No madam, I am trying to relieve the pressure on his wrist.

The younger-looking and larger of the two Greek-looking men steps forward, draws his fist back, he punches Boycie who crashes backwards and knocks a table flying.

Boycie, with a small smear of blood on his nose, starts to pull himself up from the floor, but as he attempts to stand, the woman in the crowd steps forward and raises her handbag. She brings the handbag crashing down on Boycie's head. He falls back on the floor.

Mike and Trigger look at each other incredulously.

Woman Call the police!

Mario Yes, madam, of course.

Del *(To himself)* Oh no, not the police. Alright, there'll be no need. I am an officer of the law!

Del strides through the crowd.

Woman *(To the young Greek)* I thought they were taller than that.

Del I'm a small town policeman.

Del now drags Boycie up and puts an arm lock around him. He forces Boycie's face against the window.

Albert *(To Rodney)* Do you get the

Chain Gang

impression all is not going according to plan?

Boycie What are you playing at?

Del Just keep it shut and we might get out of here with our collars intact. *(To Boycie)* OK, sunshine, you are nicked! Come on, out you go! *(To woman in restaurant)* Rest assured, madam, when we get him down the police station we'll give him a bloody good hiding. Alright you, out!

EXT. STREET OUTSIDE RESTAURANT. DAY. FILM.

Del and Boycie exit as the ambulance screeches to a halt outside the restaurant.

They now run across the van where Mike and Trigger are now standing.

Mike What happened?

Del Arnie's had a connery.

Albert You mean he's dead?

Del No, no, he's still alive. The ambulance got here just in time.

Trigger So where's the money and the gold?

Boycie Where do you think it is? It's in Arnie's holdall! Why did you make us leave the restaurant?

Del Because they've just called the Old Bill. Arnie's got seven and 'arf grand of your unlaundered money. Plus a case full of gold from a VAT fraud! Do you want to tell the police that it's really yours?

Boycie Why didn't you try and get the case off his wrist?

Del God bless me gently! You tried that – didn't you? – and you got a punch in the nose and a whack over your head for your trouble. What do you think I am, a wally or something?

Rodney So how we gonna get it back?

Del It's alright. We'll go to the hospital. All we gotta do is find out what time the visiting hours are. It'll be cushty!

We now see the ambulancemen carrying Arnie out on a stretcher. He is covered with a blanket and is unconscious. The briefcase is still chained to his wrist and is placed on top of his body.
They carry him into the back of the ambulance. One of the ambulancemen stays in the back, the other closes the doors and rushes to the cab.

Rodney We don't know which hospital they're taking him to.

Del We'll follow 'em. Mike, your car's pretty nippy. You do the following.

Mike Right, mate.

We see a council truck and a couple of workers putting clamps over the wheels of Mike's car.

I don't believe it, I've just been clamped!

Del Rodney, follow that ambulance!

Rodney climbs into driver's seat and starts the engine.

Del indicates the back door to the others. They move to back. Del reaches out to handle of back door only to find it racing away from him in a cloud of exhaust fumes.

The van races away in pursuit, leaving the rest of the consortium standing on the pavement.

What a plonker!

INT. TROTTERS' LOUNGE. DAY. STUDIO.

Boycie is dabbing his injured nose with a damp cloth. At this point his nose should have turned to a sore red colour.
Del paces the room puffing on a cigar. Mike and Trigger are seated and worrying.

Mike Right, I'm gonna make a couple of phone calls, Del.

Del Leave that phone alone, Michael. No one touches it.

Mike I've just been clamped! I've gotta get

the authorities, sort it all out.

Del Look, I'm expecting a very important phone call any minute now from Rodney or Arnie at the hospital. You just sort your car out tomorrow.

Boycie What's good for a broken nose?

Trigger A baseball bat, knuckleduster.

Boycie I mean, my nose might be broken!

Del Will you shut up going on about your hooter? Or I'll ram this up for a splint! *(Brandishing a metal pen. Rodney enters the flat)* Alright Rodders? What's happened?

Rodney We followed the ambulance down to St Stephen's Hospital.

Del St Stephen's Hospital. Right, now we know where to visit.

Albert No, that's where we lost 'em!

Boycie You lost 'em?

Rodney Yep, they just went straight down the Fulham Road.

Del Oh Gordon Blue! I mean, how could you possibly lose an ambulance! It's a ruddy great big white thing with a flashing blue light on the top! And in case your peepers ain't too clever, it's fitted with an air-raid siren!

Rodney It can also go straight through red lights!

Albert He tried his best Del, but by the time the lights had changed, the ambulance was miles away.

Boycie So what we going to do now eh? All our money and our gold is lying in some matron's office.

Del It's alright, Boycie, don't worry. Listen, we'll... we'll phone every hospital and ask if he's there.

Mike No, no, no. Hospitals won't give you that sort of information over the phone.

Del Alright. Well, we'll drive round them all, then!

Trigger Well, that's gonna take for ever. There must be 25 hospitals in London.

Rodney Oh thank Gawd for the Tory Party, otherwise there could have been 30!

The phone begins ringing.

Del Albert, answer that! If that is Rodney's girlfriend, tell her to phone back later!

Albert answers the phone.

Look, it doesn't matter how long it takes as long as we find him, does it? We can share the hospitals out. I mean, we've all got cars.

Mike I ain't, mine's been clamped!

Del Shuddup whinging, Mike.

Albert Del, it's some Indian doctor from Arnie's ward!

Del Well, tell him I haven't got time to talk to him now. I'm trying to find out...

Boycie Get on that phone!

Mike Don't let him ring off!

Del Ssshhh!! Hel... hello doctor. Yes, this is he. Arnie... yes, Arnold! Yes... Oh yes, I knew the deceased very well... we... deceased? Do you mean to say that he is dead?

Rodney Oh I love him! I just love him!

Del Yes, it has, it's come as a very nasty shock. Yes of course I'll do anything I can to help his widow... Well yes, she's bound to be a bit distraught. *(To the others)* Arnie's passed on.

Boycie What about our loot?

Del Doctor, I was just wondering. Arnie had about his person a couple of little keepsakes of mine. I wondered if you had found them... It's 250 18-carat gold chains and £12,500 in used notes. His widow has taken all his belongings? Yes, do you happen to know where she lives? Yes, I am a friend of the family but they moved recently, you see... But in case his widow don't get in touch with me about funeral arrangements. I know you're not supposed to give out addresses to any Tom, Dick or Harry but this is different... Doctor, look, I'll give you a good drink! No... Hang on! He's rung off!

Boycie Did he give you her address?

Del He couldn't tell me, it's confidential!

Chain Gang

Boycie How are we going to find her, then?

Del I don't know yet!

Rodney I… I could go down to the town hall and find his name on the electoral list.

Del Well done, Rodders, that's good thinking.

Trigger No! He only moved here recently from Lambeth. He wouldn't be on the list yet.

Del You dipstick!

Rodney Well, alright, I'll go down to Lambeth Town Hall, then.

Del Well done Rodney! Go on, go to Lambeth.

Rodney Right. Arnold what?

Del Eh?

Rodney What's his surname?

Del Dunno. I never caught his surname! Well, does it matter?

Rodney Well, of course it matters! They're not gonna be down on the electoral list as 'Arnie and Pat' are they?

Boycie This is something else!

Mike What about the One Eleven Club! They'll have his full name and address on his membership form!

Rodney Yes, yes.

Del No, no. He wasn't a member. he used to drop the doorman a few quid to get in.

Boycie We could go to the coroner's office and check the list of recent post mortems.

Trigger They wouldn't do a post mortem on someone with a history of heart trouble.

Mike He had a history of ticker trouble?

Del They said he'd be alright if he stuck to the right diet.

Rodney And to be fair, he didn't have nothing to eat in the restaurant!

Boycie God in heaven, what has he done to us? He's pulled us into a twelve and a half thousand pound deal with a geezer who's been shown the yellow card!

Del We'll be alright if we can trace his widow.

Albert I've got an idea.

They all stop and look at Albert before continuing with their argument.

Albert The phone!

Rodney Oh God! He's hearing things now!

Albert Arnie was the last one to dial out on this phone! He called his wife. At their house, remember?

Boycie So what?

Albert This phone's gotta redial button. If you press that you'll get straight through to Arnie's house.

Del just looks at Albert. and then takes his head and kisses him on the forehead-before pressing the button.

Del *(Listening)* Right, right.

Mike How we gonna explain it to her eh? It looks a bit bad turning up just before the funeral laying claim to most of his estate!

Boycie No, it's alright. Arnie told her that he'd sold the chains to Del. So they'll be no problem!

Del Ssshhh! Wait a minute! Ssshhh! Hello? Hello, hello? I'm awfully sorry to bother you in your hour of darkness, but I was a friend of Arnie's and I was just wondering… sorry? Oh, oh sorry, sorry. Beg your pardon. Sorry to have bothered you. Bye! Strange, innit? I've just got through to the Highcliffe ruddy Hotel, Guernsey!

Rodney Aaargh! Sorry, Del Boy. Look, I only called to see whether Cassandra got there safely. *(Points at Albert)* He told me to do it.

Boycie And that's it, innit? We've done our money and it's vanished into thin air!

Del Boycie!

Boycie I am going to see if I can buy myself a little doll that looks something like you. And then I'm going to burn it!

Del Chin up! Boycie! We'll find a way.

Mike I am gonna get my car unclamped, Del. Thanks for everything.

Del You're giving in Michael. You musn't

give in. Remember what Churchill said, you know, he said up the Alamo! I'm sorry, Trig, that your aunt Reen had to pawn her necklace. Shall I give her a ring and explain?

Trigger Oh no, don't do that, Del. She doesn't know she's pawned it yet!

Del So how's the weather in Guernsey?

Rodney *(Cheerfully)* Oh, she said it was… It's pissing down Del.

EXT. GATWICK AIRPORT/INT. VAN DAY. FILM.

We see the Trotters' van with Rodney driving and Cassandra in passenger seat driving away from airport.

Rodney So how was it?

Cassandra The hotel was horrible, the weather was lousy, the food was rotten and the people were boring.

Rodney Oh good.

Cassandra And you were right. Some of them did hold an orgy.

Rodney You're kidding?

Cassandra No, honestly. I stayed for about an hour and then I got fed up.

She laughs then leans across and kisses his neck.

Rodney No, no Cassandra, not while I'm driving!

BUSY LONDON STREETS. INT. VAN. DAY. FILM.

Cassandra How was your week?

Rodney Okay, a business contact dropped dead, another one was beaten up in a restaurant and then we were on the brink of making a fortune and ended up losing everything. Average sort of week really.

Cassandra Well, as long as you kept yourself busy, that's the main thing. Oh God, I hate this sort of thing…

The car in front has pulled up because an ambulance is parked outside a classy Chinese restaurant and is blocking the way.

The same two ambulancemen as before exit from restaurant with Arnie on stretcher. He has the blanket over him and the briefcase chained to his waist.

Cassandra What's the matter, Rodney? You look like you've seen a ghost.

INT. NAG'S HEAD PUB. NIGHT. STUDIO.

We see Del and Trigger seated at table and in deep conversation. Del explaining.

Del He done us in South-East London. Rodney saw him in South-West London. He's doing it all over town!

Trigger Yeah… You'd think he'd be taking things easy in his condition, wouldn't you?

Del No, Trig… God help us! There's nothing wrong with him. I mean, he's not a sick man, is he? I mean, he's a conman!

Trigger So you don't reckon he's really ill?

Del That is what I suspect.

Trigger But that night in the club he looked a bit sick.

Del Yeah, but he was talking to you, weren't he?

We see Denzil has entered.

He is wearing his lorry-driver's clothes.

Denzil Alright, fellas?

Del Oh hiya, Denzil.

Denzil Can I get you a drink?

Trigger Er, no, I'm alright.

Del Yeah, same here.

Denzil Can I get you one? Can I join you?

Del No, it's a bit awkward at the moment, Denzil, you know. We are in conference.

Denzil What?

Del We're in conference.

Trigger I thought we was having a chat.

Del This is a conference.

Denzil Listen, Del, I haven't got long. I've got the truck outside. I'm off to Germany tonight. I've got a consignment to bring back.

Del Oh well, that's alright, then, Denzil. Go on, have a nice trip.

Chain Gang

Denzil Are you ill or something? I've just said I'm going to Germany and I will be bringing a load back and you haven't even asked what it is!

Del Yes, I know, Denzil. But I'm a bit busy at the moment, y'know. I'll talk to you later.

Denzil Oh well, see you do. I might have a deal for you.

Del Yeah, alright, mate. See you in a minute.

Denzil Boycie, eh? Got time for a chat?

Boycie Some other time, Denzil. Some other time.

Denzil shrugs and moves to bar. As he does so Mike appears.

Denzil Wotcher Mike...

Mike See the barmaid, Denzil. I'm busy.

Denzil Rodney, how you doing?

Rodney Yeah, bit tied up at the moment, Denzil. I'll talk to you later, alright?

Denzil reacts. He smells his armpits.

Denzil Rodney, why are people ignoring me? What have I done to them?

Rodney Nothing, nothing. It's just there's a bit of heavy stuff going down at the moment. D'you know what I mean? Oh by the way, Denzil, this is Cassandra, my...

Cassandra Choose your words carefully, Rodney.

Rodney My friend. And Cassandra, this is Denzil.

Cassandra Nice to meet you.

Denzil You too.

Rodney Right. Well, I'll leave you two to have a little chat, then. See you later.

We cut away to the conference table.

Del Come on, hurry up, sit down, Rodney. Sit down.

Mike But I was under the impression that Arnie was a good family man. I mean, all he ever spoke of was his wife, Gary and young Steven.

Del Yes, I know, and I'm under the impression that Gary and young Steven are about

six foot tall and they like to dress up as ambulance men.

Boycie What, you mean it's their ambulance? No, can't be, Del. Remember when Arnie come over bad in the restaurant? It was the staff that phoned for an ambulance.

Del Yeah, and didn't it arrive quick?

Boycie Yeah! Come to mention it, it was a bit lively.

Del I phoned that restaurant this afternoon and the manager told me that minutes after Arnie's ambulance arrived, another one turned up. The real one.

Rodney We reckon they do it with split-second timing, right. At one o'clock Arnie does his dying swan act. And at three minutes past one his boys turn up in their ambulance, then it's off into the wide blue yonder.

Del No one's gonna question a couple of medical orderlies, are they? Carrying a sick man out of a restaurant?

Mike And no one can follow the ambulance because –

Mike, Del & Rodney It goes through red lights!

Boycie And you can pick up these old ambulances anywhere.

Del I know. It's beautiful, innit?

Trigger So what's Mr Stavros got to do with it all?

Del Mr Stavros don't exist, Trig.

Trigger Well, Arnie seemed to know him pretty well.

Del No, he only did that. He invented him, didn't he? Just to get us on the... Explain it to him will you Rodney?

Rodney Yeah you see...Oh it's too boring, tell him Mike..

Mike Forget it Trig.

Boycie It doesn't help me my money back. I'm still convalescing from open wallet surgery.

Del At least we know that Arnie and the dough are still out there somewhere. It puts us in with half a chance. I put the word out

79

that I am interested in buying some gold chains.

Denzil approaches the table on his way out.

Denzil I'll see you fellas, I'm off.

Consortium Yeah, see you, Denzil.

Denzil Nice talking to you, Cassandra.

Cassandra You too, Denzil. Safe trip.

Del I bring this meeting to a conclusion, gentlemen. All I can say is: just keep your ears to the ground, right? Trig, that just means listen out; it doesn't mean get on your hands and knees and… Come on, Rodney, let's go. See you, chaps.

Del and Rodney make their way to Cassandra's table.

Mike See you, Del.

Rodney Sorry to leave you talking to a total stranger.

Cassandra Don't worry, Rodney. Even strangers can be fun – I found that out in Guernsey. *(Smiles)*

Del Look at his face, now look, look, he looks as though he's sucked on a lemon! Anyway, that Denzil's a nice bloke, though, ain't he?

Cassandra He was charming. And he actually sat down and spoke to me…

Rodney I'm sorry, I just had things to do.

Cassandra He left a message. He heard that you were interested in buying some gold chains.

Del Oh not more gold-plated Mickey Mouse gear.

Cassandra Apparently one of his brothers, Carl is it?

Del Yeah, lives over in Bethnal Green.

Cassandra Apparently he's met some guy in a casino, a retired jeweller or something, who's got 200 and…

Del Fifty!

Cassandra Yes, 250 gold chains for sale and Denzil and his brothers are buying them.

Del Where is Denzil?

Cassandra He's just left.

Del opens door and calls out into the night.

Del Denzil, don't buy them!

Rodney No, you're gonna have to shout louder than that, Del. He's half way to Germany!

Del *(Shouts louder)* Denzil, Don't buy 'em!

INT. INDIAN RESTAURANT. DAY. FILM.

We see a smartly-dressed Denzil and his brother Carl seated at table sipping a lager each. They have menus in their hands but they are not looking at them. Their attention is centred firmly on someone sitting near the window.

Arnie is seated at a window table. He is smartly dressed and has the briefcase chained to his wrist.

EXT. SIDE ROAD/JUNCTION. DAY. FILM.

We see the ambulance parked.

One of the young ambulancemen from previous scams is seated at driving wheel. The other is standing on corner of junction before returning to the cab.

Gary Can you see Dad?

Steven Yeah, he's in position. About another four minutes.

Gary Right. And this time you make the phone call. It's always me who has to pretend to be the hospital doctor. 'Did you know the deceased very well?'

Steven OK, I'll do it.

INT. INDIAN RESTAURANT. DAY. FILM.

Denzil and Carl look at each other and react.

Arnie I'm sorry, I'm not feeling well. Could you get me an ambulance?

Chain Gang

EXT. INDIAN RESTAURANT/ INT. AMBULANCE. DAY. FILM.

The ambulance is parked outside the Indian restaurant with its back doors open.

We now see Arnie, eyes closed feigning unconsciousness, being carried out on stretcher.

The siren sounds and the ambulance roars away leaving a bewildered Denzil and Carl standing on the pavement. Cut to interior of ambulance.

Arnie's death-mask face now cracks into a big grin and chuckle.

Arnie Wonderful!

Arnie opens his eyes and reacts horrified. Arnie sees the grinning faces of Del, Boycie and Mike. Del and Boycie are wearing ambulancemen's uniforms.

Del What's wrong, Arnie? You don't look too well!

EXT. INDIAN RESTAURANT. DAY. FILM.

Gary and Steven's ambulance is parked outside with the back door open.

Gary and Steven, both rather worried by now, standing outside restaurant talking to one of the Indian waiters.

Gary What's up?

Indian waiter Ambulance come, he gone!

Gary and Steven look at each other wondering what the hell's happening.

They are about to close the back doors when they find Denzil, Carl and another of the brothers behind them.

Denzil Wotcher fellas.

Steven What's happening?

Denzil We're going for a little ride. Get in!

INT. DEL'S AMBULANCE. DAY. FILM.

Arnie Now take it easy, fellers. I can explain everything.

Mike We're not looking for explanations. It's all very clear.

Arnie At least let's have a chat.

Boycie Funnily enough, there was one or 12 and an 'arf thousand things we wanted to talk to you about.

Albert hands Del a large and vicious looking set of bolt cutters.

Albert Try this, Del Boy.

Del Thank you, doctor.

Arnie You don't need that to cut the chain off. I've got a key.

Del Who said anything about cutting the chain off?

Arnie reacts in a state of panic.

Calm down, Arnie, calm down. You'll give yourself a heart attack!

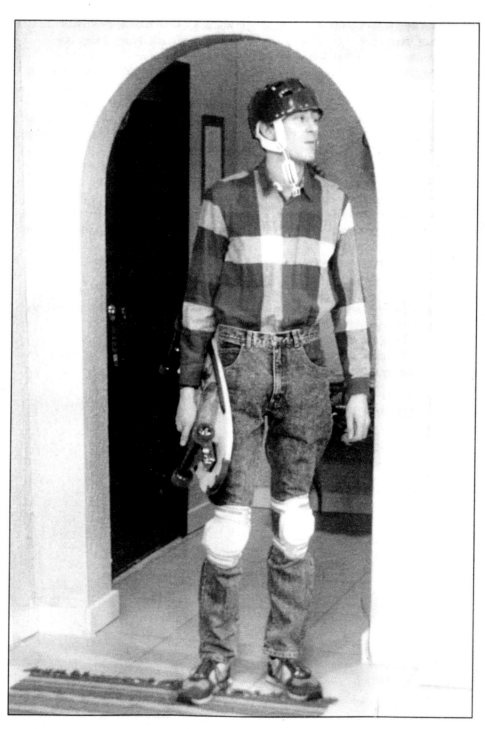

The Unlucky Winner Is...

INT. TROTTERS' LOUNGE/KITCHEN. NIGHT. STUDIO.

The lights are subdued and romantic music is coming from the stereo. On the floor and dining table there are various paintings and sketches (Rodney's artistic endeavours).

Cassandra is seated on settee. She is dressed as if she is going out for the evening and is studying some of the paintings and sketches.

Cut to kitchen. We find Rodney smartly but casually dressed. He is placing the last quartered smoked salmon sandwich on to a plate which is on a tray.
He now opens the fridge and is surprised and delighted to find a bottle of white wine.

Cut to lounge. Rodney now enters from kitchen carrying the tray with the plate of sandwiches, the bottle of wine and two wine glasses.

Cassandra I love this one. 'Marble Arch at Dawn, by Rodney Trotter, aged 14 and a half.' Oh! What's this bit? Did you paint something out?

Rodney Yeah, the Eiffel Tower.

Cassandra The Eiffel Tower? Behind Marble Arch? Is it meant to signify something?

Rodney Yes. It signifies that originally it was the Arc de Triomphe, but no one could spell the Arc de Triomphe. So I thought – I know, I'll stick a double-decker bus going past and say it's Marble Arch. And it worked. In fact my art teacher said in my school report he thought it was a master-

piece. So there, Cassandra, how does it feel to be in the company of a genius?

Cassandra If I ever find out I'll drop you a line! *(Referring to bottle of white wine)* Are you going to pour that or paint it?

Rodney starts pouring the wine.
Cassandra now produces another painting from the portfolio.
It's one of these modern, abstract pieces and neatly in the centre of it there is a label off a tin of Tesco's baked beans.
Cassandra studies it as Rodney pours the wine.

Cassandra Rodney, I know I'm going to make myself look very stupid, but does this baked bean label mean anything?

Rodney What? Yes, it does! It means Del's been putting all his competition stuff in my portfolio again!

Cassandra What competition?

Rodney Oh it's his latest line, innit? He's going in for any competition he can get his hands on. We've had spot the ball, spot the mistakes, spot the dog, everything! Oh look at this lot! Spaghetti 'oop labels, crisp packets, Maltesers wrappers!

Cassandra I didn't think Del was the type to go in for competitions.

Rodney Oh yeah. At the moment he's on the verge of winning a brand-new Ford Sierra, a free manicure for a year and a night out with Maria Whittaker.

They are both laughing at Del.

Cassandra Where is Del by the way?

Rodney Oh, both he and Albert have got dates this evening. Del's seeing some bird called Petula. He chatted her up at a boot sale.

Cassandra And who's Albert going out with?

Rodney Ah, some old dear called Elsie Partridge. He met her at bingo. She's a widow – got 11 children!

Cassandra Eleven kids!

Rodney Yeah, then her husband got fed up and died. D'you like smoked salmon?

Cassandra Love it.

Rodney Good, 'cos they're smoked salmon sandwiches. D'you want vinegar?

Cassandra simply shakes her head. She kisses him again and they embrace and fall gently back onto settee.

Now the door to Albert's bedroom opens and Albert enters lounge. He is smartly dressed in a suit and tie, or better still, a naval uniform.

Albert Did you put a plug on the microwave, Rodney?

Albert exits to kitchen.

Rodney Did you hear something?

Cassandra It sounded like your uncle.

Albert enters from kitchen reading the instructions off the back of a frozen oven-ready meal.

Albert Is our microwave 650 watts or 550 watts?

Rodney I thought you had a date with Elsie Partridge.

Albert I have. She'll be here in a minute.

Rodney Hold on! I thought you was taking her out!

Albert And I thought you were taking the girl wossname out! How are you love, alright?

Cassandra *(Straightening her clothes)* Yes, fine, thank you.

Albert I'm not spoiling my evening for you, Rodney. It's all arranged. I've got a beef risotto for the microwave and a nice bottle of wine in the fridge. *(Exits to kitchen)*

Cassandra picks up the half-empty bottle of wine from table and looks to Rodney, who gestures for her to say nothing about the bottle of wine.

Rodney *(To Cassandra)* Sorry.

Cassandra It's OK. It's the way it goes.

Rodney I know! I could drop Albert a few quid then maybe after dinner he'll take Elsie Partridge down to bingo eh? Then we could be alone.

Their licentious grins fade as we hear the front door slam and the sound of Del whistling.

Del enters from the hall wearing his trendy coat and carrying his filofax. He doesn't see Rodney and Cassandra as he moves directly to cocktail bar. In so doing he has to talk through Rodney's artwork which is strewn across floor.

Del Oh look at the state he's left this place in! You wait 'til I get my hands on that little plonker! *(Del now sees Rodney and Cassandra.)* Oh what are you two doing? You look as though you're waiting for your case to come up!

Rodney We've just been, em… discussing art, that's all.

Del Oh isn't it funny that every time he discusses art, with someone, their buttons come undone.

Rodney and Cassandra instinctively look down at their buttons. Del laughs at catching them out.

Right, Rodney, here's the keys to the van. You can take Cassandra out now.

Rodney We're not going out!

Cassandra We could pop down the road for a while.

Rodney No, Cassandra. We're staying put!

Del Rodney, could I have a board meeting?

Rodney moves across to Del.

Look Petula is coming round.

Rodney Well, Cassandra is already here! We are having a cultural evening.

Del Yes, I know, but Petula's bringing all her gear.

The Unlucky Winner Is...

Rodney Derek, I don't care if she is bringing her gear! We are not going out!

Del Look Rodders, I'm giving her a yuppy salad, ain't I? I went out first thing this morning and bought her a lovely bit of smoked salmon.

Rodney I don't care what you've bou… Alright, we'll go out, then!

Del Good boy! You know it makes sense.
Albert enters from kitchen.

Albert Where's my bottle of wine?

Del Cor blimey! Captain Birdseye's here and all! I thought you're supposed to be going out with the old woman who lived in the shoe!

Albert I am. She'll be here for dinner in a minute.

Del Din… She's not coming round here too, is she? Oh well, that's handsome, innit? Well, you might as well stay in, Rodney. We'll have a party!

Rodney Oh t'riffic!

Del D'you wanna put a record on darlin'?

Cassandra Yeah okay, anything in particular?

Del How about 'The Gang's All Here'?
Albert picks up the half-empty bottle of wine from table and examines it. He looks to Rodney for an explanation.

Rodney Sorry, I didn't realise!
Albert exits to kitchen in a huff.

Del So he's been showing you his etchings, has he?

Cassandra Yeah, I think he's good.

Del Yeah, he's alright, I suppose. You see, I like a bit more realism in my art. That's always let you down, Rodney, you see.

Rodney *(To Del)* What are you talking about? *(Picks up painting of wine bottle. Albert re-enters room)* That's realistic, innit?

Albert Yeah, and it's full!
Albert exits to kitchen.

Rodney I said I'm sorry.

Del Yeah, but, I mean, look at all the other stuff here. I mean, take a look at this one for example. 'Marble Arch at Dawn.' What a cock-up that turned out to be.

Cassandra Rodney's art teacher liked it. He said he thought it was a masterpiece!

Del No, he didn't! He said he thought it was a mantlepiece!
Del exits to kitchen. Cut to kitchen.

Albert It's alright for you to laugh. He nicked my bottle of wine.

Del Stop moaning about your bottle of wine, you old git. Anyway, Rodney didn't mean to 'af-inch it. Look, he's in love. You know we've got to learn… we've got to learn to be a bit more understanding, you see.

Albert Yeah, I suppose you're right. It was only a cheap bottle of wine anyway.

Del Exactly. Now then… 'Ere, that dipstick's only had my smoked salmon away an' all, ain't he, eh? You wait 'til I get my hands on him!

Albert Don't have a go at him in front of Cassandra. You'll just embarrass the boy.

Del You're right, Albert. I'll wait 'til she's gone, then I'll kick him up the jacksy! Any letters for me this morning?

Albert No, just a couple of bills. Nothing from them dopey competitions of yours.

Del You won't be calling 'em dopey when I win, will you?

Albert How can you win? You don't post your entry 'til a couple of days before the closing date.

Del No, because that ensures that my entry will get to the top of the pile! You know, you've gotta think about these things, haven't yer?

Albert There's a competition on the back of them cornflakes.

Del You can't win the raffle if you don't buy a ticket, can you? Listen, I'm expecting Monkey Harris to come round in the

morning. He's expecting a load of them Italian shirts from Malaya the end of the month. Tell him I'm not interested.

Albert But you are?

Del I know that. But don't let him know that. Otherwise he'll expect a fair price, won't he, eh?

Cut to lounge. The door bell rings.

Rodney I'll get it.

Cassandra What's that, another competition?

Del Yeah. I'll win this one.

Cassandra What have you got to do?

Del I dunno yet.

Rodney *(To Del)* Oi, it's Albert's old bird. *(Calls)* Uncle, your date is here. *(To Del)* What an old dragon!

Del *(Laughing)* I know! *(Looks out through open hall door and reacts)* You saucy git, that's Petula! *(Calls)* Come in sweetheart. Let's take your coat.

INT. NAGS HEAD PUB. DAY. STUDIO.

Rodney is seated at a table and is wearing his market clothes. On the table there are two women's magazines, something like 'Cosmopolitan' and 'Marie Claire'.
Cassandra is at counter ordering food.

Rodney is reading an article in one of the women's mags. The headline then sub headline reads; "Sex! A Rose Garden Or Minefield?" Rodney reads the article with a worried interest. He is now reading the second magazine. At the top of the page the headline reads: "Pregnancy And The Single Girl". Rodney reads some of it then looks up, a worried man. He places mag back on table and then sips his drink. He picks up his "Which Car?" magazine and opens it directly to a page which shows a full-page ad for Durex. The ad consists of a blow-up photo of a

condom sachet with the manufacturer's name printed across it.

Mike Right, there you go, love.

Cassandra Thanks.

Cassandra returns with meals. She hands Rodney the pie and chips.

Rodney Oh sorry, Cass, I've sort of... lost me appetite a bit.

Cassandra Why, what's wrong?

Rodney Nothing. I was just sitting here thinking about us.

Cassandra And it's put you off your food! Thanks, Rodney.

Rodney No, no, I didn't mean it like that, Cass!

Cassandra Hm?

Rodney We're pretty close, wouldn't you say?

Cassandra Sorry? *(She moves her chair)*

Rodney I didn't mean it like that. I mean, we get on really well.

Cassandra We have our moments.

Rodney Well, it's them moments that's worrying me. You see, I've got a bit of a dilemma. I think maybe I ought to discuss it.

Cassandra Fire away.

Rodney Well, look, we're both responsi-ble, mature adults.

Cassandra Yes. *(She now blows down the straw and makes her drink bubble up)*

Rodney Oh that's it, forget it!

INT. TROTTER'S LOUNGE. DAY. STUDIO.

Del enters, carrying a large cardboard box. Albert follows Del in, carrying a similar box.

Albert Bloody fair, innit? A young feller like Rodney stops off to have dinner with a bird and leaves the carrying to an old chap like me.

Del *(Mocking)* They've got no respect these days.

Albert They've got no respect these days.

Del You fought in a war, didn't you?

The Unlucky Winner Is...

Albert I fought in a war, didn't I? I fought so that kids like Rodney could have freedom. And what do they do with their freedom?

Del (*Mocking*) Anything they ruddy like!

Albert Anything they ruddy like!

Del You'd better stick all those Eyetie shirts in Rodders' room.

Albert moves to front door and closes it. As he does so he finds the envelope and picks it up.

Oi, is that for me?

Albert No, it's addressed to Rodney.

Del takes the envelope and opens it. He removes the contents which consist of a two-page letter clipped to a holiday brochure which shows a Mediterranean beach and the word 'Mallorca'.

Del Oh well, same thing. Let's see what he's been gettin' through the post. Now then... 'Dear Rodney Trotter, thank you for your contribution to bla bla...We are pleased to tell you bla bla'

Albert What's wrong?

Del Well, d'you remember that competition I sent off?

Albert You've sent off hundreds of 'em!

Del The Mega Flakes competition.

Albert Yeah. What about it?

Del Well, what they wanted you to do, you had to draw or paint a world-famous landmark, right? Well, world-famous landmarks are not my speciality; I'm more of a portrait man meself. So, just for a laugh, I sent off the old 'Marble Arch at Dawn' in Rodney's name, and guess what? He's only won!

Albert You're pulling my leg!

Del No, no, look, straight up! Have a butcher's at that, look. They're giving away ten top prizes of a week's holiday in the Mediterranean and Rodney's copped for one! I always said that was a good painting, didn't I? I mean, it's the realism, you see,

that's always been Rodney's strength.

Albert Aah, I'm well pleased for the boy. He's never won anything in his life.

Del No, only a couple of 'Ugly Bird' contests when he was younger. And look where they're sending him – Mallorca!

Albert 'A luxury suite in a five-star hotel, á la carte menu and a week's spending money for the winners and their guests.'

Del Their guests! Their guests! Of course, it's always a holiday for two, innit? Oh yes, I could do with a break! Oh yes, a bit of sunshine'll set me up a treat.

Albert now turns to second page of letter.

Albert That's strange!

Del What is?

Albert Have you read page two?

Del Well no, not yet.

Albert Well, I think you'd better.

Del Oh no! I don't believe these wallies!

Albert Bit of a mix-up at their head office I suppose. Bloody shame innit? You were looking forward to that holiday as well, weren't you?

Del Yeah.

Albert Still, at least Rodney never found out, and what he don't know won't hurt him. You better phone the cornflakes people and tell them.

Del Yeah, I'll phone 'em and say thank you very much, see you in Mallorca.

Albert But you can't go ahead with it!

Del You don't wanna put money on that do you? Listen, me and Rodney have never had holidays like other people. I can't say bonjour to a chance like this without a fight! It's a holiday, it's sunshine – it's free!

Albert Have you read that second page properly?

Del Yes, I've read it! Look, me and Rodders can wing it! We've got over worser problems than this.

Albert Well you'd better tell Rodney and

see what he says.

Del I will tell him, but not straight away. I'll chose my moment carefully.

Albert Would you prefer me to break the news?

Del No, I'd prefer you to mind your own business and keep well out of it.

Albert You know me, son, I never interfere. But I think it's only right to tell the boy.

Del Yes, what we have here, Uncle, is a case of je ne sais pas pourquoi.

Albert What's that mean?

Del Well, roughly translated it means; 'He who sticks his nose into a beehive will get more than a nostrilful of honey!' Are we understanding each other?

Albert I'm saying nothing, son.

Del Cushty.

INT. NAG'S HEAD PUB. DAY. STUDIO.

Rodney I'd better be getting off.

Cassandra What are you and Del up to today?

Rodney He's picking up a gross of Italian shirts off Monkey Harris and I'm down the market selling kiddies' dolls. *(Pats the old suitcase which is standing next to him)* I won't be always doing this.

Cassandra Doing what?

Rodney Well, selling crap down markets. I'll get my diploma in computer science soon. Then things will change.

Cassandra You don't have to prove anything to me, you know that don't you, Rodney?

Rodney Well, you've got a good job in a bank, ain't yer? Your dad's a successful businessman and me, well, I'm an apprentice fly-pitcher! I mean, let's be fair, Cass, a girl like you, she could marry some really rich good-looking bloke.

Cassandra If I was to meet a handsome, wealthy young man and he asked me to marry him, d'you know what I'd say?

Rodney What?

Cassandra I'd say, "Ciao, Rodney!" And you wouldn't see me for the tinted windows of his Porsche. But until that time I'm happy to drag along with you.

Rodney So you're not just saying that?

Cassandra No, honestly.

Rodney *(A great sigh of relief)* And there's me fretting, eh?

Cassandra I've been going out with you longer than I went out with any of my other boyfriends. And do you know why?

Rodney 'Cos they all packed you in?

Cassandra Right! And because I love you.

Rodney Oh! Well, I love you too, Cass.

We now see Mike is clearing the table next to them and has heard this.

Mike What a load of old cobblers! *(Moves back to the bar, mumbling)* It makes you wanna throw up!

Cassandra Why do you always come to this pub?

Del enters.

Rodney It's the atmosphere, I suppose.

Del Rodders!

Rodney Yeah, on me way now, Del.

Del No, no stay where you are. Michael – champagne!

Del arrives at the table.

Have I got news for you, bruv. You, Rodney Trotter, have only won a competition!

Rodney Alright, what is it, a wind-up?

Del No, no, this is God's-honest. Look, there it is, in black and white. What can't speak can't lie! Look at that, look at that!

Rodney I don't believe this is happening to me! Bloody 'ell! Oh sorry.

Cassandra That's alright. Where's the other page?

Del Eh?

Cassandra Well, it says: 'please turn to page two'.

Del Ah, yes, that's alright, no… I've left that in the flat.

The Unlucky Winner Is...

Rodney It's not a mistake?

Del No, no, it's all pukka. They're looking forward to meeting you in Mallorca! They wanna take publicity photographs and everything. You're gonna be on the back of millions of cornflake packets!

Rodney Am I?

Del Yeah, you and the other nine winners, yeah.

Rodney A Mediterranean holiday, eh? I've never won anything before in my life, have I?

Del No, apart from them 'Ugly Bird' comp… No, he's never won anything in his life.

Cassandra You clever old thing! I didn't even know you'd been in for a competition.

Rodney Well, no, it was… Del, I never went in for this competition!

Del No, no, I did it for you. It was a painting competition, you see, so I sent off the old 'Marble Arch at Dawn', and it's come up trumps!

Cassandra What did the other page say?

Del Er… nothing… er… it was all about sightseeing and excursions and all that sort of thing. 'Ere listen, I'll get the champers, alright?

Del escapes to the bar.

Rodney A holiday for two in Mallorca, eh?

Cassandra Mm.

Rodney Can you imagine it Cass? A luxury suite, five star hotel.

Cassandra Á la carte menu!

Rodney Spending money! A whole week of total freedom. Nothing to do but sit back in the sunshine and gaze at the blue skies and golden beaches – and then dance the night away in the warm Mediterranean air.

Cassandra God, it sounds wonderful!

Rodney Will you miss me?

Cassandra Bound to. But I expect I'll find something to replace the excitement of your presence – you know, knitting, something like that.

Rodney Can you get a week off work?

Cassandra Yeah, I'm owed some holidays.

Rodney Right! What about your parents?

Cassandra I thought it was only a holiday for two.

Rodney You know what I mean. How are they gonna feel about you going on holiday with me?

Cassandra Rodney, mum and dad like you, they trust you.

Rodney Do they? I'm not sure I like that.

Del returns with a bottle of champagne and glasses on a tray.

Del Here we go. There we go. I'll tell you what, Rodders, we'll be having champagne for breakfast every morning when we get to Mallorca. And all down to Larkin. There you go darling. I'll tell you what. I just can't wait to get there.

Rodney reacts, he hadn't reckoned on this. He looks to Cassandra for help. She lowers her eyes, sensing that this is a family matter.

Rodney Er… well, thing is, Del.

Del Come on, drink up, drink up, 'ere come one. Cheers! celebrate!

Rodney Cheers. It's just that, you know, this holiday is for two, and I… I was thinking…

Del No, no, no. It's not for two! It's for three people.

Rodney Three?

Del Yeah.

Rodney You sure?

Del 'Course I'm sure. I read it… it was on the page that I thre… I left in the flat.

Rodney Three's a funny number, innit?

Del Oh yeah, three's very funny. Always has me in stitches does three. How about you?

Cassandra Three's not bad, but seven's my favourite, it creases me up.

Del Oh, seven's a killer.

Rodney What I mean is, these things are usually done in twos, ain't they? I mean,

you see it on the telly, don't you – *Bob's Full House*, *The Price Is Right* and all that game – a holiday for two! So why's this one for three?

Del I don't know. Ask the people at the cornflakes factory.

Cassandra Maybe it's 'cos it's Mega Flakes. You know? They do everything bigger.

Del There you are, see, she's cracked it. I'll tell you what this means, Rodney.

Rodney What?

Del It means that Cassandra can come with us, eh?

Rodney Yeah, hadn't thought of that.

Cassandra Thank you. Love to.

Del Yeah well, what is it eh? Just – what three weeks to the off? Just enough time for us to get some new clothes. You get your bikini-line sorted out, and then we are away. Lovely Jubbly!

Rodney Yeah great! Three people?

Del Yes, three, Rodney, just three, three. Just don't keep on about it, alright?

Cassandra How does Albert feel about you two going off and leaving him?

Del Albert is over the moon about it. Gives him seven clear days to row in with Elsie Partridge. She'll be round the flat before you can say olé!

Cassandra Excuse me.

Rodney Oh right. *(Kisses her on the cheek)* look… er… I'll see you later, OK? Take care.

Cassandra I'm just going to the ladies.

Rodney Sorry! I thought you were going back to…

Del is laughing at Rodney as Cassandra exits.

Del You wally!

Rodney Shut up. Look, I'm glad she's gone. I want to have a little chat with ya, you know? I've got a bit of a problem. Well, it's more of a worry.

Del What, is it about the holiday?

Rodney Well, yeah, sort of. Er… Holiday's

heightened my concern, you know? Made the problem a little more urgent kinda thing.

Del What is it, then?

Rodney Well, it's…

Rodney picks up the 'Which Car?' mag. He surveys the bar to make sure no one is looking. He places the mag under table and opens the page to Del.

Del What, Ford Escorts?

Rodney Eh? No…

Rodney finds the right page. He opens magazine so that Del and us get a quick glimpse of the condom ad. He closes it quickly.

Del Oh I see. Look bruv, you don't have to worry; they're not really that size in real life.

Rodney I know that! God… I know they're not that… bloody 'ell! What I mean is, me and Cassandra, are getting closer all the time, you know? Well, I mean, we haven't done nothing yet.

Del No? I thought you was on the firm with it.

Rodney No, no, no, it's nothing like that. But you, well you know let's face it, with the best of intentions these things can get beyond our control.

Del Yeah. Way beyond mine.

Rodney Exactly. So I feel that in this day and age, er… what with what's happening in the world, it is every responsible adult's duty to, well…

Del Go equipped?

Rodney Well yeah, if you like.

Del Yeah, well, no… that's very wise and mature of you, Rodders, that is. So what's the problem?

Rodney Well I… I keep going to buy 'em…

Del And…

Rodney Well, there's a sort of stigma attached to 'em.

Del No, that's just a piece of silver foil. You chuck that away.

The Unlucky Winner Is...

Rodney I don't know why I ever involved you in this. I mean, well… in this day of AIDS and all the warnings on the telly and in the press and all that, people are still embarrassed to go and buy 'em. I mean, me, I seem to think that it's only seedy little blokes do it.

Del Hm.

Rodney Will you go and get 'em for me?

Del On your bike! Get 'em yourself!

Rodney I've been trying to do that for a long time, but whenever I go into the shop it's either a lady serving me or me bottle goes! Look at this. *(Produces four combs, a tub of vick and some photographic film)* This morning I bought four combs, a tub of Vick and a film for a Kodak Instamatic!

Del Yeah, but they sell them everywhere these days. You can get 'em in the… in the butcher's, the bike shop, in Patel's Multimart – they're by the phonecard counter. They even had a machine in here you could get 'em in once. You know, except it got jammed with a drachma. Have you discussed it with Cassandra?

Rodney Well, of course I haven't! What d'you think I…? Hold up, she's coming back!

Del Alright? Want some more champagne darling?

Cassandra No, I've got to get back to work in a minute. I'll stick with the fruit juice.

Del I'll get you another one.

Rodney Cass. What I was saying earlier about our blossoming relationship.

Cassandra What about it?

Rodney Well, when one is in a situation like ours – one…

Cassandra Or in our case, two.

Rodney Or in our case two. Should be careful.

Cassandra Careful on what?

Rodney That we don't become three!

Cassandra Oh! I see what you mean!

Rodney Yeah… I… I do hope you don't think I'm being a bit presuming. I… I just thought, well, we are going on holiday together and, you know, in that atmosphere of sunshine and freedom and, well, sharing the hotel suite, our relationship might… could – well, who knows? – ascend to a more physical plane.

Cassandra Yes, I suppose so.

Rodney Yeah?

Cassandra Well, who knows what might happen? You haven't been discussing this with Del, have you?

Rodney Well… no, course I haven't, no. What d'you think I am?

Cassandra Good!

Del now shouts across from the bar.

Del Oi, Rodders! You're in luck. Mike's had a new machine fitted in the gents.

Mike I'll get you some change, Rodney.

INT. ARRIVALS AREA. PALMA AIRPORT. DAY. STUDIO.

We see Del, Rodney and Cassandra exiting from customs area.

Del Where are they, then?

Rodney The courier said meet at the desk.

Cassandra There it is.

Above the desk is a large 'Mega Flakes' logo. All of the group wear rosette-type badges which carry the logo and their names written in magic-marker.

An Englishman wearing short-sleeved shirt and a tie is walking among the group asking questions and ticking off names on his clipboard.

Rodney Right! Pour the sangria, José, we have arrived!

Rodney takes Cassandra's arm and they are about to move towards desk.

Del Just a minute, hang on.

Rodney What's up?

Del Listen, just before you go and check in… erm… this prize ain't quite as straight-forward as it seems.

Cassandra Rodney did win, didn't he?

Del Oh yes, yes, yes. Oh yeah, well, it's all pukka and above board and all that. I mean, we're here, ain't we? You know, we've got all the tickets and everything, yeah?

Cassandra So what's the problem?

Rodney *(Is now studying the group with a puzzled expression)* That's strange, you know.

Cassandra What?

Rodney Well, I noticed it on the plane but it didn't sort of register. They're all mums and dads. They've all brought their kids with 'em.

Cassandra What's strange about that?

Rodney Well, except for me, right, all the winners are parents.

Del No, it's not the parents that are the winners, Rodney. It's the kids.

Cassandra What do you mean?

Del Well, Rodney's painting won first prize – in an under-15-year-old category.

Rodney Say it again!

Cassandra So they think Rodney's 15?

Rodney Is that right?

Del No. They think you're 14.

Rodney Fourteen? They think I'm 14?

Inside Cassandra wants to explode with laughter but, for Rodney's sake, she controls herself. But as she looks at him it becomes too much.

She turns away quickly with a tiny snort or yelp or whatever.

Why didn't you tell me this back in England?

Del Well, I thought it might cast a little cloud over the holiday. Look, Rodney, I sent your painting off in good faith. I mean, I didn't know there were lots of categories. But it was you – not me – you were the one that wrote on it 'Rodney Trotter, aged 14 and an 'arf'. So the organizers must have put you in the kid's category. So it's your fault for writing on it.

Rodney But how was I to know that in 12 years' time you were going to enter it for a cornflakes competition?

Del Well, how was I supposed to know that you'd win, eh? 'Ere, it doesn't matter. Now, come on, come on, you're gonna waltz through it.

Cassandra has regained her composure and turns back to them just in time to hear Rodney say;

Rodney Waltz through it! How the 'ell am I gonna pass for 14?

Cassandra turns away again convulsed with laughter.

Will you stop doing that, Cassandra.

Cassandra Sorry.

Rodney Act your age.

Cassandra collapses with laughter at this. (To Del) This is your fault. I'm gonna break your bloody neck!

Del Just look, just look over there look, look. Some of those lads, look, they're over six foot tall. I mean, 15- and 16-year-olds, they look much older these days than they used to. And you've got the added advantage of your boyish good looks.

Cassandra nods but is still hiding her face to conceal her laughter.

Rodney That's why there was three tickets, innit? One each for Mummy and Daddy and one for the sprog.

Del Well, you can't expect 13- and 14-year-olds to go abroad on their own, can you?

Rodney And what exactly is your role in all this?

Del Well, when the cornflakes people phoned up they said that you had to be accompanied by your parents. So I said – and I... I don't know why I did it, I must have been flustered at the time – I said that I was your dad.

Rodney My dad! Did you hear that, Cassandra?

The Unlucky Winner Is...

Cassandra Yeah! And who the hell am I supposed to be? His mum?

Del Shh! Shh! Keep it down! I said that Rodney's real mother had sadly passed away. I mean, that's the truth innit? And I said that I had met a younger woman who has become a very important part of my life.

Cassandra And is that supposed to be me?

Del No, it's that fat bird over the back there! Yes, it's supposed to be you.

Cassandra So, according to you, I'm supposed to be Rodney's common-law stepmother?

Rodney God, please tell me this is a bad dream.

Del You're only pretending aren't you? I mean, you ain't gotta check behind his ears or pick him up from school or nothing like that, have yer?

Cassandra I think we should go and tell them the truth.

Del Just a minute, dopey, just a minute. We're here, now, aren't we? If we all keep schtum we can have a lovely free holiday.

Rodney But if they find out we're lying they'll chuck us out the hotel.

Del And if they find out we're telling them the truth, they'll chuck us out of the hotel. Now return flights are not for another week, so what we gonna do? They'll probably stick us in a Spanish half-way home.

Rodney Del Boy, at some point during the week, they are gonna realise I am not 14.

Del Yeah, but we'll be back in the hotel by then, won't we? There'll be nobody there to ask questions? Come on, we're on holiday, eh?

Cassandra Well, whatever else it turns out to be, it's an experience.

Del Good girl, good girl, that's right. You know it makes sense, don't yer? That's it now come on, come on, then, come on, let's get over there and check in, come on. And try and act a bit mumsy.

Cassandra What d'you mean, mumsy?

Del Just be a bit mumsy, that's all.

Del and Cassandra move off towards the desk. As they arrive Perkins is talking to some of the parents.

Perkins We'll be leaving in about five minutes, OK? It's only a half-hour journey to the hotel, so we should be there in plenty of time for lunch.

Del Excuse me. Trotter party..

Perkins Oh, Mr Trotter, good. We've been waiting for you.

Del Hello there.

Perkins Alan Perkins. Pleased to meet you both. Now, here are your rosettes...

Del Oh lovely.

Perkins Mrs Trotter, Mr Trotter, and this one's for young Rod... He's a big lad, isn't he?

Del Yes, his late mother was a very tall woman. Six foot three.

Perkins Really?

Del Oh yes.

Perkins Extraordinary. Oh well, here's your badge, Rodney. *(Hands Rodney a pin-on metal badge which has 'The Groovy Gang' printed on it)* You are now a life member of the Groovy Gang.

Rodney The what?

Perkins The Groovy Gang. It's just an idea we came up with to help the kids feel really part of it. Every time one of the organizers says, 'Are you having fun?' all you kids shout back, 'Groovy'.

Cassandra turns away to avoid Rodney seeing her laugh.

Del *(To Perkins)* Well, don't worry, don't worry. He'll soon get the hang of it.

Perkins Yes, fine. Well, we'll... er... be off in a moment.

Del Yes thank you.

Rodney I don't believe this is happening to me!

Del We'll be on the coach in a minute, be

93

at the hotel in 'arf an hour and then you're free to do what you want. Nice, and easy bruv, nice and easy.

Carmen OK! All the members of the Groovy Gang over here.

Rodney Oh no!

Carmen We're all going to the hotel on the Fun Bus. Not with all the old fogies.

Del, playing the part, chuckles along with the other parents.

Del Sauce, eh?

Rodney is horrified to see Del joining in.

Rodney You're enjoying this, ain't yer?

Del I'm just playing along with them.

Perkins Mums and dads, if you'd like to follow me, the coach is just outside. We've laid on a little welcoming reception back at the hotel. I'm sure that none of you would object to a glass or three of sangria.

Del That's lovely, Alan. Go on, then, Rodney, go on, off you go.

Rodney What?

Del You're supposed to be with the Groovy Gang.

Rodney I don't want to be with the sodding Groovy Gang!

Del Come on, Rodney, don't spoil it now.

Cassandra They're looking over here.

Carmen I'm still waiting for a... Rodney Trotter.

Del Over here, sweetheart! Here he is.

Carmen Come on, Rodney don't be...

Carmen's smile dies as she reacts to Rodney. She has never seen a taller or more mature-looking 14-year-old.

Del Hurry up, Rodders, they're getting suspicious.

Rodney I'm not going.

Perkins Is he not a good mixer?

Del A good mixer? He's like a Kenwood Chef when he gets going.

Carmen Come on, Rodney, come on, Rodney, don't be shy. You'll soon make friends. We're all going for a jumbo hamburger and double French fries.

Del That's his favourite.

Cassandra Don't get any ketchup down your shirt.

Rodney Et tu, Cassandra?

Cassandra shrugs helplessly to Rodney in a 'what can I do?' manner.

Del We'll see you back at the hotel, then, Rodney. *(His arm goes round Cassandra's waist)* Come on, darling.

Cassandra *(Clenched teeth)* Don't push your luck, Derek.

Carmen leads Rodney across to the rest of the Groovy Gang, where there is a little girl of about thirteen. She fancies Rodney.

Little girl Do you like Bros?

Rodney No.

Carmen All together, are you having fun?

Groovy Gang Groovy!

Carmen That's better. Let's go.

INT. SPANISH HOTEL BEDROOM. DAY. STUDIO.

Cassandra's suitcase is open on bed. She is now fuming at the sudden turn of events. She is dumping the clothes into cupboards, etc., and slamming doors and drawers.

Del enters through main door in a rather sheepish manner. Their eyes meet. Del smiles. Cassandra glares.

Del Alright?

Cassandra slams a door.

Nice here, innit? I've just been down to reception. I've bought us some Spanish state lottery tickets.

She slams a drawer.

There's some for you, I put your name on and everything. And there's some for Rodney there, look, and there's some for me. Never know your luck eh? We're on a winning roll, ain't we?

Cassandra Tell that to poor Rodney.

The Unlucky Winner Is...

Del Oh look, don't keep going on about it. You're gonna spoil the holiday for us you will. Listen, have you had a look round? What's here? Oh that's very nice.

She slams something else. Del pops his head into second bedroom.

That must be Rodney's room. It's got a picture of Prince on the wall.

Cassandra If that's Rodney's room, where am I supposed to sleep?

Del Well… well, I assumed that you and Rodney… No, alright. I'll sleep in there.

Cassandra Okay, so you sleep in that room. But, I repeat, where am I supposed to sleep?

Del Well… well, I thought that you and Rodney… Or maybe not!

Cassandra I'll sleep in there. You and Rodney can have the honeymoon bed.

Del Alright, alright, anything you say, sweetheart, anything you say. I just thought it might be a bit strange when the old maid comes in. You know, see me and old Rodney tucked up on the king-size.

Cassandra It would look even stranger if she found Rodney sleeping with his step-mother!

Del I didn't think of that. I'd better go and cancel breakfast in bed. Do you want me to take that picture of Prince down off the wall?

Cassandra Just leave it, Derek. You've helped Rodney and me enough already.

Del Oh look, I thought the cornflakes people would leave us alone to enjoy our holiday. I didn't know they were going to conscript Rodney into the Groovy Gang. I mean, why are they doing it?

Cassandra Mr Perkins explained it to us. It's so the youngsters won't get bored and parents can have a rest. I won't see him all week, will I?

Del Yes, of course you will. He's bound to get a spot of leave. *(Looking our of apartment window)* Here y'are. There they all are now. Hey, Rodney, don't go mad!

Cassandra Where are they?

Del They just went down over that hill there.

Cassandra That was quick, wasn't it?

Del They were on skateboards. Rodney was the leader, he was right out in front. Leader of the pack.

Cassandra Oh my God!

Knock at the door.

Del Hello?

Carmen May I come in?

Del Yes, come in.

Carmen enters. She is wearing her official uniform.

Carmen Hello, Mrs Trotter.

Cassandra *(Forgetting that she is the temporary Mrs Trotter)* Oh! Good afternoon, Carmen.

Carmen Is Rodney here?

Cassandra No, he's not here at the moment.

Carmen Oh he's still out enjoying himself.

Cassandra Yes.

Carmen Well, it's just to let him know about the junior disco on Wednesday night. But I'll come back later and tell him then. Bye for now.

(Exits)

Cassandra *(Turns to Del who is at doors to balcony)* Did you hear that?

Del He enjoys a little dance.

Cassandra It's a junior disco.

Del Well, alright, we'll say he's ill.

Cassandra Oh what, more lies?

Del No. When Rodney finds out, he's bound to be a bit Tom and Dick anyway. Right, I'm gonna have a wash then we go down and get something to eat, alright?

Cassandra But what about Rodney?

Del Oh that's alright. We'll pick him up down there somewhere.

Cassandra Yes, just look for the nearest sandpit.

Del exits to bathroom laughing at Cassandra's line which she didn't mean to be funny. From inside the bathroom we hear the sound of running tap-water and Del singing "Spanish eyes".

Now the main door opens slowly and Rodney enters. He wears a skate-boarder's protective helmet, elbow and knee pads and carries his skateboard under his arm.

Rodney is forcing himself to stay calm, his face is serious – deadly serious. He stares at Cassandra, daring her to laugh. Cassandra fights not to laugh at this vision before her. Rodney points a warning finger at her.

Cassandra What have you been doing?

Rodney I've been skateboarding, Cassandra.

Cassandra Oh I see.

Rodney Where's Del?

Cassandra He's having a wash.
Rodney moves to bathroom door and knocks gently.

Rodney *(Calmly)* Derek?

Del Is that you, Rodders?

Rodney Yes, I'm back. Could you come out, please. I'd like a word with you.

Del Won't be long, bruv.

Rodney *(Still calm)* No, could you come out now?

Del No, I've got me pants off, Rodney!

Rodney Well, it's quite urgent, Del.

Del Alright. Give us five minutes, I'll be with you.

Rodney Sorry about the bad language, Cassandra.

Cassandra What bad language?

Rodney *(Explodes)* Get out here now, you bastard, I'm going to kill you!

Del Oi, oi, oi. What's up with you?

Rodney I'll tell you what's up with me... Thanks to you I am now a 26-year-old man who just came second in a skateboard derby!

The Unlucky Winner Is...

Del Second? You were in the lead when I saw you!

Rodney I fell off!

Del I told you not to go mad.

Rodney I also have a 13-year-old Bros fan called Trudie who's got the hots for me. And tomorrow I start the first of three cycling proficiency lessons and I'm gonna kill you!

Del Calm down, Rodney! You're acting like a big kid.

Rodney Bastard!

Del I'm not coming out 'til you've simmered down a bit.

Rodney Well, I'll wait. I don't care if it takes all bloody week. I'm gonna get you, Derek Trotter, I'm gonna get you!

Cassandra Have you seen the view?

Rodney No!

Rodney exits to balcony putting his skateboard down somewhere and removing his helmet as he does.

He throws himself down in balcony chair and stares angrily out at the view.

Cassandra Would you like a drink?

Rodney Strychnine, please.

Cassandra Ice and lemon?

Rodney at last cracks a tiny smile.

Rodney *(Shows her a graze on his arm)* That's where I come off. Poxy lizard!

Cassandra Shall I clean it up for you?

Rodney No.

Cassandra It could turn septic.

Rodney Good.

Cassandra *(Now sees someone down by pool)* Is that Trudie waving at you?

Rodney Yeah. *(Gives a tiny, embarrassed wave back)*

Cassandra controls her laughter and exits to bedroom.

She moves to the bar or cocktail cabinet to get Rodney's drink. As she does so Del exits from bathroom cautiously.

Del Has he come to his senses yet?

Rodney Git!

Del Veinites, alright veinites. Look, Rodney, look, do you think if I knew this was gonna happen that I would allow us to come over here?

Rodney Well, of course you would! 'Cos you don't give a toss about anybody else as long as you're having a good time.

Del Oh, that hurts, Rodney! No, that hurts! That's like a... like a knife going right through my heart, that. I may be many things but I'm not selfish. *(Cassandra passes drink to Rodney but Del intercepts it and starts to drink it)* Cheers, darling, thank you very much. Anyway, they probably fixed up all the entertainments today to make you feel at home. The rest of the week is your own, most probably.

Rodney Oh no. I was given the full itinerary. Tomorrow after my cycling lesson, we're all off to the splash 'n' slide. Then Wednesday in the morning we're going go-karting. Then in the afternoon we have a ping-pong championship. Then on Thursday me and the rest of the Groovy Gang are out all day painting Palma Cathedral.

Del What, in matt or vinyl?

Rodney You're enjoying every bloody minute of this, ain't you?

Del No, I'm not, I'm not. I'm just trying to lighten the atmosphere. Honestly if you keep up this mood you're going to ruin this holiday for me.

Rodney Listen to me, you git. The...

Cassandra Arguing's not going to help!

Del It's your fault for telling him about the junior disco.

Rodney Junior disco?

Cassandra I didn't say a word.

Rodney I ain't going to a junior disco!

Del It's alright, Rodney, it's alright, you don't have to. Me and your stepmum have sorted it all out. We're gonna say you've got gut-ache!

Rodney Oh no, don't say I'm ill!

Del Why not?

Rodney They've got a great fat nurse to look after us!

Del But you like uniforms, don't you eh?

Rodney Yeah, but you wanna see her. She'd have to go on a diet to get into the Roly-Polys! God, what a choice eh? I can either have all day with Trudie in me earhole going on about Matt and Luke or have Sister George rubbing me belly!

Del Tricky one, bruv!

Rodney You are enjoying this, ain't you?

Del No, honest. I'm trying to help.

Cassandra You're deliberately saying things to annoy Rodney, aren't you?

Del Alright, I won't say another word! Right, that's it, I'm just gonna go out and have a walk round the town, alright?

Cassandra I didn't know you liked uniforms…

Rodney No, no, it's just him mucking about.

We hear a knock on main door.
Del opens it to Perkins and Carmen.

Carmen Is Rodney back yet?

Del Rodney, the Arkela is here!

Perkins We just thought we would… er… take the opportunity to… er… check your passports.

Del What d'you want to check our passports for?

We must have the strong feeling that Carmen and Perkins are suspicious of Rodney's age and are doing their own investigation. They share little suspicious looks and are edgy.

Carmen It's simply Spanish regulations.

Perkins Immigration laws. I'm sure you understand.

Del Do you know where our passports are, dear?

Cassandra Oh yes. I'll just get them.

Rodeny gestures Del over to him.

Rodney *(Whispering)* My date of birth's on my passport.

Del *(Whispering)* It's alright, don't worry, I doctored it.

Rodney Oh thank… You've done what?

Del It's alright it was only written in biro so I altered the last two numbers to make it look as though you were born in 1975. Right?

Rodney I don't believe…

Cassandra Here they are.

Carmen and Perkins give the passport a cursory glance and hand it straight back to Cassandra.

Perkins Thank you.

Now they do the same thing with the second passport only they hand it back to Del.

Carmen Thank you.

Del Thank you.

Carmen Thank you.

Del Thank you.

Now they open Rodney's passport (this is one they've been looking for).
They study it long and hard. Now they both look up at Rodney, suspicion written all over their faces.

Perkins Well, everything seems to be in order. Sorry to have bothered you.

Carmen Yes. Rodney, don't forget about the junior disco on Wednesday night. We start at 7.30 pm. It's great fun. We have break-dancing and spot prizes.

Rodney Smashing.

Del shows them to the door. Perkins and Carmen exit.

Del Listen, I reckon we ought to keep our heads down for a while, until the coast is clear. I'll tell you what I'll do. I'll order some room service.

Rodney What? No, no…

Del Eh?

Rodney I mean, we're alright now, ain't we?

Del Eh?

The Unlucky Winner Is...

Rodney Why don't you go out for a little while? You know you look like you could do with a bit of fresh air.

Rodney gestures with his head, 'Go out leave me and Cassandra alone'.

Del *(Gets the message)* Oh? Yeah, yeah. Now you come to mention it I do feel, you know, a bit claustrophobic! Well... I'll leave you two alone, then, shall I? Oh, and Rodney?

Rodney Yeah!

Del *(A kind of loud and secret whisper right across the room)* They're in my flight bag!

INT. HOTEL BAR. NIGHT. STUDIO.

This is a few nights later. Once again the decor is expensive and tasteful. Upstage we have large double doors which are open and lead into disco.

Inside the disco we can see members of the Groovy Gang and other youngsters from the hotel. They are dancing to 'The Birdie Song'. We get the impression that they are formed in a large circle and the circle is moving slowly in an anti-clockwise direction. We can only see half of the circle and it is without Rodney. Cassandra is seated alone at table. Del is at bar collecting drinks.

Del So he said he fell with her... Listen, come on... Listen, you two better go. I'll see you later, alright?

Girl Ta ra, mate. Thank you.

Del *(To Cassandra)* Alright?

Cassandra No! I thought Rodney and I would be spending a romantic week together. I have spent most nights sitting in our room alone. All I've seen of him is brief glimpses as he and the Groovy Gang rush off to the crazy golf or the evening film show. Oh my poor Rodney!

Cassandra turns towards disco and reacts. We now see through the open doors to disco that the Groovy Gang's dancing circle has moved round and Rodney is now in view and follows the movement of the others in an embarrassed, self-conscious way. He does all the action to 'The Birdie Song'. He now does a double-take as he sees Del and Cassandra.

Del gives him an encouraging smile and the thumbs up sign. Rodney glares back and gives a v-sign.

Del That's charming, innit? He'll lose Brownie points for that one. Still seems to be enjoying himself, don't he?

Cassandra Rodney's not enjoying himself! Last night he cried.

Del Why do you think he's carrying on with this pretence, eh? Certainly ain't doing it for me, 'cos if me and Rodders had been here on our own we'd have been out on that street ten minutes after landing! He's only doing this for you, sweetheart.

Cassandra Me?

Del Yeah. He told me.

Cassandra Really?

Del Would I lie to you? He only wants to see you having a good time. He wants to see you enjoying the sunshine. He's only trying to make you happy. So the least you can do is put on a smile for him. Let him know his sacrifices have not been in vain.

Cassandra I didn't know.

Del No, well there you are. Didn't want to tell you but, you know, you forced me hand. Oh here he is. Alright, Rodders?

Rodney *(To Trudie)* I'll be back in a minute!

Cassandra Having fun.

Rodney Groovy! Ah, you didn't get me a drink then?

Del Eh?

Rodney Well, not to worry. I'll get my own.

Del Alright! Don't get stroppy about it,

Rodney Can I have a large Bacardi and coke, please?

Del And an orange cordial with ice and a straw, please.

Rodney Del, I'm gonna tell them the truth. I can't take it anymore. Let 'em chuck us out in the gutter if they like, I just don't care.

Del That's alright. Go on, go on. You just think of number one, eh? What about that poor mare? She's having the time of her life on this holiday.

Rodney Are we both talking about Cassandra?

Del Yes, we are. She just told me.

Rodney But last night she told me she hated it! She said she'd rather be self-catering in Beirut!

Del She's only saying that for you. 'Cos she thinks you got the 'ump because you had to go into these ping-pong championships and hamburger-eating contests. She's only backing you up. But secretly she's really enjoying herself. Go on, you go and ask her.

Rodney I didn't know that.

Del No, well I didn't want to tell you but, you know, you forced it out of me.

Rodney sits down next to Cassandra.

Rodney So, you enjoying yourself?

Cassandra Yeah, I'm having a great time. You?

Rodney Yeah, cosmic. I wish we were staying here for a fortnight. You enjoying yourself, Del?

Del Not bad.

We now see a woman enter and survey the bar. She is in her early 30s, good figure but slightly brassy in make-up, hair-style and dress.

Yeah, I'll be with you in a minute, sweet-heart! Promised to take those two girls to a nightclub. May be back late – tomorrow lunchtime, sort of! I've emptied my flight bag. See ya!

Del exits with woman.
Rodney and Cassandra smile at each other.
Carmen calls from the disco doors.

Carmen Rodney, Rodney. It's the finals of the break-dancing championship.

Rodney God!

Cassandra It's up to you. D'you fancy watching?

Rodney Watching? I'm in it!

INT. HOTEL BAR. DAY. STUDIO.

Del enters looking dishevelled – as if he has just surfaced from a hectic night. Rodney and Cassandra are seated at bar looking at a newspaper.

Del Juan. Can I have a pina colada with ice and Alka Seltzer?

Upon hearing his voice Rodney and Cassandra move down the bar to him.

Rodney Del.

Del Yeah?

Cassandra Where have you been?

Del Sorry, dear. Me and that woman I took out last night found we had a lot in common. What are you two dancing about for?

Rodney You know you said we was on a winning roll?

Del Yeah?

Rodney It weren't a roll, my son, it was a bloody avalanche! *(To Cassandra)* Sorry.

Cassandra It's OK.

Del What are you talking about?

Rodney We've won.

Del I'm not with you Rodders.

Rodney We've won!

Del What, the break-dancing contest?

Cassandra D'you remember the day we arrived at the hotel? You bought some Spanish state lottery tickets. Well…

Rodney and Cassandra We've won!

Del You're winding me up!

Rodney No. No, look. *(Shows Del the newspaper and ticket)* Carmen gave us this

The Unlucky Winner Is...

paper to swat the flies with. Cassy did Spanish at school and she noticed the result. Look.

Del Bloody hell!

Rodney *(To Cassandra)* Sorry.

Cassandra S'alright.

Rodney It's a million pesetas, Derek!

Del A million? You know what this means, don't you Rodney? We've done it! We're millionaires! I always told you didn't I?

Rodney You've always said it!

Del Yes, this time next year...

Rodney and Del We'll be millionaires!

Cassandra But it's only a million pesetas.

Rodney and Del Only!

Del Listen, darling. I don't care if it's pesetas, roubles or Hungarian luncheon vouchers! We're rich!

> *Del and Rodney embrace and jump up and down in joyous celebration.*
> *Breaks into song.*

Oh! If I was a rich man...

Rodney and Del Yoo doo doo doo doo doo doo doo... All day long I'd... doo doo.

> *Del sudden stops, panic written all over his face.*

Del Hold on, hold on! Ah, we're in Spain!

Rodney I know.

Del And we're foreigners!

Rodney So?

Del Well, there might be some, some Spanish law saying foreigners can't pick up Spanish kitties!

Cassandra Then why did the man sell you the tickets if he knew you couldn't win?

Del To earn himself more commission.

Rodney Oh no! Come on, Del, not even you would... *(Realises Del would)*

Del Eh?

Rodney My God, they've got a rule!

Del Yeah!

Rodney I just know they've got a rule!

Del Mr Perkins – Alan.

Perkins Oh, there you are! I've been looking for you everywhere! I've just heard the marvellous news. Congratulations!

Del Yes, yes, thanks. I wonder if you would sort of, double-check that for us, would you?

Perkins Of course, pleasure. Yes, no doubt this is the winning ticket. If you like I'll ring the regional office of the lottery organizers and stake your claim.

Del I was a little bit worried, we were worried about us being foreigners.

Perkins How do you mean?

Cassandra Well, is there a rule that says non-nationals aren't allowed to win the lottery?

Perkins I don't believe so. We sell tickets here in reception to guests from all over Europe.

Rodney Well, can you check the rules for us?

Del Yeah, look, they're on the back there somewhere. They're all written in Spanish or someinck! Yeah.

Perkins Yes, of course. No... No... That's okay... Ah! It says, "Non-citizens of Spain must present their passport and any necessary visa documentation with their winning ticket when making a claim". You've just won a million pesetas!

Del and Rodney Ay! Wow! Ooohhh! Do be do be do be do...

Perkins Oh dear!

Del Do do...

Perkins Oh dear, oh dear, oh dear!

Del Something wrong, Alan?

Perkins I don't quite know how to break the news. I'm afraid you can't claim a penny of this money, Mr Trotter.

Rodney But we've got the winning ticket!

Del Yeah!

Cassandra We've checked these numbers a hundred times!

Del Yeah, you just double-checked it yourself!

Perkins Yes, the numbers are correct. It is the winning ticket, alright. The problem is it's got Rodney's name on it. You see, under Spanish law nobody under the age of 18 is allowed to gamble.

Del Yeah, but look at him. They'd never guess he was under age.

Perkins That's what we've been saying all week! But Rodney would have to present his passport. I've seen it myself and it states quite clearly that he was born in 1975..

Del He wasn't... Look, he's not... I mean... I don't believe this is happening to me.

Perkins I can imagine how you feel, Mr. Trotter. I'm as disappointed as you.

Del I bet you're not pal!

Perkins I'm sorry. I'm so dreadfully sorry. *(Perkins exits)*

Rodney You berk.

Del All is not lost Rodders. We'll simply tell them the truth.

Cassandra I don't think that's a good idea Del. By telling the truth, you would be pleading guilty to forging an official document, Rodney would be pleading to entering the country illegally and I'd have a hard time proving I wasn't an accessory before the fact. They'd all carry custodial sentences.

Del What?

Rodney We'd all go down the Kermit!

Del There's gotta be a way... There's gotta be a way.

Del has an idea. He begins to smile.

Rodney Oh no! What are you gonna do?

Del produces a biro pen.

Rodney You're not gonna have another go at my passport! It'll look like a kindergarten scribbling pad by the time you've finished!

Del Not the passport, Rodney, the ticket. I'm gonna change 'Rodney' to 'Del'.

Rodney How the hell can you change Rodney to... Oh God!

Cassandra Bloody hell! *(To Cassandra)* Sorry.

Rodney S'alright.

NB: The ending of this original draft differs from the final transmitted programme.

The Unlucky Winner Is...

Sickness and Wealth

INT. TROTTER'S LOUNGE. DAY. STUDIO.

Rodney's computer is on the table.
Del, wearing his market clothes, is laying asleep on a chair.
From the kitchen we can hear the tinny sound of an old spin dryer.

Rodney Oh come on, Cassandra... Yeah, I know you've got your studying to do. Can't we just go out for a quick drink or a pizza or something, then you can do your studying when you get home. Well, you know it's 'cos I like being with you. I sort of miss you when we're apart... Alright, I'll tell you the truth. I'm bored stiff in this flat... What? No, that's Albert, he's got himself a new spin dryer, well it was new once! He bought it cheap 'cos of the bomb damage. Yes, at the moment it's jumping around the kitchen like a Dalek with St Vitus's dance. Del? He's laid out asleep in the chair with his dodgy stomach... Yeah, he's still getting them pains. Well, he's going out later for a vindaloo... no, well to him, you see, it's a sort of alternative medicine... I don't want to go out with him for a curry... I'll spend the evening in. Albert's got that old bird of his coming round – Elsie Partridge, I told you about her. We'll most probably play some Max Bygraves platters and then sit and talk about our ailments. Pity Del's going out, he'd have liked that. Oh well, that's very nice of them. Well, tell your parents thank you very much, I'd love to come to tea tomorrow. Seven o'clock tomorrow, lovely... Well, I'll see you tomorrow evening then.

We see that Del is sound asleep. Rodney smiles, satisfied that he will not be overheard.

You know I love you. Don't I tell you often enough? Do you love me? Oh very funny, Cassandra, I'm laughing this end as well... Alright, alright, I'll see you tomorrow.

He blows a kiss down phone. Now another kiss, then a third one.

Albert enters from kitchen surrounded by a great cloud of steam.

Albert Here y'are son. I bought a Chinese take-away earlier, I've just warmed it up. We've got fried pork, fried rice and... something.

Rodney How can you stay out in the kitchen with all that steam and noise?

Albert I'm an old naval stoker, ain't I? That's nothing to me. I remember coming round Cape Horn once, I was on this merchantman.

Rodney The things you and your mates got up to!

Albert A merchantman's a ship.

Rodney Oh!

Albert It was so hot and steamy in the boiler room that when I come out I was shrivelled like a prune.

Rodney Oh, that's what caused it.

Albert I hate it when you're in a sarky mood, Rodney! D'you reckon Del Boy should eat all this fried food? He's been getting a lot of jip with his guts lately.

Rodney There's nothing wrong with him. He had a similar thing years ago. We rushed him into casualty one night. They had ECG machines out, doctors and nurses everywhere. Then he burped! That was it, a miracle cure.

Albert Well, perhaps you're right. I'll get the knives and forks.

Rodney moves computer from table. Instead of the usual computer beep we hear a short, low buzz (like a warning). Del automatically rubs his belly.

Del Sorry. You alright, bruv?

Rodney Yeah, how you feeling?

Del Triffic, Rodders, brill. What's all that whirring noise?

Rodney That's Albert's spin dryer.

Del His what? *(Del goes to kitchen and opens door)* Oi, what is your game? What are you doing buying this old junk? Here, look at it, it's knocking all the paint off the units.

Albert comes out of kitchen.

Albert I got it as an investment, Del. It cost us 50 pence to get our clothes dry at the laundromat. I bought that off the bloke upstairs for a score.

Del You dozy old twonk! That's the one I sold him last week for a tenner. Why didn't you come and ask me first?

Albert I didn't like to bother you, boy. Not with you being ill.

Del Ill? I'm not ill. There's nothing wrong with me.

Albert But you got that stomach trouble again.

Del It's not stomach trouble. It's just pains, normal pains.

Albert Well, you came in tonight and flopped straight down on that sofa in agony.

Del No, you don't understand Unc, it's called PMA.

Rodney PM... I thought only women got that.

Del No no Rodney, that's PMP. PMA means positive mental attitude. That's my buzzword. It's what us yuppies have got. See, what I was doing was laying on the chair psyching myself up for the challenge of tomorrow.

Albert So what was all the sweating and holding your belly about?

Del Oh that was nothing. There's nothing wrong with me... Rodney, go to the bathroom and fetch us some Andrews Liver Salts, will you?

Rodney goes into kitchen.

Albert I'll do you a plate of Chinese, Del. Gawd knows what those local takeaways are gonna do when they know we're gonna move.

Del *(Now worried, almost fearful, like a man facing a confession)* Move?

Albert Didn't you see that letter? It arrived this morning. It says on the envelope it's from the council housing department.

Del Oh, that? Yeah, I read it.

Albert Is it about them letting us buy this flat?

Del No, it is not about them letting us buy this flat. It's about them evicting us from this flat.

Albert Evicting us?

Del Ssshhh! I don't want Rodney to know about this. I haven't paid the rent on this place for the last three months.

Albert Cor blimey! I knew things were a bit tight but I didn't know they were that bad.

Del It's all gone wrong for me, Albert. All me investments have gone sidewards. Rodney's been down the market for over a week trying to flog these exclusive women's fashions. But all the frost and sleet seems to have put 'em off buying summer dresses. I've been tucked up on some of my other investments and at the end I just couldn't afford to pay the rent.

Albert No, but you're still drinking those pina coladas in the wine bars. You're still eating in the curry houses and the bistros.

Del That is all on the slate. I've gotta keep me image up. Once your competitors get an inkling that you're going down the pan, they start queue-jumping to pull the chain. And that plonker Rodney ain't helping me.

Albert Yeah, I see what you mean. Don't worry about it, Del.

Del Don't worry about it! I ain't had a decent night's kip for the last two weeks worrying about it. It's with me everywhere, all the time.

Sickness and Wealth

Albert Something'll turn up right out of the blue, you'll see. He who dares wins, eh?

Del *(Half-hearted, almost defeated)* Yeah, he who dares wins. Oh you cowson.

Albert You've gotta see a quack with that belly of yours.

Del There's nothing wrong with me. They're just normal pains. You keep the doctors away from me, Albert. I don't like doctors.

Albert You could go and see that Scottish quack – what's his name? Dr Meadows. He's not like a normal doctor, he's sort of human. You know you can talk to him. He's like a mate.

Del Look, I do not want to go and see Dr Meadows 'cos there is nothing wrong with me. Alright?

Albert It's your life son.

Del Yes, it is my life and I don't wanna hear no more about it.

Albert Alright son, I won't say another word on the subject.

Rodney enters with the tin of Andrews.

Albert Don't you think Del Boy ought to go to the doctor's with his belly?

Del Oh Gawd!

Rodney He won't go to the doctor's, though, will he? 'Cos he is terrified of doctors.

Del I am not terrified of doctors. The reason I am not going to see Dr Meadows is 'cos there's nothing wrong with me.

Rodney makes the sound of a chicken clucking.

You're starting to wind me up, Rodney. I'll get a glass for this.

Albert You seeing Cassandra tonight?

Rodney No, not tonight, Unc.

Del No, he's going round tomorrow night for tea.

Rodney That's right. Her mum and dad said I could... You git, you was earwigging my conversation.

Del 'Of course I love you, Cassandra. I tell you often enough, don't I?' *(Blows three kisses)*

Rodney That is out of order, Derek.

Del is laughing as he enters kitchen without noticing the steam. Now, from in kitchen (oov) we hear him cry out in alarm.

Rodney That's not fair is it? It was a private conversation.

Albert Why'd you speak to her from the living room? It's a cordless phone, Rodney. You could have talked in one of the other rooms.

Rodney Like where? I couldn't use my bedroom 'cos the walls are so thin the people next door can hear, and I can't use the kitchen 'cos you've got R2D2 break-dancing in there.

Albert You could use the bathroom.

Rodney The bathr... Albert, I cannot hold a romantic conversation surrounded by damp towels, Del's soggy espadrilles and a bog with no lid. Besides, it's freezing in that bathroom.

Albert You've noticed that as well, have you?

Rodney Well you can hardly fail to notice it, can you? Our bathroom window gets condensation on the outside.

Albert Why d'you think that room is so cold?

Rodney Well, I don't know, do I?

Albert Now listen, son, listen. You may call me a silly old sod...

Rodney You're a silly old sod.

Albert Look, be serious, Rodney. Us sailors are superstitious, it's sort of an affinity with the supernatural, and I think there's a presence in that bathroom.

Rodney A presence?

Albert When you're in the shower, don't you feel there's someone else there with you?

Rodney Yeah but there usually is. Del's having a shave or you doing your toenails.

Albert The reason that room is so cold is it's possessed.

Rodney *(His protest is feeble)* Oh leave off, Unc.

Albert Elsie Partridge is a medium. She knows all there is to know about the supernatural, and she said she could sense a presence in that bathroom.

Rodney Blimey!

Del enters from kitchen, carrying a glass.

Del It's like a sauna out there. Switch that thing off.

Albert It'll be finished in a minute, Del. D'you want to put anything in it for you?

Del Yes, your head.

Del pours himself a brandy.

Rodney Have you ever noticed how cold our bathroom is?

Del Yeah, yeah I have. It does get a bit tatas out there, don't it?

Rodney When you're in there, right, do you ever get the feeling that you're not alone?

Del You mean as if there's someone else there with you?

Rodney Yeah.

Del What, sort of a strange feeling?

Rodney Yeah.

Del Like as if you're being watched?

Rodney Yeah.

Del No! Why? Do you?

Rodney No, no. It's Albert reckons it's possessed.

Del Possessed? Do me a favour. Give us a couple of months and it might be repossessed.

Del now stirs a spoonful of Andrews into his brandy.

Albert Elsie Partridge reckons it's haunted.

Del starts laughing into his drink. This in turn gives a twinge in the stomach.

Del Oh stop it, will you? You're making me hurt!

Albert Elsie Partridge is a medium.

Del Is she? Well, you better whip that round to her, then. That should fit her a treat.

Albert I'm not talking about her dress size. She's a spiritualist. She can contact the departed.

Del Yeah, I bet that's where she pulled you.

Albert She has powers, Del. She is one of the true communicators. Back in the early Sixties she used to hold regular meetings in that hall above John Colliers. People come from miles around to listen to Elsie. They paid thousands of pounds to use her powers of communication.

Rodney I think there is more to this occult lark than meets the eye, Del.

Del Do me a favour, Rodders. No self-respecting ghost is gonna haunt our bathroom, is it? Specially after he's been in there.

Rodney Then why is it always so cold?

Del It's either one of two reasons, Rodney. One, it could be as you two say that the phantom of the karszy has struck again. Or, two, it could be something to do with the fact that the council has put our extractor fan in the wrong way round.

Rodney Oh yeah. They were supposed to come back and mend it, weren't they?

Del Ghosts and ghouls! You two slaughter me.

Del exits to the bedroom area.

Albert I suppose that extractor fan could have something to do with it.

Del now enters from the bedrooms area. He is deep in thought as he walks across to Albert.

Del Thousands of pounds?

Albert Eh?

Del You said they paid that Elsie Partridge thousands of pounds?

Albert Yeah. But she never took a penny of it, Del. She used to send it all to Battersea

Sickness and Wealth

Dogs' Home. I bet she wished she'd have kept some of it now she's only got her pension to live on.

Del But they still paid her all that lovely money, though?

Albert Yeah, they'd pay a fortune to talk to their... No, no Del. She's retired now.

Del Maybe she'd like a part-time job.

Rodney No, just drop it, eh Del?

Del Don't you see what this means? You were right.

Albert Was I?

Del You said something would turn up out of the blue. And this is it. Me and Elsie Partridge, what a combination. The old-age pensioner with a priceless gift and a successful yuppy who's brassic flint. We could make a fortune for each other. I do believe that this is God giving me a sign. *(Looks up to heaven and smiles piously, now stricken by stomach pains)* Cor blimey.

> *Rodney and Albert grab him and force him down into chair.*

Albert Sit down here, son.

Rodney What can I get you?

Del Pina colada – lots of ice.

THE NAG'S HEAD PUB. NIGHT. STUDIO.

> *Nerys is serving behind bar.*

Jevon Here Boycie, can we have a word?.

Boycie What is it?

Mike She's here.

Mickey You remember that old Cortina you said me and Jevon would never sell?

Boycie What Cortina's that then?

Jevon That two-tone one – blue and rust. Well me and Mickey flogged it today.

Boycie But that Cortina was a death-trap. You should be ashamed of yourselves!

Mickey But you sold it to us!.

Boycie Did I? Oh so I did. It weren't a bad little run around I suppose. Are you and Jevon partners or something?

Jevon Yeah, we're doing a bit of trading.

Mickey We're specialising in anything.

Boycie Why don't you pop down my showrooms in the week? I've got a few old bangers out the back you could have a go at.

Jevon Yeah, thanks Boyce.

Mickey Here, would your Marlene be interested in a Crimplene dress with great big flowers all over it?

Boycie Well of course she wouldn't.

Mickey Oh that's a shame,'cos Rodney Trotter's got loads of 'em.

Mike If there's anything else you want, Mrs Partridge, just give me a shout. *(To Boycie)* She's here.

Trigger Who's here?

Mike That spiritualist woman. Here, to tell you the truth, Trigg, I'm having second thoughts about letting Del use upstairs for this seance.

Boycie You don't honestly believe in all that mumbo jumbo, do you Michael?

Mike I don't actually believe it. I just don't like taking the chance.

Boycie Michael, if Elsie Partridge really could raise the dead, half the money lenders in Peckham would be employing her. No, no, it's all a load of old tosh. Only a simpleton would believe in it.

Trigger I believe in it.

Boycie Say no more. *(To Mike, referring to Trigger)* He still leaves a glass of milk and biscuits out on Christmas Eve.

Nerys My mum went to seance once. She got a message from the other side. It said she would meet a tall bald man who would change her fortune. A week later she got mugged by a skinhead.

Mike There you go Boycie, you can't argue with that can you? There's got to be something in all this supernatural stuff.

Trigger My old gran was a bit of a medium. A few years after my grandfather died she made contact with him.

Mike Oh yeah? What did he say?

Trigger Nothing.

Boycie Nothing?

Nerys Well he was dead wasn't he?

Mike Yes, but she'd just made contact from across the veil.

Trigger For the last 15 years of his life they didn't talk to each other.

Nerys And he kept the row going?

Trigger Yeah. Well, he was a stubborn man.

Boycie Well, they must have been interesting seances. A mad medium and a spook with the hump. Hold up, here comes the Ghostbusters.

We see Del, Rodney and Albert enter.

Del A pina colada for me Nerys, and the usual for everyone else.

Mike Del, a word.

Del Alright, Michael. Yes, coming, coming.

Mike Are you paying for these drinks or what?

Del Michael, please.

Mike This slate of yours, Del, is getting out of hand, Del. That Mrs Partridge has just arrived, right, and she's had food and drink all on your slate.

Del Don't worry about it, Mike.

Mike Over the last few months you've had more cocktails than James Bond and a fried lunch every day and all on the slate.

Del Gimme a couple of weeks and I'll sort it out with you.

Mike You've had about 10 packs of cigars all on the slate and even the rent for the room upstairs is on the slate.

Del Unless your attitude changes Michael, I may have to consider taking my business elsewhere. Look, sit down. I've been sailing the good ship Trotter through a little patch of fiscal turbulence, right? But as soon as I get old Elsie Partridge firing on all four cylinders I'll be laughing. I mean, within a month from now she'll be bringing 'em back to order. I've worked out a little price list. Neighbours and family friends, three

quid. Relatives a fiver, spouses and pets a tenner each, and a score for Elvis Presley. This time next year I'll be a millionaire. Just think what this is going to do to you, Michael. She'll be drawing them in from the four corners of the kingdom, right? So not only will you be getting the rent for the room upstairs but once the show is finished all the pilgrims'll be down here having a jolly-up won't they? Your takings'll treble overnight. You know it makes sense, Mike.

Mike Yeah, I s'pose so.

Del Sit down, Boyce.

Mike I'm still worried, though.

Del Oh leave it out, Michael.

Mike We're dealing with the powers of darkness here. I mean, are we gonna end up with the table and chairs flying round the bar?

Del No more than a normal Friday night.

Del and Boycie laugh.

Mike You realise that this pub is built on the site of a public grave where the victims of the great plague were buried?

Rodney Oh well, that's all we need ain't it, them popping up to celebrate Agincourt, innit?

Nerys They'd all be covered in boils and scabs and things.

Boycie It'll be like a Singing Detective look-alike contest, won't it?

Rodney I agree with Mike. We're messing around with the supernatural. There's no telling what evil forces we might evoke.

Trigger Yeah, you could have Satan himself come crashing through the wall.

Del Well, it's lucky Rodney's wearing his old jeans, innit?

Del and Boycie laugh.

There are three loud thumps upon the ceiling.

Del I think that's her sign to say she's ready..

Rodney Well, it might not mean that.

Sickness and Wealth

Del Either that or she's got cramp in her wooden leg. Come on, Rodders, come on, let's go.

INT. UPSTAIRS ROOM OF NAG'S HEAD PUB. NIGHT. STUDIO.

Elsie Partridge is seated at a round table. She is in her mid-sixties and is a very sweet and genuine lady. She takes her 'gift' and the proceedings very seriously. Rodney, Boycie, Albert, Mike and Trigger are seated around the table. Del carries the last chair to the table and sits down.

Elsie Now, I think it's time we began. May I ask you once contact has been made to refrain from interrupting. Now, hands on the table. Fingers touching. Concentrate.

Elsie now stares directly ahead. Her head drops to one side and rests on her shoulder.

Elsie now begins moaning lowly.

Mike What's she doing?

Trigger She's going… *(moans)*

Mike I mean, why is she doing it?

Albert She's gone into a trance.

Mike Thank Gawd for that. She had one of my pies earlier.

Elsie straightens her head and opens her eyes. She now appears quite normal.

Elsie The spirits are with us. A man has stepped forward. A tall, elderly man wearing a black coat and a black hat. He wished to speak to someone called Audrey… No, no, Aubrey.

Del Aubrey?

Rodney shrugs.

We see Mike and Trigger look at each other, mystified.

Boycie I am here.

Rodney Aubrey?

Boycie It's my middle name.

Trigger You never said your name was Aubrey.

Boycie Nor would you if your name was Aubrey.

Elsie This man seems agitated. He's brandishing a piece of paper. Have you any idea who it could be?

Boycie No. This piece of paper, it's not a logbook for a Cortina, is it?

Elsie No, it's a photograph. A black and white photograph. It shows this man, but years younger. There's an odd-looking boy standing next to him, five or six years old, evil face.

Del Boycie, it's you and your dad.

Boycie Yeah, of course. He's the only one who ever called me Aubrey.

Elsie There is a sadness about the photograph, as though something is missing. Of course, your mother isn't with you.

Boycie No.

Elsie Had she passed over to the next world?

Boycie No. She was taking the photo.

Elsie I see. This man – your father – is worried. He says you must be a good father, you must look after your child.

Boycie Is he having a pop at me or something?

Albert Elsie. Boycie and his wife Marlene can't have kids.

Del They've been trying for years, you know, but nitto.

Rodney Yeah, they've had tests, things frozen, everything.

Mike The hospital's just about given up with him.

Trigger He's low on something.

Boycie Do you mind not discussing my personal life in front of strangers? *(To Elsie)* You tell my old man to keep his nose out of my business. He was always having a go at me for not giving him a grandchild.

Del Come on now, take it easy, Aubrey.

Boycie And you can wrap up for a start. I'm gonna get a drink. It's a load of old

rubbish anyway. I don't believe in any of it.

Boycie exits.

Albert Are the spirits still with us, Else?

Elsie Yes, yes, yes. They're still here. Close the circle. Someone else has stepped out. It's a woman. Tall and slender, long golden-brown hair.

Del reacts – he knows it is his mum. He looks to Rodney who also suspects this.

The fingers covered in ruby and gold. Bracelets adorn the wrists.

Del You know who that is, don't you?

Trigger Sounds like Jimmy Saville.

Del Jimmy Saville! That is our mother.

Trigger Sorry, Del boy, Dave.

Del, fuming, looks to Rodney.

Rodney Jimmy Savile!

Del Yeah, that's right, bruv. Bloody cheek.

Elsie She says she is proud of her children.

Del and Rodney smile to each other.

She says you have both worked hard to succeed. But never mind. She wants to know that she is with you always.

Del and Rodney smile to each other.

Wherever you are, whatever you are doing she is looking over you. She says you mustn't mourn her any longer. She is happy. She says she is at peace and...

Rodney Mrs Partridge.

Del Don't interrupt, Rodney.

Rodney I just wanted to clear something up. When she says she's looking over us all the time, right, well, she don't mean all the time does she?

Elsie Well I'd think the spirit world would have its own ideas on discretion.

Rodney Yes, I was just wondering.

Del Yeah!

Elsie She is concerned for you, Derek.

Del Me? What about me?

Elsie She is concerned for your health.

Del I'm alright, Mum, never been better.

Elsie She says you are not well. She feels your pain.

Del Ah no, that's just a bit of jip, that's all, Mum. Most probably an onion bhaji lodged somewhere.

Elsie She wants you to go and see a doctor.

Del There's nothing the matter with me.

Elsie She insists.

Del No, I don't want to go and see a doctor. You know I don't like doctors.

Elsie Oh they're becoming distant. They're drifting away.

Albert Can't you get 'em back, Else?

Elsie Is there anybody there? If anybody is there, talk to us. Say something.

Nerys *(To Mike)* Lager's off.

Del, Rodney, Albert, Mike, Trigger and even Elsie Partridge scream with alarm. This in turn makes nervous Nerys scream with alarm.

You made me jump.

Mike What d'you think you made us do?

Nerys Well, I had to tell you I've got customers waiting down there.

Mike Alright, alright, I'm coming.

Albert I'll get your coat, Else.

Albert exits.

Elsie moves to collect her handbag thus leaving Del, Rodney and Trigger alone.

Trigger So what you gonna do, Del?

Del About what?

Rodney About the message from Mum.

Del Oh do me a favour, Rodney. You didn't believe all that, did you?

Rodney Well, you seemed pretty convinced. At one point I thought you were gonna suck your thumb and throw a paddy.

Del I was only doing that for Elsie's sake. I mean, she's a genuine old lady who most probably believes she is getting these messages. But at the end of the day it's a load of old rubbish.

Trigger Yeah, I think Del Boy's right, Dave. I mean, she got a message saying that Boycie's gotta look after his kid.

Sickness and Wealth

Del Yeah, that's right, and everyone knows that Nelson's Column's got more chance of knocking out a nipper than Boycie.

Rodney So you're not going to the doctor's?

Del No, I am not going to the doctor's 'cos there is nothing wrong with me.

Rodney See you in the bar, Unc.

Del, Rodney and Trigger exit.

Del Come on down, Rodney.

Rodney I'll only take you…

Albert *(To Elsie)* Thanks for doing that, Else.

Elsie That was the first time I've ever lied to someone at a sitting. I only gave Derek that message because you asked me to.

Albert I'm grateful. He wouldn't take any notice of me and Rodney. The only one he'd ever listen to was his mum.

INT. NAG'S HEAD PUB. NIGHT. STUDIO.

Del, Rodney and Trigger enter.
Mike is putting up a poster: "The Seance. Make contact or money back. Tuesday 17th January. 7.30. Admission £2.50."

Del Right then, come on, Rodney, here, Nerys. Where are them posters? Rodney stick these up in the window. The sooner the devotees know about them the better.

Marlene *(Deeply concerned)* Del.

Del Wotcher Marlene, hello. What you doing here?

Marlene Boycie's just told me what that Elsie Partridge said.

Del Now don't you start. I've been having enough trouble with Rodney and Albert. There is nothing the matter with me.

Marlene I'm not talking about your illness. I mean what she said to Boycie.

Del Look, darling, you don't wanna take any notice of what Elsie Partridge says because it's all a con, you see.

Marlene No, you don't understand. I'm having a baby.

Del *(Frozen with fear)* What?

Marlene I've just had it confirmed at the hospital.

Boycie So what do you think of that?

Del clutches his stomach as the pain returns.

Rodney Quickly.

Marlene Well what's up with him then?

Rodney Sympathy pains. A lot of men go through phantom pregnancies.

Boycie I thought that only happened to the father.

Trigger gives Boycie a little smile.
Boycie reacts.

INT. DOCTOR'S SURGERY. NIGHT. STUDIO.

Dr Shaheed, an Indian woman of about 30, is seated behind the desk, making a few notes.

There is a knock on the door.

Doctor Come in.

Del I'm sorry, is Dr Meadows about, the Scottish doctor?

Doctor No, Dr Meadows left general practice two years ago. He's working at the local hospital. I've taken over from him. I'm Dr Shaheed.

Del You're a woman.

Dr Shaheed looks in a mirror.

Doctor Well, well, so I am. Nobody ever tells me anything these days. You're Mr Trotter.

Del I know.

Doctor Well, come in, take a seat.

Del moves reluctantly to desk.

What's the problem?

Del Me? Oh nothing at all.

Doctor You're not ill?

Del Never felt better.

Doctor Mr Trotter, I have a waiting-room full of sick people. Now, what is it? You want a certificate?

Del No, no, I don't want a certificate. I mean, I'm self-unemployed. No, it's just…

it's hardly worth bothering you with.

Doctor Why don't you let me be the judge of that? What's the problem?

Del Well, I've been getting a bit of a Cynthia.

Doctor Cynthia?

Del Pain. *(Chuckles)*

Doctor *(Doesn't get it)* Where do you get this pain?

Del Well, all over, really. This morning I got it in the lift going down to the…

Doctor No, no. Where on your body?

Del Oh right. Get it in the old New Delhi.

Doctor New Delhi?

Del Yeah, the belly, the belly. You're not from round these parts, are you?

Doctor No, I'm from New Delhi.

Del Really? Not much point calling you in an emergency then, is it? *(Laughs)*

Doctor *(Doesn't laugh)* I mean I was born in New Delhi and now I live in Peckham.

Del Yeah, I know. It was just a joke, you see.

Doctor Oh yes, very good. What sort of a pain is it?

Del Well… it hurts.

Doctor Yes, but is it a sharp pain or a dull pain?

Del Well, it's a bit of both, really.

Doctor Would you strip to the waist, please, Mr Trotter.

Del No, no, it's alright, doc, there's no need for that. Just gimme some painkillers.

Doctor I'd like to examine you. Please strip to the waist and lie on the couch.

Del reluctantly moves towards couch which is behind a screen.

Do you smoke, Mr Trotter?

Del Not just now, thank you, doctor.

Doctor I wasn't offering, I was enquiring.

Del Oh, I see. No, I don't smoke. Well, I have one cigar a year on Christmas night, but I'm trying to cut down.

Doctor I don't think one cigar a year will do you much harm. Do you have any trouble passing water?

Del I had a dizzy spell going over Tower Bridge once.

Doctor You have bouts of dizziness?

Del No, no. It was a joke, doctor.

Doctor I think it would be best if we stopped all the joking, I'm finding it rather confusing. Do you ever suffer with constipation?

Del No, regular as clockwork.

Doctor You have plenty of roughage in your diet?

Del Nothing but roughage. Muesli, brown bread, all that. I'm a very organic person.

Doctor That's very good. Even in this day and age you'd be surprised the number of people still exist on fried foods and takeaways.

Del Eurgh! Not me, doc. I'm like a walking Grobag. When they bury me there'll be rhubarb everywhere within six months.

Doctor walks behind screen and reacts.

Doctor Mr Trotter. When I said strip to the waist, I meant the top half.

Del Oh, sorry.

DOCTOR'S SURGERY. NIGHT. STUDIO.

Doctor You can put your shirt back on now, Mr Trotter. I hope my stethoscope wasn't too cold for you?

Del Round here, we call 'em deafascopes.

Doctor Really? Why?

Del Well, if you can't hear nothing, either your deaf or we're dead!

Doctor Are you a heavy drinker, Mr Trotter?

Del Me? No I'm teetotal. Well, I have the odd mineral water, skimmed goat's milk that sort of thing.

Doctor You have a very high pulse rate.

Del Oh thank you, doctor.

Doctor No, I'm concerned about it. I mean, it's almost as if you're frightened of something.

Sickness and Wealth

Del Frightened, me? No, I don't know the meaning of the word. No, I know what it was. I jogged down here to the surgery from the gym this evening.

Doctor Ah, that would explain it. I wish all my patients were as health-conscious as you, Mr Trotter.

Del Oh mais oui, mais oui. What d'you reckon the pains are then, doc?

Doctor To tell you the truth I'm not sure. I'd like you to go down to the local hospital and have a few tests done.

Del OK. I'll make an appointment tomorrow morning then, shall I?

Doctor No, I'd like you to go now.

Del Now? What? D'you mean this minute?

Doctor Yes. You may have a grumbling appendix. Now I emphasize the word 'may'. If that should prove to be the case we have to remove it as quickly as possible.

Del You mean cut it out?

Doctor Yes, I mean cut it out.

Del But it might not be me appendix?

Doctor Maybe.

Del So if it's not me appendix, what else could it be?

Doctor Well, let's not speculate.

Del Let's hope it's me appendix then, shall we? I don't have to go by ambulance, do I?

Doctor No, but I don't want you jogging there. You can call a minicab. *(She turns her back to Del and collects some files.)*

Del No, that's alright. I'll give my brother a bell. He'll drive me down there.

Doctor I'll call the hospital and tell them you're on your way.

She turns, arm outstretched to pick up receiver from her desk phone.
She reacts as Del has already picked it up and is about to dial.

Doctor I'll use the phone in reception.

Del Yeah, alright then, doc. Rodney? Hello Rodders, it's me, Del Boy. Yes, I'm here at the doctor's. Yes, listen. There's nothing to worry about, but I want you to come down here and give me a lift down to the hospital… Yeah, I've got to go there right away. Listen, listen. I said there's nothing to worry about. I don't want you driving here at a hundred miles an hour and having an accident, nothing like that… No I can't phone for a minicab! I don't care if *Neighbours* has just started. Look, I am at the quack's and I just want you to help me a bit… I don't wanna go on me own… Yeah, alright, I'll see you in a minute.

INT. THE NAG'S HEAD PUB. DAY. STUDIO.

Mike What can I get you, Rodney?

Rodney A lemonade with ice, non-alcoholic lager top and a small rum, please.

Mike Any news from the hospital?

Rodney No, not really. He ain't got a grumbling appendix. They don't seem to know what it is. Still, they're keeping him in, running tests on him and keeping him under observation.

Trigger Must be horrible that.

Mike What?

Trigger Well, lying in bed all day with someone standing there looking at you.

Rodney No, Trigg, they don't just keep… Yeah, must be horrible.

Mike Years ago I had a mate like that. Doctors couldn't find out what was wrong with him.

Rodney And he died, did he?

Mike Yeah… *(Realises what he has said)* Oh no, I'm not saying that Del's got that.

Rodney Well let's hope not, eh? Listen, Mike. We're going to visit him this evening and he asked if you'd do him a bacon sandwich with lots of brown sauce 'cos he can't stand that hospital food.

Mike But it'll be all cold and greasy by this evening.

Rodney Yeah, that's how he likes it, and he also said would you send up a bottle of

coke and put some Bacardi in it, so as the old matron won't suss it?

Mike Leave it to me, Rodney.

Rodney moves to table where we see Cassandra and Albert.

Rodney places the drinks on the table and sits. Nothing is said between them.

Cassandra Cheer up a little bit, Rodney. I mean, Del's in the best place, isn't he?

Rodney Oh yeah, he's in the best place. I just wish they knew what was wrong with him. Maybe on second thoughts I don't wanna know what's wrong with him.

Albert When I was stationed out in New Guinea...

Rodney and Cassandra Oh God.

Albert A crew-mate of mine went down with a mysterious tummy bug just like Del's. The finest medical brains in Jayapura couldn't make out what it was.

Rodney No? *(To Cassandra)* Your dad still thinking about buying that new Jag?

Cassandra He's looking at one tomorrow.

Rodney Yeah?

Cassandra Yeah.

Albert Until this American surgeon arrived on the scene. He twigged it straight away.

Cassandra And what was it?

Albert Green parrot's disease.

Rodney Well, that's certainly worth knowing, Albert. thank you very much.

Cassandra Are you going to tell the doctor in charge of Del's case? You know, he might not have thought of it.

Rodney No, that would have been one of the first things he would have thought... How the hell's Del gonna get green parrot's disease in Peckham?

Albert Well, I admit it's a long shot. I'm just grabbing at straws, I s'pose.

Rodney Yeah, yeah, we all are Unc. I'm sorry.

Albert I'm gonna put a drop of blackcurrant in this.

Cassandra Can I visit Del with you this evening?

Rodney Yeah, okay. It's worth the journey just to see his pyjamas. He's never been ill before. Well you know, he's been ill but he's never been in hospital. He's terrified of 'em. He got stabbed once outside a dance hall. There was blood all over his shirt, a four-inch gash in his shoulder. But he never went to hospital.

Cassandra He didn't have it treated?

Rodney No he did it himself. TCP and a flannel.

Cassandra Did he know the person who did it?

Rodney Yeah.

Cassandra And I bet he didn't report it to the police?

Rodney No. Well, he couldn't really. He was engaged to her at the time. I prayed last night, prayed Del wouldn't die.

Cassandra Rodney, that's not going to happen.

Rodney No, no, I know. Soon as I done it I thought, 'That's stupid, Del ain't gonna die... He's not the type.'

INT. HOSPITAL WARD. NIGHT. STUDIO.

On Del's bedside table we have a few get-well-soon cards and a large bottle of Coca-Cola. Rodney, Cassandra and Albert are seated round bed.

Del So anyway, they took some more samples this afternoon. Sample of me blood, sample of me... samples of every-thing. Now I'm supposed to fast for 24 hours.

Cassandra Well, why's that? Are they running more tests tomorrow?

Del Yeah. I tell you what, I'll be 12 pound, three gallons lighter than when I come in, I know that.

Sickness and Wealth

Now, from beneath the bed covers, Del produces the bacon sandwich that Rodney asked for in previous scene.

Rodney What you doing? You're not supposed to be eating that.

Del I know, Rodney, but this fasting makes you hungry.

Cassandra But it could affect the results of the tests.

Albert Give over gel. It's only a bacon sandwich and a bit of brown sauce.

Del Exactly, Besides, it was in the local paper a while back, this is one of the few hospitals in Britain that has not been equipped with a bacon sandwich detector!

Rodney I don't believe you, Derek! When a doctor says you're supposed to fast for 24 hours then you should fast for 24 hours.

Del Well, what you bring this sandwich in for then?

Rodney 'Cos I didn't know you were supposed to be fasting. And you're not supposed to be drinking that either. It's got Bacardi in it.

Del Ssshhh! Keep your noise down, will yer? Listen, with the sort of measures Mike gives, there's less spirits in that than there was at our seance. Oh that reminds me. Wasn't last night the pukka seance night?

Rodney *(Half-hearted)* Yeah.

Del Did it all go well?

Rodney Er... not quite as well as we'd expected.

Albert It was a total cock-up from where I was standing.

Del Well, somebody tell me.

Cassandra Well, you know those posters you put in the pub windows with The Seance and the ghostly face?

Del Yeah, yeah.

Cassandra Well a lot of people got the wrong impression. They thought The Seance was a group.

Rodney The place was packed with punk rockers. There was Special Brew everywhere, people shouting 'Aceed', all that.

Cassandra They were expecting to see an 'Iron Maiden'-type band.

Rodney Then Elsie Partridge walked out in her hat. They weren't best pleased, Del. Fortunately she remained in a trance throughout the riot.

Albert She was still in it this morning when I went round to her flat.

Del Innit amazing? I only organised that seance out of the goodness of my heart. I just wanted to help people to overcome their loss, and how do they thank me? They chuck it back in my face!

Rodney Still, at least you tried.

A bell rings.

Albert Visiting time's over. Can't say I'm disappointed, I hate these places, death and sickness everywhere.

Del Yeah, they ain't all they're cracked up to be, Unc. Take care. *(Kisses Cassandra)* Bye-bye, sweetheart. *(Referring to Rodney)* Thanks for coming. Look after him now, will you?

Cassandra Yeah, I'll see he's alright. I hope you feel better soon, Del.

Del There's nothing wrong with me. I don't know what I'm doing in here.

Rodney I'll see you tomorrow, mate.

Del *(To Cassandra and Albert)* Yeah. *(To Rodney)* Hang around a minute, bruv.

Cassandra and Albert exit.

Del is smiling as he waves goodbye to them.

Rodney I'll see you outside. What's up?

Del *(Suddenly changes into a frightened schoolboy)* I'm scared, Rodney!

Rodney Oh come on, Del. You're in hospital.

Del That's why I'm scared!

Rodney I mean, can you think of a better place to be?

Del Yes, down the market, in the pub, anywhere but here. I think I might know what's wrong with me.

Pause.

Rodney What?

Del I think I might have… you know.

Rodney You mean?

Del No.

Rodney What! Not…

Del Yes.

Rodney Don't be silly. What makes you think that?

Del Because the doctors found out I was a bachelor and they started asking questions about my social activities.

Rodney Bloody 'ell.

Del It's alright. I didn't tell 'em nothing. I made out I was like an amateur monk. But I've been lying here thinking about my past.

Rodney What's the point in depressing yourself?

Del I've bin thinking back to some of the birds I've knocked about with. Cor blimey, Rodney, some of 'em have bin round the track more times than a lurcher.

Rodney Del, you're just being irrational.

Del What about that unisex hairdresser's, down the high street?

Rodney Well, what about it?

Del Well, I went in there last month for a trim, didn't I? And I thought I was going to get one of the dolly birds in the miniskirts, you know, and all that, but who did I get? They gave me some mush called Jason.

Rodney So?

Del So, say he was a bandit.

Rodney I don't believe… Del, you cannot go around making accusations against innocent people. Anyway, you can't catch it off a comb.

Del No, but say he nicked my neck with his razor or something.

Rodney So long as he doesn't kiss it better, you're laughing, ain't you?

Del Then there's Uncle Albert – blimey, he's been round the world more times than Phileas Fogg. There's no telling what he might have picked up. And there's you and that computer.

Rodney My computer?

Del Yes. I was reading about all those computer viruses.

Rodney Look, calm down, right? Look, I understand your concerns and fears. But you're just letting your imagination run away with you. If you'd had 'that' or anything as serious as that, they would have known by now. They're experts you know.

Del Yeah, yeah. I didn't think of that, bruv. It can't be that serious, can it?

Rodney Well, of course not. So you just remember that next time you're lying here at night, thinking of all them women and male hairdressers you've known…

Del They've got a spare bed downstairs if you're interested.

Rodney I'll see you.

They share a smile. Rodney stands to leave. Del leans back in bed. We now hear Del moan as if in great pain. Rodney rushes back to him.

Rodney Del, hold on. I'll get the nurse. Nurse! Hold on, Del, don't you die. Don't you bloody die.

Del I'm not gonna die, you plonker. I've just sat on me bacon sandwich.

INT. HOSPITAL WARD. DAY. STUDIO.

Del is sitting upright in bed. A tray holding his lunch is across his lap. A nurse arrives at Del's bed.

Nurse Aren't you eating that?

Del No, I'm not in the mood, sweetheart.

Nurse That's fresh fish.

Del I know it's fresh, it just winked at me.

Nurse I'll have to tell matron.

Del No it's alright. It didn't really wink at me.

Sickness and Wealth

Nurse No, I mean if a patient doesn't eat his food I have to report it.

Del Oh go on, then, you go and grass me up. I'm not frightened of the old cow. Oh, by the way, any news of my application for a bed bath?

Nurse Sorry.

Dr Meadows enters. He is in his mid-to-late thirties. Meadows is a dedicated doctor who relaxes with the occasional punch-up.

Dr Meadows You've gotta make a decision, Mr Trotter. We can either save you or the baby.

Del Robbie Meadows, you old git.

Dr Meadows Please, Del, not in front of the staff.

Del Oh yeah, sorry. Dr Meadows, you old git. What brings you up here?

Dr Meadows I've got good news and bad news, Del. The good news is they've put me in charge of your case.

Del What's the bad news?

Dr Meadows I specialise in amputation.

Dr Meadows laughs like a drain.

Del *(A very false and weak laugh)* Oh that's a good 'un. Here, d'you still get down the One-Eleven Club?

Dr Meadows No, not any more, Del. I packed gambling in, it's a mug's game. D'you still go down there?

Del Oh yeah. Anyway, how comes they've put you in charge?

Dr Meadows It was an accident, really. I just happened to be talking to some colleagues when the name Derek Trotter cropped up. So I asked if I could read your GP's report and have a look at your tests. I was amazed. I found myself reading about this non-smoking, teetotal, celibate vegetarian health freak. I thought, 'Can this be the same Derek Trotter that I know and begrudgingly admire? That uptight, wheeling-dealing, pina colada lout? The Castella king, the curry connoisseur? The same man who has lived his life on nervous tension, fried bread and doubtful women?'

Del And was it?

Dr Meadows Yes, it was. Why did you lie to your GP, Del?

Del 'Cos she's a doctor.

Dr Meadows I don't understand.

Del Well, you never tell doctors the truth, do yer? Otherwise you'll end up in hospital.

Dr Meadows But you are in hospital.

Del No, but I didn't mean that to happen, did I? I just wanted her to give me a bottle of jollop.

Dr Meadows Del, if you'd told the truth in the first place, my colleagues could have diagnosed your problem in a quarter of the time. As it was, they thought they were dealing with the perfect man – but all the time it was you! It confused them Del. It threw 'em onto the wrong track.

Del Well, I told her I did admit to having a cigar at Christmas time.

Dr Meadows What about the other 10,000 throughout the rest of the year? Oh that reminds me, we found your cigar-holder in the body-scanner.

Del Oh cheers Robbie. Must have fallen out of me robe.

Dr Meadows We know what's wrong with you, Del.

Del Right... Let's hear the worst. I can take it, I'm not frightened. Don't pull any punches. I want it straight from the shoulder.

Dr Meadows Yeah, I think it's best in the long run. Well, basically, Derek, there's nothing wrong with you.

Del Oh, oh thank God! Thank God. Thank Allah, thank Buddha. Thank you, thank you, God.

Dr Meadows Relieved, eh?

Del Well, you know. So what about all these pains I've been getting?

Dr Meadows You have an irritable bowel.

Del Well, I'm not surprised with you lot pulling me about.

Dr Meadows No, no. That's what your condition is called. You have irritable bowel syndrome. It's nothing serious. I'll put you on a course of drugs. Your condition has been caused by your lifestyle. The late nights, the booze, the nicotine, the fried fast foods. Do you ever think about all the saturated fat floating round your arteries?

Del I try not to. It puts me off me grub.

Dr Meadows One of the major contributory factors of this syndrome is stress. A lot of yuppies suffer from it.

Del Yeah?

Dr Meadows Del, I took the liberty of phoning the director of housing about your rent arrears.

Del How d'you find out?

Dr Meadows I phoned your flat. I'm sorry, mate, I had to find out what the hell was going on. I spoke to your uncle. The council have agreed to give you some breathing space, a bit of time to get yourself together.

Del Cheers, Robbie.

Dr Meadows You've been given a warning, Del. Nature's little way of telling you to eat muesli for breakfast. Cut right down on the drink and cigars. Start eating wholesome, real food and above all else learn to relax. Doctor's orders.

Del Whatever you say.

Dr Meadows Pop this into the pharmacy on your way home.

Del I can go?

Dr Meadows Yes, and don't come back. I want you convalescing for the next three weeks. I don't want you working or getting excited. Sit in a chair, eat boring foods and live a boring life.

Del Well, that'll be easy. I can talk to my Uncle.

Dr Meadows See you around, Del.

Del Yeah, and... thanks, Robbie. *(To*

himself) I knew there was nothing wrong with me.

Dr. Meadows smiles and exits, and the relief and gratitude comes flooding out. Del's bottom lip quivers. He momentarily puts his hands to his eyes. Then quickly pulls himself together.
(Telling himself off) Silly old sod.

INT. TROTTERS' LOUNGE. DAY. STUDIO.

Del is sitting in armchair watching TV. He is wearing pyjamas and has a blanket over his legs. He is bored, bored, bored, bored, bored.

Albert enters from kitchen carrying a breakfast tray.

Albert Here you are, Del, breakfast.

Del Oh good. What is it?

Albert It's muesli.

Del Blimey! It looks like something that's bin swept out of a pigeon loft.

Albert You can at least try it.

Del eats some of the muesli.

Del It tastes like it's been swept out of a pigeon loft. I can't eat this for the rest of my life. I'd rather croak it than eat this rubbish.

Albert Well, don't get excited, you'll bring your pains back on. All the quack said was you've got to get a sensible diet, and muesli's just part of it.

Del Alright, alright, Unc, alright.

Albert I'll do you a cup of tea, son.

Albert exits to the kitchen. Del reaches for his pack of cigars.

Del How many cigars am I allowed a day?

Albert She said three.

Del How many have I had?

Albert Four.

Rodney enters from hall.

Rodney Alright?

Del Yeah, triffic, Rodders.

Rodney Oh what's up with you now?

Del I am not ill, okay? All that happened

Sickness and Wealth

was that I caught a syndrome. But you two are treating me like an invalid.

Rodney We are not treating you like an invalid, Del, we are just trying to do our best by you.

Del Yes, I'm sorry, Rodders.

Rodney That's alright. *(To Albert in kitchen)* Albert I've got the Complan. *Rodney places the packet of Complan on the table and then turns to Del* So you feeling relaxed?

Del Yes. All over, thank you.

Rodney Good, 'cos I have got some really great news.

Del What's that?

Rodney Guess what? I'm getting married!
Del clutches his stomach as the pain returns.

Rodney Albert!

Seance

Tuesday 7:30pm at the Nag's Head

Be astounded by the spookily mystical powers of Peckham's very own 'Madam Elsie' – the phone-book of the supernatural.

Seances, Exorcisms, Bar Mitzvhas

spiritual clients include:
Cleopatra, King Arthur, Marilyn Monroe (of Tooting Bec)
Elvis, Anne Boleyn & Black Beauty (the original one)

INT. THE NAG'S HEAD PUB. DAY. STUDIO.

Rodney is seated at table with Albert. He wears his market clothes. His expression and general demeanour indicate that he has recently suffered a great disappointment. He is gutted in the extreme.

Albert, Boycie and Trigger are at counter. Mike is behind the bar. Boycie is regaling them with more boring stories of fatherhood and his unborn child.

Boycie So then the obstetrician takes me and Marlene into this room and they've got a scanning machine, you know, one of them things they can see right inside the womb.

Mike Yeah?

Boycie Suddenly on the screen we saw a shape. It was amazing.

Mike What was it?

Boycie It was a baby. What do you think it was, a Cornish pasty?

Mike I mean, was it a boy or a girl?

Boycie I don't know. They don't give you a close-up! But I could just tell by the proud way it held its head that it was my child.

Trigger Blown all them rumours to bits then, ain't it?

Boycie Yeah, that's right. The doctors said... What rumours?

Trigger Well, a lot of people thought Marlene was imagining it, you know, like a phantom pregnancy.

Boycie Oh no, I've seen the proof. It's all pukka. But there's still a long way to go; the baby's head is not engaged yet.

Mike But Rodney Trotter is. Look at him, poor little sod.

Trigger If he's like this now, what's he gonna be like come the wedding?

Boycie I've heard two of the bridesmaids are Samaritans.

Albert Come on, cheer up, son. It ain't the end of the world. So you've failed some silly little exam.

Rodney I did not fail some silly little exam.

Albert You didn't pass, did you?

Rodney What I'm saying is, there was nothing silly about it! It was a very important exam. If I had passed that I would now have a diploma in computer science. It would have been the foundations of a real career. Instead of which I have all the prospects and future of a Sinclair C5. I just wanted to be somebody in Cassandra's eyes. With that diploma I could have applied for a proper job.

Albert Look on the bright side, son. You'd have most probably failed the interview.

Rodney I've already passed the interview.

Albert How d'you mean?

Rodney You promise you won't say a word to Del? Cassandra's dad's offered me a position in his company. See, he's expanding the computer section and he wants me to help run it. 'Course, he was under the impression that this diploma exam was a foregone conclusion.

Albert Who told him that?

Rodney Me. But that's not the only thing. See, me and Cassandra, we found a flat. It's really nice, you know, modern. The only thing is we've got to put down a six-grand deposit. Cassy's taking two thousand out of her savings, her mum and dad are giving us two grand as a wedding present and it's up to me to find the other two. Where am I gonna find two grand? With my savings and salary we'll be lucky if we get a

weekend in a time-share tent. It was gonna be so good until that bloody exam.

Albert You can do one of two things, Rodney. You can go down the council and see if they've got a place or you can sell your share of the business to Del for £2,000.

Rodney That's a good idea, Unc. I hadn't thought of that. Yeah, I'll go down the council this afternoon.

Del enters.

Del Take a look at this, bruv. I've got an executive mobile, solid state of the art. It's all do to with statalites or something. Anyway, they normally retail at £199.99. I got them for 25 nicker each.

Rodney Where'd you get them from?

Del You know that Mickey Pearce and Jevon? They started trading, you know, so I said I'd help them out. I've got a hundred of them.

Rodney A hundred? Well, that's £2,500. I didn't know we had that sort of money in the firm.

Del No, no, no. I've got them on sale or return, haven't I? What I don't sell I return. Lovely Jubbly. So how did it go last night?

Rodney How'd you mean?

Del Well, down at the night school. You got the results of the exam.

Rodney Oh… er… Mr Jamille said he hadn't had a chance to look at everyone's work yet.

Del You've passed, Rodney. I can just feel it. With your diploma and my yuppy image we're on our way up and to celebrate the occasion I've just been down the printers and I have ordered 200 of these – Trotters Independent Traders headed notepaper. This'll let them know we're around.

Albert What's all those initials?

Del Modern business people only speak in initials, don't they? They've got FT, *Financial Times*, BA, British Airways, GLC, General

'Lectric Company. And we've even got a list of company directors.

Rodney Oh yeah, you and me.

Del Yeah.

Rodney What's these initials after my name? DIC.

Del No, that is Diploma in Computerisation, Rodney. Yeah, it's got impact, yeah, they'll see our high profile coming a mile off.

Rodney Del, thanks to your high profile we now have a company called TIT and a director with DIC after his name.

Del No, no, no. That stands for Trotters Independent Traders and DIC is Diploma in… TIT. I see what you mean Rodney. I know, I'll give the printers a bell on my executive mobile phone.

Mike arrives with three glasses of sparkling wine.

Mike Compliments of the stud.

Del Cheers, Boycie. What about that then Mike? An executive mobile phone. I can let you have this for what I paid – 40 nicker.

Mike Forty eh? Nice-looking model.

Del It's top of the range.

Del presses the 'aerial release button'. The aerial shoots out and knocks one of the glasses of wine over.

Mike Blimey! That aerial's a bit urgent, ain't it?

Del It's called instant aerial. It's a feature of this particular model, you see.

Del now presses out seven digits.

In the background we can see that Trigger and Boycie are watching the racing on TV.

As Del presses the phone buttons so the TV channel changes each time. Del, Rodney, Albert and Mike have their backs to screen so they don't realise what is happening.

Little Problems

Boycie and Trigger are facing the screen and so are not aware of Del's phone.

The screen changes from horse racing to a BBC2 programme to 'Rainbow' to the Channel 4 logo to a BBC2 programme back to horse racing.

Del waits for call to be answered. We hear a high-pitched whine from phone.
I know what's happened, the statalite has moved out of position. Hang about, there'll be another one along in a minute.

Mike I think I'll stick to the phone in the public bar, Del.

Del Alright, 35 quid. I don't mind losing a fiver for a mate. *(To Rodney)* Don't worry. This time next year we'll be millionaires.
Del puts aerial in. TV goes off.

INT. TROTTER'S LOUNGE. DAY. STUDIO.

We have two or three large cardboard boxes upon which is printed:
"Voxphone exexcutive. The go anywhere phone."
Del, now in his Gordon Gekko gear, is plugging various leads into the back of his VCR (as per episode Danger UXD) Albert is watching him.
Rodney is getting ready to go out, and has just finished drying his hair or something.

Albert I thought Rodney said that video recorder could only work on continental electric?

Del Yeah, that's why I popped over to Calais earlier and got myself a couple of bucketfuls. No, it's alright. Here, you know that Chinese kid who lives over in Desmond Tutu house? He's a bit of a boffin when it comes to the old electrics so I got him to fit an adaptor to it.

Rodney The Chinese kid?

Del Yeah.

Rodney The one you always said was stupid?

Del There's nothing stupid about him Rodney, he's a genius! I hear your diploma exam wasn't as easy as you thought it'd be.

Rodney Who told you? Albert?

Del No, no, it wasn't. I bumped into that Mr Jamille, that teacher at your training college.

Rodney Del, everything I did in that examination was correct – well, except for one minor miscalculation. You see, we had to program a computer with a mock flight plan. It was supposed to be an unmanned space probe. Stupid. We was given all the information, you know: navigational data, analyses of payload ratio to engine capacity.

Del Yeah, well, you need all that, don't you?

Rodney Yeah, yeah. But I got a bit confused between litres and gallons right? We don't have much dealing with continental measurements, round here in Peckham, so I didn't program enough fuel and my probe fell slighty short of Venus.

Del Yeah, he mentioned something about Dartford. Listen, soppy, you don't actually know that you haven't passed. I mean, no one's told you that you've failed.

Rodney Del, I don't need a weatherman to tell me when it's peeing down. Mr Jamille handed out all the diplomas the other night except for me.

Del Well, you know, maybe he was busy, maybe he hadn't got round to looking at yours yet.

Rodney Please don't patronize me. Look, I naused it up and that's all there is to it.

Del Right, OK. You know best. Oh, by the way, Mr Jamille asked me to give you this. *(Produces a rolled diploma complete with red tie)*
He wanted me to apologise for him and say he was very sorry but he'd been very busy an' he's only just got round to marking your work.

Albert All that whinging and whining and you'd passed all the time.

Rodney I don't believe it!

Del I'm proud of you, Rodney. Well done.

Rodney Oh cheers, Del.

Del Now you can get your new job, can't you?

Rodney Yes, I won't have any problem… Who told you that? Albert?

Del No, it was not Albert; Cassandra's dad told me.

Rodney You've met Cassandra's dad?

Del Well, yeah, he's got that little printing firm and I wanted to get them letterheads printed, and I thought I'd take the business down to him, you know, keep it in the family. He's a nice bloke as it happens, Alan, we had a nice chat and a drink.

Rodney But Cassandra's dad don't drink.

Del Oh no, but this was a special occasion, wasn't it? The heads of two great house-holds meeting for the first time. Well, it was a bit like a summit, so anyway we had a couple of scotches and that's when he told me he'd offered you the job.

Rodney You're not upset, are you? 'Cos I mean I'm breaking the partnership up.

Del Eh? Oh our partnership, no, that's alright, Rodney, you've made the right decision. No you've got to go with that Alan 'cos you know he can offer you a future which is more than I can. Anyway, you've got to have a proper job to get a mortgage for your new flat.

Rodney Yeah, I suppose… Who told you that? Was that Cassandra's dad?

Del No, Albert. So what you doing about the deposit then?

Rodney Oh I dunno, mate. Where am I gonna get £2,000?

Del Off your big brother.

Rodney What?

Del I'm giving you £2,000 as a wedding present.

Rodney Where are you gonna get that sort of money?

Del I'm owed it, ain't I? I'll just call in my debts.

Rodney What, you mean I can tell Cassandra and her dad?

Del You can tell the *Daily Mirror* if you want to.

Rodney Well. That'll be her. Cheers!

Knock at the door. Rodney goes to answer the door.

Albert Where are you gonna get all that money from?

Del Well, d'you remember a long time ago I sold them video recorders to Boycie? Well, he still hasn't weighed in with the old dosh-aroonies. So I'll get the money off him and give it to Rodney and it'll all be rez de chassé, as they say in the Dordogne.

Rodney and Cassandra enter.

Rodney Look who's here.

Del Hello, sweetheart.

Cassandra Hello, Del. Alright Albert.

Albert Hello, love.

Cassandra You passed.

Rodney Mmm.

Cassandra Oh you clever old thing.

Rodney Oh well, you know, it was nothing. Oh by the way, would your ask you dad how he'd like the deposit paid? You know, cash or cheque.

Cassandra You got the 2,000?

Rodney Of course.

Cassandra I don't think he cares if it's cash or a cheque.

Rodney Oh well, that's cool.

Del You off out tonight, sweetheart?

Cassandra Yes, we're going to see an Italian film.

Del Oh getting in the mood for your honeymoon in Rimini, eh?

Cassandra *(Embarrassed)* Oh shut up.

Rodney Del.

Del laughs.

Little Problems

Rodney exits.

Albert Here, how you gonna understand that film if it's all in foreign?

Cassandra No, it's got English subtitles underneath.

Del Oh Albert wouldn't bother with the subtitles.

Cassandra He can speak Italian?

Del No, he can't read.

Cassandra *(Has picked up Del's voxphone)* Oh that's a coincidence. My dad's just come home with one of these.

Del Has he? Oh well, there's a thing. Hope your mum's pleased.

Cassandra Well, no, he came home absolutely plastered.

Del No!

Cassandra I've never seen my dad drunk before..

Del No. Well, I've got to get on with this.
Del pushes button on VCR and there is an electrical flash. Del switches TV off.
Oh that stupid Chinese kid. I knew I shouldn't have trusted him with it.

Albert He's only a kid isn't he?

Del But he said he could do it!

Rodney Right, I'll see you later, then.

Cassandra Bye.

Del Yeah, enjoy the film.

Cassandra Thanks.
Rodney and Cassandra exit to hall.
Albert picks up the diploma.

Albert Here, I'm really pleased Rodney's got his diploma. Lucky you bumped into that Mr Jamille, innit?

Del Yeah.

Albert How much d'you give him?

Del Hundred and fifty.

INT. NAG'S HEAD PUB. NIGHT. STUDIO.
This is a week later. Del is at bar with Mike and Trigger. He is still trying to flog a voxphone to Mike.

Del It comes complete with batteries plus a little attachment for fitting it to the dashboard of your car, the works, and all for 35 nicker.

Mike Del, watch my lips very closely. I do not want one. Only an idiot would buy one of those things. You got one?

Trigger No, I haven't... I'm thinking of getting one though.

Del Well done, Trigg. I'll show you how it works, shall I? Excuse me, gentlemen, business calls.
Del moves across to Boycie.

Boycie Hello.

Del I think it's about time you weighed in with the money for those video recorders I sold you.

Boycie Del, I have told you before I am not paying you for them. They don't work.

Del Listen, I've solved that problem. There's a little Chinese kid over on my estate, now he's an electronics genius, now you give me the three and a half that you owe me and I'll get him to fit adaptors on all your machines. They'll sell like hot cakes.

Boycie Derek, I am skint.

Del Oh don't give me that, Boycie, please.

Boycie It's the truth! Marlene's pregnancy is costing me an arm and a leg. She's at a dodgy age for knocking out her first chavvy. She needs to be under constant surveillance by a very expensive group of medical experts. She's already had a week in a private ward.

Del Can't she go on the National Health?

Boycie Well, of course she can't. I can't expect my wife to mix with all those ordinary patients. Have you seen the way some of them dress?

Del Look, I've got Rodney's wedding coming up. I need that money.

Boycie I am just potless, Del, and that is no lie. I will pay you that money as soon as things pick up.

Del It'll be too late by then!

Boycie I am sorry, Del Boy. You cannot get blood out of a stone. Oh talking of blood, I heard the Driscoll brothers were looking for you.

This is exactly the same as being told that the Kray twins wanted a word.

Del Driscoll brothers looking for me? What they looking for with me? I never deal with the Driscoll brothers. I make sure of that.

Boycie Well, perhaps they want to look at Rodney's wedding list?

Del Very funny.

Boycie Half a shandy, please, Michael.

Del is more curious than worried at this point. We now see Alan Parry (Cassandra's dad) enter. He is in his early to mid-forties, smartly and expensively dressed. Despite his success he had not lost his cockney accent. He is a nice, genuine sort of bloke who gets great pleasure out of these rare opportunities to return to his roots. He has a small red mark or bruise above one of his eye-lids.

Alan I guessed I'd find you here, you toerag.

Del Alan, what a pleasant surprise. *(To the others at bar)* Here, look who's here. Cassandra's dad, Rodney's future father-in-law.

Alan How d'you do? Nice to meet you.

Mike Let me shake you by the hand, Alan. You're a brave man taking a Trotter into you family.

Alan Rodney's alright, I like him.

Del That's right. He's one in a million. Now you come and sit down over here, Alan, get away from all this riff-raff. What you drinking?

Alan Just a lemonade for me, thanks Del. That drink I had with you last week, it knocked me sideways. I hardly touch the stuff these days, and Pam, my wife, she doesn't really agree with drinking.

Del You could always out her, you know,

get yourself a younger model.

Alan Yeah, but she's been with me for so long she's almost one of the family. Go on, I'll have a small scotch, but that's me lot.

Del Alright, then. Can I have a small scotch and the usual for me, please. Here, what you done to your eye?

Alan Oh yeah, the aerial on that phone you sold me came out a bit fast.

Del Oh yeah? Well you had been on the sherbets, though, eh? Anyway, what you doing around here?

Alan I'm just a bit bored, Del. There's something wrong with our television.

Del Oh?

Alan So I thought I'd pop round here and have a chat about the wedding arrangements. You know, I think you should make some sort of contribution to the proceedings.

Del Oh yeah, of course.

Alan I mean, what sort of a hall do you think we should hire?

Del Well, you know, I don't think we ought to go mad, you know, it's only a registrar office wedding, ain't it, eh? No, actually, he's got a very nice hall here, you know, and it's cheap.

Alan D'you know if I had my way that's exactly where we'd hold the reception – a good old knees-up in a pub and plenty of jellied eels.

Del Well, this place is perfect, innit? And it's cheap.

Alan Yeah, yeah. But my wife Pam, she's gone all up-market on the idea. She wants to hold the reception in a cricket club pavilion or the country club. Oh yeah, she's got it all planned out. It's all Dom Perignon and caviar.

Del Oh yuck.

Alan Not a jellied eel in sight. So what do you think?

Del Well, I reckon you ought to put your

Little Problems

foot down, you know. How much is this gonna cost me then?

Alan Cost you? Oh Del, it's not gonna cost you a penny. My only child's getting married and I'm paying for the lot.

Del Yeah, but I thought you said you wanted me to make a contribution.

Alan Yeah, with ideas and opinions.

Del Oh well, actually, your missus has got a point, hasn't she? You know, I don't think that you and me ought to be selfish, should we? After all, it is for the happy couple, it is their big day.

Alan You don't like those sort of surroundings, do you? I mean champagne, caviar, country clubs.

Del Oh no, Alan, I hate it, I hate it, all put on. I mean, them people just do things for effect.

Mike arrives with a small scotch for Alan and a very exotic looking cocktail for Del (it's more like a floral tribute).

Del Here's to the big day.

Alan Yeah.

INT. NAG'S HEAD PUB. NIGHT. STUDIO.

This is an hour or so later.
Alan is not there. Del is standing at bar talking with Mike.

Mike Boycie, Trigg, your minicab's here.
Mickey Pearce and Jevon enter.
Mickey has his arm in a sling and Jevon is limping badly. But their faces are unscathed.

Mickey Del.

Del You two still haven't got the hang of those revolving doors, have you?

Mickey Can we have a word, Del?

Del Yeah, 'course you can, yeah. Michael, get Mickey and Jevon a drink, will you?

Jevon Those mobile phones we gave you. You got the money for them yet?

Del Of course I haven't. I haven't sold 'em yet.

Jevon Oh Christ!

Mickey Oh bloody hell!

Del What's up with you two, eh?
Trigger, Boycie and Alan enter from the door that leads upstairs.
They are holding Alan, who is drunk.

Alan Del, I'll see you, Del.

Del Yeah, cheers, Alan. Glad you enjoyed the drink.
Boycie, Trigger and Alan exit.

Mike Here, Del, that's a stroke of luck. He's hired my hall for the wedding reception and I'm doing all the food and drink. Where am I gonna get jellied eels from?

Del I don't believe it!

Mickey See, those phones weren't ours.

Del We could have had a nice country club.

Jevon We had them on sale or return, same as you.

Del We could have been eating caviar instead of Mike's scotch eggs.

Mickey Del, they want their money.

Del I'm a caviar person, me, you know, most probably. Who wants their money?

Jevon and Mickey The Driscoll brothers.
Boycie enters.

Del The Driscoll brothers?
Boycie, and other people in pub turn and look in Del's direction.
(Now quieter)
You two have been dealing with the Driscoll brothers?

Jevon Only with those mobile phones. We thought they'd be a good seller.

Del They done your arm didn't they? And your Gregory. That is their trademark, they don't touch the face but they knock the hell out of the body.

Mickey Danny Driscoll said this was a friendly warning. I'm sorry, Del, we had to tell him you'd taken the phones.

Jevon They've got it in their heads that you're trying to con them. They're looking for you, Del.

Del I know, I know. I've had a warning. But let me tell you this: if I end up supporting a flyover on the M26, I guarantee you two are gonna be in the next junction.

Let us see Mickey and Jevon's reaction. I'll get your drinks.

Del moves to bar.

Boycie Alright, what is all this about the Driscoll brothers?

Del Nothing, nothing at all. Listen, if the Driscoll brothers come in here asking for me, you ain't seen me, alright?

Mike Listen, I've heard of the Driscoll brothers, Del, but I've never seen them. What they look like?

Boycie Well, one of them looks like he was evicted from the planet of the apes.

Del Yeah, and the other one reminds me of Cliff Richard.

Mike What, he's younger than his years?

Del No, he's got one of them faces you'd like to slap.

Mike Here, Trigg, did you get Alan off home alright?

Trigger Yeah. There was almost an accident. The minicab driver nearly reversed into the Driscoll brothers' car.

Del The Driscoll brothers are here? What door they coming in?

Trigger Well, I dunno. They're just getting out the car.

Mike Upstairs, Del! Hide in the hall.

Del, Mickey, Jevon and for some unknown reason Trigger, rush to door that leads upstairs.

Now two heavy guys enter (these are the enforcers) followed by Danny Driscoll. He is middle forties, tall and dressed in the time-honoured way of London villains, three-piece suit, lairy tie, gold watch chain hanging across his waistcoat, overcoat draped over his shoulders.

Danny Boycie, how nice.

Boycie Hello, Danny. Your brother not with you?

Danny Yeah.

Now Tony Driscoll steps out from behind Danny. He is a younger and much smaller man, a pugnacious little sadist.

Boycie Oh wotcher, Tony.

The Driscolls walk over to the bar.

Boycie Drink?

Tony No. Is that right Marlene's up the spout?

Boycie Yeah.

Danny *(Shakes his head sadly)* Dear, dear, dear. Well, you let us know the moment you find out who done it and we'll sort him out.

Boycie Yeah, righto, Danny.

Now Danny laughs.

Boycie put on a laugh.

Yeah, good one, Danny, good one.

Tony Del Boy around?

Mike No, no. I ain't seen him this evening.

Danny Well, that's funny. His van's in the car park and -- what's this? *(Referring to Del's cigar and cocktail which are still on table)* A Castella, a Malibu reef. Are you sure he's not around? Think hard, guv'nor.

Mike Well, he may have been in earlier and then he left.

Danny I see. You just had this place decorated?

Mike Yeah.

Danny Shame. I wanna buy everyone in this pub a drink, whatever they want. Now here's a pound and I want change. *(Stares at Mike, daring him to argue)*

Boycie Large cognac, please, Michael.

Mike reacts

INT. NAG'S HEAD. UPSTAIRS HALL. NIGHT, STUDIO.

There is a hole in the wall which acts as a makeshift bar.

At the far end we have a low stage with

Little Problems

curtains either side. We now see the
curtain on left of stage move.

Del Keep still, will you?
We cut to behind curtains.

*We find the four desperadoes standing
behind curtain. Jevon is nearest to edge
of curtains. Mickey is next to him. Then
Trigger and finally Del who is furthest
away from curtain's edge.*

*Del's voxphone is in the breast pocket of
his jacket or his trendy green trenchcoat.
We can see the top of the voxphone
clearly. For the first time Del realises that
Trigger is with them.*

Del *(Quietly to Trigger)* Trigg, what you
doing here? It's got nothing to do with you.
What are you doing here with us?

Trigger *(Hadn't thought of this either)* I
dunno really. You said quick upstairs so I
just went.

Del shakes his head sadly.

*We see the entrance doors and hear
footsteps approaching. The door is
kicked. It shudders on its hinges but
doesn't open.*

Danny There's a doorknob there, Tony.
Why don't you just turn it like a human
being?

*The door opens and Tony, Danny and the
two heavies appear.*

*Danny looks immediately towards curtain
and smiles to himself, he gestures with
his head towards curtains. Tony doesn't
understand the gesture. His face says
"What?" Angrily, Danny gestures again
but more sharply with his head. Tony
now understands, and takes one of those
long poles used for opening high
windows and approaches the left hand
curtains.*

*He now thrusts the pole at head height
towards the curtain. The curtain between
Mickey and Jevon's head protrudes with
the thrust of the pole. He now thrusts
pole at hip height. The curtain between
Del's legs protrudes with the thrust of
pole. His frustration becomes too much.
Accompanied by a manic scream he hurls
the pole at the right hand curtain. It
smashes into curtain and clatters to floor.*

Danny Let's try the bogs.
*The four move towards entrance door.
We cut to behind curtain.*

Jevon They're going!

Mickey *(Whispers)* We're in the clear.
*Trigger taps Del's chest – the voxphone.
Trigger has in fact hit the 'aerial release'
button.*

*There is a tiny whirring sound, and
almost instantaneously with the tap the
aerial shoots up Del's nose.*

Del Aaaurghh!
*We see Danny and Tony who were about
to exit, stop at the door.*

*We now see the curtains on left of stage
moving violently. Mickey and Jevon
appear. They smile wildly and are terrified
by Danny. Now Trigger and Del appear.
Del still has the voxphone stuck up his
nose and is struggling to dislodge it.*

Danny He's got one of our phones up his
nose.

Tony That's a good idea, innit?

Del *(Pinched nose sound)* Yed, dank you
Danny. I dust dot dis done duck up my dose.

Danny Tone, help the man.

Del Do, dat's alwite.
*Tony moves to Del and yanks the phone
free. It comes free accompanied by a
loud 'pop'.*

Del Aaargh! Thanks for your help, Tony.

Danny I thought I said I didn't want to see

your faces round here any more.

Jevon Yes, Mr Driscoll.

Mickey Thank you, Mr Driscoll.

Mickey and Jevon leave quickly.

Tony That goes for you too.

Trigger Yeah, but.

Del Go on Trig, see you later.

Trigger leaves.

Tone You owe us £2,000. You got the money?

Del No, of course I haven't got the money. I haven't sold the phones, yet, have I?

Danny Don't give us that, Derek. Them two youngsters Ebony and Ivory took the phones from us over three months ago.

Del Three months? I didn't know that, Danny.

Danny Do you think we're stupid? *(Looks at Tony)* Do you think I'm stupid?

Del No.

Danny Those two munchkins work for you and you're doing a bit of a Fagin, but you picked the wrong ones this time. If you don't come up with the two grand I'm gonna take his collar and lead off and let him loose on you.

Del Hang on! You got it wrong, you've got it all wrong. I tell you what: you can have all the phones back.

Danny I don't want all that old rubbish back.

Tony They used to make our telly go funny.

Danny And that model's old now, and at least one of them's been up your hooter.

Del You've got to give me a bit of time. I mean, you two ain't short of a couple of grand.

Danny And you know why we ain't short of a few bob?

Del No.

Danny 'Cos we don't let debts linger. Can we explain something to you, Del? When me and Tony were kids we was very, very poor. Our old man used to work in the

stables in one of them big mansion houses. He used to work from six in the morning 'til eight at night and what for? A pittance.

Tony A shilling a day and a horseshit sandwich.

Danny Then one day there was a robbery at the mansion. The bill arrested our old man, but there wasn't any evidence, was there?

Tony That's right – just fingerprints.

Danny Just fingerprints.

Tony And eyewitnesses.

Danny Couple of eyewitnesses... They found the jewels on him.

Tony It was a plant.

Danny Yeah. It was a right fit-up. He died in a police cell with a fractured skull. They said it was a suicide attempt that went wrong, or right, whatever way you look at it. They claimed he tried to hang himself with his braces and smashed himself to death on the ceiling. Do you believe that?

Del No, no, I don't.

Danny The day he died, Tony and me swore that no one would ever dump on us and we would never, never be poor.

Del Wait a minute! After your dad died you two went to a young offenders' home, and who was it that used to look after your old mum with some hooky groceries and a bag of coal and all that – it was me, weren't it, eh? Come on, you owe me. No, I mean, you owe me at least a bit of time.

Danny He's right.

Tony No, he aint.

Danny We owe him.

Tony I don't think we do.

Danny Tony, we had an agreement – I do the thinking, you don't. Alright, Del, you got yourself a bit of time.

Del Cheers, cheers, Danny. When will I see you again?

Danny Dunno. We'll surprise you.

Del Good. I'll look forward to that.

Little Problems

Danny Get the money.

Del Right.

Danny Either you pay us or we pay you.
*The Driscolls and the heavies move
towards exit door.*

*As they do so Boycie arrives. He seems
surprised to find them still there.*

Boycie Oh hello, Danny. Just popped up to
see if you needed any help.

Danny No, I think we handled it pretty well
on our own. Be seeing you soon.
The Driscolls and heavies exit.

Boycie moves to Del.

Boycie Del, Mickey Pearce has just told me
you got some electrical equipment off the
Driscolls.

Del Yes, that's right.

Boycie It's not those video recorders you
sold me, is it?
*Del is about to say 'no' when he realises
that he's missing a chance to get some
money.*

Del N… Yeah!

Boycie God, do the Driscolls know?

Del I haven't said anything, you know, yet.

Boycie Well, you're not gonna tell them I
got them, are you?

Del Look, they wanna give someone a
good hidin'. Tell us what it was like, won't
you, Boycie?

Boycie (*Produces three packs of notes still
in bank wrappers*) Here… Here's most of
the money I owe you.

Del I thought you were skint?

Boycie I thought I was but then I suddenly
happened to find three grand in my pocket.
Square it with the Driscolls. Keep them off me.

Del Leave it to me, Boycie. What are
friends for?

INT. THE NAG'S HEAD PUB. NIGHT. STUDIO.
This is Rodney's stag night.

*All the gang are there. Mike, Boycie,
Trigger, Mickey Pearce and Jevon.*

*A comic is on stage doing a stag night
routine – or at least most of his gags are
about marriage and aimed at Rodney.*

Comic So remember, Rodney, marriage is
like a self-service restaurant – you get what
you want, you see what your mates got and
you want some of that.

Denzil I remember my stag night, Rodney.
It was about one o'clock in the car park and
I was just about to stagger home when they
jumped out on me.

Rodney Who, who jumped out on you?

Denzil I dunno. It was pitch black. Anyway,
they super-glued a learner sign to me pants
and run off and left me.
Del and Rodney are laughing.
I didn't mind the learner sign. I just wish
they'd let me have me trousers back.

Rodney (*Laughs a drunken laugh*) What!
You didn't, you didn't have no trousers on?

Denzil No, Rodney, no.

Albert I'm just popping out.

Del Albert, just a minute. While you're up
there, put another score in the whip.
*Albert moves round bar and makes his
way towards the gents. From the stage
the comic spots him.*

Comic Oh look, there he goes, hi-hoe.
Alright mate?
*Albert sneers in return and continues
towards door.*
Fancy putting your head on upside down!

Albert I fought in the war.

Comic What? The Boer War?
Albert exits.

The Driscolls enter.
Go on, get out of here, you miserable old
so-and-so. Here listen lads. There was this
fellow, he was really short. I tell you how
short he was. He got a job at Mothercare as

a bouncer, that's how short he was. He was so short, well, he...

Tony gives him a look that could kill from fifty paces.

The comic reacts, frightened.

Well, he wasn't that short... A tall feller, he was very tall...

Danny Driscoll reacts.

No, he wasn't tall, he was a woman.

Denzil Del, I don't wish to spoil the surprise, but the Driscoll brothers have just arrived.

Del Oh have they? Well, let them wait a while.

Denzil Do you need any backup?

Del No, it's alright, Denzil, thanks. Thanks a lot. No, don't worry. I've got their money.

Rodney Are you... Are you having a good time, Del?

Del Yes, yes, I'm having a blinding time, Rodders, yeah, yeah.

Rodney I get married in two days' time.

Del Yeah, I know you do. You wanna keep off the sherbet, otherwise you're gonna have a hangover in Rimini.

Rodney Oi, Del at the cerem...

Del Ceremony yeah, right...

Rodney ...ceremony, will they... they won't say my middle name will they?

Del No, no. He'll just call you, you know, like Rodney Trotter...

Rodney I wanna thank you, Del. You've done everything for me in my life.

Del Yes, alright. Shut up, Rodney.

Rodney When I was a kid, he brought me up, when I was a nipper.

Denzil Yeah, I know, Rodney. I remember.

Rodney He looked after me my brother did. I mean, if it wasn't for him, right, I could have been a drunk... or I could have been a snu-gliffer or anything. And I tell you something else about this man: he's giving me £2,000 for a deposit on my flat.

Del is smiling. The smile dies and turns

to a look of horror as he remembers his promise.

Del *(To Denzil)* I forgot that.

Denzil Oh hell.

Tony Driscoll beckons Del. He indicates outside.

Del Rodney, alright now, you stay here, right? You just listen to the man, alright? Back in a minute.

Del crosses to the Driscolls and exits.

Comic Course, my wife, she used to sell ice creams in the cinema. When we got married she went up the aisle backwards. She was lovely. We were driving home one night and she said, 'Would you like to see where I had the operation?' I said, 'Yeah'. She said, 'See the hospital up there on the hill...'

Rodney I'll tell you. Del, right; he's the bested bloke in the world.

Denzil Yeah, I know. Listen, Rodney, sometimes people say things that they mean, what they really mean is...

Rodney What you mean?

Denzil Well, sometimes they promise things and they really mean to keep that promise, but other things stop them from doing it.

Rodney looks at him long and hard. Then bursts out laughing for no apparent reason.

Denzil looks away defeated.

INT. THE TROTTER'S LOUNGE. NIGHT. STUDIO.

It is in darkness except for light coming from the hall which leads to the bedrooms.

We hear a key in the front door and Rodney enters. He is trouserless and has a learner sign super-glued to his boxer shorts. He is drunk and seething.

Little Problems

He pauses in the centre of the room and tries to focus in the half-light. He now staggers from the corridor to the bedrooms area.

INT. CORRIDOR TO BEDROOM AREA/BATHROOM. NIGHT. STUDIO.

Rodney Del!

Rodney staggers towards the bedroom area.

We hear Del from inside bathroom. He makes the kind of sound people make when they've had too much to drink.

Rodney Del! Del! Are you in the bathroom?

Del Yeah, yeah.

Rodney Thanks for walking out and leaving me like that.

Del Sorry! I had too much to drink. I come over bad. I'm still feeling a bit rough.

Rodney Oh and thanks for not getting me that money. Denzil explained that you had something more important to spend it on! You promised me. I've told Cassandra and her mum and dad and everything. I said I've got the money. What am I gonna look like now, eh? I'll tell you what I'm gonna look like now. I'm gonna look like a right tit-head, that's what I'll look like.

Cut to the bathroom, this is also in half-light.

We just see Del's face, maybe in the mirror. He is sweating and heavy-eyed, just like someone who's had too much to drink.

Del Your money's on the table.

Rodney What?

Del Your deposit money. It's on the table.

Rodney reacts to this news. Not sure whether to be overjoyed or suspicious. He staggers towards the lounge.

We now see that Del is bare-chested. His body is covered in bruises, scratches and cuts, courtesy of the Driscoll brothers. He bathes his wounds with a flannel and a basinful of cold water. Each touch of the flannel on his wounds make him wince with pain.

Rodney enters from lounge holding a bundle of notes.

Rodney Del?

Del Yeah?

Rodney Thanks.

Del It's alright, bruv. It was a pleasure.

Rodney Del... I'm sorry, right?

Del Oh leave it out, you tart.

Rodney You're still gonna be my best man, aren't you?

Del Yeah, 'course I am.

Rodney We'll have a good old knees-up eh?

Del I think I've had enough of that for one night, Rodney.

Rodney And I tell you what – we'll have a good old sing-song.

Del Yeah, as long as you don't mind me sounding like the Bee Gees.

Winces as he dabs one of his cuts

INT. REGISTRY OFFICE. DAY. STUDIO.

Rodney and Cassandra are standing in front of the table.

The registrar and clerk are behind table. Del is standing a few yards behind Rodney and to his right (or is it left?) One of Cassandra's friends, who is also acting as witness, is standing a few yards behind Cassandra.

We see Alan and Pam (Cassandra's parents). Pam, in her early forties and very smartly dressed. As Alan described her, she is slightly up-market. They both smile on benignly. Behind them are

Wedding Invitation

Mr & Mrs Alan Parry

Request the company of

Boycie and Marlene

to join them in the
celebration of the marriage
of their daughter Cassandra Louise
to Rodney Trotter
on the 13th February 1989
at the Peckham Registry Office
Peckham, London SE15 at 1.00pm

and afterwards at the
Nag's Head, Peckham, London SE15

R.S.V.P 10 Grove Road, Blackheath

Little Problems

Cassandra's friends and relatives.

On the Trotters side we have Albert, Boycie and a five-month pregnant Marlene, Trigger, Denzil, Mike, Mickey Pearce and Jevon. Mickey and Jevon are with girls.

Registrar I do solemnly declare.

Rodney I do solemnly declare.

Registrar That I know of no lawful impediment.

Rodney That I know of no lawful impediment.

Registrar That I may not be joined in matrimony to this woman, Cassandra Louise Parry.

Rodney That I may not be joined in matrimony to this woman, Cassandra Louise Parry.

Registrar Do you have the ring?
Rodney and Cassandra turn to their witnesses for the rings. Del hands Rodney the ring. This is all done with great decorum. Rodney and Cassandra place rings on fingers.

Registrar Now repeat after me: I call upon these persons here present.

Rodney I call upon these persons here present.

Registrar To witness that I, Rodney Charlton Trotter…
The Trotter side starts laughing. We actually hear Boycie, Denzil, Mickey and Jevon repeat the word 'Charlton'. Rodney reacts with 'I knew this would happen' reaction. Del turns away and grins, but this makes his ribs hurt and he winces. Cassandra smiles and turns away. The registrar coughs gently to try and bring some order.

that I, Rodney Charlton Trotter…
We hear more guffaws and squeals from the Trotters' side. Del, despite his smile, is gesturing for order.

Registrar *(To the Trotter side, nicely)* I would appreciate it if the guests would conduct themselves in a manner more becoming to this occasion, thank you.

Rodney That I, Rodney Charlton Trotter.
There are more laughs and squeals from the Trotter side.

Registrar Take this woman, Cassandra Louise Parry, to be my lawful wedded wife.

Rodney Take this woman, Cassandra Louise Parry, to be my lawful wedded wife.

Registrar Now repeat after me: I call upon these persons here present.

Cassandra I call upon these persons here present.

Registrar To witness that I, Cassandra Louise Parry.

Cassandra To witness that I, Cassandra Louise Parry.

Registrar Take this man, Rodney Charl… Rodney Trotter.

Cassandra Take this man, Rodney Trotter.

Registrar To be my lawful wedded husband.

Cassandra To be my lawful wedded husband.

Registrar Now you have both made the declarations required by law and you have made a solemn and binding contract with each other in the presence of your witnesses, you are now husband and wife. You may kiss the bride.

Rodney Thank you.
Rodney and Cassandra kiss. Cassandra's parents and relatives observe this with sweet and maybe emotional smiles. The Trotters side greet it with cheers, wolf whistles, etc. Rodney is embarrassed by the whole thing.

The Registrar now offers Rodney the pen to sign the marriage certificate.

INT. NAG'S HEAD HALL UPSTAIRS. NIGHT. STUDIO.

Pam Now the moment you two get back from honeymoon, you must call me.

Cassandra Look, we haven't even gone yet.

Alan Don't you be late for your first day at work, Rodney.

Rodney No, I'll be there, Alan.

Pam You'll have to come round to dinner.

Rodney Oh thank you, Pamela.

Alan We could invite Del.

Pam Er... well.

Rodney *(Sensing her embarrassment)* He'll most probably be busy.

Pam Yes.

Alan Well, I'm seeing him on Wednesday. I'll ask him.

Pam You're not going to get drunk again?

Alan No. He's taking me to a pie and mash shop.

Pam What for?

Alan For pie and mash.

Cassandra I think I'll just go and say goodbye to a few more people.

Cassandra and Rodney move away.

Pam What's happened to you? Ever since you've met Rodney's brother you've become like a born-again hooligan. It's thanks to you that my daughter's wedding reception is being held at this ghastly pub, all champagne and welks; there's spoons of jellied eels everywhere.

Alan That's because I like jellied eels. Look Pamela, I've worked all my life. I'm a successful businessman in charge of a successful business! And if I fancy eating the occasional bowl of jellied eels, I will eat the occasional bowl of jellied eels.

We see Del in background. He hasn't heard any of this.

Del Hey, Alan, there ain't many of them jellied eels left, I'd get stuck in if I was you.

Alan crosses back to get jellied eels.

Del joins Rodney.

Cassandra See you in a minute.

Del Are you off then, bruv?

Rodney Yeah, going in a minute.

Del Just wanted to... er... just wanted to say, Rodney, that I'm really very proud of you. You've got it all now, ain't you? New job, new flat, new wife, new life.

Rodney Yeah. We had a few good years, eh?

Del Some good times.

Rodney Some right laughs, eh?

Del And a couple of tears. But that's all part of it. I just wish that Mum ...

Rodney Oh no, shut up! You'll have me going.

They now just look at each other. It's almost as if one of them's emigrating.

Rodney now embraces Del. Del shouts in pain.

Del Oohhh.

Rodney What's wrong?

Del I got a bit of a bruise. I don't know how I got it.

Cassandra Goodbye, Del, and thanks for everything.

Cassandra hugs Del.

Del That's alright sweetheart. Listen, will you do something for me?

Cassandra What?

Del Be gentle with him.

Cassandra Oh shut up!

Cassandra and Rodney move towards exit. Rodney pauses at door and looks at Del, then exits.

Marlene appears.

Marlene I didn't know Rodney's middle name was Charlton.

Del Oh yeah, it was me mum. She was a fan.

Little Problems

Marlene Oh what? Charlton Heston?

Del No. Charlton Athletic.

Marlene Duke, get off that table. You gonna have a dance with me Del?

Del Not right now Marlene, under this shirt I am covered in scratches and bruises.

Marlene Who you been going out with then?

Del It's a long story.

Marlene How come you never got married, Del?

Del Me? No, I'm too shrewd for that game.

Marlene You got engaged, though, didn't you? Lots of times. So why didn't you marry any of them?

Del I dunno. It was Rodney, I suppose.

Marlene Rodney stopped you getting married?

Del Well, back in them days Rodney was just a kid, you know, and I had to bring him up.

Marlene You were like a mother and father to him.

Del Yeah, I breast-fed him for the first six months. No, it's just that all the birds that I went out with they wanted to get married but they didn't want to bring Rodney up, especially the way he went through shoes. So what was I supposed to do? Marry them and stick Rodders into care? Nah, I elbowed them. It's family, innit?

Marlene You should be proud of yourself. He turned out a real good 'un.

Del Yeah, he's a diamond. A forty-two-carat diamond.

Boycie Come along, Marlene. *(To Del)* I wanna have a word with you during the week. You should see what that Chinese kid has done to my video recorders.

Marlene See you, Del.

Del Bye-bye, sweetheart.

Marlene Bye.

Del Bye, sweetheart.

Marlene Come on, Duke.

Del Cheerio, Boycie.
Albert follows.

The last few stragglers are leaving the hall. They call or wave goodbyes to Del. Now, save for the sleeping jock, Del is alone in the hall. The record 'Holding Back the Years' by Simply Red is playing.

He looks around the empty hall and thinks back to the good times and the not so good times. He thinks of Rodney's new found happiness. He thinks of his own future and doesn't like the taste.

He knows he'll never be that millionaire. But there is one tiny spot, deep in his heart, that refuses to let his hapless dream die. And that is the spot that Del now goes to.

He holds his head up defiantly as the repeated chorus from 'Holding Back the Years' plays across his face. ("I'll keep holding on").

Mike appears and breaks Del's concentration.

Mike Cassandra's dad's been ill in the toilet.

Del I told him not to eat all them jellied eels.

Mike I've got to lock up, Del.

Del Yeah, alright, Mike. Thanks very much for a very nice do.

Mike Cheers, mate.
Mike moves towards the sleeping jock. Del walks to exit door with the record playing over.

INT. TROTTERS' LOUNGE. NIGHT. STUDIO.
This is two weeks after the wedding. The flat is in darkness.

We hear key in front door.

Now Del enters from hall. He is dressed in his market gear and carries the suitcase.

The cordless phone begins ringing.
Del Hello, Trotter Independent Traders... Oh it's you, Albert... er... no, it's alright, I've only just got in, yeah. Where are you... oh you're round at Elsie Partridge's are you? Oh yeah, got your plates of meat under the table there, ain't you, eh, you saucy old goat? What? No, no, they're back from their honeymoon. Yeah, I saw Rodney this morning racing off to work. Yeah, he looked great, he did, nice three-piece suit, smart tie, yeah, and his executive briefcase, yeah, the lot... You what? No, no, I didn't have chance to speak to him. I was in the van and he came racing past on his bicycle... The honeymoon? Yeah, I think that went alright, yeah. He was as white as a sheet... You what? Oh yeah, you off down the Legion tonight, are you... Me? No. Well, I'm alone. Well, no, no. I'm not alone, really; it's just the way I'd like it to be... No, no thanks very much, Albert. I appreciate the offer but I'm not in the mood for dominoes tonight... Yeah, I'll *see* you when I see you.
The door to hall opens and a very tired Rodney enters.

He is wearing the clothes Del described – a three-piece suit, a smart tie, a trendy raincoat and is carrying an executive-style briefcase. He has bicycle clips around his ankles.
Rodney *(Tired)* Alright?
Del *(Stunned to see him)* Yeah, triffic, Rodders.

Rodney flops down in armchair.
Rodney I am exhausted.
Del Yeah you look a bit cream crackered. What is it? Executive stress, is it?
Rodney No, it's that bike. The wheels hardly go round, the chain's come off twice and the front light don't work. Where d'you get it from?
Del I dunno. It's been in the garage for years.
Rodney *(Yawns)* What's for tea?
Del I ain't got a clue have I? Can I say something to you? Give you a piece of advice that may hold you in good stead in the, you know, future?
Rodney Yeah, go on, then.
Del It's just that, well, how can I put it? *(Shouts at him)* You don't live here no more.
Rodney *(A momentary pause before it sinks in)* Oh, bloody 'ell! She'll go loopy.
Rodney exits, closing door behind him. He now rushes back in and grabs his briefcase.
I'll phone you, right?
Del Yeah, righto, bruv.
Rodney exits, closing door behind him.
Rodney Take care, Del.
Del You too, Rodders.
He now rushes back in and grabs his bicycle clips.
Rodney I'll see you.
Del See you around.
Rodney exits, closing door behind him. This time we hear the front door slam. Del has a great big smile. He now knows that things aren't going to be as bad as he imagined. No matter what happens, Rodney will always be around.
What a plonker!

Little Problems

SERIES SEVEN

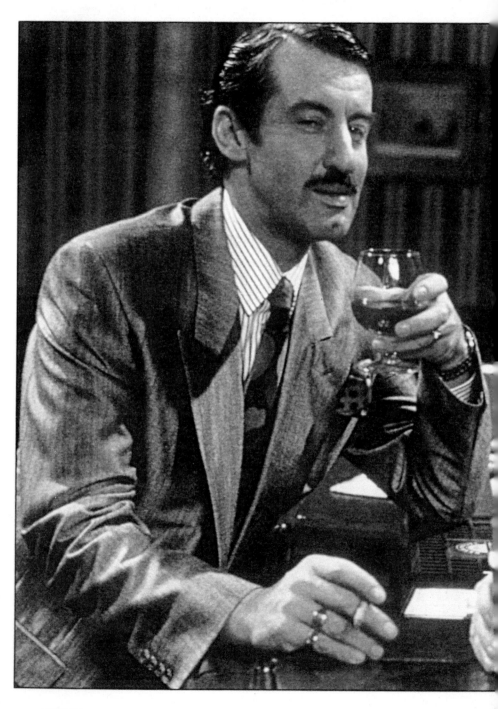

The Sky's the Limit

INT. TROTTERS' LOUNGE/BEDROOM AREA. DAY

The table is laid for a healthy breakfast: half a grapefruit, a packet of All-Bran, toasted granary bread, a pot of tea and a jug of orange juice. Also on the table is a tray which holds a cup and saucer (fine English china with a floral pattern) and an old white mug. There are also a couple of newspapers.

The 'bed' on the settee is neatly made. Albert, in dressing gown and pyjamas, is pouring tea into the cup and mug, as he does he sings a modern pop song.

Cut to hallway of bedroom area. Three doors: Del's bedroom, Rodney's bedroom and the bathroom. The door to Del's room opens and Raquel, wearing a nightdress and dressing gown, peers out towards the lounge where she can hear Albert singing and whistling. Del appears behind her. He is already power-dressed for the day.

Del Well, go on then!

Raquel Albert might come out here any second!!

Del So what? You're only going across there to the bathroom, Raquel. It's hardly a life-or-death sprint across no man's land!

Raquel But what if he sees me? He doesn't know I'm staying in here with you. He still thinks I sleep in Rodney's old room and Rodney sleeps on the settee! We'll have to tell him the truth, Del!

Del Yeah, I s'pose you're right, sweetheart. If it'll make you happy, you tell him.

Raquel Me? I'm not telling him! It's embarrassing! He's your uncle, you tell him!

Del Alright, I'll tell him. He don't bother me. Quick! Get back, he's coming!!

Raquel and Del exit to bedroom and close door.

Albert enters from the lounge carrying the tray and the newspapers.

He knocks on Del's bedroom door.

Tea up, Del Boy.

Del opens door.

Del Morning, Unc.

Albert hands him the floral-patterned cup and saucer and the newspapers.

Albert Morning, son. There's yer papers. *Financial Times* and *Exchange And Mart*.

Del Cheers, Albert. I'll check the Tokyo closing prices at the breakfast table.

Albert Yeah, please yerself, boy.

Albert carries the old white mug across to Rodney's door and knocks.

Albert *(Calls)* Raquel! Cup of tea, love... You awake? Raquel? I'll leave it outside for you, love.

He places mug on floor outside door and moves towards lounge.

INT. TROTTERS' LOUNGE. DAY

Del is seated at table sipping his tea and reading the papers. Albert enters.

Del *(Sniffing the air)* Something smells good, Albert.

Albert I'm just doing meself some egg and bacon. Whatd'you want for breakfast, something healthy or something nice?

Del *(Looks disdainfully at the half of grapefruit, etc)* Yeah, do us a fry-up. But be a bit lively, though. I don't want Raquel seeing. She's into all this high-fibre cobblers.

Albert *(Is about to enter kitchen)* You managed to have a talk with young Rodney yet?

Del *(Busy reading newspaper)* What about?

143

Albert What d'you mean, what about? He's left his wife and come back to live here!

Del I know. But he's a full-grown adult now, so what am I supposed to say?

Albert I don't know. You could appeal to his common sense.

Del Oh yeah? Then after lunch I'll go out and find Shergar!

Albert It's no laughing matter. Cassandra's gone to live in a foreign country!

Del No, she ain't! She's gone to Spain. She's only there for a week. Her and her mum are just getting away from it all at the family villa. Talking of their family villa, I'm family now, ain't I? I could do with a break. I'm having a drink with Cassandra's dad tonight: I'll have to have a word with him.

Albert He's down the pub every night boozing!

Del Cassandra's dad?

Albert I'm talking about Rodney!

Del Oh, gonna say, Alan's teetotal. Having a drink with him is like going on a pub crawl with Betty Ford. Look, you don't wanna worry about Rodney. He's just a bit confused at the moment.

Albert Yeah, he looked a bit confused when he come in last night. Confused as a newt! Still, at least he's making a bit of effort. *(Indicates settee)* Look, he made his bed before he went a work.

Del Er... actually, Unc, Rodney didn't sleep on the settee last night.

Albert *(Too loud for comfort)* Where'd he sleep then?

Del *(Reacts to the loudness)* He slept in his old room.

Albert I thought Raquel slept in there!

Del *(Cringing at the loudness of this conversation)* Er... No!

Albert *(OOV)* Where'd she sleep then?

Del *(Mumbles)* I don't believe him!! *(Calls)* She slept... er... somewhere else.

Albert Oh I see!

Del breathes a sigh of relief, believing Albert now understands the situation.

Albert Where?

Del Gordon Bennett! *(Calls)* If you could raise your voice by half a decibel they might be able to hear you in the Doodoyne!

Albert enters from kitchen carrying a plate of sausage, egg, bacon, etc.

Albert You mean she slept with you.

Del Well... Yes! Here, don't you go saying nothing to her about it!

Albert Don't she know, then?

Del I mean, it might embarrass her!

Albert No wonder you're looking so chirpy! *(Laughs)*

Del That laugh! Sounds like someone trying to push-start a Lada!

Albert Here y'are, you can have my breakfast, build yer strength up. I'll cook meself another one.

Del Cheers, Albert, you're a lifesaver. Lovely Jubbly!

Raquel enters from the bedroom area, dressed casually for shopping. Del quickly pushes his plate of food over to Albert and pulls the grapefruit to him. Raquel moves to table.

Raquel Morning, Albert.

Albert Morning, love. Nice to see you back on yer feet.

Raquel looks to Del.

Del gives a facial shrug which says 'Yes, I've told him.'

Albert D'you feel up to a bit of breakfast?

Raquel No thanks. *(Referring to Albert's breakfast.)* I don't know how you can eat that sort of rubbish, Albert.

Del The Trotter family have been eating that sort of rub... food for generations.

Albert It never did us any harm. My dad lived 'til he was 81.

Del 81, see? That's a good age.

Albert It weren't for him. He died!

The Sky's the Limit

Del Yeah, I know. I meant… blimey! Raquel's right. I can't eat fried food any more. Gimme a nice grapefruit anyday.

Raquel Good, that's what I like to hear. You've got some egg on your chin.

Del just about resists swearing at being caught out by such a silly mistake. He wipes the evidence away.

Raquel A doctor told you to stay off fried food!

Del Yes, and a doctor told Snow White to eat more fruit, and look what happened to that poor cow! Alright, I know you're concerned for me, sweetheart, and I'm grateful. I'll leave it alone in future. Are you eating?

Raquel No, I wanna get down to the shops before they're too packed.

Del Come on, I'll drive you down there. I've gotta load of printing to deliver to Boycie. See you later, Albert. And you know what you can do with that rubbish! *(Quietly.)* Put it in the oven – in the oven.

Del, carrying his filofax and mobile phone, and Raquel exit to hall and front door. Front door closes. Albert is about to carry the plate into the kitchen when the door to the bedroom area opens and Rodney pops his head in. He looks typically hung-over – hair a mess, stubble and the whites of his eyes a light shade of crimson. He is wearing boxer short, socks and an 'I ran the world' T-shirt.

Rodney Del gone to work?

Albert Yeah. I thought you had as well!

Rodney No, I… er… I sort of overslept when I woke up.

Albert D'you want some breakfast?

Rodney Yeah, I wouldn't mind a… *(Sees the remains of Del's breakfast and reacts)* Ah, God! A glass of orange'll do.

Albert exits to kitchen with plate.

Albert You'd better get a move on, Rodney, it's gone nine.

Rodney Well, to be honest, Unc, I don't feel well enough to go today. Would you ring 'em and say I won't be in?

Albert *(OOV)* What's wrong with you, then?

Rodney *(Holding head)* It's me stomach. It's sorta aching.

Rodney picks up phone and begins tapping out numbers.

Rodney I think I've got a viral condition. There's a lot of it about.

Albert enters from kitchen minus the plate.

Albert Yeah, especially among the regulars at the Nag's Head.

Rodney I have not got a hangover if that's what you're thinking! Alright, I had a drink last night.

Albert And the night before, and the night before that! *(Takes phone from Rodney)*

Rodney Oh shuddup! Ask for the personnel department.

Albert *(On phone)* Oh, hello. Could I have the personnel department, please? *(To Rodney)* They wouldn't have the likes of you in the armed forces.

Rodney Lets me out of World War Three then, dunnit?

Albert *(On phone)* Oh, good morning. I'm calling on behalf of Rodney Trotter. He won't be into work today because he's… eh? What d' you mean, 'Who is he'?

(To Rodney)
Who are you?

Rodney Who am I? The cheeky… Tell her I'm the head… the head of the computer section!

Albert *(On phone)* He's the head… the head of the computer section!

Now Albert chuckles at something the other person has said.

Albert Yeah, that's him!

Rodney looks up through bleary eyes with a 'what the hell are they laughing at?' expression.

Albert Well, he won't be into work today. He's got a bellyache.

Rodney (Horrified, mouths the words) Bellyache?

Albert (On phone) Don't know, dear. He might be a bit egg-bound.

Rodney (Turns away cringing) Oh God!

Albert (On phone) Yes, thank you, dear. Bye (To Rodney) Alright?

Rodney Alright? What d'you mean, alright? Why d' you tell her I've got a bellyache?

Albert That's what you've got, innit?

Rodney No, it is not!

Albert You said you had an ache.

Rodney I have!

Albert In yer belly?

Rodney Yes!

Albert Well, ain't that a bellyache?

Rodney No!

Albert Well, I must have got the wrong end of the stick, Rodney!

Rodney Bellyaches are what you have when you're tryna get out of school sports day! Heads of computer sections have viral conditions!

Albert Well, whatever it is, they know you won't be in today.

Rodney I don't think I can ever go there again for the rest of my life! Egg-bound!

Del's voice is heard from hall.

Del Albert, where have I left the keys to my van?

Del enters from hall.

Del Quick, get that breakfast on the ta... (Surprised then suspicious as he sees Rodney) I thought you'd gonna work!

Albert He's not going a work today.

Del Why not?

Albert He's got a viral condition.

Del What's that?

Rodney A bellyache.

Del Must have come on sudden, Rodders! You weren't feeling any pain at all last night!

Rodney I know what you're thinking!

Del I bet you don't!

Rodney Just 'cos I had a couple of drinks; you automatically assume I've got a hangover!

Del Have you looked in the mirror this morning? Well, I tell you, Rodney, you are not the fairest in the land! You look like you've just come back from a Club 18–30 trip to Chernobyl!

Rodney Chernobyl's not too far from the truth! My love life has taken on a distinctly Russian ambience of late. Freezing bloody cold and the goods rarely turn up!

Albert You don't wanna believe all you hear about the Russians. During the war.

A low moan of dismay from Del and Rodney.

Albert ... I was in the Soviet Union for a while.

Rodney Oh no, we're back in the USSR!

Del They wouldn't let you into the Soviet Union! Gawd, they wouldn't let you into the plumbers' union!

Albert I was dry-docked in Murmansk for over a month! And I met quite a few Russian girls — and I'm telling you they was hot stuff!

Rodney Oh leave off, Albert!

Del He could have a point, Rodney. I mean, look at that love-bite on old Gorbachev's head!

Del and Albert laugh. Rodney starts to laugh but it hurts.

Del Help us look for them keys, Rodney. I've gotta drop that stuff off at Boyce's. Albert, iron that pink shirt of mine. I'm meeting Alan for cocktails this evening.

Rodney Alan? What, Cassandra's dad?

Del Yes, Rodney. Your father-in-law, your employer! I don't know how much longer he's gonna stand for your old fun and games. How many days you had off recently with hangovers? You're gonna push that

The Sky's the Limit

man's loyalty too far.

Rodney I'm ill!

Del Yeah, I'll tell him you've got the two-bob bits.

Rodney A viral condition sounds better.

Del And what do I say to him about this situation with you and Cassandra?

Rodney Tell him I'm working on it.

Del Oh that should cheer him right up, shouldn't it?

Rodney stands and moves round the room looking for Del's keys.
Del notices Rodney's limp.

Rodney Where d'you leave yer keys?

Del I don't know. Have a look in my bedroom. *(Now genuinely concerned)* Rodney, bruv, d'you want me to make an appointment with the doctor?

Rodney No, no, I'll be alright.

Del But you're limping.

Rodney Yeah, me sock's soaking wet. Someone left a mug of tea outside my door.

Del looks at Albert.
Albert gives an embarrassed grin then exits to kitchen.

EXT. BOYCIE'S BACK GARDEN. DAY

Duke is bounding around the finely manicured lawns chasing a ball and barking. Boycie, wearing pyjamas and dressing gown, is standing by his satellite dish and studying it with a frustrated expression. He looks up to the sky, as if checking the path of the next satellite, and adjusts the dish accordingly. Marlene is in the background putting Tyler into his buggy. She is dressed for a day out.

Marlene Are we going out for the day or aren't we?

Boycie Yes! We're going out for the day! But I am waiting for the engineers to call to check this thing over. They were supposed to be here at nine. Look at it, quarter to ten and no sign of 'em! Del Boy was supposed to bring my printing round as well. I suppose he's too busy with that woman – what's her name?

Marlene Raquel.

Boycie Yeah, the stripper.

Marlene She is not a stripper! She's an actress!

Boycie Oh really? Well, the last time I saw her she was acting the part of a stripper. *(Laughs)*

Boycie adjusts the aerial again.

Marlene Isn't it working yet?

Boycie Yes, it's working. It's just that I can't line it up with the satellites. *(Looking skywards)* I mean, how am I supposed to know where they are?

Marlene You'd think they'd make 'em fly a bit lower, wouldn't you?

Boycie Well, it wouldn't be a bad ide…

Marlene *(In babyish talk)* Look, Tyler. There's your daddy playing with his new toy. Doesn't he look stupid?

Boycie This is not a toy, Marlene! You are looking at £2000 worth of state-of-the-art technology!

Marlene That didn't cost you £2000! You got it 'ooky!

Boycie *(Cuts in quickly)* Ssshhh, ssshhh! For Gawd's sake, Marlene! We've got a chief inspector living next door!

Marlene I know. That's who you got it off of. Why couldn't we have got a cheap one from Dixons like everyone else?

Boycie Because this is not for pleasure! This is a hi-tech investment in my video-leisure company. This thing can pick up the whole of Scandinavia. I can then record films of the more adult variety and distribute them among my more discerning clients.

Marlene You mean perverts.

Boycie Well, if you wanna get medical about it, yes!

Bronco, the decorator, calls from the front door.

Bronco Boycie, you got a minute?

Marlene *(Referring to Bronco)* He wants paying. And no messing around! You pay him! I know what a tight sod you are. And be nice to him. *(Indicating temple)* You know he's had problems!

Boycie Alright, I'll be nice to him. *(Bends down as if to kiss Tyler)*

Marlene Don't get your face too close. It scares him!

Boycie exits through open French doors.

The Sky's the Limit

EXT. BOYCIE'S FRONT GARDEN. DAY

Bronco places a few dust sheets and pots outside front door.

Boycie, now irate, exits from front door.

Bronco I've just finished.

Boycie Oh you're finished alright. Look what you've done to my vestibule! There's paint on me carpet, paint on the chandelier, paint on me Chippendale telephone seat!

Bronco You can't help a drop or two of paint!

Boycie A drop or two! It looks like someone's held an acid party in a Dulux warehouse!

Bronco Well, I'm sorry you're disappointed. What shall I do with the bill?

Boycie Stick it! Where the mice won't get at it! I'm not paying!

Bronco Hang about, Boycie. We had an agreement! You owe me 400 quid! We shook hands on it.

Boycie I know. I had to wash the paint off afterwards! You either adjust your fee to take account of all the damage, or contact my solicitor. This is the last time I have a cowboy working on my property!

Bronco I am not a cowboy!

Boycie Not a cowboy! I've got spur-marks on me grandfather clock!

Boycie exits to house, slamming front door closed.

Del's van pulls into driveway.

Bronco is now shouting through the letterbox.

Bronco I don't like being called a cowboy! No one's ever called me that before!!

Del *(Pleased to see him)* Bronco!

Bronco Oh, wotcher, Del.

Del How's yer luck, pal?

Del approaches Bronco carrying his filofax and mobile phone.

Bronco I've just bin working for Boycie, that's how bad it is! You'll never guess.

That tight-arsed bark's only refusing to pay me! Accused me of being a messy worker.

Del Well, you are a little bit sloppy, ain't yer, Bronc? Mean, look at them overalls.

Bronco But I'm a painter and decorator!

Del I know, but I only sold 'em to you Tuesday!

Bronco I asked Sandra to run 'em through the washing machine, but the landlord's cut our electric off.

Del Landlord? I thought you bought a little flat down Lordship Lane?

Bronco Building society evicted us.

Del So where are you now?

Bronco We're in a bed-and-breakfast hotel out near the airport.

Del Oh, well, handy if you like planes, innit?

Bronco Yeah, we're at the end of the main runway.

Del Cushy! Here, how's your little Kylie these days?

Bronco She broke her arm.

Del No!

Bronco Climbed up on a chair to look at a plane.

Del It's a bit grim, ain't it, Bronco?

Bronco Maybe I should tell Boycie, eh? Give him a sob-story.

Del A sob-story to Boycie! That's the man who cheered when Bambi's mum died!

Bronco I don't understand my luck lately. If it can go wrong, it's gone wrong! A roof I re-tiled has just collapsed. Last week I rewired a bloke's flat, yesterday it caught fire… Oh, by the way, here's my business card in case you ever want anything done.

Del Cheers, I'll keep it handy.

Del screws the card up and throws it behind him without Bronco seeing.

Bronco I've worked hard to build up this business, and I've always led an honest life.. Well, I've kept out of trouble for the last five years, ain't I?

Del Oh yeah. But being banged up in Wandsworth prison helped, didn't it?

Bronco And why did I go away?

Del Because you have a tendency to nick stupid things! I mean, you were caught speeding down Streatham High Road in a knocked-off JCB! Look, mate. You've got a few, you know, problems, and…

Bronco What'd you mean, problems?

Del Well, that psychiatrist said you had some sort of paranoia.

Bronco You can't take any notice of him, Del. He always had it in for me.

Del Yeah, didn't think of that. *(Produces a wad of money)* Listen, Bronco, d'you wanna few quid to tide you over?

Bronco No. Nice of you, Del. I'll get me money one way or the other. See you around.

Del If you need any help, give us a bell… Stay lucky.

Del winces at what he has just said. Bronco drives out in his van. Del rings front door bell. Boycie opens door.

Del I've brought your printing round.

Boycie He's gone, has he? Good. He's been decorating my vestibule – made quite a good job of it, as it happens. I'm well pleased.

Del *(Astounded)* But you've refused to pay him!

Boycie No, no, Del Boy. I've refused to pay him the agreed price. It's principle. I kick up a fuss, he don't want the aggro or the publicity so he knocks 50 per cent off for good will. He gets a living wage and I save two hundred notes… It's good business.

Del But Bronco's got Sandra, Kylie and Rachmann to keep going!

Del opens back of van. It is loaded with cardboard boxes on which is printed: 'Parry-Print'.

Boycie *(Gestures to house)* Does this look like the Social Security to you? I mean, who is he, anyway?

Del He's yer brother-in-law!

Boycie D'you think I like having a certified nutter working in my house? I only give him the job to help him out. Talking of in-laws, it's bloody handy Rodney working for his father-in-law's printing firm. I mean, look at all this at half-price, eh? Does Alan know about this?

Del He wouldn't mind if he did. Rodney is totally in charge now. That firm couldn't operate without him.

Boycie Yes, I always had faith in the boy.

Del Yeah, so did I. You've ordered a lot this time, ain't yer?

Boycie *(Picking up one of the boxes)* Yeah. I thought I'd get in now before Rodney gets the sack.

INT. THE NAG'S HEAD. NIGHT

The bar is sparsely crowded. Albert is playing the piano – 'Red Sails in the Sunset' – but none of the customers takes any notice. Mike, leaning on the counter and looking in Albert's direction, appears to be in a reflective mood.

Trigger, in his suit, is seated at the bar.

Mike *(To Trigger without actually looking at him)* I've been thinking about getting one of them electric pianos.

Trigger Yeah? They sound a lot better, don't they.

Mike That's right. And you can switch 'em off. Still, at least my ban on his singing has worked. Last night it was Trotter the younger and his dopey mates. Were you here last night?

Trigger Most probably.

Mike There was Rodney, Mickey Pearce and that Jevon, dancing and poncing around pretending to be Ninja Turtles. They'd all had far too much to drink.

Trigger Don't want that sort of thing in a pub, do yer?

Mike No, you don't!

The Sky's the Limit

Albert *(Starts singing the last verse)*
Red sails in the sunset, way out on the sea,
oh carry my loved one, safe home to me.

Trigger He's singing.

Mike I know.

Trigger Does he know you banned him?

Albert takes a bow. One person applauds out of politeness and he joins a couple of old boys playing dominoes.

Del, now wearing a different suit and the pink shirt he had asked Albert to iron earlier, enters carrying his aluminium briefcase and the mobile phone.

Del *(To Mike and Trigger)* Au revoir to you both.

Trigger Del Boy.

Mike What you having?

Del Give us a peach daiquiri and a chipolata sandwich. Any sign of Alan? He's supposed to be meeting me here for a drink.

Mike He ain't been in so far.

Trigger *(To Del)* Saw Boycie about 'arf an hour ago. He didn't even stop to say hello. Seemed in a right mood.

Del I bet Marlene's taken the Velcro off his Y-fronts again.

Alan enters, hurrying.

Alan Sorry I'm late, Del. Pam just phoned from the villa.

Del No problem, Alan. What are you drinking?

Alan Just a tomato juice for me.

Del Add a tomato juice to my order, Mike. We'll be at the table.

Alan Del, you've most probably been wondering why I asked to meet you tonight.

Del Been wondering? Well, of course not! I couldn't think of anything more natural than relatives having a drink together.

Alan Relatives?

Del You and me. We're family, aren't we?

Alan Well, we're... kind of related – sort of.

Del No sort of about it, Alan! When your Cassandra married a Trotter you all became Trotters – maybe not in the eyes of the law, but certainly in the eyes of my heart. Oh yes, Alan, you are my family. Anything of mine is yours for the asking – and I'm sure it works the other way round... dunnit? This villa of yours...

Alan *(Cuts in quickly)* What happened to Rodney today?

Del Rodney? Oh yes. He's got a touch of viral condition.

Alan Yeah, the lady in personnel said he had the two-bob bits.

Del Oh, it's worse than that, Alan. He really is very poorly.

Alan You called the doctor in?

Mike arrives with drinks.

Del I wanted to but he just wouldn't let me. It's his uncle's influence. Rodney's trying to be a British bulldog.

Mike Last night he was tryna be a Ninja Turtle.

Del reacts.

Alan D'you mean Rodney was down here last night?

Mike Down here? He was down here, up there, all over the place! Drunk as a sack, he was! If he hadn't been spending so much on drink I'd have thrown him out. *(Returns to bar)*

Del This viral condition comes on very sudden.

Alan Alright, Del. Cards on the table. This situation with Rodney is what I really came to see you about. So tell me, what the hell is happening?

Del He's... he's drinking too much and pretending he's enjoying it.

Alan That's why he's been having so many days off work recently.

Del Yeah. Most of the time he's feeling and looking horrible. I've told him. If he carries on much longer he'll be a dead-

ringer for Keith Richards. I mean, he looks like an extra from Hallowe'en already.

Alan What d'you think's brought it about?

Del Who knows? Sorta life he's been leading, I suppose. Late nights, booze, women, drugs.

Alan Rodney?

Del Oh Rodney! Oh sorry! Thought you meant... Well, it's obvious, innit? It's this thing between him and Cassandra.

Alan Yeah, that's what I feared. I always had such high hopes of them two. What with her experience at the bank and all her studies, Cassandra's had a very good business grounding and she's got an alert mind and lots of original ideas. And Rodney's... Rodney's a very trustworthy person.

Del Oh he's a diamond, Alan, a diamond.

Alan Exactly. I'd always hoped that one day I could leave the business to them two knowing that I'd left it in good hands.

Del Like a dream come true, innit? I mean, you could fall off the perch in peace, couldn't you?

Alan Well, I wasn't actually talking about falling off the perch, Del. I meant I could retire.

Del Oh, of course!!

Alan Pam and I have always planned to settle down in our villa in the sun.

Del You'd have no worries, would yer? If Rodney and Cassandra got in trouble with the business I'd always be around to take control.

Alan Er... well... we're about the same age, Del, so by that time you'd be retired too.

Del Didn't think of that... Well, I could spend a few months over in the villa with you and Pam.

Alan Oh yeah. Wait 'til I tell her.

Del You and Pam, me and Raquel. You can just picture it, can't yer?

Alan Yeah.

Del We'd have a right laugh. Few sangrias, bit of fried squid. Lambarda the night away. Lovely Jubbly! Shall we have a drink to celebrate it?

Alan No, no, I don't touch it nowadays.

Del Talking of your villa...

Mike *(Calls from bar, holding telephone receiver up)* Del. Call for you.

Del Who is it?

Mike Someone called Blonco or Bronco.

Del Sorry about this, Alan. It's a very, very important business associate of mine.

Mike I'd hurry up if I was you. He sounds like he's had a skinful.

Del *(An embarrassed smile to Alan)* Do excuse me.

Del goes to phone. Trigger turns to Alan.

Trigger You never know what you've got 'til it's gone.

Alan Eh? Yeah, I suppose you're right, Trig.

Trigger I know how much it can hurt. I had a relationship break up a few years ago. She worked at my council depot.

Mike She was a lady road-sweeper?

Trigger Oh no! She was management – real high-flier. You had to go to her when you wanted a new broom. Linda. Nice girl. Had a funny eye. Never knew if she was looking at me or seeing if the bus was coming. Anyway, she heard about this little hotel out near Henley-on-Thames and she said to me, 'How about spending a weekend there?' *(Winks)*

Mike and Alan are hanging on the next words.

Del *(On phone)* So what sorta money we talking? I'll pop round and have a look at it, Bronc.

Mike *(To Trigger)* Yeah?

Trigger What?

Alan Well... Was it a nice weekend?

Trigger Yeah. Well, at least I thought it was... but she didn't wanna see me no more after it.

The Sky's the Limit

Alan Well… er… I don't like to pry, Trig…

Mike No, it's a bit personal.

Del (*Hand over mouthpiece of phone*) What happened?

Trigger She got jealous. I heard later, through friends, that she wanted to go with me.

Alan Give us a large scotch, Mike.

INT. TROTTERS' LOUNGE/HALLWAY/ BALCONY. DAY

Raquel is hoovering the rugs. Del is talking to someone on his mobile phone. The balcony doors are open.

Del (*On phone, as if struggling to hear above sound of hoover*) Eh? Speak up, Leroy.

Albert enters from bedroom area.

Albert (*Points to spot on floor in front of balcony doors*) There's still a bit of mud and dirt over here, love.

Raquel Thank you, Albert!

Albert Pleasure, dear.

Albert exits to kitchen.

Del (*On phone*) Say it again, Leroy… Eh?… Raquel, sweetheart. Switch the J. Edgar off, will you? I'm on the mobile blower.

Raquel Sorry! (*Switches hoover off*)

Del (*On phone*) Now, what was you saying? Eh? Can't hear you, Leroy! Can you hear me? Eh? (*Mumbles*) Stuff this for a game of soldiers. (*Presses* OFF *button*)…Oh dear, we got cut off. Gawd knows what he wanted.

Raquel Del. Can I ask you something?

Del Anything you like, darling.

Raquel Before I moved into this flat how did you keep the place clean?

Del We didn't.

Raquel What I'm trying to say is: I seem to spend all my time hoovering.

Del Well, have a break. There's a lot of ironing to be done in the kitchen.

Del turns away, grinning.
He stares at mirror and splashes his face with aftershave.

Raquel (*Smiling. She knows he's joking*) For your sake I hope that's a joke, Trotter! Otherwise you'll be drinking that aftershave!

Del Sit down, put yer feet up. I'll make us a nice cup of tea… Albert, put the kettle on and make some tea.

Rodney enters from hall, dressed in a suit and carrying a briefcase. He is not in the best of moods.

Raquel You home for lunch, Rodney?

Rodney No. Alan's given orders for me to go and pick Cassandra up at the airport. (*To Del*) Oh by the way, I met Leroy this morning. He was complaining like mad about that mobile phone you sold him. I told him to give you a ring.

Del Oh right, thanks, bruv. So, you had a little chat with Alan?

Rodney No, he left a message with his secretary. Alan wasn't at work today. He's got some sort of virus.

Del (*Casual and innocent*) Oh?

Rodney Why's he want me to pick Cassandra up?

Raquel Well, I think it's a good idea! It'll give you and Cassandra a chance to have a chat.

Rodney I'm not talking to her! She weren't talking to me before she left, so I'm not talking to her now!

Raquel Oh, grow up, Rodney!

Rodney It's got nothing to do with you, Raquel! (*At Del*) Or you!

Del Don't have a pop at Raquel!

Rodney Well, both of you stay out of my life! (*Exits to balcony*)

Del That is one touchy little sod, that is!

Raquel Don't come down too hard on him. He's going through a bad patch.

Del Yeah? He'll be going through a bleed'n' window if he don't mend his ways!

The front door bell rings.

Raquel I'll get it. (*Exits to hall*)

153

Raquel opens door to Boycie. They
appear not to like each other.

Boycie Oh it's Raquel! You look so
different fully clothed.

Raquel Hello, Boycie. I suppose I've got to
ask you in?

Boycie Yes. I'd like to get away as quick as
possible. I've left my Mercedes parked
downstairs and you know what they're like
on this estate. They'd have the wheels off a
Jumbo if it flew too low.

Raquel Well go on then, go in.

Boycie You're too kind.

Cut to lounge
Boycie and Raquel enter.

Del *(Still in a mood over Rodney)* What
d'you want?

Boycie Oh dear. Do I detect an atmosphere
in chez Trotter?

Albert It's most probably Del's aftershave.
(Catches the glare from Del) I'll make the
tea. *(Exits to kitchen)*

Raquel I think I'll go out to the balcony
with Rodney. I could do with the air. *(At
Boycie)* I suddenly feel rather nauseous.

Boycie reacts as Raquel exits to balcony.

Boycie You've got one in a million there,
Del Boy.

Del I know! So what brings you round?

Boycie Well, you may have heard, Derek,
that recently I acquired a rather expensive
piece of electronic hardware. A television
satellite aerial receiver.

Del No, I didn't know.

Boycie Oh yes. And I'm not talking about
one of these 150 quid Micky Mouse jobs you
see glued to the side of reclaimed council
houses ruining the beauty of the stone
cladding. Oh no, I'm talking two grand, hi-
tech, state-of-the-art sophistication.

Del Steady on, Boyce, you're making
me jealous.

Boycie You're not the only one. Yesterday
some git nicked it!

Del You're kidding?

Boycie When I went out in the morning it
was standing there in my back garden.
When I came home later.

Del It wasn't!

Boycie You catch on fast, Del.

Del So what you telling me for?

Boycie Because the word is a very similar
satellite receiver was seen entering this
estate tied to the back of a lorry. So if any
of your ... er... contacts should offer you an
almost new aerial dish, then buy it for me as
cheap as possible. Offer 300, but I'll go to
500 at a push.

Del You wanna buy your own property
back? Why don't you go to the gendarmes?

Boycie *(Nervy)* I thought I'd save a lot of
time doing it this way. Know what I mean?

Del Yeah, I know what you mean. I'll keep
me ear to the ground. If I hear anything I'll
give you a bell.

As Boycie moves to hall door, Raquel and
Rodney enter from balcony.

Boycie Goodbye, Raquel. Glad to see
you've settled in so well.

Raquel Is your son about 11 years old with
a Mohican haircut?

Boycie Good God, no!

Raquel Well, who's that sitting in your
Mercedes?

Boycie reacts and exits through hall and
front door.
Del and Rodney laugh at this.

Del You feeling any better?

Rodney Yeah. Sorry about just now.

Del Forget it... What you gonna do then?

Rodney Dunno.

Raquel D'you want your marriage to
work?

Rodney Yeah.

Raquel Really? Honestly?

Rodney Yeah, really, honestly. I want me
and Cass to go back to the way we used to
be. If she wants to pursue her career and

The Sky's the Limit

has to go to functions and seminars at the *(spits the word)* bank, then I don't mind any more, I really don't.

Del Well, how about telling her that? 'Revenons à nos moutonst' as the guv'nor of the Bastille said as the flames licked round his old April. It's French for 'I've gotta do something, quick!'

Rodney With Cassandra, I had a woman I loved. A woman who said she loved me… Now I find myself halfway between paradise and Nelson Mandela House… I just want her to understand and believe that I mean what I say! I've tried everything in my power to convince her. I feel as if I've taken the mountain to Muhammad only to find he's already bloody got one!

Rodney's anger forces him up from chair to balcony.

Del *(To Raquel, indicating Rodney and the fact that this should be a private conversation)* I'll er…

Raquel Yeah, go on.

Del exits to balcony.

Rodney is leaning against the guardrail looking out at the world. At this point we can see only half of the balcony.

Del Why do you think Alan asked you to pick Cassandra up from the airport?

Rodney 'Cos he weren't feeling well.

Del No. It's because Cassandra and her mum have bin sitting by their swimming pool in Spain having the same conversation that you and me just had. She feels exactly the same as you do.

Rodney Cassandra?

Del No, her mum! Of course Cassandra!

Rodney Really?

Del Really… You've got some money, ain't you?

Rodney *(At first emphatically then remembers who asked the question)* Yeah, I've got money! Well, you know, some!

Del Well, I've got an idea. I know the manager of a luxury hotel not all that far from the airport. I used to go there sometimes during the mating season. Now he could set you up in the bestest suite in the hotel, the full works. So when Cassandra flies in – all suntanned and relaxed – you could be waiting with a lovely bouquet and the keys to the bridal suite. A mini-honeymoon – 18 months after the first.

Rodney D'you think it'll work?

Del Yer best whistle, a splash of Brut, you'll be home and dry!

Rodney Go on then, I'm game!

Del Good boy. You know it makes sense. I'll give him a bell.

Rodney Listen. You know I said I've got some money? Well, since I've been working for Alan I've been doing really well. I know you've been struggling a bit lately, so if you want any, it's there.

Del Oh, Rodders. You are the jewel in Mum's crown, Rodney, you really are!

Rodney Oh shuddup!

Del It's nice of you, bruv, and I appreciate it. But I ain't doing too bad. I've got money coming in from that half-price printing… *(Gestures to the unseen side of balcony)* and I should make a nice bit of bunce on this thing.

The other half of the balcony is taken up by a large satellite aerial dish. Although it should look very similar to Boycie's dish there should be a few subtle differences.

INT. A LUXURY HOTEL SUITE. NIGHT

Only the bedside lights are on. The main door is opened by Rodney, who is carrying his flight bag. Rodney surveys the room and is pleased by what he sees. Henry, the concierge, enters carrying a bottle of champagne in a bucket of ice.

Henry Good evening, Mr Trotter. I am Henry, your concierge. Your brother

phoned and said you would be requiring our very finest suite, complete and utter privacy and a full English breakfast.

Rodney Oh yes, thank you.

Henry As this booking is of an intimate nature I think it would help to maintain a degree of privacy if we dealt only in cash.

Rodney Oh yes, of course.

Henry That will be £150 then.

Rodney A hundred and f...! Oh right, fine.

Rodney produces some notes from his wallet.

Henry As a special surprise, Derek also ordered champagne on ice. Only the very finest champagne he said. Money is no object.

Rodney Oh that was nice of him.

Henry That will be another £70 please.

Rodney *(Handing more money over)* He can be very generous at times, can't he?

Henry I believe you have a guest joining you?

Rodney Yes.

Rodney begins testing the springs of the bed.

Henry So it's a special evening?

Rodney Yes. My wife will be landing in about an hour.

Henry I see. Well, don't worry, if she should call at the hotel I'll say I've never heard of you.

Rodney No, you don't understand. My wife is my guest.

Henry Your wife? Oh well, it takes all kinds! Would you like me to order you a bouquet of flowers?

Rodney No thank you, my brother got me a bouquet of flowers. They're out in the va... car.

INT. AIRPORT LOUNGE. NIGHT

We see Rodney is standing in a large crowd at the arrivals area. He is holding a large bouquet of pink flowers. Rodney forces his way out of the crowd in the arrivals area and makes his way across to an information desk. In front of the desk travellers are demanding information. Behind the desk the ground staff are trying to deal with customers as best as possible. Rodney calls to a stewardess who is talking on phone.

Rodney Excuse me, miss.

Stewardess Just one moment, sir. *(On phone)* I'm afraid the flight from Geneva has been cancelled, madam... I shouldn't think it will be arriving until sometime tomorrow... I'm very sorry. *(Replaces receiver. To Rodney)* Can I help you, sir?

Rodney Have you any idea when flight 475 from Malaga will be arriving?

Stewardess I'll just check. *(Punches up information on computer screen)* 475... That flight should be landing in about ten minutes, sir.

Rodney Oh good.

Stewardess In Manchester.

Rodney Manchester?

Stewardess I'm afraid it was rerouted.

Rodney But I'm waiting for my wife! I've got a hotel suite – I've got a bottle of champagne – I've spent nigh on 200 quid waiting for this flight!

Stewardess I'm very sorry, sir. As you can see, the airport's in absolute chaos at the moment. Your wife was lucky to take off at all. *(The phone rings. She answers)* Information, can I help you?

Rodney turns away, shoves the bouquet into a litter bin and walks towards the exit doors.

INT. NAG'S HEAD. NIGHT

A disconsolate Rodney is seated at table having just returned from airport. He is eating a packet of pork scratchings. Raquel is seated next to him and trying

The Sky's the Limit

to cheer him up. Del is at the bar ordering a drink. Trigger is seated further along the bar.

Raquel The important thing is she landed safely.

Rodney Yes, in Manchester! I mean, so much for my surprise! Nearly 250 quid it cost me! I thought by now me and Cassandra would be sitting in our honeymoon suite sipping champagne and… and looking at her holiday snaps. D'you know how much tonight cost me?

Raquel About £250.

Rodney Two hundred and fifty quid it cost!

Cut to bar

Del Michael. Give us a non-alcoholic lager for the stud over there. *(Indicates Rodney)*

Mike What's up with him tonight? Looks like he's just come back from a funeral.

Mike places the open bottle of lager on counter.

Del In a way he has! I can't say too much, Mike. It's all very personal and private. Let's just say Rodney thought he would be enjoying the fruits of love and he's ended up with a packet of pork scratchings. Raquel and moi will have a glass each of your very finest cognac.

Mike Celebrating something, are we?

Del At this very moment, Michael, I have 500 smackeroonies en route to this pub tucked up safely in Boycie's pocket.

Mike Boycie's paying out 500 notes? What's happened? He had a whack on the head or something?

Del We'll say no more about it, Michael – wheels within wheels – pour passer le temps, as they say in Nice. Keep the change, Mike.

Del takes the drinks to the table.

Del There you go.

Rodney Cheers. I had such high hopes for tonight.

Del I know. I could see it when you walked in.

Rodney Thanks for ordering that champagne on ice, Del.

Del No problem, bruv. He gave you the best stuff, didn't he?

Rodney Oh yes, 70 quid's worth.

Del Good. A lady like Cassandra only deserves the best. Bloody pity she's up in Manchester, innit?

Rodney Yes, it is.

Raquel Still, you can talk to her tomorrow. And she'll know you went out to the airport to meet her, her dad'll tell her.

Rodney Yeah, that's true. At least I made the gesture and that's what counts.

Albert enters and joins them.

Albert Cassandra's up north.

Rodney I know she is! How'd you know?

Albert She just phoned from Manchester airport, wanted you to know she was safe and not to worry.

Raquel Where'd you say Rodney was?

Albert I said he was spending the night at some hotel.

Del But did you tell her which hotel?

Albert I couldn't remember its name so I gave her the phone number.

Rodney But you told her I'd gone to meet her at the airport?

Albert Of course not! It was supposed to be a surprise!

Rodney and Del speak together.

Rodney You daft old sod!

Del You garrity old git!

Rodney She'll phone the hotel to discover that I've booked the honeymoon suite in the name of Mr and Mrs Trotter!

Del She'll think he's gone caseo with some tart for the night! I don't know how you're gonna talk your way out of this one, Rodney. .

Rodney If you hadn't suggested booking into a hotel for the night, none of this would have happened!

Del I didn't hear you object too much! It was your hormones that were on turbo, not mine!

Raquel Look, why don't you phone Alan? He's bound to speak to her soon so he can explain.

Rodney Good idea, Raquel. I'm going back to the flat and phone him.

Del You can use my mobile. *(Pause)* Best go back to the flat and phone him.

Raquel You can give me a lift back, Rodney. *(To Del)* You coming?

Del *(Indicates counter where Boycie has just arrived)* Not yet, sweetheart. My money's just walked in.

Rodney, Raquel and Albert exit.
Del joins Boycie.

Del Don't hand that 500 quid over in full view of everyone – I've heard intensive care ain't all it's cracked up to be.

Boycie You're in no danger whatsoever, Del Boy. I ain't handing you a penny.

Del Now just a minute, Boycie! I got your satellite dish back for you.

Boycie No, you didn't, Del. At this very moment in time, my satellite dish is standing in my back garden and picking up a very exciting episode of *Wagon Train* from Helsinki.

Del But you said it had been nicked!

Boycie That's what I thought. But I discovered this evening that, while Marlene and I were out for the day, the engineers took it away for repair.

Del Well, what's that thing I've got on my balcony?

Boycie I don't know, Del. And to be perfectly honest I couldn't give a monkey's toss.

Boycie walks away laughing.

INT. TROTTERS' LOUNGE. BALCONY. NIGHT
Albert is seated in armchair trying to correct the fuzzing and sissing on TV

screen. *Rodney is on the phone waiting for his call to be answered. Raquel is scanning a black address and phone book (Del's little black book). Del, an exotic cocktail in hand, is pacing the floor in agitation.*

Rodney *(Impatiently on phone)* Come on, Alan, answer!

Raquel I can't find anyone called Bronco in your address book.

Del Even if you found his name it'd do no good. He moved a little while ago.

Raquel There's a lot of women in here.

Del Eh? Oh, just acquaintances.

Raquel Why have you put stars by some of their names?

Del *(Shrugs innocently)* Gawd knows. Long time ago. *(Snatches book from her)* Let me have a look.

Rodney *(Switches phone off)* He's not in. I bet he's driving up to Manchester to pick Cassandra up. I can just see it all now. She'll tell Alan I've booked into a hotel with another woman – he'll sack me. Cassandra'll divorce me... *(To Albert)* ...and it's all your fault! *(To Del)* And yours!!

Del Oh shuddup, you tart! I've problems of me own.

Albert So have I! I just cannot get a picture from your satellite dish!

Del Just leave the telly alone, will yer? I've gotta get in touch with Bronco, find out where the idiot got that receiver from.

Albert I thought you said he gave you his card.

Del He did. And I filed it somewhere behind Boycie's geraniums.

Rodney If only that airport hadn't been in such a mess her plane would have landed at Gatwick and everything would have been great. I bet the air-traffic controllers have gone on strike in France again.

Del That's it, Rodney, that's where he's moved to.

The Sky's the Limit

Raquel France?

Del No, Gatwick! He's in some little bed-and-breakfast hotel.

Raquel But you can't remember what it was called?

Del No. It was named after someone famous.

Rodney Well, that's narrowed it right down, hasn't it? Uncle, could you pop in my room and fetch my 37 volumes of famous historical characters? We'll soon have this sorted out, Del Boy.

Del Don't get bloody sarky with me, Rodney! A painter! That's it, it was named after a painter! Well, come on, Bamber, this is your area.

Rodney Yeah, alright. A painter… Michelangelo?

Del No.

Raquel Rembrandt? Picasso?

Del No, no.

Rodney Rubens? Van Gogh?

Del No.

Rodney Botticelli?

Del No.

Raquel Turner?

Del No, no. A famous French painter.

Rodney A French painter? Why didn't you say he was French?

Del I just told you he was French!

Rodney Bloody 'ell!

Raquel Monet?

Del No.

Rodney Manet?

Del She just said that!

Rodney No, she said Monet

Del That's what I mean! Pay attention, Rodney!

Albert Adolf Hitler used to be a painter.

Raquel I don't bel…! How long's he been French?

Rodney And who in their right mind would call their place the Hotel Hitler?

Raquel A famous French painter. Lautrec?

Del No.

Rodney Renoir?

Del No! French!

Rodney Degas, Boudin, Pissaro, Seurat, Tissot?

Del *(A moment's hesitation)* No!

Albert Schubert.

Raquel Schubert?

Rodney Schubert! You soppy old…

Del *(Cuts in)* That's it!! The Hotel Schubert!

Raquel Schubert?

Del Well done, Unc. *(Scanning Yellow Pages)* I don't know, he's got all these GCEs and it takes an old sea dog to come up with the answer.

Rodney You said a French painter! Schubert weren't French!

Del No?

Rodney And he weren't a painter!

Del *(Finds number in Yellow Pages)* Ah, here it is! *(Starts punching out numbers on phone)*

Raquel *(To Albert)* Schubert was a German composer!

Albert Austrian, actually.

Rodney How did you know?

Del Shut up! I'm on the blower. *(On phone)* Oh good evening. Could you put me through to Mr Lane's room, please? Thank you.

Raquel Shall we just leave the satellite dish and watch the ordinary telly?

Rodney Yeah, let's watch the news. They might have another report on the ecological destruction of our planet – anything to cheer me up.

Del *(On phone)* Bronco? It's Del Boy. Listen, pal, about that satellite dish you sold me. Where exactly…eh? What you apologizing for? Alright, alright, you were desperate and you had a funny turn. I can understand that. Rodney's living back with us… Well, of course I know what it is! It's obvious what it is! It's a satellite receiver! What d' you

mean, that's what you thought as well? Bronco, why you crying? It's a what? Where the hell'd you get it from? Oh my God! Oh hell's bloody bells! *(Switches phone off in state of shock)*

Albert So where's he get it from?

Del Eh? He can't remember.

Raquel Del, look here. Look at this.

Raquel is watching the news on TV. Without taking her eyes from the screen she gestures for the others to come and look. Richard Whitmore is reading the news.

Richard The radar transmitter dish *(A photograph of the same dish Del has on the balcony appears on screen)* similar to the one shown here, was stolen from the end of Gatwick's main runway in the early hours of yesterday morning. The theft brought Gatwick airport to a standstill and has caused chaos throughout Europe and left thousands of returning holiday-makers stranded.

Rodney, Albert and Raquel turn and look at Del. Del grins sheepishly and shrugs.

Raquel You caused that! You've brought Europe – a whole continent – to a standstill!

Del I didn't mean to!

Rodney That's why Cassandra's plane couldn't land. That's why she's stuck at Manchester airport instead of in my honeymoon bed! And that's why my marriage is all but finished!

Del Haven't you ever made a mistake? I mean, you thought it was an aerial dish an' all, didn't you??

Cut to balcony.

Del and Rodney enter from lounge and stare at the dish.

Del *(Now desperate)* I'll tell you what I'll do, Rodders. I'll give it back tomorrow!

We now hear the sound of jet airliner somewhere in the night sky. Immediately two lights (red and yellow) somewhere on dish begin flashing alternately. An electronic buzzing noise is unheard, as if the machine has come alive. The dish now swivels around as if lining up with the incoming plane.

Del and Rodney are horrified. They look skywards towards the approaching jet. They now look back at the dish and realise it has homed in on the plane.

Del *(Screams to Raquel and Albert in lounge)* Switch it off!

The Sky's the Limit

The Chance of a Lunchtime

INT. THE TROTTERS' LOUNGE. DAY

Del, in dressing gown and silk pyjamas is pouring three cups of tea. Two of the cups and saucers are on a tray which also contains a plate of jam biscuits. The other cup is on the table.

Del *(Calls towards kitchen)* Albert, I've poured you a cup of tea. It's on the table.

Albert Righto, son.

Del takes his newly lit cigar from ashtray and clenches it between his teeth as he carries the tray, with both hands, towards door to bedroom. The door is closed. Del lifts his left elbow up towards door handle. In so doing his head comes down and the end of the cigar goes into the tea in one of the cups. Del opens the door then returns to the table. He removes the offending cup from the tray and places it on the table. He takes Albert's fresh cup of tea and places that on tray. He exits to bedroom.

INT. DEL'S BEDROOM. DAY

The room is decorated in what Del believes is a sophisticated style. The bed has side tables built into the modern swirling brass headboard. One bedside table contains the built-in controls for his radio, the other table contains the built-in controls for hidden lighting. None of them works. The bed is covered in black satin sheets and these in turn are covered by a mock tiger-skin bedcover. On the walls hangs one modern painting of a nude woman, a painting of a Ferrari sports car and a Turner print. On the pine and brass dressing table stand numerous bottles of aftershave and deodorants. On the floor stand two or three large cardboard boxes. Raquel, in a nightdress, is sitting up in bed reading Shakespeare's As You Like It. *Del enters carrying the breakfast tray.*

Del Here you go, sweetheart. Always start the day off with a nice cup of Darjeelin', that's my motto.

Raquel Thanks.

Del So what are you up to today?

Raquel Nothing much. *(Referring to book)* Just gonna sit around and try and learn this. I wish I'd never agreed to this audition in the first place. I'll never get the part anyway.

Del You're giving in before you've even started.

Raquel You don't know how nervous I get at auditions.

Del Listen to me You will be wonderful. She who dares, wins! Alright?

Raquel If you say so, Del. *(Kisses him)* Thanks. You know, you're the only one who's ever really given me encouragement. My ex-husband used to laugh at me. To him, ambitions and dreams of wonderful things were a waste of time.

Del Oh no. You must never lose sight of your dream! When I was 18 I decided that I was gonna be a millionaire by the time I was 21.

Raquel Really?

Del Yep… and when I was 21 I said I'd be a millionaire by the time I was 30… and when I was 30… *(Referring to the biscuits)* D'you fancy a Jammy-Dodger?

Raquel Mm, please. I've never told anyone this, but, d' you remember I was in America for a while? Well, while I was there they were putting on *Aida* at the Met. So I applied for a part in it. I didn't get it – there

were union problems and I wasn't very good. But for a while, my head was filled with big theatre. You know, New York, Broadway – all that! Stupid…

Del No, no. You didn't get it but you had a go! Anyway, reckon it could have been for the best.

Raquel How?

Del Well, *Aida* at the Met! I just couldn't see you playing a policewoman.

Raquel No, it's… Perhaps you're right. Although I wouldn't have had to do much research. My husband was a policeman.

Del *(Spits his tea out)* Your old man was a copper?

Raquel Yeah. Didn't I ever say?

Del No. *(Looks worryingly towards the cardboard boxes)* D'you ever see him?

Raquel No, I haven't seen him for years and years. Why?

Del *(Lays back on headboard in relief)* Oh! Just curious.

There is a knock on bedroom door.

Rodney Am I interrupting something?

Del No.

Rodney Oh well, better luck next time. *(Enters)* I'm off to work. See you later.

Del I'm going round your flat today to repair your front door. Have you spoken to Cassandra since she got back off holiday?

Rodney Er… no.

Raquel Why don't you ask to meet her, talk things over quietly between yourselves?

Rodney If she wants to make the first move, then fine. Other than that – nito!

Del But she's only just got back from Spain!

Rodney So?

Del Well, can I at least give her a message from you?

Rodney Yeah. Say hasta la vesta.

Rodney exits.

Del Vesta? That's boil-in-the-bag curry, innit?

Raquel No. It's Spanish for boil-in-the-bag curry.

INT. HALL TO RODNEY'S/CASSY'S FLAT/OUTER FOYER TO BLOCK. DAY

Del, wearing jeans and a working shirt, has just fitted a new, plain front door to the flat. Cassandra, looking tanned from her recent Spanish holiday and dressed casually, is standing in the outer foyer watching Del tighten the final screw into the lock.

Cassandra Promise you'll let me pay you for doing this, Del.

Del I wouldn't hear of it, darling. You brought me that bottle of duty-free back from Spain, that's all the payment I need. Me and Raquel will celebrate with that soon.

Cassandra What are you celebrating?

Del Raquel is having lunch today with her show-business agent. She's up for an audition. Shakespeare's *As You Like It.* Can't go wrong with Shakespeare, can yer? He's my favourite.

Cassandra Well, wish her the best of luck for me, won't you?

Del 'Course I will… *(Referring to door)* There you go, sweetheart. This new front door'll put a couple of grand on the value of your flat.

Cassandra *(Smiling)* Yeah, I'm sure it will, Del.

Del Genuine French pine, that is.

Cassandra It said on the bottom, 'Produce of Angola'.

Del Yes, French Angola! I'll whip round tomorrow and varnish it for yer.

Cassandra No, you don't have to do that.

Del It's the least I can do after what happened… I mean, it's not very nice coming back off holiday to find yer front door smashed in, is it?

Cassandra I must admit I've had better welcome homes.

The Chance of a Lunchtime

Del Still, at least no real damage was done. Right, let's try it.

Del turns the key in the lock and pushes the door. Door doesn't budge. Del gives Cassy a smile of encouragement and now pushes harder.

Del That's a good sign, that is.

Del now puts his shoulder to the door. With a scrape and a squeak the door opens about half an inch.

Cassandra D'you think the door's too big?

Del Possibly. But as my old mum always said: if you've gotta have one, have a big 'un. You see, the wood will shrink with time. A couple of weeks from now this'll look like it was made to measure. *(Finally opens door)* There you go – cushty.

Cassandra Thanks for everything, Del.

Del *(Placing his tools in his bag)* You don't have to thank me! We're family, Cassandra. You're my sister-in-law.

Cassandra Yeah. Don't know for how long though.

Del You and Rodney still at battle stations, are you?

Cassandra Seems like it. We haven't spoken for ages.

Del Well, I think Rodney's had a change of heart.

Cassandra What makes you say that?

Del We were having a chat earlier, and he said he still loves you… very deeply.

Cassandra Rodney said that?

Del Oh yes. He asked me to ask you whether you'd be prepared to meet him tonight.

Cassandra Where?

Del A little restaurant over Wapping way. I've got the address here. *(Produces scrap of paper)*

Cassandra That's not Rodney's writing.

Del No, he told me the address and I wrote it down. What shall I tell him?

Cassandra Yeah, alright then. I've got nothing better on.

Del Lovely Jubbly.

Cassandra But tell him not to think he can buy me a bottle of wine and then walk straight back into this flat!

Del He knows that, Cassandra. I think he wants to – you know – woo again. I'll tell him you'll be there. Seven thirty?

Cassandra Fine. But how am I gonna get back into the flat tonight? I don't know if I'm strong enough to open the door.

Del No problem. Rodney'll be with you. Bonjour for now.

Del exits, carrying his tool bag.

INT. TROTTERS' LOUNGE/HALL. NIGHT

In the room are three large cardboard boxes with Anthachime printed across them. Underneath this, in smaller print, is Made in Macau. Del, power-dressed for the evening, is seated at the table fitting batteries into one of the Anthachime devices (those doorbells that play various national anthems). Albert is seated in an armchair. Raquel, smartly dressed as she has recently returned from her lunch appointment, enters from kitchen.

Raquel You didn't do any shopping today then, Albert?

Albert No, that cup of tea I had this morning made me feel a bit rough. Anyway, I thought you did the shopping now.

Raquel I've been out to lunch with my agent!

Albert Well, there's some egg and bacon in the fridge.

Raquel Del doesn't like fried food!

Del *(At the very thought of fried food)* Euurgh!

Raquel *(To Del)* Well, I'm sorry, but it'll have to be egg and bacon.

Del Tch! Oh well, that's the way it goes. I'll have four rashers.

Raquel OK.

Del So when's this audition of yours?

Raquel Tomorrow. I'm auditioning for Rosalind.

Albert Rosalind who?

Raquel The part of Rosalind! I've got to learn the whole of Act Three, Scene Two by tomorrow morning. How the hell am I supposed to do that?

Del I'll help you.

Raquel How d'you mean?

Del I'll rehearse with you. You know, I'll read the other parts so you can get used to it.

Raquel You?

Del Yeah! I used to do a bit of acting when I was at school. Bloody good I was an' all. You get the old book out and we'll start when I get back from the pub.

Raquel Alright, then. Thanks. I'll get the dinner on.

Raquel exits to kitchen.

Albert You used to act at school?

Del Yeah. I played the landlord in the Nativity play. There was little Del Boy, 'No room at the inn'. Finally Joseph persuaded me to let 'em kip in the stable. I tried to charge him one and six for the night and got the cane. Those were the days...

A key in the front door is heard. Del rushes out to hall.

Rodney is just about to enter when Del stops him by holding the door.

Del Ring the bell, Rodders.

Rodney Eh?

Del Ring the bell.

Rodney Why? I've got me key!

Del Just ring the bell.

Rodney *(A heavy sigh)* Alright.

We hear the bell chime playing the American national anthem. Del walks slowly back into the lounge, listening to and obviously moved by the music. An incredulous Raquel enters from the

kitchen. The front door slowly opens and Rodney, dressed in his office clothes, enters the hall as if in state of shock. He looks up to where the Anthachime box is situated. He enters lounge as the anthem finally ends.

Del *(Salutes)* Vive la France!

Rodney What is that thing?

Del Brilliant, innit? It plays 36 different national anthems.

Raquel 36 different nat...! You are kidding, aren't you?

Rodney No, he's not kidding, Raquel. I can see it in his eyes.

Albert How'd you know they're genuine national anthems?

Del 'Cos it says so on the box! What can't speak can't lie.

Albert Well, I've seen umpteen Olympic Games and I ain't heard half the tunes that doorbell plays.

Del Well, of course you haven't! I mean, how many gold medals have Fiji and Borneo won? But if they had pearl-diving and putting the shrunken head in the Olympics then you'd hear their anthems. Talking of shrunken heads... Rodney, can I have a private word?

Raquel exits to kitchen as Del draws Rodney away for a quiet word.

Rodney What is it?

Del I was round your flat today fixing the front door. I think Cassandra's had a change of heart.

Rodney Yeah? What makes you think that?

Del We were having a chat and she said she still loves you... very deeply.

Rodney Cassandra said that?

Del Yes. She asked me to ask you whether you'd be prepared to meet her tonight.

Rodney Where?

Del I've got the address written down here. *(Hands Rodney the scrap of paper)*

The Chance of a Lunchtime

Rodney That's not Cassandra's writing.

Del No. She told me the address and I wrote it down… What d'you reckon, then?

Rodney Yeah, alright. I've got nothing else to do.

Del Lovely Jubbly.

Rodney But I hope she don't think she can buy me with a bottle of wine and walk back in my life.

Del No, no. I think she wants to, you know, woo again. I've booked the ta… she's booked the table for 7.30, so you'd better get a move on.

Rodney Yeah, I'll get showered… And – thanks, Del.

Del What you thanking me for? I'm just the messenger.

Rodney I feel… sort of… nervous.

Del What you gotta be nervous about? She's your wife.

Rodney Yeah. Just be meself, eh?

Del No, try and make an impression.

Rodney Yeah. Of course. You staying in tonight?

Del I'm going down the Nag's Head later. Mike and Trigger wanna buy one of these doorbells.

Rodney D'you want me to drop 'em off at the pub on me way out?

Del No, I've gotta do it, Rodders. See, they don't know they wanna buy 'em yet. When I get back me and Raquel are gonna rehearse her new play.

Rodney Right. *(Almost exits to bedroom area then stops in doorway. Turns back)* Del rehearsing a play?

Albert Raquel's up for some audition.

Del It's one of Shakespeare's famous plays.

Rodney And you are gonna rehearse it with her?

Del Yeah.

Rodney *(A great big grin spreads across his face)* Oh cosmic! Can't you do it now

before I go out?

Del Of course not!

Rodney Why not? I'd like to have a la-a-look – see how it's done.

Del You can't expect an actress of Raquel's calibre to start rehearsing at the drop of an 'at! She has to have motivation! She has to search for her character. It's all about feel and sensitivity, and that takes time, Rodney… Besides, she's only just put the rashers in the pan.

INT. THE NAG'S HEAD. NIGHT

The pub is quite crowded. Del is at the bar demonstrating one of the Anthachimes, which is playing the German national anthem, to Mike. Del listens proudly to the music.

Del What d'you reckon then, Michael? Brilliant, innit? No more of that 'Avon calling' cobblers. You can have the old stars and stripes playing.

Mike You expect me to have one of them things on my front door?

Del You're keen on the idea, ain't yer?

Mike Del, they're cheap and tacky!

Del I've got one on my front door!

Mike Yeah, you most probably have. You'd need a brain by-pass to have one of them things fitted.

Trigger How much you selling them for, Del?

Del Funny you should say that, Trig. They retail at £36.50. It's yours for 13 quid and that includes batteries and fitting.

Trigger Go on then. I'll have one.

Del Good boy, Trig. You know it makes sense.

As Trigger pays Del, the sound of raucous female laughter is heard from a 38-year-old peroxide blonde woman, Trudy, who is standing some distance away with a couple of men. Trudy has obviously had too much to drink.

Del I thought you'd banned laughing in this pub.

Mike With that sort I have. The two blokes have been plying her with drinks since six o'clock. I think they're fed up with it now.

One of the two men approaches bar.

Man Would you call her a cab?

Mike Yeah, something like that.

Man No, no. Would you phone for a minicab? The lady wants to go to Battersea.

Mike Yeah, leave it to me. I've got an understanding with British Telecom. I make a phone call and they charge me for it.

Mike moves off to make call.

Del *(To the man, gesturing after Mike)* You'll have to forgive him, it's his religion. He's an orthodox tight-arse.

The man returns to Trudy and his friend.

Del So what you bin up to, Trig?

Trigger I went down to my sister's house at the weekend. It was her 42nd birthday.

Del Oh, cushty… No, no, hang on a minute. She's five years younger than you. That means she's only 39.

Trigger I know. But she's a typical woman. Lies about her age.

Del Yeah!

Trigger So how's the family?

Del Oh mustard. Raquel's boning up for an audition – a Shakespeare play.

Trigger Yeah? Will it be on telly?

Del No, no. Not this particular one. Most probably the West End, something like that.

Trigger Hope she don't change.

Del Raquel? Why would she change?

Trigger Well, they start mixing with all them posh actors and the next thing you know they've changed.

The Chance of a Lunchtime

Del No, not my Raquel.

Trigger My sister went out with an actor once. He played the cat in *Puss-in-Boots*. She suddenly thought she was more intelligent than the rest of the family.

Del Yeah, but if you remember, Trig, you had the same problem with your goldfish… Oh, look who's here!

Marlene is standing at the other end of the bar, her back to Del as she talks to one of the locals. Del moves along the bar and touches her up.

Marlene Oops! (*Sees it's Del*) Oh, you!

Del How are you, sweetheart?

Boycie is standing by the entrance with the baby buggy and witnesses Del touching up his wife. He leaves the buggy with a couple of women who are talking to the baby.

Del How's the baby?

Marlene Oh he's lovely. He's there with Boycie.

Boycie Good evening, Derek.

Del Wotcher, Boyce. Just saying hello to Marlene.

Boycie Yes, I noticed you approach my wife and shake her warmly by the 'arris!

Marlene Oh shuddup, you miserable sod. He's just having a laugh.

Del Just a giggle. What are you having?

Boycie I'll have a large cognac. Marlene will have an orange juice. She's driving my son home in a minute.

Del Michael. A cognac, an orange juice and my usual.

Marlene I've got some pictures of the baby here.

Del He's a little champion.

Boycie He's got my eyes, ain't he?

Del Na! His eyes are all warm and smiley.

Boycie So are mine.

Marlene My mum always said you had vampire eyes.

Boycie Well, she should know, the old bat!

Del He's got eyes like mine. He's got Mike's mouth, Rodney's nose and Trigger's ears.

Boycie What are you saying?

Del Nothing! Honest.

Marlene Talking of Rodney. How is he now?

Del He's alright, darling. He's having dinner with Cassandra tonight – trying to patch things up.

Marlene Oh good. I suppose you've missed him, eh, Del?

Del Who?

Marlene Rodney. I mean, you must have missed him when he left your partnership.

Del Oh yeah, I missed him like George Michael missed Andrew Ridgely.

Del, Boycie, Mike and Marlene laugh at this. After a few seconds Trigger joins in – he doesn't know why.

Tyler starts crying.

Marlene Won't be a minute… Don't worry, Tyler, Mummy's coming.

Boycie That woman's as soppy as a lorry-load of monkeys. I came home this evening to find that some salesman has flogged her a door bell that plays 36 national anthems.

Trigger I got one of them.

Boycie Yes, I'd have put money on that, Trig! The difference is I live in a mock-Georgian mansion in the Kings Avenue. Our neighbours are not gonna appreciate being awoken by the sound of *Long Live Swaziland* every time the milkman calls.

Del He still calling, is he?

Boycie Yeah. And she's… And she's ruining that boy of mine – spoiling him rotten. We've got the most expensive nanny in the world, a 300-quid-a-term crèche and Marlene's just put in a takeover bid for Toys-R-Us! On the other hand, having a baby's changed my life. I used to be so happy. Now I'm up half the night stuffing

Bonjella in his mouth, I'm too tired to sell me cars and I ain't been to the Masonic lodge for a month. You don't know how lucky you are.

Del Not luck, Boycie. It's called shrewdness. Never again, that's my motto. I had all that Farex and Ostermilk lark years ago when Rodney was a sprog. I wouldn't wish that on my worst enemy – though I used to say a little prayer for you an' Marlene.

Marlene *(Calls)* I'm off home, Boyce. Don't be too late.

Boycie I'll be about an hour. You'll know it's me. I'll play *Mexico Forever* on the front door.

> *Marlene turns the buggy round so we can see Tyler.*

Marlene Wave to your daddy.

> *Tyler waves.*
> *Boycie, Del, Mike and Trigger all wave back to the baby.*
> *Boycie reacts.*

Boycie *(Gulps his drink back and walks off to join Marlene)* Ain't funny! Ain't bloody funny!

> *Del and Mike collapse with laughter.*
> *Trigger grins.*

INT. TRENDY RIVERSIDE RESTAURANT. NIGHT

> *A smartly dressed Rodney is seated at one of the tables overlooking the river nervously awaiting Cassandra's arrival. He turns to see Cassandra and stands. Cassandra arrives at the table.*

Cassandra Hello.

> *They kiss politely.*

Rodney Oh hi.

> *A waiter takes Cassandra's coat.*

Cassandra Thanks.

> *They sit.*

Rodney *(To the waiter)* Thank you. *(To Cass)*

Rodney So, how was Spain?

Cassandra Oh, you know, OK.

Rodney Good. Do anything interesting?

Cassandra Not really. There was just mummy and me at the villa. To be honest it was a bit boring.

Rodney I can imagine! No, I don't mean being in your mother's company is boring! I mean, she's not a boring person!

Cassandra I know what you meant.

Rodney Good... *(Calls to the waiter)* Excuse me. *(To Cassandra)* Would you like a glass of something?

Cassandra I'll have the same as you.

> *A waiter arrives.*

Rodney It's mineral water.

Cassandra That makes a nice change. I was told you'd been drinking heavily.

Rodney *(An embarrassed laugh for the waiter's benefit)* Heavily! Silly! *(To waiter)* Could I have a glass of mineral water, please? *(To Cassandra)* I think your father was exaggerating slightly, Cassandra.

Cassandra Daddy didn't tell me. It was Del.

Rodney Yeah, well... Maybe I did go a bit overboard after – you know – we left each other.

Cassandra You mean you left me!

Rodney Same thing.

Cassandra No it isn't! I didn't go anywhere, Roddy. I was at the flat waiting for you. You just didn't come home!

Rodney Look, we came here to discuss things, not to argue!

Cassandra You started it!

Rodney No, I didn't! I went home while you were on holiday. I didn't know you'd put new locks on the door!

Cassandra Yes, I should have told you. But that was no reason for you to kick the door in!

Rodney I didn't kick the door in! I sorta *(does shoulder gesture)* that's all!

Cassandra Why d'you go back?

Rodney I wanted to surprise you.

The Chance of a Lunchtime

Waiter arrives with glass.

Cassandra You did surprise me! I didn't expect to come home and find my husband had kicked the front door in!

Rodney *(Embarrassed smile to waiter as he takes glass)* Oh thank you very much. *(To Cassandra)* Look, I've got as much right to enter that flat as you! We've got a joint mortgage, remember, from the bank?

Pause.

And what about that girl you took out?

Rodney I didn't take any girl out!

Cassandra You asked a girl out!

Rodney That was just to make you jealous. But it was a stupid idea and I never went through with it although, at this moment in time, it strikes me as one of my better moves!

Cassandra Well, this is obviously going to be a total waste of a good evening! Just think of all the more interesting things I could be doing – like washing my hair.

Rodney What about me? I've passed up the chance of seeing Del rehearse a Shakespeare play! People would pay a fortune for something like that, and I could have got it for free!

Cassandra I came here this evening hoping that you and I could find some common ground on which we could base our future! But it's just pointless! I'm glad I found out this early in our marriage what you're really like! Your drinking, your bouts of violence! God, I can just imagine my future with someone like you! You really are the silliest, pettiest, most childish person I've ever had the misfortune to marry.

Rodney *(Realises what she is really saying. With growing confidence)* You fancy me, don't you?

Cassandra *(Tries to hide her smile)* No, I don't!

Rodney Yes, you do, you little flirt, you!

Cassandra *(Laughing)* Oh shut up!

Rodney What I meant by surprising you was, I wanted to be in our flat when you got back. Not just to say welcome back, but be living there! That's why I got angry when I couldn't get in. Why d'you change the locks on the door for?

Cassandra Because you walked out!

Rodney I know, but I only went to post a letter!

They both laugh.

Cassandra Oh I hate you! I wanted this to be serious. I wanted to really tear into you!

Rodney Oh that's why you asked to meet me?

Cassandra I ask to meet you? You must be joking! Roddy, you're the one who did the asking.

Rodney No, Del came home and said you wanted to meet me. You even suggested this venue.

Cassandra Rodney, Derek brought a message round from you. He said you wanted to meet me at this rest…!

They both now realise they have been set up.

Cassandra Del!

Rodney Yeah, Del! Git!

Now neither of them can help but smile at Del's audacity.

Cassandra So, what do we do now?

Rodney *(Shrugs)* Dunno… D'you fancy showing me yer tan?

Cassandra Yeah, alright.

The waiter arrives.

Waiter Can I take your order?

Rodney No, I've lost my appetite.

Cassandra Same here.

The waiter shrugs and exits.

Cassandra *(Hands Rodney a key)* That's the new key.

Now there is urgency – they both want to get home.

Cassandra I've got to go round to mummy and daddy's. I've left some of my stuff at their house.

Rodney You won't be too long, will yer?

Cassandra No, an hour or so. D'you remember your way home?

Rodney I remember.

Cassandra In case you get confused, we've got a new front door.

Rodney *(Smiles and nods)* I'll see you in bed in half an hour.

Cassandra Roddy!

Rodney Sorry!

Cassy exits.

INT. THE NAG'S HEAD. NIGHT

Del, Mike and Trigger are at the bar. Del is eating a hot dog. Trudy's laugh is heard again.

Trigger *(Referring to Trudy)* You're gonna have trouble with that one, Michael.

Mike Don't I know it? The sooner that minicab arrives, the better!

Del Disgusting, innit, eh? I like a lady to act like a lady. I can't stand to see a woman staggering round a pub dropping crisps everywhere.

Trigger I remember your mum.

Del Yeah! What d'you mean?

Trigger She was a lady, weren't she?

Del Oh yes, Trig. She was a lady. She was the first woman in Peckham to smoke menthol cigarettes.

Trudy laughs.

Del *(Referring to Trudy)* I mean, just look at the state of that! I don't know how any bloke could admit to knowing her, let alone being seen in her company...

Trudy *(Calls)* D-e-l!

Del turns to look at Trudy.

Del Blimey!

Trudy leaves the two men, rushes over and throws her arms round Del's neck.

Trudy How are you, darling?

Del *(Doesn't know her from Eve)* Oh, triffic!!

Trudy How long's it been?

Del How long's what been?

Trudy Since we last saw each other?

Del Have we met?

Trudy You don't remember me? Trudy!

Del Trudy? Were we engaged?

Trudy Yes!

Del Cor blimey! You've changed, sweetheart.

Trudy Ain't we all, love? Hang on, I'll just get my drink.

Trigger I don't remember her among your fiancées.

Del Yeah, 1970. We were engaged for about a month.

Trigger So it was one of your longer engagements?

Del Yeah. We broke up after Rodney's pet mouse nested in one of her wigs. The last time I saw Trudy was on a caravan site in Sheerness. In the middle of the night our caravan got hit by lightning. She went running out in the rain – no drawers and a polo-neck jumper. I've gone off that hot dog, Mike!

Rodney enters.

Rodney Del – we're back together. Me and Cassy, we've made it up.

Del Well done, Rodders. I'm pleased for you, bruv.

Rodney Mike, there's a minicab outside for someone.

Mike That'll be for your ex-fiancée, Derek.

Mike Take her out, will yer?

Del Yes, yes, gimme a minute.

Rodney *(Looking across at Trudy. To Del)* Not another fiancée!

Del I couldn't help it! I was young! You ain't left Cassandra out in the van, have you?

Rodney No. She's gone to get some things from her mum and dad's house. I thought

The Chance of a Lunchtime

I'd pop in and tell you that I won't be home tonight.

Del No, Rodney. You *will* be home tonight.

Rodney Oh yeah, my real home! *(Hands Del a key)* There's your key back. Thanks for – you know – having me…

Del Oh it was a… a pleasure, Rodders.

Rodney Cassandra didn't ask to meet me, did she?

Del Na. I lied.

Rodney You're a conniving git!

Del Did the trick though, didn't it?

Rodney Yeah! Thanks, Del. Oh I've just seen Raquel and Albert getting off the bus.

Del She's coming here? Oh Gawd! She musn't see me with Trudy. Raquel gets very jealous.

Trudy returns to Del and cuddles him.

Trudy Tell me everything that's been happening!

Del We ain't got time, sweetheart. Your cab's waiting for you.

Trudy Well, why don't you come back to my place? We can talk about old times.

Del I can't right now, Trudy. I've gotta bit of business to attend to. Rodney, on your way out, escort this young lady to her cab, will you?

Rodney Yeah. Come on, then. *(Takes Trudy's arm)*

Trudy I'll see you, Del. D'you come in this pub often?

Del No, it's the first time I've ever been in here, innit, Mike?

Mike That's right.

Rodney leads Trudy out.

Del Cor blimey! Talk about *Fatal Attraction*.

THE NAG'S HEAD. EXT. NIGHT

The minicab is waiting at the kerb. Rodney and Trudy exit from pub. She has her arm round Rodney's shoulder. He has his arm round her waist in an effort to keep her upright. Trudy stumbles slightly.

To stop herself from falling she puts both arms round Rodney' s neck. He has both arms round her waist. They are now at the taxi. From a distance it would look as if they were kissing.

Trudy Is this your car? It's a lovely car.

Rodney tries to open the back door.

Rodney Mate! Can you open the back door, mate?

Rodney now reacts horrified as he sees Cassandra stopped by the pub in her car. Cassy does a double take as she sees Rodney and Trudy. Rodney shakes his head towards Cassandra as if to say 'No, it's not what you think!', Cassandra looks as if she is about to burst into tears, guns the car forward with a screech of tyres and roars off into the night.

Rodney Cass! Cassy!

Trudy slips to the ground, giggling.

Trudy Rodney!

Rodney walks away.

INT. THE OUTER FOYER, ROD AND CASSY'S FLAT. NIGHT

Rodney, desperate and out of breath from running, enters from the door leading to the stairwell. He finds his front door key and fits it into the keyhole. He cannot open the door.

Rodney *(Calling)* Cass! Cassandra! Unlock the door! Look, Cassy, we've gotta talk! That woman was nothing to do with me! She was some old sort Del was engaged to years ago! Cass, let's at least talk!

He bangs on the door.

Rodney Cassandra!

Rodney lays his head forlornly against the door. He now presses the doorbell button and immediately one of Del's anthachimes plays the French national anthem. Rodney turns from the front door and, with the anthem playing in his ears, exits to the stairwell.

THE TROTTERS' LOUNGE. INT. NIGHT

Del and Raquel are rehearsing As
You Like It. *Albert is in an armchair in
front of the TV, which is on but has
no sound.*

Raquel *(As Rosalind, reading from the
book)* By no means sir, Time travels in divers
paces, with divers persons, I'll tell you who
time ambles withal, who time trots withal,
who time gallops withal, and who he stands
still withal.

Del That's bloody good, Raquel.

Raquel *(As herself – not wishing to lose the
momentum – holding the book out for Del
to read)* Orlando! Orlando!

Del Oh right! *(Finds his place in the book.
Now in 'Richard the Third' voice)* I prithee,
who doth he trot withal?

Raquel *(As herself)* What are you doing?

Del I'm acting.

Raquel Well, don't! Just read it!

Del I thought I'd put a bit of passion into it.

Raquel No, I don't want you to. Just read
it.

Del Alright. *(Reads from book in his normal
voice)* I prithee, who doth he trot withal?
That alright?

Raquel Yes. *(As Rosalind)* Marry, he trots
hard with a young maid, between the
contract of her marriage, and the day it is
solemnis'd, if the interim be but a se'nnight,
time's pace is so hard, that it seems the
length of seven year.

Albert When you gotta learn this by?

Raquel Tomorrow morning.

Albert *(Laughs his laugh)*

Raquel Oh Del! He's right! I'm gonna
make a real mess of this audition.

Del No, you won't; you'll be terrific – won't
she, Albert?

Albert 'Course you will. And even if you're
not, what have you lost?

Raquel What do you mean, what have
I lost?

Albert Well, it's only a bunch of nancy
actors doing a play that no one can make
head nor tail of!

Del *(To Raquel)* There you are! That's made
you feel better, ain't it? *(To Albert)* You
dozy old twonk! This is authentic culture, so
keep yer gob shut. *(To Raquel)* Shall we
continue?

Raquel You sure you don't mind
doing this?

Del Of course not! I'm enjoying it. It's a
blinding play.

Raquel Thanks. Shall we start at the
beginning?

Del *(Tiny moment of panic)* No, no. Let's
shift on a bit, eh?

Raquel *(As Rosalind)* With a priest that
lacks Latin, and a rich man that hath not the
gout; for the one sleeps easily because he
cannot study, and the other merrily…

*The front-door bell is heard playing
the American national anthem. Del exits
to hall.*

Del Saved by the door bell.

Cut to hall

*Del opens door. A dejected Rodney
enters, having just returned from his
own flat.*

Del What are you doing back here? I
thought you were staying at yer own flat!

Rodney We've broken up.

Del Broken up? You've only been together
an hour! What happened?

He follows Rodney to lounge.

Cut to lounge.

Rodney She saw me standing outside the
Nag's Head with me arm round bloody
Trudy!

Raquel You had your arm round another
woman? Well, no wonder she's thrown you
out! It serves you right, doesn't it, Rodney?

Rodney Trudy was nothing to do with me!
She was… *(Del eyes Rodney not to say any
more)* She was… just a friend!

The Chance of a Lunchtime

Raquel Oh just a friend, eh? How many times have I heard that? I've got no pity for you; in fact you disgust me! It wouldn't do you any harm to take a leaf out of Del's book.

Del Yeah.

Raquel *(To Del – referring to book)* I'm gonna study this in the bedroom.

Del Alright, sweetheart. See you in a little while.

> *Raquel exits to bedroom.*
> *Rodney glares angrily at Del.*

Del Don't look at me in that tone of voice, Rodney. I didn't know Cassandra would see you. Anyway, what was you doing with your arm round Trudy?

Rodney Stopping her from falling flat on her bleedin' face!

Albert D'you reckon Cassandra'll tell her dad?

Del No. She'll keep it personal between her and Rodney.

> *The phone begins ringing. Del and*
> *Rodney look at each other – they know*
> *it's Alan.*

Del *(Cont)* *(Answers phone)* Trotters Independent Traders PLC...

(Falsely pleased) Alan.

Rodney *(Whispers)* Don't say I'm here!

Del *(On phone)* No, Rodney's not in.

Rodney *(Whispers)* Don't say I'm out!

Del You just said... *(On phone)* What I mean is he's not in the room. He's asleep in bed... Yes, of course. I'll give him the message. *(Switches phone off)* He said he wants to see you in work tomorrow, first thing in the morning.

Rodney Oh Gawd!

Del Don't worry. It's probably something to do with business. Me and Raquel are gonna carry on rehearsing in the bedroom. If you hear any funny noises, it'll most probably be me doing me speech at Agincourt.

> *Del exits to bedroom.*

Rodney Alan's gonna sack me.

Albert He can't sack you.

Rodney Of course he can. He owns the firm.

Albert That printing shop of his is overloaded with work. He's got orders coming out of his ears. Everyone's working overtime and weekends.

Rodney So what are you saying? He'll wait 'til the rush is over?

Albert During the war...

Rodney Oh please, Unc – not the U-boat and the fjord again!

Albert ... we docked at Valletta, on our way to Greece. We had a chief communications officer on board, Tubby Fox.

Rodney Funny name for a ship, innit?

Albert That was the officer's name! Well, old Tubby liked to live it up then. He got the chance and one night he was on duty when the skipper caught him in the radio room – a bottle of gin in one hand and a Maltese girl in the other. He put him on a charge and started court-martial proceedings.

Rodney Albert – is there any point to this story or are you just rambling?

Albert The navy had a wartime rule – only commissioned officers were allowed to control the radio room.

Rodney Yeah, he's just rambling.

Albert Now, Tubby was the only communications officer on board. So d'you know what he did?

Rodney I don't care what he did!

Albert He resigned his commission. Which meant?

Rodney I don't know.

Albert It meant the ship couldn't sail! The captain had no choice but to refuse to accept Tubby's resignation! Once he'd done that, he couldn't proceed with the court martial. It was checkmate.

Rodney Oh I see! They needed him more than he needed them?

Albert Exactly! What I'm trying to say is: realise your own importance. Tubby Fox did, and he went on to captain his own submarine-hunter.

Rodney *(Now relieved and much more at ease with his situation)* Yeah! You're right! Cheers, Unc.

Rodney exits to bedroom

Albert *(Talking to himself)* He died in Palermo harbour. Dropped a depth-charge – in nine feet of water.

(Shakes his head sadly at the memory)

INT. A TRENDY CAF[E] / EXT. STREET (CHURCH HALL) DAY

Del, power-dressed, with briefcase and filofax, is seated at a window table reading the Star, a cup of coffee on the table. He looks across the road at a small church hall, a sign outside of which reads: 'Auditions. 10.30–13.00.' Raquel leaves the church hall with Adrian the director. They both laugh as they make their way towards the café. Del quickly opens his briefcase, puts the Star inside and produces the Financial Times.

INT. PARRY PRINTING WORKS. DAY

Rodney approaches Alan's office. He is holding a letter and appears apprehensive. He knocks on the door, then he summons up some courage and enters. There is no-one there so Rodney places the envelope on Alan's desk.

INT. PARRY'S PRINTING WORKS/EXT. ALAN'S OFFICE. DAY

Rodney enters from Alan's office. As he does so, we see Alan approaching. He seems happy and excited.

Alan Rodney!

Rodney Oh... er... Alan. I've left a letter for you on your desk.

Alan Yeah? I'll deal with it later. I wanted to talk to you.

Rodney Yeah, Del said you wanted to see me.

Alan Look, er... You remember we had lunch with Ron Carey from the Harvey's mail-order people?

Rodney Vaguely. It was months ago.

Alan Well, we've got the contract!

Rodney You're kidding!

Alan A three-year deal. We print all their junk mail, their catalogues and their office stationery.

Rodney That's massive.

Alan You're telling me! I think we can safely say we'll be eating turkey again this Christmas.

Rodney No, I mean, how are we gonna handle it? We've barely got the staff or room to cope with our present workload.

Alan We take on more staff and move to a larger workshop. That's what I wanted to see you about. I've been looking at some new premises. I'd like you to see 'em.

Rodney Right! Where are they?

Alan You know that new industrial estate out at Nunhead...

EXT. PARKING AREA AT BACK OF PARRY'S PRINTING WORKS. DAY

Alan and Rodney exit and are approaching Alan's Jaguar.

Rodney Alan. About last night.

Alan Last night?

Rodney What happened between Cassandra and me.

Alan Oh that? Well, needless to say Pam and I were delighted at the news.

Rodney Delighted?

Alan Cassandra came home and told us that you two were back together.

Rodney Oh yeah! But I wanted to talk to you about what happened after that.

Alan Rodney, I'm a man of the world but I'm also Cassandra's father. I don't wanna know what happened after that! Know what I mean?

Rodney Yeah!

The Chance of a Lunchtime

INT. THE TRENDY CAFE. DAY

Raquel and Adrian enter the café and go to the bar. Del joins them. She immediately sees Del and, at first, seems surprised and a bit put out at his presence.

Del Alright, sweetheart?

Raquel What are you doing here?

Del Oh well, you know. I just happened to be passing. I thought I'd pop in and give you a lift home.

Raquel Del, this is Adrian, he's the director. Adrian, this is Derek, he's... he's a friend.

Adrian Pleased to meet you, Derek.

Del And you, Ade, and you. So how'd she do?

Adrian At the audition? Very well,

Del Cushty. *(To Raquel)* See. Told you it would be no problem.

They are moving to bar.

Raquel You shouldn't ask questions like that!

Del Oh shuddup. You're too picky, that's your problem.

Adrian What can I get you?

Raquel A small dry sherry, please, Adrian.

Del Yeah, same here.

Adrian *(To bar person)* And I'll have a kir. So are you in the business, Derek?

The barman pours the drinks.

Del The business? Oh, show business! Not exactly.

Adrain But you're involved in some way?

Del No... I'm an importer-exporter. Fine antiques, quality objets d'art, mobile telephones, that sorta thing.

As Adrian picks up the sherries, Jules, the set designer, enters . He is 25, trendy and gay. He wears tight black leather trousers, an expensive, armless T-shirt and an earring. His hair is dyed blond and he wears a hint of make-up. A nod and a smile is exchanged between Jules, Raquel and Adrian.

Del *(Continuation of previous speech)* Funny you should mention it. While we're on the subject, Adrian, I am at this moment promoting a brand new line in computerised communications systems which I think could be right up your street. It's a musical doorbell. You press the button and...

Adrian *(Cuts in)* Derek, this is Jules.

Del turns straight into Jules's face and reels away quickly as if taken by surprise.

Del *(Shocked)* Ooh!

Adrian Jules is our set designer. Jules, this is Derek, Raquel's... er... friend.

Jules Hi.

Del Alright?

Jules *(To bar person)* Gimme some vitamin C. I feel absolutely wrecked.

Del, Raquel and Adrian move away from bar with drinks in hand. The bar person pours the orange juice.

Del Shall we go to the table?

Adrian Yeah, fine. I'm gonna grab something to eat first.

Raquel I feel a bit peckish as well.

Del And me.

Raquel *(Whispers harshly at Del)* Go and sit at the table. I need to talk to him.

Del Alright!

Raquel and Adrian move to the salad bar. Del sits at window table. He watches Raquel and Adrian, who are at the buffet table, chatting, and laughing. Jules now plonks himself down opposite Del.

Jules They think I can design magnificent stage sets on peanuts! I mean, these people don't have a budget. It's more like a whipround.

Del Yeah, know what you mean. It's a bark, innit?

As he sips his sherry he becomes self-conscious of the small, feminine sherry glass.

Jules Feel my hands.

Del Eh?

Jules Feel my hands. Go on, feel 'em.

Del *(Touches Jules' palm tentatively)* Oh yeah, 'orrible, ain't they?

Jules That's callouses! I'm the set designer yet I have to help unload the lorries. Did I go to art college for three years for that?

Del 'Course not!

Jules No.

Del simply doesn't know how to continue this conversation.

Del See the match the other night?

Jules Match? What match?

Del England v Yugoslavia.

Jules No, I'm not really interested in football.

Del Well, you're lucky! You were dead lucky! Some of the decision that ref gave were criminal. We wos robbed, absolutely robbed. They showed the match on *Grandstand*. I said to my brother they should have had it on *Crimewatch*.

Jules I tell you what I did watch. That Elizabeth Taylor film *Cat On A Hot Tin Roof*. Isn't she the most beautiful creature ever?

Del Yeah, it's a shame she got fat, innit?

Jules Oh but her bone structure! And her eyes! And her hair. Derek, her hair just cascades everywhere. I wish I had hair…

Dels now sees Rodney and Alan in the Jag outside in the street, parked at a garage right outside the café. Rodney spots Del and smiles, but his smile dies as he sees Jules sitting opposite Del. Jules is going on about Liz Taylor. His wrists have become limper and he is touching his eyes and hands. As Alan now looks with curiosity at Del and Jules, Del realises what they might be thinking and shakes his head at them. Alan and Rodney look at each other and then drive off.

INT. THE TROTTERS' LOUNGE. NIGHT

Raquel, seated, is reading a typed letter. She seems worried. Del is at the bar pouring champagne. Albert is in an armchair, and Rodney is just finishing his dinner.

Albert You've told us about 30 times already. I've never seen this place, but I feel like I could give you a guided tour.

Rodney Well, I'm excited! I tell you, Alan is going places.

Del He ain't the only one who's going places! I'll get all the hounds along for your opening night, Raquel…Raquel?

Raquel Oh sorry. What d'you say?

Del I said, I'll get all the boys there for the opening night. Boycie, Trigger, Mike. We'll give you a big cheer when you walk on. Make that Adrian mush think you've got a fan club already.

Raquel OK. Thanks.

Albert Well, cheer up, gel. You got the part, didn't you?

Raquel Yeah, I got the part, Albert.

Del *(Hands Raquel a glass of champagne)* There you go, darling.

Raquel Not for me, Del.

Del But we're celebrating your good news.

Raquel I've got this letter to read. It's all the details of the play. I'd like to read it with a clear head. I'll see you in a little while.

Raquel exits to bedroom.

Albert What's up with her?

Del Dunno. She's bin acting a bit off ever since she came out of that audition. Maybe it's being with that actors' crowd! Perhaps she feels she's a bit better than us now.

Rodney Raquel's not like that!

Del You don't know, Rodney. A cravat and a codpiece can turn a girl's head.

The phone begins ringing.

The Chance of a Lunchtime

Rodney answers it.

Rodney *(On phone)* Hello… Alan. I've just been telling Del and Albert about our new premises… What letter? *(Horrified. He'd forgotten the letter)* Oh that letter? Let me explain. You see, it was a token – a sorta gesture. The situation that existed then between Cassandra and I may have been causing you some embarrassment, and I wanted you to know that I was fully aware of it… Yes… Mm… Fine… Let me get this straight, Alan. When you say you've accepted my letter of resignation, what exactly do you mean? I see… Yes, thank you. *(Switches phone off)*
Rodney just stands there, rigid with shock.

Del You handed in a letter of resignation?

Rodney Sort of!

Del I don't understand, Rodney!

Rodney I… er… thought it was best.

Del You stupid little plonker! That's the best job you've ever had or are ever likely to have, and you've chucked it away!

Rodney Listen. I am in control of my own destiny! I am my own man and I make my own decisions in this world.

Del But why did you resign?

Rodney *(Indicating towards Albert)* Because he told me to!

Albert Me? I didn't say a word.

Rodney You told me about that officer on your boat who resigned and saved himself from a court martial.

Albert But that was different, son.

Rodney How?

Albert Well, he got away with it!

Rodney I didn't think Alan would accept my resignation!

Del But he did!

Rodney I know he did! I thought I was too important to the firm.

Del But you weren't!

Rodney *(Shouting at Del)* I know I weren't! Bloody know that now, don't I?

Del Alright, calm down. I'll have a word with Alan, see if I can get him to change his mind.

Rodney Too late. He's already got someone to take my place.

Del That was quick, weren't it?

Albert Bet your life he jumped at the opportunity.

Rodney What's that supposed to mean?

Albert No, no. I meant the bloke who's taken your place!

Rodney Oh yeah, he jumped at it alright! It's my assistant.

Del What, that young kid?

Rodney Yeah.

Del The spotty one? Only left school last year?

Rodney Yes.

Del Elvis?

Rodney Yes.

Del And he's doing what you were doing?

Rodney Yes.

Albert I heard that boy was an onion short of a stew.

Rodney Who told you that?

Albert You did.

Rodney You must have misunderstood me, Albert. Elvis is not daft.

Del There's no danger of him winning *Blockbusters* though, is there? *(To Albert)* He's the one who thought sugar diabetes was a Welsh flyweight.

Rodney Look, he's just filling the gap until Alan finds someone of my expertise to take over.

Albert It's just strange they should replace you with a silly boy.

Rodney Just stay out of it, Albert!

Del Oi, Oi, Rodney. You can't talk to an old hero like that!

Rodney Well, he's getting on my bloody

179

nerves, keeping on and on about it.

Del You're just trying to pass the buck, Rodney. Well, it won't work. This is all yer own doing. You had a lovely wife, a lovely flat and the bestest job in the world – and you blew it!

Rodney *(Cannot find an answer)* Who was that bloke you were having lunch with today?

Del It was one of Raquel's arty friends.

Albert What bloke's that then?

Del Just stay out of it, Albert.

Del and Rodney turn their backs on each other.

INT. DEL'S BEDROOM. NIGHT

Raquel, in dressing gown, is seated on the edge of the bed staring at the floor. Del enters in pyjamas and dressing gown.

Del You OK?

Raquel Yeah, fine.

Del picks up the typed letter Raquel had been reading earlier.

Del You read yer letter about the play?

Raquel Yeah, I've read it.

Del Look, sweetheart. If we've had a row, will you at least tell me about it?

Raquel We haven't had a row! Everything's fine.

Del No, it isn't. Ever since you met that Adrian and Jules and all the others at the audition, you've been different towards me. I mean, what is it? Maybe I'm not as good as your actor cronies, eh? Perhaps I embarrassed you!

Raquel Don't be stupid, Del!

Del I saw your face, Raquel. When Adrian talked to me about *Hamlet* and I said I preferred Castellas, I saw your face! So when d'you begin rehearsals?

Raquel The tour doesn't start for another three months.

Del Oh well, gives you plenty of time to meet more of them intelligent, sensitive actor people, don't it?

Raquel Derek, will you get it into your thick skull: I'm not trying to meet intelligent and sensitive people, I'm happy with you!

Del So what's the problem? Tour? You said it was a tour!

Raquel That's right. It's a nine-week tour of the country.

Del I didn't know you had to go away! I thought it was just a play – you know, local... Oh I see it all now. Your head's filled with big theatres again! Applause, applause, the show must go on!

Raquel We're not appearing in theatres.

Del Well, if you're not appearing in theatres, what are you appearing in?

Raquel Schools!

Del Schools?

Raquel Yes, schools. It's a co-project by the Education and Arts Council. We're supposed to take Shakespeare to the inner cities. Imagine what it might have done for me.

Del Oh yeah. A few years from now you could have bin a dinner lady.

Raquel Don't become like the others, Del. Putting down every little dream I have.

Del I'm not putting yer dreams down, sweetheart. You know I'd never do that. I don't want you to leave me! I'm frightened you won't come back!

Raquel I'm not going anywhere, Del. I'm turning the offer down.

Del No, no. You mustn't do that. It's a good opportunity, Raquel. I was just being selfish.

Raquel I can't do that tour, Del.

Del Why not?

Raquel Because I've read the play again and again and at no point does Shakespeare mention that Rosalind – is pregnant.

The Chance of a Lunchtime

Del Well, that's poetic licence... innit... Did you say you was pregnant?

Raquel *(Nods slowly)* I've done all the tests and... everything. It's certain.

Del Blimey!

Raquel Are you angry?

Del Angry?

Del, who still hasn't smiled, opens the bedroom door.

Del *(Calls)* Albert! Get out of bed, you lazy old sod, and open the biggest bottle of champagne you can find! Tonight we celebrate!

Raquel You're not angry?

Del Angry? I'm gonna to be a daddy! I wanna phone everyone I know: I wanna have a party – I want someone to put on a fireworks display for us!

Rodney, in pyjamas and dressing gown, arrives at the open bedroom door.

Rodney What's all the fuss?

Del Rodney... Just stay where you are.

Albert arrives at bedroom door.

Albert What's happening?

Del Let me ask you two a question. *(Pointing at Raquel)* How many people can you see standing there?

Albert and Rodney look at each other.

Albert Well... one.

Del I can see – two.

Del and Raquel smile lovingly at each other and embrace.

Rodney You know what this means, Albert?

Albert No.

Rodney Well, either Raquel's pregnant or Del's pissed.

Stage Fright

INT. THE NAG'S HEAD. DAY

Raquel is standing talking to Mike and Trigger at the bar. Del, power-dressed, with mobile phone and briefcase, is seated at a table reading a letter. Rodney is sitting opposite Del, eating a sandwich. Albert is reading the letter over Del's shoulder.

Del I don't believe it! When did this arrive?

Albert This morning.

Del Well, why didn't you let me know sooner?

Albert I couldn't get in touch with yer. You've been out all morning. I thought you might have popped home for elevenses.

Del How many times I gotta tell you, Unc? Elevenses is for wimps. I'm out there on that yuppy tightrope, nerves on red alert. A beta-blocker and a dream, that's me. I eat on the move, mobile phone in one hand, a Pot Noodle in the other.

Albert I tried to call you on yer mobile phone.

Rodney That's why Del ended up with an earful of noodles.

Del Oh look, the boy from the blackstuff's woken up!

Rodney Look, just 'cos I'm out of work, there's no need to rub it in! For all you know my recent misfortunes could herald a watershed in my life and I could go on to greater things.

Del Oh yes! You've broken up from your wife, walked out of a beautiful home, resigned from a highly paid job and pulled the chain on your career. That's just the sort of springboard you need for the future, innit?

Rodney Something'll turn up.

Del That's what General Custer said! And something did turn up! Another bloody load of Indians!

Albert You should be giving Rodney a bit of encouragement.

Del What d'you think I'm doing? I'm worried about him! A few weeks back he had cash on the hip and a glowing future. Now he's skint and the only thing that's glowing is his liver!

Albert What happened to that golden handshake he got from the printing firm?

Del He's kissed that all up the wall, ain't he? Blown it all on Cuba libres and lairy suits.

Rodney I don't believe this git! He has the audacity to sit here moralising with me while holding a letter from the magistrates' court saying his case has been brought forward!

Del Yeah, well one of them things, innit? Everyone has to go to court once in their life.

Rodney Once in their…! They've given you yer own parking place!

Del Don't try and change the subject, Rodney!

Albert I think what Del's trying to say is: for the last month or so you've been living back at the flat. In the past that was *alright*, but now Raquel is pregnant.

Del And it shows, don't it? See that little lump? That's my embryo.

Rodney, revolted, puts his sandwich down.

Del See, a few months from now there'll be no space in the flat.

Rodney She'll be that big, will she?

Del I mean, that room of yours will be turned into the nursery. This is a perfect opportunity for you to go out and find yer own bachelor pad, innit?

Albert He's waiting for the council to offer him something.

Del Oh, cushty. Well, with any luck we might be able to throw a combined party. Rodney's house-warming and my son's 21st!

Rodney For your information, Derek, the council phoned this morning with an offer of accommodation.

Del No! Really?

Albert It's true, Del. I was there when he got the call.

Del Well, that's terrific news, Rodney. Well done, bruv.

Rodney They've offered me an LDA.

Del An LDA! Well, things are looking up!

Rodney I'm viewing it this afternoon.

Del If you need any furniture, give us a shout. Young Towser's doing a very nice line in quality reject three-piece suites.

Rodney Right. Could come in handy… Del, can I ask you something?

Del Of course, bruv. Anything.

Rodney What's an LDA?

Del Dunno!

Albert Well, it's an abbreviation for something.

Rodney I know it's an abbreviation for something! But what? L-D-A. Maybe it stands for Luxury Detached Abode?

Del Yeah! I doubt it, but maybe! I'll get the drinks.

Rodney Not for me. I'd better go home and change. I'm meeting the council mush in an hour.

Del Best of luck, bruv.

Rodney exits. Del crosses to the bar, where Mike is talking to Raquel. Trigger is next to Del.

Trigger Wotcher, Del Boy. Alright?

Del Yeah. Mike, same again, please.

Mike Hang on, Del. *(To Raquel)* So you thought of a name yet?

Raquel No! It's too early for that.

Mike It's best to sort it out early. Saves rows later.

Del Mike! *(Holds glasses out)*

Mike Yeah, hang on a minute, Del.

Mike *(To Raquel)* So how's this gonna affect your career?

Raquel What career?

Mike *(To Raquel)* I thought you was an actress and a singer and all that.

Raquel Yeah. Well, I think in my condition I'll put my career on hold for a while. Like 15 years or so.

Trigger *(To Raquel)* That reminds me. You know the Down By The Riverside Club?

Del Yeah. I'm thinking of going and getting a drink there. Mike, when you're ready!

Mike I've only got one pair of hands, Del! *(To Raquel)* I remember the night I came home and my wife told me she was two months pregnant. I was a cocktail waiter at the time.

Raquel Ah! It's a moment you'll never forget.

Mike That's right. I remember it especially, 'cos I'd just come home from three months on a cruise ship.

Raquel Oh! Sorry.

Mike Oh no, it was a nice cruise. Do you wanna see the snaps?

Trigger A mate of mine from the council's depot's singing there tonight.

Mike and Raquel continue chatting as Trigger talks to Del.

Del What?

Trigger At the Down By The Riverside Club. Tony Angelino.

Del Who?

Trigger Tony Angelino. That's his stage name.

Del Sounds like a good evening, Trig. A few drinks, scampi in a basket and the singing road-sweeper. Cushty.

Trigger He's not a road-sweeper! *(As if to impress)* He's on the dust.

Stage Fright

Del Oh well!

Trigger He sung there once before, about six years ago.

Del He's back by popular demand, is he?

Trigger Yeah. He's got a terrific voice. He's gonna be a big star one day. Fancy coming down there tonight?

Del No.

Mike *(To Del, referring to Raquel)* What you hoping for?

Del The same again if you're not too busy!

Mike I mean the baby.

Del Oh. It's a boy.

Raquel How do you know? It might be a girl.

Del No, no. It's a boy. I know it is!

Mike Don't forget, you can hold a very nice wedding reception up above here.

Del and Raquel share a look as Mike goes for the drinks.

Del *(To Raquel)* Let's go and sit down over there.

They move towards a table.

Del Have you told any of your family yet?

Raquel I've written to my parents.

Del I was thinking more about your husband.

Raquel My solicitor's still trying to trace his whereabouts. We've been apart now for seven years so divorce'll be no problem.

Del Well, as soon as that comes through we'll get hitched.

Raquel Sorry?

Del We'll tie the knot.

Raquel But I might not want to marry you.

Del What you mean, you might not wanna marry me? Don't be silly.

Raquel I'm not being silly! You haven't even asked me.

Del Haven't ask…! Cor blimey, Raquel! You're… Well, you are, ain't yer? Where I come from action speaks louder than words.

Raquel Would you keep me in the style that I've become accustomed to?

Del Of course I would.

Raquel Well, there's no way I'm marrying you then!

Del Listen to me. We're gonna have a blinding future together.

Raquel Are we?

Albert begins playing piano.

Del Yes, we are. Everything's beginning to fall into place. Business is going well and I've got lots of new projects in the old pipeline. *(Checks watch)* I've got a meeting in half an hour's time with an old mate of mine who owns one of these dinner and dance clubs. I think he's heard about them 300 packets of crisps I've got in the garage.

Albert is playing and singing 'Slow Boat to China'.

Del Listen, he's playing our song… badly. I've got a really good feeling about the future. I tell you, Raquel, this time next year I'll be a millionaire.

Raquel Alright then, I accept.

Del Good girl! You know it makes sense.

Raquel Maybe tomorrow we could go out and get an engagement ring?

Del Not tomorrow, sweetheart. I'm in court.

Raquel reacts – this is news to her.

INT. THE STARLITE ROOMS. DAY

There is a small dance area with tables around it. To one side is a long bar, and there is a stage. A cleaning lady is hoovering the carpet. Behind the bar sits Eric the manager, a tough-looking cockney, Del enters.

Del Eric! How are you going, pal?

Eric Talk about Marley's ghost! Del Boy! You're looking prosperous.

Del Yeah, can't complain. Well, I can, but no one listens.

Eric I've heard good things about you, Del. You're making your mark in the parish. I'm pleased for you. I like to see people get on.

Last time I saw you, you were really struggling – driving round in some shitty little three-wheeled van. *(Laughs at this)*

Del *(Laughs along with Eric)* Those were the days, eh? Er... actually I kept hold of that van – nostalgia – all that. I just use it for business.

Eric What's yer main motor, then ? A little sports coupé? *(Pronounces it 'coop')*

Del Yeah, something like that. I ain't seen you for... what? Five, six years.

Eric Is it that long?

Del It was just after that little misunderstanding we had.

Eric I don't remember that.

Del Yeah. You thought I'd done you out of 500 quid.

Eric Well, you did, didn't you?

Del No, no. I explained it to you at the time. It was just a misunderstanding.

Eric Yeah, well. We'll let sleeping dogs lie, eh, Del?

Del Yeah, all in the past, eh, Eric? You've done this place up nice.

Eric Yeah, it's doing some business as well.

Del Cushty! I'm pleased for you. Anyway! What d'you want? You left a message with my answer-machine.

Eric I thought it was your uncle.

Del Same thing.

Eric Got a bit of a problem, Del. Tomorrow night the club's been booked for a birthday-party cabaret, all the exes. I had a young singing duo lined up, but they've let me down at the last minute. I've phoned round all the local agents *(produces a sheet of paper)* That's what I've been offered so far.

Del *(Reading the paper)* Well, that looks alright to me.

Eric No. I need a singer, Del. Someone who knows what they're doing. Now I heard recently that you're living with some bird who used to do a bit of nightclub singing.

Del Raquel? Yeah, she's done a bit of singing. But she packed it all in ages ago.

Eric Would she fancy coming out of retirement for one night?

Del She's three months pregnant, Eric. I couldn't ask her to do something like that.

Eric It's hardly hod-carrying, Del. I mean, all she's gotta do is four or five songs.

Drl No. She told me once before about the nervous tension she used to suffer before she went on stage. I couldn't ask her to do that.

Eric That's a shame, Del. I've got a contract here just waiting to be signed by someone.

Del I'm sorry, pal. I'd liked to have helped you, but... Raquel's given the business up. It's her life. I can't go interfering with her wishes. You don't want any cheap packets of crisps, do you?

Eric No, what I want's a singer. I'd have made it worth her while – 600 quid for one night's work ain't to be sneezed at.

Del *(Produces a pen to sign contract)* She'll need a backing group!

As Del signs we see Eric grin an evil, vengeful grin

INT. THE TROTTERS' LOUNGE. DAY

Del is seated at the table trying to eat his lunch. Albert is also seated at the table eating lunch. Raquel is seated across the table shouting at Del.

Raquel What d'you mean you promised him?

Del What could I do, sweetheart? It's a mate in trouble.

Raquel I don't care who it is, Del! I'm not doing it!

Del But I gave him your word.

Raquel Well, you had no right to!

Del It's 300 quid, Raquel!

Raquel I don't care how much it is, Derek! I'm not doing it!

Del Come on, sweetheart! Eric's in right lumber. He's been in touch with all the agents – he even showed me the list they

Stage Fright

sent him. So far he's been offered 12 strippers, 18 blue comedians, a trained dog act and Lionel Blair.

Raquel So what's wrong with that?

Del Nothing's wrong with it. It's just that Eric wants you!

Albert But she's three months pregnant.

Del I ain't asking her to be a belly-dancer, am I? Just sing a few songs. *(Referring to her belly)* Anyway, it doesn't show. Turn round, sweetheart. There are, it don't show. You've got a lovely figure and a beautiful voice. And that is a gift, Raquel, and you should share that gift with the world.

Raquel Or a bunch of drunks in the Starlite Rooms! Del, I've never sung in a real nightclub before!

Del You showed us that poster of when you appeared on the same bill as Otis Redding at the Talk of the Town, London.

Raquel It was Laurie London at the Talk of the Town, Reading.

Del Well, same thing, innit?

Raquel No, it is not! That was the one and only time I've ever appeared alone on stage. It was a nightmare. I forgot the words, I forgot the tune, it was just a nightmare! People actually cheered when they announced last orders. The only other times I've been on stage has been in a double act. I was with the magician, the Great Ramondo. I was in that duo, Double Cream. See, I don't mind that. There's someone there to support you. Someone there to share the blame.

Del Well, I'll sort you out a singing partner.

Raquel It's not as simple as that! You have to get to know each other – rehearse – find out whether we can harmonise and whether we're even compatible.

Del We'll do all that!

Albert When's the show?

Del Tomorrow night.

Raquel Tomorrow night! It's impossible!

Del *(Produces a contract)* Look I've signed a contract guaranteeing that I will supply the cabaret. It's legal and binding.

Raquel *(Reading the contract)* The Trotter International Star Agency!

Del That's me. I've diversified.

Raquel Why did you sign a contract before you'd even spoken to me?

Del Because I never for one moment thought that you would let me down. Rodney – possibly. *(Referring to Albert)* Him – like a shot, but you? No. Still, I shouldn't be too surprised. It's the story of my life, really. My dad let me down, walked out and left me to fend for meself. My mum died. It weren't her fault, but I actually felt that she'd let me down as well. It's funny the things that go through yer mind when you're only 16 and… alone. Maybe that's why I've always played it straight with people. I've always been open and upfront because I hate the thought of other folk feeling let down – the way I did.

Albert *(Has been looking at the contract)* It says here he's paying you 600 quid!

Del *(Under his breath)* You mouthy old git!

Albert You said 300.

Del Yes. And isn't it obvious why I said that?

Albert No.

Del Because… because… because I realised that a fee of £600 would make Raquel even more nervous than she already was. So I tried to take the sting out of it – smooth the edges down – relieve the pressure – by saying it was only 300.

Raquel *(Kisses him gently on the hand)* Thank you.

Del So you're gonna do it for me, are you?

Raquel But who will I be singing with?

Del Trust me, Raquel, trust me. I will never put you wrong. We'll go through some of my LPs, pick out a few classics.

Raquel But these songs have gotta have musical arrangements. We need a pianist.

187

Del Well, that's no problem, is it? Albert!
Albert *(With a big, optimistic smile)*
Yes, Del?
Del Get the Yellow Pages, we'll sort out a musician. *(To Raquel)* What d'you say?
Raquel I'll think about it, Del.
Del Cushty!
Raquel I'm just thinking about it, Del! No promises.
Del Of course not. But in the meantime you have a little practice, eh? Get the old voice in trim – just in case.
Raquel Yeah. Alright – just in case. I'm gonna make some coffee. Anyone else?
Albert I'll have a cup, dear.
Del And me, sweetheart.
Raquel exits to the kitchen.
Del She's gonna knock 'em bandy, Albert. You wait and see.
We hear Raquel singing in the kitchen. At first she is singing reasonably quietly.
Raquel Do you know the way to San José, I've been away so long I'm going home to San José
Del Listen to that. Voice like an angel. *(Calls into kitchen)* Sing up, darling, don't be shy.
Raquel raises her volume and continues singing the song. Del does a little dance to her singing.
Del Lovely Jubbly!
Rodney enters from the hall, wearing a suit and looking very depressed.
Del Raquel's singing at the Starlite Rooms.
Rodney Yeah? Her voice don't half travel, don't it?
Del No, I mean, she's in the kitch… What's up with you?
Rodney I've just been to view the council's offer of accommodation. And you were right, Derek, LDA does not stand for Luxury Detached Abode.
Del I had a feeling.

Rodney LDA stands for Low Demand Accommodation.
Albert What's that, then?
Rodney It's a place where no one else wants to live!
Albert What they like?
Rodney Well, they're er… *(Referring to flat)* They're like this!
Del You saucy little git! *(Shouts into kitchen)* Keep the noise down, Raquel! We can't hear ourselves think out here!
Rodney You should have seen the place they offered me. It was like a time-share apartment on Albert Square.
Albert Did you take it?
Rodney Of course I didn't!
Raquel enters from the kitchen.
Albert Well, you've gotta find a place of your own soon, Rodney. *(Referring to Raquel)* A few months from now she'll be having a kiddie.
Rodney Yes, I know! But at the moment the council's my only hope. I'm out of work and have no money coming in, so I can't afford to look in the private sector.
Raquel I don't wish to sound brutal, Rodney, but why don't you get another job?
Rodney starts laughing uproariously at this. After a few seconds Albert starts laughing as well.
Rodney It's not that funny, Albert! *(To Raquel)* With my history the only chance I have of future employment is to go out and find my own window-cleaning round.
Raquel I'm sorry, I don't understand. You left your previous employment of your own accord. You weren't sacked, you resigned. So where's the problem?
Rodney It's not as simple as that, Raquel. *(Accusingly)* Is it, Derek?
Del You see, sweetheart, Rodney's only ever had one real job – working for

Stage Fright

Cassandra's dad – the job he's just resigned from.

Raquel But I thought prior to that he was a partner in Trotters Independent Traders.

Rodney starts laughing again.

Del Yes, he was – and sorely missed when he left. But you see, Trotters Independent Traders was never what is legally known as a pukka business. We never quite got round to registering our name at Companies House. It helped us cut down on a lot of paperwork…

Rodney … and income tax and VAT.

Del Yes… So officially Rodney left school at 16 but didn't get his first job until he was 26. The only other time he showed up on a government computer during that decade was when he received a suspended sentence for possession of cannabis.

Raquel *(To Rodney)* And you don't fancy window-cleaning?

Rodney No. I don't like heights.

Albert Couldn't you specialise in bungalows?

Rodney Shuddup, Albert!

Raquel Alan's bound to give Rodney a glowing reference.

Del We know that, sweetheart. But where's he gonna say he was for the other 10 years – in the toilet? No, it's a problem. It's a shame you can't get a job in something that really interests you… Like… Well, music. You like music, don't you?

Rodney Yeah.

Del Even if it was a part-time job.

Rodney Yeah, that'd do.

Del Something like… a road… manager.

Rodney *(Laughs ironically)* Where would I get something like that?

Del You never know your luck, Rodders. You just never know your luck.

EXT. THE DOWN BY THE RIVERSIDE CLUB. NIGHT

The club is by the river. It is a large and brightly lit prefabricated building, its lights reflecting in the river. Somewhere a tug hoots. From inside the club we can hear the muffled tones of Tony Angelino singing 'Fall in Love'.

Tony I've been in love so many times. Thought I knew the score,

The van pulls into the crowded car parking area, which is rough and rutted.

Tony But now you've hurt me Oh so bad, I can't take it any more. And it looks like I'm never gonna fall in love again.

Del, overcoat draped round shoulders in what he believes is show-biz agent fashion, alights from the van. Rodney, dressed in a suit and tie, alights from driver's side. He looks towards the club and listens to the song. He closes his eyes as a great dread comes over him. Del loves the sounds he is hearing. As they move to the entrance we see a sign outside: 'The Down By The Riverside Club Welcomes Tony Angelino – The Singing Dustman'.

Tony *(Loud and powerful)* F… a… ll in love, I'm never gonna – fall in love. I'm never gonna fall in love again.

INT. THE DOWN BY THE RIVERSIDE CLUB. NIGHT

Tony Angelino, a drummer and a guy playing a sophisticated synthesizer are on the smallish stage. Tony is 35, slim and tanned and has black, curly Tom Jones-type hair. He is wearing a pair of sunglasses. His shirt is open almost to his navel, and he is wearing tight black trousers and a belt with a massive gold buckle. Something is hanging inside his trousers which could easily be an 8" salami. Around the stage are 8 or 10 tables occupied mainly by 50-year-old women.

189

Most of the villainous-looking men are hanging around the bar.

Tony *(Singing)* All the things I heard about you, I thought they were only lies. But when I saw you with another man, I just broke down and died. And it looks like I'm never gonna fall in love again.

Del and Rodney enter and move to the bar.

Del *(To Rodney, referring to Tony)* He's good, ain't he?

Rodney Good! He's bloody awful!

Del You don't know what you're talking about, bruv. Look at all the old dears. They'll be chucking their corsets on the stage in a minute.

Tony F... a... ll in love. Please don't ask me to, fall in love. You see, I'm never gonna fall in love again.

The song ends to rapturous applause from the ladies.

Del Listen to that, they love him. If I put him and Raquel together I'm on a right winner.

Rodney But she's pregnant!

Del Only a little bit!

Rodney You're just exploiting her, ain't yer?

Del She's earning out of it, and earning well! We've all gotta do our little bit to bring money into the flat.

Rodney Yeah. Well, I reckon it's all wrong.

Del It's got nothing to do with you, Rodney. You are just my road manager – part-time at that! I've explained your duties – you drive 'em to rehearsals, get the tea and sandwiches and sweep up when they've finished.

Rodney Am I allowed to voice any opinion on repertoire, presentation, arrangement, interpretation?

Del No.

Rodney Right. I will do exactly as you say. And no bloody more! You won't hear another word out of me on the matter!

Del Good.

We hear the opening bars to 'Delilah'.

Tony *(Singing)* I saw light on the night that I passed by her window.

Rodney It's old-fashioned, Del. Who's gonna pay money to listen to this?

Del *(Indicates the women)* Well, they have, ain't they? *(Indicates the men)* And so have they! You seem to think that popular music is all about the top 10. Well, it ain't – 80 per cent of the people in this country are middle of the road and this is what they like to hear. I mean, John Denver and Roger Whitaker never get on *Top Of The Pops*, but they still sell millions of records a year. It's serious bunce, Rodney, serious bunce. And this is my chance of getting a piece of the action. Raquel and Tony could become the new... the new Carpenters.

Rodney Or plumbers, or brickies.

Del Peters and Lee.

Rodney Ooh!

Del Sonny and Cher.

Rodney Chas and Dave.

Del Renee and Renato.

Rodney Mills & Boon.

Del *(He hasn't heard any of Rodney's insults)* You got that contract?

Rodney Yeah. *(Produces contract)* I don't know if it's all legal. I ain't been trained in that sorta thing.

Del You've got two GCEs Rodders, that'll do for me. (Reads contract) Yes, lots of 'hereinafters' and 'forthwiths' – lovely Jubbly.

Tony finishes his act with the final couple of lines of 'Delilah'.

Tony *(Singing)* Forgive me, Delilah, I just couldn't take any m... o...

Tony taxes his bows to great applause.

Tony Thank you. Thank you so much. You've been a wonderful audience.

Tony makes his way to the side of the stage.

Stage Fright

The synthesiser-player takes the mike.

Synth-player Ladies and gentlemen –
Tony Angelino.

Tony exits with a bow and a wave.

INT. CORRIDOR/SMALL PRIVATE WASHROOM. NIGHT

*As Tony exits Del and Rodney are waiting
for him. Del has the contract in his hand.*

Rodney He'll never sign that contract.

Del He'll sign it, Rodney... Tony, lovely performance.

Tony Thanks.

Del (*Holds the contract and a pen out*)
Would you?

Tony (*Believing it to be an autograph*)
Of course.

*Del points to where he wants the
signature to go. Tony signs and
moves off.*

Del (*Blows the ink dry. To Rodney*) Easier
than you thought, weren't it?

Rodney I don't believe you did that!

Del He who dares, Rodders! (*Calls*) Tony,
can I have a word, son.

Del catches him up in the corridor.

Del Bit of business to discuss. I've got a
few bookings lined up for you.

Tony Yeah? Come in here. We can discuss
it while I'm getting changed.

*Tony opens the door to the washroom.
Del and Rodney enter as two lady fans
approach Tony in the corridor.*

First woman Tony, can I have your
autograph?

Tony I'll be back in just a minute, honey.

Tony enters washroom.

Tony (*To Del and Rodney*) Chicks!

Rodney Oh. Local hen-party, is it?

Tony No. Actually, it's the local Women's
Institute. Still, you've got to keep them
happy, eh?

Del My name's Derek Trotter of the Trotter
International Star Agency, Peckham. Call me
Del. This is my roadie, Rodney.

Tony What's this all about, Del?

*During Del's next speech, Tony removes
his cuban-heeled boots and instantly
shrinks by three inches.*

Del I am putting together a middle-of-the-
road duo. You and a very talented young
singer named Raquel Turner.

Tony bends down to take his boots off.

Del I have a confirmed booking at the
Starlite Rooms with a option for a long-term
contract...

Tony stands up.

Del ... if you're good enough.

Tony You're kidding me? The Starlite
Rooms?

Tony hands his wig to Del.

Del You got a manager, Tony?

Tony Er, no.

Del Well, you have now, son.

*Del goes to shake Tony's hand, but Tony
pulls a salami out of his trousers and puts
the salami in Del's hand. Del then gives
Rodney the salami.*

Rodney Eurgh!

He throws it away.

*Tony is now at the basin, washing off the
quick-tan make-up. Del is standing next
to him washing his hands.*

Del I can't understand how a bloke with a
voice like yours ain't been snapped up. Can
you, Rodney?

Rodney (*About to go into a long speech*)
Well...

Del (*To Tony, referring to Rodney*) See, he's
as mystified as me!

Tony Nobody's told you anything about
me, then?

Del No. Is there something I should
know?

Tony (*Drying himself, obviously hiding
something*) No, no.

*Tony's face is now the same pasty white
as his body.*

Tony When's this booking for?

Del Tomorrow night. Yes, I know it's short notice and you and Raquel have got a lot of work to do rehearsing together, working out yer repertoire and what 'ave yer. But I've got faith in the two of you. You're a pro and so is she. I'm offering you a £100 for tomorrow night.

Tony No? The most I've ever been paid is 50 quid.

We see Del's 'why didn't I keep my mouth shut' expression.
Rodney smiles at Del's discomfort.

Rodney Well, you're in the big time now.
By now, Tony has removed his skin-tight trousers and is wearing a pair of ordinary slacks. He steps into a pair of slip-on shoes as he buttons up his very ordinary shirt. Tony packs his stage clothes and props away in a canvas flight bag.

Del You're rehearsing first thing in the morning. I've booked a room at the Jesse Jackson Memorial Hall. I'll give your road manager a list of classic hits I want you to rehearse.

Tony (Slight panic) No, no. There are only a few songs I can sing, Del.

Del And that's why you hardly ever get any bookings.

Tony No, it's not that! It's because I...

Del Well, what?

Tony Nothing.

Del Your problem is you're frightened of a challenge. But now you've got me behind you. You must trust me, Tony. I won't put you wrong. I'll play it straight down the line with yer. No secrets, no small print. All you've gotta do in return is trust me. Do you trust me, Tony?

Tony Yeah. OK, Del.

Del Good boy. You know it makes sense.

Tony Will you be at the hall in the morning?

Rodney No, he's in court tomorrow.

Del Yes, I'm witness to – something.

Tony (Referring to contract) You want me to sign that?

Del (Holding up contract) No, you've already done it, son.
As Del opens the door, Tony is left wondering 'When did I sign that?'

Cut to corridor. Del, Rodney and Tony enter.

Rodney (To Tony) See you in the morning.
Rodney and Del exit.
Tony takes pen from a lady fan and is about to sign his autograph.

Tony What's your name?
Lady elbows him out of the way aggressively.

Fan Get out of the way, you. Where's Tony?
Calling into washroom.

Fan Tony, Tony!

INT. THE NAG'S HEAD. NIGHT
Raquel and Albert are seated at a table. Boycie and Mike are seated at another table. Del and Rodney enter.

Rodney I can't believe that was the same bloke.

Del Yeah. It's just costume props. They all use 'em. You don't think Mr Spock's ears are his own, do you? (Now at table) Great news, Raquel. I've found your singing partner.

Raquel Oh God!

Del What? He's terrific, ain't he, Rodney?

Rodney Eh? Yeah.

Del You gotta see him to believe him, ain't you, Rodney?

Rodney Yeah.

Del He's got a tremendous voice, great stage presence and oodles of charisma. He's a star in the making, Raquel, and I'm talking international.

Albert Where d'you learn about him?

Rodney He works with Trigger at the council depot.

Stage Fright

Raquel Is that true?

Del Sean Connery was a dustman.

Raquel And is he like Sean Connery?

Del Well, he wears a wig. I'll get the drinks. Give us a hand, Rodney.

They move to the bar. As they approach, we see the smiling Mike and Boycie nudge each other in a 'Here he comes' manner. They are going to wind Del up.

Boycie Del Boy! I hear you're in court tomorrow.

Del Ssh!

Boycie Don't do a lot for your yuppy image, does it?

Del Oh I don't know. It's quite trendy nowadays. All the Big Bang boys did a bit of stir.

Rodney Yes, it's very fashionable in the City. Computer fraud, insider dealings, stock manipulation.

Mike What you up for, Del?

Del Fly-pitching. It's a 50 quid fine and a slap on the wrist. Occupational hazard when you're upwardly mobile.

Boycie I hear Raquel's up the spout? Congratulations

Del Thank you, Boycie. Michael, our usual and whatever you two are having.

Boycie Of course, it ain't easy being a father.

Del No, I remember the trouble you had. All them test tubes and what have you.

Boycie *(Cuts in)* I am not talking about that, Derek! I mean looking after your child's welfare, planning for his future... Have you thought about all that?

Del My kid'll be alright. Don't worry about it, Boyce.

Mike Then there's the pregnancy itself. That can be nine months of hell.

Del With your missus I imagine it was, Mike!

Boycie Of course I was lucky. Marlene gave birth after only eight months.

Rodney Yeah, well they say it's quicker by tube...

Del We've just come back from the Down By The Riverside Club. We heard Trigger's mate singing. He's good, ain't he, Rodney?

Rodney Yeah...

Mike Perhaps Trigger could recommend him to Eric. *(Laughs)*

Boycie laughs.

Del Eric? What, from the Starlite Rooms?

Boycie Yeah, the one who don't like you. Something to do with 500 quid.

Del That was years ago!

Boycie But that man holds a grudge. Anyway, he's got 24 hours to fill a cabaret spot for tomorrow night.

Mike He'll never do it. I mean, the word's out now.

Boycie Well, he'd better come up with something. I've heard Eugene Macarthy's really looking forward to it.

Mike and Boycie laugh.

Del tries to hold back the feeling of a nauseating panic.

Rodney Who's Eugene Macarthy?

Boycie A local villain and not a very nice man. Rumour has it that the SAS pays Eugene protection money.

Del But what the hell's Eugene gotta do with all this?

Boycie Didn't you hear?

Del What?

Boycie Well, Eugene owns the Starlite Rooms.

Del No, no. Eric owns the club!

Mike Eugene bought him out three months ago.

Del looks horrified.

Boycie I mean, there was no boardroom negotiations, offer and counter-offer. Eugene gave Eric choices – take it or I'll nail you to a door. Eric – realising that he was dealing with a man who puts out death sentences on Muslims – took it.

Mike Anyway, tomorrow night is Eugene's mum's 82nd birthday. So he's throwing a

party at the Starlite Rooms for her and all the nasties.

Del No, it can't be right, Mike. Eric's still at the club!

Mike He's just the manager now.

Boycie Yeah, and part of Eric's managerial duties is booking the cabaret. But every time he booked an act Eugene didn't like, he would be promptly nailed to the nearest door.

Mike So he came up with a brilliant solution. He started employing the services of local entertainment agencies, so if Eugene was displeased he took his wrath on the agent. Eventually, the agents held a meeting in a convalescent home and decided to boycott the Starlite Rooms.

Boycie So unless Eric finds a mug to supply the cabaret for Eugene's mum's party, B&Q'll be selling another door.

Del and Rodney move to the bar.

Del We're in a little bit of trouble here, bruv.

Rodney Yeah... We?

Del We've signed a contract guaranteeing to supply the cabaret!

Rodney I've signed nothing! I'm just the sweeper and the tea-boy!

Del I've been thinking about what you said. You deserve a more creative role in all this.

Rodney And I've been thinking about it as well, and I don't wanna more creative role! Gimme the broom, the teapot and the 50 quid and I'm happy!

Del Well, thank you very much, Rodney.

Rodney It's my pleasure, Derek!

INT. DRESSING ROOM AT THE STARLITE ROOMS. NIGHT

A very worried Raquel is seated in front of the mirror wearing her stage clothes. There is a knock at the door.

Raquel Come in.

Rodney, dressed up for the evening, enters.

Raquel *(Desperate)* Is Del here yet?

Rodney No. I phoned the flat but there's no reply. Perhaps he's still in court.

Raquel But it's nine o'clock!

Rodney Maybe the jury's still out.

Raquel Don't be stupid, Rodney! He's only been charged with unlicensed trading!

Rodney Well, he's not here anyway.

Raquel I can't go through with this.

Rodney Why not?

Raquel What do you mean, why not? You were at rehearsals this morning. You know what happened! Tony's... got a problem.

Rodney Well, they might not notice.

Raquel Of course they'll notice! How can they not notice?

Rodney You've gotta go through with it for Del's sake! Eugene Macarthy's out there with his mum!

Raquel Who's Eugene Macarthy?

Rodney He's not nice people, Raquel.

Raquel Well, you go and tell Eugene Macarthy and his mum that the cabaret's off!

Rodney Me? I'm just the roadie! Sweep up and make tea, that was my instructions. D'you fancy a cup of tea?

Raquel No, I don't!

Rodney D'you want anything swept up?

Raquel No.

Rodney Well, that's me finished.

Rodney exits.

INT. THE STARLITE ROOMS. NIGHT

Diners are sipping brandies and puffing on after-dinner cigars. The men all look like villains. Rodney moves to the bar. Del, in evening suit, arrives.

Rodney Where the hell have you been?

Del My case got put back to last. They fined me 65 quid then I discovered I'd left me wallet at home. So I phoned Sinbad and told him to bring it down. He only got a bus! I'm banged up in the cells waiting for

Stage Fright

Albert and he's out there in the Friday night rush hour on a bleedin' bus! Anyway, I popped home, changed me suit and…

Rodney *(Cuts in)* Will you shut up for a minute? We have got problems!

Del Problems? What sorta problems?

As Rodney is about to explain, Eugene Macarthy appears at Del's shoulder. Eugene is 45, big and never smiles.

Eugene Del Boy.

Del *(Startled by Eugene's sudden appearance)* Eugene! How lovely to see you.

Eugene Eric informs me that you're supplying tonight's cabaret? I hope it's good, Del. It's my old mum's birthday and I don't wanna see her disappointed.

Del Have no fears, Eugene. It's the best, the very best. Would I give your mum anything less? *(About to introduce Rodney)* Oh by the way, this is…

Rodney *(Cuts in)* I'm the road manager. I just make the tea and sweep up. I'm nothing to do with the artistic contents or anything like that.

Eugene Well, here's to a good evening.

Del Yes. Sit back and enjoy, Eugene.

Eugene moves off towards his table. Eric, in evening suit, appears on stage and takes the mike as the backing duo quietly set up their equipment in the background.

Eric Ladies and gentlemen, welcome to the cabaret hour! Before I introduce our stars for the evening, may I just say happy birthday, Mrs Macarthy – Eugene's mum. Happy birthday, Lil.

We see Mrs Macarthy – she is 82 and, like Eugene who is sitting next to her, never smiles. All the other diners raise their glasses and say, "Happy birthday, Lil".

Eric We're proud to present tonight a couple of young British singers whose names you may not be familiar with. But if you were a resident of a certain town in Nevada, USA, their names would be on the tips of your tongues. For they have just finished a sell-out season on the same bill as Barry Manilow at the world-famous Desert Inn, Las Vegas!

Applause.

Rodney Where's he get all that crap from? *(He looks at Del)* What a stupid question.

Eric And we're proud to say that of all the venues to start their British tour they have chosen the Starlite Rooms, Peckham. So a big welcome for – Raquel and Tony.

Applause as Raquel and Tony take the stage. Del applauds wildly and whistles. Rodney claps politely.

Raquel's nerves now appear to have gone. She is the complete professional.

Raquel *(Sings)* I was alright for a while. I could smile for a while. But when I saw you last night, You held my hand so tight, When you stopped to say hello, And though you wished me well, You couldn't tell, That I'd been cry…ing, over you, Cry…ing, over you, Then you said so long, Left me standing all alone, Alone and crying… crying… crying… cry…ing. It's hard to understand, But the touch of your hand, Can start me crying…

Del She's bloody good, ain't she, Rodney?

Rodney Cosmic!

Tony begins and acts like a Tom Jones with dramatic movements and over-the-top gestures.

Tony I thought that I was over you, But tell me now, what can I do? I love you even more, than I did before, So, dah'ling, what can I do…oo? You don't love me,

And I'll always be,
Cwy...ing, over you...

Raquel looks in Del's direction with a glare.

*Eugene and his mum are staring at the
stage but their expressions tell nothing.*

Tony Yes, now you are gone,
And from this moment on,
I'll be cwying.

Raquel Crying.

*We see Eric grinning smugly at Del's
discomfiture*

Tony Cwying.

Raquel Cwy... crying.

Tony Cwy...ing.

Raquel and Tony Cwy...ing...Cwy...ing
O...ver y...o...u.

*The number ends to a deafening silence.
Nobody in the audience knows what to
make of it.*

Rodney *(To Del)* What d' you reckon, then?

Del I... I... I'll see you later, bruv.

*Rodney begins to clap. He is joined by a
few others and finally the whole
audience applauds politely. Del exits.
Raquel's glare follows him.*

INT. THE TROTTERS' LOUNGE. NIGHT

One hour later.

*Del is facing the floor, agitated, fright-
ened, puffing nervously on a cigar and
sipping a cocktail. Albert is seated in
an armchair.*

Albert So how comes you didn't know he
had trouble with his Rs?

Del Because he never told me! All he said
was he only enjoyed singing certain songs.
You can see what he meant now. He only
sings songs without Rs in 'em!

Albert So he chose the songs for tonight?

Del Well... I mean... I didn't know, did I?
Gawd knows what Eugene and his mum
thought! *(Looks at door to hall)* I never did
like that front door anyway.

*The front door closes and Rodney and
Raquel enter from the hall.*

Raquel *(To Del)* You bastard! You just
walked out and left us!

Del Well, what did you expect me to do?
Go over to Eugene's table and say, "That
was different, weren't it?" Did you carry on
with the performance?

Raquel Oh yes, Derek, we saw it through
to the death. *Please Welease Me,
Congwatulations* and *The Gween Gween
Gwass of Home.*

Rodney Followed by a medley of wock
'n' woll!

Del This is not funny, Wodney – Rodney!!

Rodney I thought it was hilarious!
(Referring to Albert) I ain't laughed so much
since he caught his beard in the food mixer.

The front door bell rings.

Del Answer that, Albert. If it's Eugene,
tell him I've just gone to get the hammer
and nails!

Albert *(Calls towards front door)*
Who's there?

Tony *(OOV)* Can I speak to Mr Twotter?

Raquel It's Tony. Let him in.

*Albert opens the door to Tony, who is
wearing his stage clothes.*

Tony I've come for my money!

Del I'm up to my eyes in it at the moment,
son. We'll talk about it tomorrow.

Tony No, not tomorrow. I want my money
now! I did the performance, didn't I? I did
the wepertoire that you... you insisted on.

Del But I didn't know you couldn't
pronounce your Rs!

Tony What does that matter?

Albert It matters quite a lot when you're
singing songs with Rs in!

Tony But I don't sing songs with Rs in!
And if a song has got an R in it I change
the lywics!

Del Well, why didn't you change the
lywics tonight?

Stage Fright

Tony How can I change the lyrics to *Cwying*? The bloody song's called *Cwying*!

Raquel Tony and I did everything you asked us to do, Del, so pay the man his money. And while we're at it, you owe me money as well.

Del Let's talk about it tomorrow, sweetheart.

Raquel Listen, Trotter, you're not cheating me!

Del Oh! It's alright for me to be cheated though, innit?

Rodney Who's cheated you?

Del (*At first he cannot answer this… Now referring to Albert*) He charged me £1.40 for fares! I only realised as I was putting me dickie bow on, he's got a free bus pass! And I can't see the Starlite Rooms paying me anything after tonight's disaster! I'll end up out of pocket!

Tony We signed a contwact!

Del Yes, but my brother drew that contract up and he included a get-out clause, didn't you, Rodders?

Rodney No.

Del Why not?

Rodney 'Cos you didn't tell me to. Anyway, I'm not a lawyer. I make the tea and sweep up, remember? And you owe me 50 quid!

Del produces a wad of notes.

Del (*Hands Tony some money*) Here are… (*Hands cash to Raquel*) There you go, darling.

We see that Del has only a fiver left. A look is shared between him and Rodney.

Rodney (*In an assertive, angry manner*) We'll talk about this tomorrow!

Del Anything you say, Rodney.

Tony You know what you've got, Del? You've got an 'ism'.

Del An 'ism'? I ain't got one of them, have I?

Rodney Dunno, there's a load of old crap in that garage.

Tony You're not alone with your pwejudice. We've got sexism, wacecism, sizeism and ageism. Well, I'm a victim of pwonunciationism! I've got a good voice! I've got a good style. I've got a perfect tone. But just because I pwonounce my Rs differently fwom the west of you I can never be a star! Just because of my pwonunciation you've dumped me!

Del And how'd you think I feel? I got lumbered with a 'star' whose props come from (*Indicates feet*) Lilley & Skinner (*Head*) Crown Toppers (*Groin*) and Mattesons!

Tony But you can always find another singer. I'm stuck with my pwoblem. No one who pwonounces Rs like me have ever become successful.

Albert There's Roy Jenkins and Jonathan Ross.

Tony Exactly… (*He opens his mouth as if he has something important to say, then realizes there is little point…*) Don't matter… See you, Del.

Del Take care, son.

Tony Waquel.

Raquel Bye, Tony.

Tony Wodney.

Rodney gestures goodbye. Tony leaves.

Del Well, don't look at me like that! I didn't create this pronunciationism! It's them – the public! I think you should be able to say what you want and how you want. It's a free country.

Albert Del's right. It ain't his fault.

Del Thank you, Unc. Help yourself to a brandy.

Albert moves to bar. The phone rings.

Del (*Without thinking, he answers*) Hello? (*Reacts and curses himself for answering*) Eugene! How nice of you to call. Actually I was gonna give you a bell in the morning… Yes… Yes, I did notice that. Funny enough,

I've just been discussing it with my road manager… Mmh! Did she? Well, I can't say I blame her… Really? How is she now? Good… Yes… Of course… I'll be there first thing in the morning… Bonjour, Eugene. *(He switches the phone off and ponders the conversation)*

Rodney D'you wanna hide eight pairs of pliers in yer pocket?

Del *(To Raquel)* He wants to book you and Tony on a five-week contract!

Raquel He what?

Del His mum liked you.

Raquel You're kidding!

Del No, straight up. He said she ain't laughed so much in years!

Del rushes to the window and opens it. He calls down towards the tower block's entrance.

Del Hang about, Tony! I've got you some more bookings! Stick with me, son, I'll make you wich!

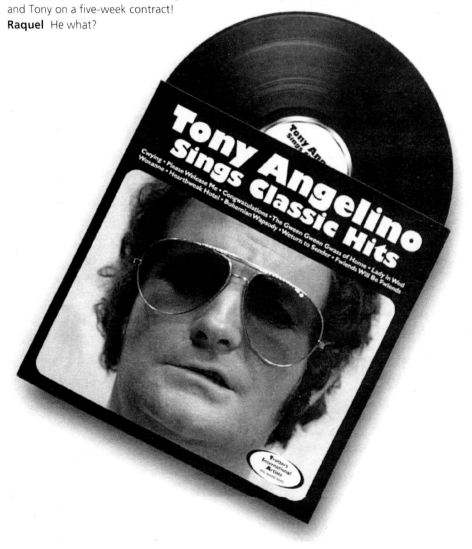

Stage Fright

 200

INT. A NIGHTCLUB

A sign reads "Auditions. Please report to back door". The owner and manager of the club (both tough-looking characters of 45) are seated facing the stage, on which a 20-year-old girl is singing accompanied by the club's pianist. Seated at the bar are Del, excited and power-dressed, and Rodney, bored and casually dressed. The girl is singing 'Feelings'.

Del *(Quietly to Rodney)* She ain't a lotta cop, is she?

Rodney I honestly ain't got a clue, Del. I don't even know why you brought me here.

Del Well, you're out of work, Rodney, so what else would you be doing at 10 o'clock in the morning? Laying in your pit playing tent! I thought you'd like to come along here and give Raquel a bit of encouragement.

Rodney Encouragement? Have you heard the song she's chosen for her audition? I mean, it's ridiculous, stupid!

Del I chose that song!

Rodney Did you? Well, that explains it!

Del It's a beautiful song.

Rodney It's hardly appropriate.

Del Of course it's appropriate. The old numbers are coming back.

Owner *(Calls to the girl singer)* Yes, thank you, love, thank you. Next. *(Calls)* Raquel Turner.

Raquel enters the stage and smiles nervously to Del and Rodney. Del smiles proudly. Rodney returns the nervous smile.

Owner *(To Del)* Are you her agent?

Del Yes, I am. *(Hands owner his introduction card)* Derek Trotter of the Trotter International Star Agency, Peckham.

'You want 'em, we got 'em.' That's our motto. D'you know Shirley Bassey?

Owner Well, not personally.

Del *(Winks and crosses his fingers)* Like that, like that!

The pianist plays the opening bars to 'Chapel Of Love'.

Raquel *(Sings)* I'm going to the chapel and I'm gonna get married. Going to the chapel and I'm gonna get married

She now turns slightly and we see she is five months pregnant.

We see the shocked reactions of the owner. He looks to Rodney and Del.

Owner *(Calls to Raquel – loud)* Next!

Del is bemused, Rodney embarrrassed.

THE TROTTERS' LOUNGE. DAY

Albert is lying asleep in the armchair. There are two large cardboard boxes, one on top of the other. Large printing on the box reads 'Futafax. The fax machine of tomorrow – today'. Stencilled across the boxes is the word 'reject'. Beneath this is a white square of glued-on paper upon which is printed 'Lot 41'. On the bar is one of the fax machines. The machine begins printing out a message with much flashing of red and green lights and overloud printing sound. It prints out a short message. Now all the lights go out, accompanied by an electronic beep which slowly dies. The front door opens. Albert immediately wakes up, is out of the chair and running a carpet sweeper over the rug. Rodney and Raquel enter from the hall.

Rodney Alright, Unc?

Albert Phew, I haven't stopped since you went out. How'd the audition go?

Raquel Don't ask! Just don't ask! He got me up on the stage and got me singing "I'm going to the chapel and I'm going to get married". Look at me!

Del enters.

Del I think it was your choice of song, Raquel. Next time we'll choose something more modern. Maybe a Madonna number.

Raquel How about *Like a Virgin*?

Del Yeah, something like that!…Here, you shouldn't be standing up for too long in your condition. Come and sit down. Try this one, it's nice and warm. *(Del looks at Albert)*

Albert grins nervously.

Raquel I was gonna make some tea.

Del Don't worry about that. I'll make a pot of tea. Rodney, make a pot of tea.

Rodeny How come I've gotta do it?

Del Because Raquel's pregnant and your Uncle's knackered!

Rodney Yes, and I'm supposed to be out of work!

Albert But it's not compulsory, Rodney. The government do allow you to make a pot of tea.

Rodney What I'm saying, Unc, is, what about Brian Epstein there?

Del I've got all my correspondence to catch up with.

Rodney What, one letter! And that's for Raquel!

Raquel I'll make the tea.

Raquel exits to the kitchen

Del It's alright for some little dipstick who's got nothing better to do than jolly it up down the pub every night and crawl out of bed when he hears the theme to *Home And Away*! But me, I'm a trailblazer, a captain of industry. I'm dealing with clients who run organizations that are household names.

Rodney Yeah, like Parkhurst!

Del None of my mates are in Parkhurst, Rodney!

Rodney A captain of industry! More like a bloody stowaway! You get off on this yuppy image, don't yer? I mean, what's the latest brainwave? Fax machines.

Albert They're handy things to have, Rodney!

Rodney For normal people, yes! But he don't know anyone who's got another fax machine! That's why, in the two months he's been wired up to the worldwide digital miracle, he ain't had one message! *(Looks at machine and reacts)* You've got a message on your fax machine, Del.

Del Ah! How's it feel to be a plonker, Rodney? This could have come from anywhere! New York, Rome, Toronto! *(Reads message)* It's from Mike at the Nag's Head. See, he had the foresight to buy one of my machines and he's double-glad he did! *(Reads more of the message)* Cor, he's a moaner, ain't he? 'Machine not working pro…' What's he want for 45 quid? What about this, then? I've only been invited to a school reunion.

Albert You're kidding.

Del No, straight up. It's the pupils of class 4C who left the Martin Luther King Comprehensive in 1962. *(To Albert)* That used to be the old Dockside secondary modern. That's a turn-up for the book, innit? I'm gonna see all my old mates.

Rodney D'you suffer with seasickness?

Del No, why?

Rodney It can get choppy on that Isle of Wight ferry.

Del This is the last time I tell you, Rodney, my mates are not in bloody Parkhurst! Anyway, the reunion's tonight at the Nag's Head. *(Calls)* Here, Raquel, you'll never guess!

Del exits to the kitchen.
Raquel is rereading the letter and looking deeply worried.
Del enters.

The Class of '62

Del My old school are only having a reunion tonight at the Nag's Head. What's up?

Raquel Nothing.

Del There's something bothering you, ain't there? I can tell. Is it the audition? 'Cos that geezer was well out of…

Raquel *(Cuts in)* No! Nothing to do with that. It's this letter. It's from my solicitors. They've managed to trace my husband and told him that I've started divorce proceedings.

Del Good… And what's he say about it?

Raquel His solicitors said that he is considering his response.

Del There's nothing he can do about it, sweetheart. I mean, you broke up with him eight years ago. In all that time have you ever seen him or heard from him?

Raquel No, nothing. But you don't know him like I do! He can be horrible when he wants to be! I wish you'd never suggested starting divorce proceedings.

Del Look, don't worry about your old man, Raquel. He can't hurt you, darling. He don't even know where you live. And even if he did, he's gonna have to get past me first. So let's just leave it to the solicitors, eh? Let them… solicit. I want our relationship to be pukka – married and all the exes. *(Indicating her lump)* I know that little faceache in there weren't planned, but, well, he's here now.

Raquel Or her.

Del Or her. And if I was any more happy about it I'd be dangerous. You and him…

Raquel *(Cuts in)* Or…

Del *(Cuts in)* … her – you're the best thing that's happened to me since… well, since my mum died.

Raquel ponders this compliment.

Del D'you understand what I'm saying?

Raquel Well… I think so.

Del So stop worrying, eh? Promise?

Raquel Alright, Del, you know best.

Del Good girl. You know it makes sense.
He kisses her gently.

Del You know I'd do anything for you – anything.

Raquel Alright. Promise me you won't get drunk with your mates tonight.

Del On your bike.

ROOM ABOVE THE NAG'S HEAD. NIGHT

Food and drinks are laid out on a table. Del and Denzil are seated and looking bored and uncomfortable. Boycie is pacing and checking his watch. Rodney is seated in the corner sipping a beer and smoking a roll-up.

Boycie This is bloody ridiculous. The reunion was supposed to start at 7.30 and look, it's almost 8.10.

Denzil Who's organised all this?
Mike enters carrying more food.

Mike Ain't he here yet?

Denzil Who?

Mike Your host. The bloke who paid for all this. He said he'd arrive late. He wants to make a bit of an entrance – surprise you all.

Del Come on, Michael, who is it? You can tell us.

Mike I don't know, Del. He just came in yesterday and said he wanted to book a room for a school reunion. That reminds me, I wanna have a word with you about that bloody fax machine you sold me!

Del Yes, yes, Michael! I'm rather busy at the moment. I'll fax you about it during the week.

Boycie *(To Mike)* So what was this bloke's name?

Mike I didn't catch it.

Denzil But didn't you write his name on the receipt and in your accounts?

Mike Er, no, I forgot.

Boycie In other words, he paid in cash?

Mike Yeah.

Denzil What's he look like? Was he tall?

Mike Yeah, tallish.

Del Did he have a scar running down from the bridge of his nose to his mouth?

Boycie And his right ear was missing?

Mike Not that I noticed.

Del It's not our old headmaster, then.

Denzil How can it be our old headmaster? The doctors said he'd never be allowed back into society.

The door slowly opens. They all look towards it with apprehension.

Trigger enters.

Del, Boycie and Denzil Trigger!

Trigger Alright?

Del Wait a minute. Maybe Trigger organised this!

Boycie Oh turn it up, Del Boy. Trigger couldn't organise a prayer in a mosque.

Trigger I got lost on me way here.

Denzil How could you get lost? You've been coming to this pub since you were 16!

Trigger No, I found the pub alright. I meant I couldn't find this room. *(To Mike)* I've been in your dance hall for the last hour.

Mike But all the lights are out!

Trigger I know.

Boycie You've been standing in the dark for an hour?

Trigger Yeah! I thought we were all gonna jump out and surprise someone.

Mike But there was no one else in there.

Trigger But I didn't know that, did I? The lights were out! How you going, Dave?

Rodney Alright, Trig.

Mike Well, I'll send your man up as soon as he arrives. In the meantime, enjoy yourselves.

Mike exits.

Rodney This is a bit of a mystery, isn't it? It's like something out of an Agatha Christie film.

Del, Boycie and Denzil *(Beginning to worry)* Yeah!

Trigger I used to fancy her.

Rodney I mean, think about it. Someone has arranged for you four to be in the same room at the same time…

(To Trigger) You used to fancy Agatha Christie?

Trigger Yeah. I had a picture of her on my bedroom wall.

Denzil But she was an old lady. All English country gardens and granny hats.

Del That's right. She looked like Mr Kipling's bit on the side.

Trigger Well, I fancied her. I saw her in that film *Doctor Zhivago*.

Boycie That's Julie Christie, you berk!

Trigger Yeah, well, whatever, I liked her.

Rodney *(Trying to brighten them up)* As I was saying. On a cold, rainy night in Peckham, someone has arranged for you four to be here in this room – together. No one knows who. And the most frightening aspect of the whole mystery – no one knows why! Now, think hard. Who would do something like that?

The four look at each other.

Trigger Jeremy Beadle?

Boycie Jeremy bloody Beadle!

Rodney Don't be stupid!

Del Don't try and frighten us, Rodney, 'cos it won't work!

Denzil Well, I'm gonna shoot off now!

Rodney starts laughing at Denzil's fear.

Del *(Who is hiding his fear and trying to maintain safety in numbers)* You can't go, Denzil!

Denzil I wasn't at your school for long! Me mum and dad didn't even come down to London 'til I was 13! I don't feel I really qualify as one of the old boys!

Boycie Did you get an invitation?

Denzil Yeah.

Boycie Then you're stopping!

The Class of '62

Denzil It's just that I've got a thought going round my head.

Boycie Well, lend it to Trigger.

Denzil Say – just say – our old headmaster... has escaped!

This strikes fear into Del, Boycie and Rodney.

Rodney Look, I'm just gonna see how Albert is.

Del You stay right where you are! Strength in numbers, that's my motto!

Other than Rodney, they all have their backs to the door. We see the door open slightly and a man's hand enters and switches the lights off.

Denzil Oh, bloody hell!

Boycie What's happening?

Del Alright, alright, take it easy!

Rodney Switch the lights on, Del.

Del Shuddup.

The door slowly opens. Silhouetted against the bright lights from the hallway is the tall figure of a man wearing a long black overcoat.

Denzil It's our headmaster! It's bend-over Benson!

Del Well, if it is he's grown another ear from somewhere.

The man steps forward into the room and switches the lights back on.
We see it is Slater.
This is the new, born-again-Christian Slater. He is decent and repentant.

Slater *(Big, friendly grin)* Surprise, surprise!
We see the horrified reactions of the guys.

Del and Boycie Slater!

Slater I had you going, didn't I? Be honest, I had you this time! Of all your old classmates you never guessed Roy Slater would be here!

Del What the hell are you doing back, Slater?

Slater Oh come on, Del Boy. I've gone to a lot of trouble here.

Boycie You mean you organised this reunion?

Slater Yeah. I was in town and I thought it'd be a nice way to catch up with me old mates. Hear Marlene's had a nipper!

Boycie *(Immediately defensive)* What about it?

Slater Well, nothing. Just congratulations. I know you and her have been dreaming of having a baby for years. It's... it's nice. And, Rodney.

Rodney *(Alarmed)* What?

Slater You've got married!

Rodney I know!

Slater Look, you don't have to be on the defensive with me, son. I'm pleased for you.

Rodney Yeah, well the marriage hasn't really worked...

Del *(Cuts in)* Don't tell him! He'll find a way of using it against yer!

Slater Look, Del, I haven't come here to upset things! It's just a little get-together, that's all. Can't we at least be friendly?

Del Friendly? With a snide like you! I wish it had been our old headmaster now!

Denzil I wish it had been Jeremy Beadle!

Boycie I thought you were in Parkhurst!

Slater I got paroled six months ago.

Trigger You back in the police force now, Roy?

Slater No, Trig. They wouldn't have me back. Not since I was found guilty of diamond smuggling and given a five-year prison sentence. The police are funny about things like that. I've been living in Colchester, working for an undertaker – hence the coat. By the looks on your faces, I wish I'd brought my tape measure. Fancy a drink?

Boycie No thanks, Roy. I've got a prior engagement with the downstairs toilet.

Del *(Referring to Slater)* Save yerself a journey. The biggest karsy's up here!

Rodney Yeah, I've gotta be off as well,

chief inspector. My uncle promised to tell me all about the war.

Slater Wait a minute! Let's get a few things straight. I'm not a chief inspector any more. I'm just an ordinary bloke. I can't do you any harm and I don't mean you any harm. I know you'll laugh, but... I've changed.

The others laugh derisively.

Slater A man doesn't go to this expense without good reason. I know this may sound ridiculous – but, if it were possible, I'd like to wipe the slate clean.

Del Wipe the slate clean! After what you've done to us in the past? At some time or another you fitted all of us up on some Mickey Mouse charge!

Slater I know, Del, I know! That's why I kept my guest list to just you lot. You're the ones who deserve my biggest apologies. I wish I could turn the clock back.

Del So do I! To about half-past six this evening, then I'd have stayed in and watched the telly! You nicked me, Denzil and Boycie once for possession of stolen property.

Boycie Yeah, and we'd bought it off you!

Slater I know. And... I'm sorry.

Boycie Sorry!

Denzil With the greatest respect, ex-chief inspector, stuff your apologies.

Rodney I remember when you followed me in the van and nicked me for doing 70 miles an hour in a built-up area. It was just my word against yours and guess who the magistrates believed! I mean, that van wouldn't reach 70 if you pushed it off a cliff!

Del reacts to this insult to his beloved van.

Slater Rodney, I'm sorry.

Rodney Yeah, well, shove it, Slater, shove it!

Denzil What about the time you planted 3,000 Green Shield stamps on Trigger and

he went away for 18 months in a young offenders' home?

Slater I'm sorry, Trig.

Trigger Oh that's alright, Roy.

Slater I always wanted to be mates with you lot but you, sort of, spurned me. I wanted to hurt you for not liking me. If you can't join 'em, beat 'em, that was my attitude. So the police force became my god. But in the end even my own colleagues got sick of me and my – ambitions! I knew my days were numbered. I began to panic. I felt as if the whole thing was coming to a premature conclusion. No pun intended, Boycie.

Boycie at first nods understandingly, then reacts.

Slater I was worried about my future – financial security, that sort of thing. So I turned to crime. I got meself involved in that diamond smuggling caper, and – as I of all people should have known – I got collared. I had three and a half years in a 10ft by 6ft prison cell to work out where I'd gone wrong in life! While in prison I found Jesus.

Del What, they fitted him up too?

Slater Well, to be more precise, Jesus found me. It was about that time I got a message to say my old man had passed away.

Del Yeah, I know, Roy. I went to his funeral.

Slater Thanks, Del. I wish I could have gone.

Trigger Why didn't you?

Denzil He most probably didn't have a black suit and a bloody big ladder on him! He was in nick, Trig!

Trigger No, I thought they let you out for acts of God like funerals and weddings.

Slater I applied for temporary compassionate release. Then my mum wrote to the governor.

The Class of '62

Denzil And he wouldn't let you out?

Slater Not after what that old cow put in her letter! You see, even my own mother's against me! Pathetic, innit? My own… Perhaps this reunion weren't such a good idea after all. You look a bit embarrassed. Go on, you shoot off. I'll hang around. I've gotta sort the money out with the guv'nor.

The good guys now look at each other, struggling with their common sense and common decency.

Del Go on then, Sla… Roy. I'll have a drink with you before I go.

Slater *(Moved by Del's magnanimity)* Thank you, Derek. What about you other fellers? Will you break bread with me?

Rodney I'd prefer a Southern Comfort.

Denzil Have you two gone mad?

Del What harm can he do? He's an undertaker's tea-boy!

Denzil Yeah, he's still putting bodies away!

Boycie You don't honestly believe he's changed, do you?

Rodney Personally, I'm not sure. But I'll always give someone the chance to prove it! *(Now as a show of unity with Slater)* Make that a double, Roy.

Denzil Alright, I'll have a lager… Trigger?

Trigger Yeah, I'll have a beer.

Boycie *(To Trigger)* How can you drink with Slater? That's the man who stitched you up with them knocked-off Green Shield stamps and sent you away for 18 months!

Trigger I know. But when I come out I got an electric blanket and a radio with 'em. *(Winks)*

Del *(To Boycie)* A cognac?

Boycie *(Nods)* And quick!

INT. THE TROTTERS' LOUNGE. NIGHT

Old photographs are scattered over the floor and sticking out of ancient shoeboxes and albums which lie among the empty beer cans.
Bowls of peanuts, half-eaten pizzas and overflowing ashtrays. Del, Rodney, Boycie, Denzil, Trigger and Slater have all had too much to drink. Albert, in his pyjamas and dressing gown, is trying to catch them up. Boycie is speaking to Marlene on his mobile phone. In the background the others are laughing at the old photos.

Boycie *(On phone)* It's simple, Marlene. You can pick me up when you drop Raquel back here. No, I am not drunk! None of us are drunk!

Rodney *(Calls)* Del is!

Del Shuddup, Rodney!

Rodney *(To Del)* You promised your loved one you wouldn't get drunk!

Albert Why do women always say 'Don't get drunk'?

Denzil It's their nature. My Corinne was always saying it – before she left me.

Rodney Yeah, and my Cassandra.

Albert My Ada was the same.

Trigger And they wonder why their marriages break up.

Slater Take my advice. The only sure way to avoid a broken marriage is don't turn up for the wedding!

They all laugh.

Boycie *(Hand over mouthpiece)* Keep the noise down, will yer. The women might hear! We don't want them thinking we're enjoying ourselves! *(On phone)* Yes, I've had a couple of drinks. It's a school reunion, innit? Alright, I'll see you in a minute. *(Switches the phone off)*

Rodney Who's for another drink?

Boycie Not for me. I'll get me coat on. Marlene'll be here in a minute.

Slater It's funny, but I've looked at all these photos of the boys, my old mates, enjoying themselves at various stages of their lives… and I'm not in one of them.

Denzil Well, you were busy, Roy. *(One photo)* I mean, when we took this one you were at police training college.

Del *(Another photo)* And when that one was taken you were in nick.

Albert I suppose it was tough for you inside, eh? Specially when they found out you were an ex-copper.

Slater You don't know the half of it. It was a nightmare. Every mealtime they lined up against the wall as I passed. 'Snide, snide!' They'd whisper. 'We're gonna get you, snide. Hope your wife can sew, Slater.'

Boycie Didn't the warders do nothing?

Slater That was the warders! The convicts really had it in for me – 24 hours a day you're watching your back – specially in the shower room!

Del Yeah, I've heard there's a few bandidos in there.

Slater Oh yeah! It's no wonder Oscar Wilde wrote a poem about it! You'd be amazed what they'd sell for a king-size fag and a box of matches. Fortunately they didn't give me any problems. I mean, these days even the poofs don't fancy me.

They all laugh.

Del Here's a photo with you in it, Roy. Look, it's the old school football team.

Boycie Look at that! How old were we? 14?...There's little Del Boy with his Roger Daltry haircut!

Del I was your midfield dynamo. I used to play like Paul Gascoigne. There's Boycie – he used to play like Bamber Gascoigne!

Trigger There's that Italian kid. Good player. What was his name?

A car horn is heard beeping outside.

Boycie That'll be Marlene.

Trigger Could you drop us off home, Boyce?

Denzil Yeah, and me.

Boycie This is not a bleedin' minicab service! Come on, then!

Trigger See yer then, Roy.

Boycie Yeah, see you Sla... Roy.

Slater We'll have a pint in the week, eh?

Boycie Well, er... we'll be in the pub sometime or another.

Slater It's a date, then.

Del I'll get you a copy made of this, Roy. This is most probably the last time you was with all your mates. Look at us. We had Denzil in goal. We had Monkey Harris at right back. There's a feeling about this photo. We had... camaraderie.

Trigger Was that the Italian boy?

Del Yeah, that was him, Trig!

Boycie Come on, Trigger!

Boycie, Denzil and Trigger exit.

Del Do you want another one, Rodders?

Rodney Why not?

Del Roy?

They turn to see Slater fast asleep on the settee.

Del I don't believe it. The Prodigal Plonker's gone to kip!

Rodney How we gonna get him home?

Albert Where's he staying?

Del Some bed and breakfast, he didn't say where. Better let him sleep it off 'til morning.

Albert That's not a bad idea. I'm gonna climb in.

Albert exits to bedroom.

Del You know, if someone had said to me that one day I'd be having a drink and a laugh with Roy Slater, I'd have said they were off their bloody heads.

Rodney I suppose he's not such a bad bloke after all.

Del No. Take away the uniform and the badges and he's just as scared as the rest of us. I'll get some ice.

Del exits to the kitchen.

Rodney sits back in the chair and looks at the soccer photo. He smiles and slowly his eyes close. His head rests on the back

The Class of '62

of the chair and he drifts into sleep.
Slater snores loudly. There are crisps,
nuts, pizzas, glasses, photos, beer cans
and bodies. The front door closes and
Raquel enters from the hall. At first she
doesn't notice Slater on the settee. She
reacts horrified to the state of the room.

Raquel I don't belie... Rodney, where's...
She now jumps back as Slater lets out a
particularly loud snore. Raquel is horrified
to find the body on the sofa.
She hear ice cubes clinking into glasses in
the kitchen. Del is singing as Raquel
enters the kitchen.

Del *(Reacts to the look on her face)*
I'm not drunk!

Raquel Where's he come from?

Del Who? Oh Roy? From the pub. I said
come back for a drink.

Raquel You rotten sod! All the promises
you made me!

Del Oh sweetheart! You didn't believe that
stuff about two halves of shandy and
midnight Mass did you?

Raquel *(Almost in tears)* You're like all the
others! Your promises mean nothing!
Bloody nothing!

Del Look, you shouldn't get excited in
your condition. It's bad for the baby! Have
a drink.

Raquel I don't wanna drink! I thought I
could trust you, Derek! I believed your
promises – all of them! 'Your husband can't
get near you, Raquel. He'll have to get past
me first!'

Del Well, that's right.

Raquel Really? Well, what's he doing lying
asleep on our sofa?

Del *(Wearing a silly grin)*
What you on about?

Raquel My ex-husband is asleep on the sofa!

Del No! That's Slater!

Raquel I know his name, Del! I was
married to him for four years!

The truth – and the full horror of that
truth – hits Del.

Del Slater? You were married to Slater?

Raquel Yes!

Del No! Not... Slater!

Raquel I wish I hadn't burnt my wedding
photos, then maybe you'd believe me!

Del Slater? But he's... Slater!

Raquel I know! Slater was my married
name!

Del But... Slater!

Raquel I told you my husband was
a policeman.

Del Yes, but his name was Inspector Slater.
Your name's Raquel Turner! Why didn't you
tell me what your married name was?

Raquel Because every time I mentioned my
marriage you said let's change the subject!
Have you said anything to him?

Del No, he doesn't know anything. Are you
sure you were married to him?

Raquel Of course I'm bloody sure!

Del Alright, alright! Look, you stay out here
in the kitchen. I'll get rid of him.
Cut to lounge Del enters from the
kitchen. Slater is fast asleep and snoring.
Del shakes Rodney.

Del *(Quietly)* Rodney! Rodders! Wake up
you dipstick!

Rodney What is it?

Del Slater is Raquel's husband.
Rodney stares at him a while then smiles.

Del This ain't a joke, Rodney! Raquel was
married to Slater!

Rodney No!

Del It's true, Rodders. I wouldn't lie about
something like this!

Rodney Does Slater know?

Del 'Course he knows. He was at the
wedding!

Rodney I mean, does he know about you
and Raquel?

Del Oh I see. No, he don't know nothing.
I've gotta get rid of him somehow.

Del shakes Slater.

Del *(At first angry tone)* Slater! *(Now to a more friendly tone)* Roy.

Slater Oh, Gawd! What's the time, Del?

Del Time you was off home. I'll get your coat.

Slater Yeah you're right… *(Indicates kitchen)* D'you mind if I get a glass of water?

Del No, no! There's some trendy water here. Tell me something, Slat… Roy. Did you come back to Peckham just to organise a school reunion?

Slater Well, not just for that. My wife's solicitors wrote to me to say she wants a divorce. So I had to come back to sort a few things out with her. I'm gonna phone her brief and see if I can make a meeting with her.

Rodney So you don't actually know where she's living?

Slater No. But her solicitors are local so she must be around here somewhere, mustn't she?

Del *(Glances towards kitchen)* Yeah!

Slater So I thought while I was here I'd look all me old mates up. And I'm glad I did, Del. It's done me the world of good, meeting you again and finding that you're willing to forgive and forget… It might sound a bit poetic or sentimental, but the cup of human kindness really does runneth o… *(Indicates photograph)* That's my wife!

Del Eh?

Slater That picture there! That's my Rachel!

Del No, no, it can't be, Roy. It says here her name's Raquel.

Slater Yeah, that was her stage name. She used to do a bit of singing and acting. What's a picture of my wife doing in your flat?

Del Well… it's er… What's that picture doing in here, Rodney?

Rodney I don't know!

Albert enters from his bedroom wearing pyjamas and dressing gown.

Albert Can't you lot get to bed? I'm tryna get some sleep in there! Is Raquel in yet?

Slater Raquel! You mean she lives here?

Del Well, it's difficult to explain, Roy.

Raquel enters from the kitchen.

Raquel Yes, I live here. Hello, Roy.

Slater Rachel!

Albert looks behind Raquel to see who the hell Rachel is.

Albert *(To Del)* Who's Rachel??

Slater I'm sorry, I just don't understand what's happening! I came back here and… Oh now I see it! You're cohabiting, aren't you?

Raquel If that's the way you want to put it, yes!

Slater *(Gestures to the three Trotters)* Well, which one?

Del You saucy git, Slater! What d'you mean, which one?

Slater *(To Raquel, incredulous and horrified)* Del?

Raquel Yes, Del!

Albert *(To Rodney)* Who's Rachel?

Rodney Shuddup!

Slater *(To Del)* So what's the full SP, Derek? Is she just another sort you've trawled in your net? Another notch on the bedstead? Or are you two close?

Slater reacts to Raquel's lump. He looks round the side of it.

Slater Where'd you get that from? You're pregnant!

Raquel Oh that's what it is! We've been wondering about this, haven't we Del?

Del Look, Roy. You and Raquel broke up over eight years ago! She's a free woman!

Slater produces a wallet, inside which are three pieces of paper. He removes one piece and then throws the wallet on the coffee table.

The Class of '62

Slater Not according to this letter from Rachel's solicitors! According to them I'm still her husband and she's still my wife!

Albert He's Raquel's husband?

Rodney Yes! Now I'd stay out of it if I was you, Unc!

Albert You know me, son. I'm saying nothing! *(To Slater)* Where'd you think she's been for the last eight years, in a convent?

Rodney I just don't believe him!

Slater No, I figured she'd have a bloke in tow and I guessed it wouldn't be Cliff Richard! You always liked to live a bit, didn't you, darling?

Del One more word, Slater, and I'll take you out on that balcony and see if the EEC have changed the laws on gravity!

Slater How'd you expect me to feel? This woman who I loved…

Raquel Oh shuddup, Roy, you're making me feel sick!

Slater This woman – my lawful wedded wife has been fertilised by a Trotter! You had the whole world to choose from, Rachel. You could have had Saddam Hussein or Pol Pot or a Siberian pimp with gingivitis and a wart on his nose! But you decided to go down-market!

Del Right, that's it. Get yer coat, you're out!

Rodney Alright, calm down, Derek!

Del Well, he's starting to annoy me, Rodney!

Albert *(To Slater)* Why did you come back, son?

Slater To see me friends, to see my family and, most important of all, to see my wife… I'm about to receive a little inheritance soon. It's a nice few grand and – I know this may sound ridiculous now – well, it will sound ridiculous now – but I was hoping that maybe you and me could… try again. A fresh start.

Del Why don't you naff off out of it, Slater?

Slater Oh don't worry, Derek. I couldn't take it back now, not in that condition.

Raquel *(Blows her top)* I'm getting out of here before I tear his eyes out!

Del You're exciting her, Slater!

Slater Yeah, I always could, couldn't I, love?

Del That's it!

Rodney puts his hands over his eyes and turns his head away as Del moves to kill Slater. With a supreme effort, Raquel holds Del back.

Raquel You'd better shut up, Roy, or I swear I'll set him on you! Calm down, Derek, please.

Del Yeah, I'm alright, I'm alright! Go on, you go to bed, sweetheart. I'll see you in a minute.

With a last hateful glare at Slater, Raquel exits to the bedroom.

There is now a potentially explosive pause.

Albert *(To Rodney)* Who's Rachel?

Del and Rodney Shuddup, Albert!

INT. THE TROTTERS' LOUNGE. NIGHT

Two hours later. The room is in darkness. Rodney is lying on the settee with just a blanket over him. He angrily punches the cushion, which is acting as a pillow, and tries to go to sleep.

The door from the bedroom area opens and Del, wearing pyjamas and dressing gown, enters and switches the lights on. Rodney shields his eyes from the sudden onslaught of light.

Del You awake, Rodney?

Rodney *(Angrily)* Well, even if I weren't I bloody would be now!

Del What's up with you?

Rodney What's up with me? You gave Slater my bed!

Del I had no choice, Rodders. Slater's hotel would have been locked for the night. I had to let him kip here.

Rodney What d'you mean, you had to?

Del Have a bit of compassion, Rodney! Can't you see the predicament I'm in?

Rodney No, I can't! All I've seen is that snidey bark Slater lying in my bed and me scrunched up on the chaise-longue again! I'm going to sleep!

Del Don't go to sleep, Rodney. I wanna talk.

Rodney What about?

Del What d'you mean, what about? About recent events! Like Slater and Raquel and me and my little baby!

Rodney Oh that.

Del If people were to find out that Slater was Raquel's husband it'd be the end of me and Trotters Independent Traders. No one would ever trust me!

Rodney But no one... Why?

Del How d'you think my business associates and clients would feel knowing that I was going caseo with the ex-wife of an ex-copper? And not any ex-copper! Slater the slag! He's hated and loathed throughout the parish! If they were to find out that him and Raquel had lived together and sl... sle...

Rodney Slept?

Del Oh go to sleep, Rodney!

Rodney Sorry.

Del I'd be a laughing stock! My image would be ruined.

Rodney Nobody's gonna think like that, Del.

Del Oh yes they would, Rodney! For someone like Boycie it'd be better than winning the pools.

Albert enters from his bedroom.

Albert I could hear talking.

Rodney It might have been us.

Albert Can't you sleep either? I've been lying in there for hours worrying about this situation. If people find out that Raquel was married to Slater you'd be finished.

Del I know that, Unc! I can hear it now. They'd be saying things behind me back. 'Orrible things. Slater's reject... things like that.

Albert Have you spoken with Raquel about it?

Del *(He is close to the large box of fax machines with the word 'reject' clearly in view)* Well, of course I haven't! It's not that poor mare's fault. I've gotta protect her from the gossip. I've gotta protect myself as well. I'm a proud man. I don't want people thinking I mess with rejects! That's why I offered Slater your bed, Rodney. I'm trying to keep him sweet. I don't want him opening his big mouth in the pub or the market. He's got a hold over me. One word from him and I'm finished.

Rodney But he doesn't know that! He doesn't realise that he is universally hated and despised and if people were to discover the truth you'd be ruined.

Albert Rodney's got a point, Del. What he's saying is: don't let Slater walk all over you. If you do he might become suspicious and start wondering why.

Del Yeah... I reckon you could be right.
Slater enters from the bedroom. He is wearing his suit trousers and a vest and carrying an empty glass.

Slater Sorry to interrupt. I've got a terrible thirst. *(Pours some mineral water into a glass)* Couldn't you sleep, Del?

Del No. In fact I was gonna bring you an early breakfast in bed, Slater.

Slater Oh that's nice of you.

Del Then I was gonna drag you by the scruff of the neck and chuck you out the bloody door!

Rodney and Albert nod reassuringly to

The Class of '62

Del in a 'we're with you' manner.

Slater Is that right? I couldn't sleep either – worrying about you. What the local reaction would be if they were to find out the truth. I don't think anyone would ever trust you again knowing you were living with the wife of an ex-copper. And not any ex-copper! Slater, who is universally hated and despised! I think it'd be the end of you.

Del looks to Rodney and Albert, who lower their eyes in a 'you're on your own' manner.

Slater Now I'd hate to see that happen, especially to a good mate like you. Because, despite the fact that you have taken my wife, the one woman I ever really loved, and tubbed her, I don't hold it against you. So, I made a promise to myself and I'm making the same promise to you. I'm gonna keep my mouth shut.

Del Right... Well, you know it makes sense. Thanks, Roy.

Slater I just hope and pray I don't have too many beers down the Nag's Head and go and let it slip. Beer always goes straight to my head. Now, champagne – champagne's different. I know exactly what I'm saying when I'm drinking champagne. But until my inheritance comes through I can't afford those sort of luxuries. It's a poser, innit, Del?

Del *(Picks up a wallet and produces a few tenners)* Here you are, Roy. Buy yourself a couple of bottles on me.

Slater Are you sure, Del? Well, that's very nice of you. I really am quite moved. *(Snatches the money)* Thanks. I'll see you all in the morning. I'm not sure how long I'll be staying – but that's not a problem, is it?

Del No, no! You're very welcome, Roy.

Slater Thanks Del.

Slater exits to the bedroom.

Albert What you gonna do, son? He's got you by the... well, like that. *(Screws his fist up in a ball)*

Del I don't know what I'm gonna do! I feel like I'm in a state of shock.

Rodney State of shock! Just be like getting hit by a John Barnes free kick!

Del Yeah, they're short and curly, ain't they? Gawd knows how much it's gonna cost to keep him quiet. I've given him 40 quid already and it's only the first evening.

Albert You might have given him four tenners, but this is Slater's wallet!

(Laughs)

Del No! It is an' all. Well, that's cheered me up a little bit.

Rodney examines the contents of the wallet.

Rodney What's all this? And there's some sort of contract from his solicitor... to Raquel! 'I, Rachel Slater (née Turner), hereby waive all my legal rights and entitlements to my husband's present and future estates.' It's one of them things film stars get their future wives to sign – a pre-nuptial agreement – well, in this case a post-nuptial agreement.

Del So that's what he really come here for, to get Raquel to waive all her rights to his money!

Albert But what money is he talking about? I thought he was skint.

Rodney Yeah, but he's got some kind of inheritance coming up. I suppose it's what his dad left him.

Del *(Reading the third paper)* No, his dad wouldn't have left him anything. He hated Slater more than us. Listen to this, "Dear Mr Slater, bla, bla, bla. I would take this oppor-tunity to bring to your notice the record-breaking high which exists on today's international diamond market. I would strongly advise your consideration to selling the 10 items you deposited with my firm some years ago. I await your instruc-tions, yours faithfully, bla, bla, bla." This is from a Bond Street diamond merchant.

Albert So what are those 10 items?
Rodney Well, they're hot-cross buns, are they! What d'you think they are? They're diamonds!
Del This is his inheritance! 10 little sparklers that Slater pugged away after the smuggling racket went up the pictures.

Del folds the papers up and places them back in the wallet.

Rodney You've got him, Del! This is concrete evidence!
Del I know, Rodders. But let's not rush things. We've gotta think about the best way to handle this.

Slater enters from the bedroom and takes the wallet which Del is holding.

Slater Oh you found it, Del. I've been looking everywhere for that. That breakfast in bed you mentioned. A couple of boiled eggs'd be nice about 9.30.
Del Yeah, cushty, Roy.

Slater exits to the bedroom.

Albert You handled that well, son.
Del How was I to know he'd come bursting in and nick the evidence? I'm gonna get dressed and take a drive.
Rodney You going to the police?
Del No, the all-night deli – we're out of eggs.

INT. THE NAG'S HEAD. DAY

Slater is at the bar, puffing on a large cigar. He is slightly drunk, an empty bottle and a full glass of champagne in front of him. He burps loudly. A look from Mike. Raquel enters carrying a bag of groceries. She sees Slater and turns quickly to leave, but too late.

Slater Rachel! *(He moves across to her)* Sorry, Raquel. Let me get you a drink.
Raquel No thanks. I just called in to see if Del was…
Slater I insist! *(He sits her at a table and moves to the bar)* Mike, another bottle if you'd be so kind.

Mike Is this one on Del's account as well?
Slater Oh yes. That's alright with you, innit?
Mike Yeah, fine. Del told me anything you want is down to him. I've heard of mates looking after each other, but this is something special.
Slater Del is something special, isn't he? D'you know he brought me breakfast in bed this morning.
Mike Del?
Slater They broke the mould when they made that man. *(Referring to Raquel)* She seems a nice girl.
Mike Raquel? Yeah, she's lovely. She's been married before.
Slater Has she?
Mike A right git, I heard.
Slater Really?
Mike Her luck changed when she met Del. He's got his faults, but his heart's in the right place. Don't tell him I said that, will you? *(Slater takes the bottle and joins Raquel at the table)*
Raquel What are you playing at, Roy? Why's Del paying for your champagne and bringing you breakfast in bed?
Slater He's just standing by an old school friend who's fallen on hard times.
Raquel When are you going, Roy?
Slater I haven't made up my mind. I'm just waiting for my inheritance to come through. Then I'm thinking of buying a house in this area. We'll be seeing quite a lot of each other in the future. D'you ever think back to our times together?
Raquel Some things remind me. Things like repeats of *Tenko*.

Del, carrying a suitcase, and Rodney enter.

Slater Del Boy, Rodney. Let me get you a drink.
Del Cheers, Roy. Make it a big bottle, won't you? *(To Raquel)* You alright, sweetheart?

The Class of '62

Raquel Yeah. I called in to see if you were here.

Del Why don't you go and sit in the van? I'm gonna sort this thing out with Slater. It might not be very pretty.

Raquel You're not going to hit him over the head with a chair, are you?

Del Of course not!

Raquel *(Disappointed)* Oh, well! I'll go and sit in the van then.

Raquel exits.

Del Enjoying my champagne, Roy?

Slater Lovely, Del. Helps me keep a clear head, and, as you know better than most, that's very important. I was gonna take Raquel shopping this morning, but she was still asleep. She always was difficult to wake up. Oops! Me and my... Just shows you how easily these things can slip out... I was thinking about hiring a car for a couple of weeks. That alright with you?

Del Why don't we sit down and discuss it, Roy?

Slater Of course, lead on.

They move to a table where Rodney is seated.

Del Before we go any further, Slater, there's something I want to ask you. You knew all along that Raquel was living with me, didn't you?

Slater Well, I don't suppose it can do any harm. Yeah, I knew. I went to the town hall and checked her name on the poll-tax register. I had to get my way into your flat to make sure it was the same woman. That's when I come up with the school reunion idea. *(Indicates the bottle of champagne on the counter)* Fetch us that bottle of champagne, Del, there's a good chap.

Del's hackles rise at this.

Rodney You've got a habit of leaving your things lying around, haven't you, Slater?

Del Like the other night when you left your wallet lying on the table. I couldn't help having a little look inside. I read that contract you wanted Raquel to sign.

Slater Only protecting me interests, Del. If it's good enough for Rod Stewart, it's good enough for me.

Rodney We also read that little welcome-home message from your friendly diamond merchant.

Del Now what would happen if we were to take that to the Old Bill?

Slater Sweet FA, Derek! You seem to have overlooked something. You may have read my personal paperwork, but that isn't proof! *(Produces his wallet with the paperwork inside)* I've still got exhibit A tucked up safe and sound in my pocket. So get out of that one, Perry.

Del This morning, just before I woke you for breakfast, I took your wallet from your coat and had another look at that paperwork.

Slater So what?

Del brings his suitcase on to the table and opens it. He produces one of the fax machines.

Del See that? It's a fax machine. It's exactly the same as the one we've got back at the flat. This is a masterpiece of modern technology. You can fax messages all over the world. And you know what else it does? *(Points to some small wording on the machine)* What does that say?

Slater *(Reads the small printing)* 'Photocopier' *(Reacts)*

Del That's right, Roy me boy, it photocopies things. Pictures, advertising bumf and letters asking what you want done with yer 10 smuggled diamonds! Things like that!

Slater *(Casual)* So you've got a copy!

Rodney Not just one. Several. I mean, say we mislaid something as important as that? Be a crime, wouldn't it?

Del You said it, bruv.

Slater You're forgetting, Derek, I know a lot more about the law than you. I've already stood trial for those diamonds. I've served me sentence. You can't be tried for the same crime twice.

Del Rodney mentioned that. So today we went down to the local newspaper offices and read all the reports of your trial. They had all the details. They'd even printed that old school photo with you in the football team. It was a Spot the Git competition.

Rodney Now according to the report, you were tried for illegally importing 78 diamonds into the country. It didn't mention anything about 10 missing diamonds. The police don't know nothing about them – yet!

Del If one of those copies was to find its way into the hands of your old mates at the Yard it would mean a new trial.

Rodney And be honest, Roy... *(Chuckles to Del)* Be honest!

Del and Rodney laugh. Slater laughs with them in a pathetic, pleading way.

Rodney You wouldn't stand a chance, would you? Not with your record. It'd be an even longer sentence this time. Six years?

Del I'd go for seven. Still, wouldn't worry you, would it, Roy? You like reunions. I bet all the boys in nick'll be glad to see you back. They might throw a little party on the roof for yer. We've faxed you right up, ain't we?

Slater Correct me if I'm wrong, but I get the distinct impression you're angling for a deal.

Del Spot on!

Slater Alright, then. As soon as I've sold the stones I'll split the money with you. I'll give you 10 per cent.

Del No.

Rodney Nope.

Slater Alright. 80–20 in my favour.

Del No.

Rodney No, sir.

Slater Come on!...70–30?

Del We don't want the money, Roy.

Rodney We don't want the m... *(To Del)* We don't want the...

Del holds Rodney.

Del You can keep all the money to yourself. All I want from you is a promise. You give Raquel her divorce and then you leave her alone – for ever! You get out of the area now! And you keep your big mouth shut. If one person finds out that you were married to Raquel there'll be a letter with a first-class stamp winging its way to the commissioner of police.

Slater And that's it? That's the deal?

Del That's the deal!

Slater Well, those terms seem acceptable to me, Derek. Very acceptable. Don't you worry. I won't say a word.

Del And I won't go near any pillar boxes.

Slater Well, then! I think we've concluded our business.

Del *(Calls)* Michael, bring us a bottle of your finest champagne – and two glasses.

Slater You will excuse me, won't you? I've got a train to catch... Would you do me one favour. When the baby's born, if it's a boy would you call him after me?

Del is about to jump up from the table but Rodney puts an arm across to stop him.

Rodney I wouldn't have thought so. It's not fair to christen a kid 'Arsehole!', is it?

Del smiles, proud of Rodney.

Slater No. It hasn't really got a ring to it, has it? Well, have a nice life, Del Boy.

Del Oh I will, Slater, I will!

Slater exits

Del and Rodney look at each other.

Del We pulled it off, Rodney! What a team!

The Class of '62

Rodney What a bloody team! Why didn't we take his money?

Del Because it's illegal.

Rodney Yeah, but... Yeah, s'pose you're right.

Del But when he's sold his diamonds, Raquel can divorce him and legally be entitled to 50 per cent of everything!

Rodney Oh, Derek! I will drink to that!

Mike arrives with the champagne and two glasses.

Mike *(As he pours two glasses)* You two celebrating something?

Del You could say that, Mike. We've just done the deal of the year!

Mike *(Spots the fax machine)* Here, that reminds me. That fax machine you sold me. The photocopier on it don't work.

Del That's funny! It don't on ours either!

Del and Rodney collapse in uproarious laughter. Mike looks on incredulously.

He Ain't Heavy, He's My Uncle

INT. THE TROTTER'S LOUNGE. DAY

Four carrier bags filled with groceries are in the room. Albert, wearing ancient Royal Navy blue shorts and white vest, is on the phone. As Albert speaks, Del enters from the kitchen and picks up a couple of the bags.

Albert *(On phone, breathing heavily)* Sorry, Cassandra, I'm a bit out of breath. I've been doing me physical jerks.

Del Oi, Gazza. Don't you tell her Rodney's still in bed sleeping off another hangover.

Albert *(Hand over the mouthpiece)* What d'you take me for, eh?

Del Give me five minutes, I'll write out a list!

Albert *(On phone)* Alright, Cassandra. I'll tell Rodney you called as soon as he gets up.

Del I don't believe him!

Albert *(On phone)* I mean in!

As Del exits to the kitchen, Raquel enters from the kitchen and picks up one of the bags. Raquel is now seven months pregnant.

Raquel Tell Cassandra I'll phone her later. I've gotta get this stuff in the freezer.

As Raquel picks up the bag she holds her back as if feeling a twinge.

Albert *(On phone)* Raquel says she'll call you later. Oh she's fine. I mean, women like being pregnant, don't they?

Del enters for the final bag.

Albert *(On phone)* And how you keeping, love? Good. Me? Oh I'm alright, dear. I've joined the over-sixties club on the estate. Given me a new lease of life, it has… Eh? Well, yes, there are women there, but I'm not interested in all that.

Del No, like a squirrel ain't interested in nuts!

Del exits to the kitchen.

Albert *(On phone)* I used to be a bit of a Casanova in my younger days. I could tell you a tale or two, Cassandra! During the war… Eh? There's someone at your door, is there? Yes, bye for now, Cassandra. Bye, love. *(Switches the phone off)*

He now looks into the mirror as he brushes his beard.

Albert *(Talks to the mirror and the phantom Mrs Lane)* Mrs Lane – or may I call you Dora? Could I have the pleasure of this next dance?

Albert begins dancing with an imaginary partner.

Rodney appears at the door from the bedroom. He wears pyjamas and dressing gown and is bleary-eyed and hungover.

Rodney *(At Albert's appearance)* Oh God!

Albert What time d'you call this, Rodney?

Rodney I call it 11.30, Unc. What time d'you call it?

Albert It's disgusting. A young man of your age getting up at 11.30 in the morning. Yer brother was up and out of here at 7.00. Then he came back and took Raquel shopping.

Rodney Yes, because Derek has got work and money-earning opportunities. And he's got a woman in his life! What about me, eh? I've got no job to go to and no wife to say good morning to.

Albert You might feel a bit more chirpy if you didn't wake up with a hangover every morning!

Rodney I have not got… *(This pains his head. Now quieter and more controlled)* I have not got a hangover! I'm fine! There's nothing wrong with me.

Albert Cassandra phoned. Just wanted to know how you were.

Rodney *(Panic)* You didn't tell her, did you?

Albert No, I said you was alright. She wants your cheque towards the mortgage.

Rodney Yeah, I'll... er... I'll sort it out.
Rodney exits to the kitchen, where he finds Del waiting for him.

Rodney Morning.

Raquel Morning, Rodney.

Del *(To Raquel, but looking at Rodney)* That reminds me, sweetheart. The video shop's got *Nightmare On Elm Street* in.

Rodney *(In his embarrassment he tries to change the subject)* Albert's been talking to Cassandra. She just phoned to see how I was.

Raquel He didn't tell her, did he?

Rodney No, he said I was all... What d'you mean, he didn't... *(He is interrupted by Raquel)*

Raquel *(Gets a twinge in her back)* Ooh!

Del *(Panicking)* You alright, sweetheart?

Raquel Yeah, I'm OK. Just a bit of backache, that's all. It happens every time we go out in your van. It's just not very comfortable, specially in my condition. I'm fine now.

Del You go and have a sit down. I'll put the shopping away. That's an order!

Raquel Aye, aye, sir. Don't forget to deliver our birthday present.

Rodney Whose birthday is it?

Del Boycie's kid. *(To Raquel)* I'll give him a bell.
Raquel exits to the lounge.

Del See, that van wasn't designed for pregnant women with shopping. And she's getting bigger by the day. She's just been banned from the Body Shop. If I could just get the engine running a bit smoother, that might help.

Rodney I've told you, they stopped making spare parts for your van years ago. I've tried everywhere – breakers' yards, spares shops, archaeologists.

Del Talking of archaeologists, you look like you've just been dug up from somewhere. What are you doing to yourself, Rodney? Why don't you take a leaf out of your uncle's book. Look at him in there. He's joined the over-sixties club and he's like a born-again teddy boy.

Rodney You're not suggesting I join the over-sixties club?

Del No. I think you'd be too old for 'em.
Del exits to the lounge, leaving Rodney to ponder his words. As Del enters, Raquel is seated, reading the local newspaper, The Peckham Echo. Accompanied by a photo of the Trotters' estate is a headline: "Muggers strike again on estate of fear".

Raquel There's been another mugging on the estate.

Rodney You don't want to believe all you read, Raquel. These things are usually exaggerated.

Del Yeah, it's a rumour put about by the 45 victims. If I had my way I'd hang 'em from the nearest lamppost.

Rodney It's almost the 21st century and he still wants to hang 'em up by the neck.

INT. BOYCIE'S SALES OFFICE/TROTTERS' LOUNGE

The phone is ringing. Boycie enters and answers it. During his telephone conversation one of his mechanics enters and searches the key rack.

Boycie *(On phone, with that modern sales enthusiasm)* Thank you for calling Boyce Autos Sales and Car Accessories. How can I help you? *(Now deflated)* Oh it's you Marlene! Yes, I'm going out to get Tiler's birthday present in a minute! Marlene, I'm trying to run a business here. If you remember, I sell quality used cars!

He Ain't Heavy, He's My Uncle

Mechanic D'you want me to take that old banger down the scrapyard?

Boycie *(Hand over mouthpiece)* If they'll take it!

Mechanic I'll get my coat.

The mechanic exits.

Boycie *(On phone)* A baby grand? Yes, of course I want him to be cultured, but for Gawd's sake, Marlene, he's only one! I don't give a toss what Beethoven could do when he was three! Tiler should start off in a smaller way. Leave it to me, Marlene. I'll surprise you. *(Replaces receiver)* Where can I get a mouth organ from?

The phone starts ringing again.

Boycie *(The same sales enthusiasm)* Thank you for calling Boyce Autos Sales and Car Accessories. How can I help you? *(Now deflated)* Oh, it's you Del Boy! How's your luck?

Cuts to Trotters' lounge.
Rodney enters from his bedroom on his way to the kitchen.

Del Never been better. I've got so much business going on there ain't enough hours in the day. I'm thinking of taking on staff.

Rodney Yeah, 'taking on' being the operative phrase!

Del Do something useful with yourself, Rodney. Go back to bed, son! *(On phone)* Listen, we've got a birthday present for the ankle-biter.

Cuts to Boycie's office.

Boycie Cheers, Del. We're having a little celebration. Just a few close and dear friends. I s'pose you and your family could come along as well if you like.

Del Oh very kind of you. Here, d'you reckon one of your mechanics could take a look at my van?

Boycie I know just the bloke. He suffered a family bereavement recently and could do with a good laugh. Sorry, Del. I just thought it was time you got yourself something more powerful.

Del Such as?

Boycie I don't know. A food mixer?

Del Listen. My old van does everything I want it to do.

Boycie Keep the van for business. I'm talking about a second car. I've been hearing about all this crime that has been taking place on your estate. Now wouldn't it be safer for your Raquel to be driving rather than walking?

Del I think you've got a point there Boycie.

Boycie You need something that suits your image. I've got a lovely Skoda out in the showroom. Two years old, 8,000 miles on the clock, genuine. You can have it for two and a half grand.

Del Two and an 'arf! That's a teeny bit out of my price range.

Boycie What is your price range?

Del About 400 quid.

Boycie 400? You can't get a walking frame for 400!

Boycie checks a couple of logbooks lying on the table.

Wait a minute. Your luck could be in, Del. I had a cracking little sports coupé come in as a part chop on a Honda Prelude. Beautiful bodywork, sound engine, a really nice runner. It just needs a bit of a clean-up, that's all. I was looking for a grand. But, seeing as it's me son's birthday and you're a mate, I'll let it go for 400.

Del Cushty! I'll come down and have a butcher's. See you later.

The mechanic, now wearing a coat, enters Boycie's office.

Mechanic *(To Boycie)* I'm off to the scrappers, then. Are these the keys?

As the mechanic goes to pick up the keys from the desk, Boycie snatches them away from him.

Boycie There's been a change of plan!

221

INT. THE TROTTERS' LOUNGE. DAY

Rodney is reading The Peckham Echo article. Albert enters from his bedroom. He is wearing a natty three-piece navy-blue pinstripe suit, with a gold pocket watch and chain, and a beautifully ironed shirt and tie.

Albert What d'you think, Rodney?

Rodney Er... I dunno!

Albert *(Talking to himself in the mirror)* She'll be putty in my hands.

A jubilant Del enters from the hall, followed by an ashen-faced Raquel.

Del Guess what? I've bought a new car! Cor blimey, Albert! For a moment there I thought it was Simon Le Bon! What are you all dressed up for?

Albert *(Checks his gold watch)* I'm playing the over-sixties domino final against old Knock-Knock at the Nag's Head later. So you've got a new car?

Del It's a little cracker. Raquel's just driven it back. It's a beauty, innit, sweetheart?

Raquel *(Very unconvinced. She seems in a state of shock)* Yeah!

Albert D'you wanna cup of tea, love?

Raquel Yeah, I need something, Albert!

Rodney So you're a two-car family now, then! Well, one car and a three-wheel van.

Del Which is one car and one three-wheel van more than you've got! Or are ever likely to have!

Rodney I wouldn't be so sure about that, Derek. There's bound to be a job in here for me somewhere.

Albert You'll have to come up with a good excuse before you get a job, son. I mean, how you gonna explain away the 10 years when you was Del's partner?

Raquel Albert's got a good point, Rodney. In all of those 10 years you weren't registered for income tax, national insurance or... or anything! Your work record shows that you left school at 16 and promptly disappeared off the face of the earth.

Rodney I've thought about that. I'm gonna say I was working for a foreign oil company in Saudia Arabia.

Del What, straight from school? One minute you're a milk-monitor, the next a petro-chemist? No, it won't wash, bruv.

Raquel Couldn't you say you'd been on safari?

Rodney Safari? For a whole decade?

Albert You could say you got lost.

Raquel A friend of mine went out with a guy who'd spent 12 years working for a safari company in Kenya.

Rodney That's stupid, Raquel!

Del Well, it's better than your paper-round-in-Arabia cobblers!

Albert Have you ever thought of joining the navy?

Rodney Well, funnily enough, Unc, no! How could I join the navy?

Del Exactly. In the old days they'd take anyone – well, they took you! But nowadays you've gotta have a cotchel of qualifications. What chance would Lawrence of Peckham stand?

Albert I don't mean in the Royal Navy. I was talking about the merchant. Just imagine it, Rodney. Monday, you sail out of Southampton Water. Tuesday, you're through the Bay of Biscay. Wednesday, you've rounded Cape St Vincent. Thursday, you dock in Algiers...

Del *(cuts in)* and Friday it's your turn in the barrel!

Rodney Eh?

Albert There was nothing like that on my vessels! A few funny ones but nothing like that! So what d'you reckon, Rodney?

Rodney If it's all the same with you, Unc, I'll take a raincheck on this one.

Albert You don't know what you're missing.

He Ain't Heavy, He's My Uncle

Rodney Suits me! I've been thinking, Del. Trotters Independent Traders has been going through a period of commercial augmentation.

Del No, I've been doing alright, Rodney.

Rodney Yeah… I mean, you're a property developer now. Well, you've bought this flat off the council.

Albert He's hardly developed it!

Raquel He put that new toilet-roll holder up. The musical one.

Rodney There you are, then! You've got your direct retail sales branch, your property division and now there's the theatrical agency side to the business. So I was thinking, things must be pretty hectic for you on the old business front?

Del You're not kidding. It's one power breakfast after another.

Rodney Yeah. It ain't all champagne and backgammon for you yuppies, is it? I heard you say earlier that you were thinking of taking on staff. So, seeing as I am temporarily between positions – and if the conditions are acceptable – I am willing to work for you.

Del No way, Pedro!

Rodney Look, I've g… No way, Pedro?

Del I don't need you, Rodders.

Rodney I could be very useful to you during this period of growth!

Del How?

Rodney Eh? Er… well… I'm a good salesman.

Del Do me a favour, Rodney, you couldn't flog a black cat to a witch.

Rodney Ah, but now I've got managerial experience.

Del Na.

Rodney I could computerise your entire business!

Del Na.

Rodney I have got executive qualifications

Del Na.

Rodney Can you lend us a fiver, then?

Raquel A fiver? I didn't realise things were that bad, Rodney.

Rodney I've had no money coming in since I resigned from Alan's printing works and I've still gotta pay half the mortgage on me and Cassandra's flat. It's skinted me. I've had to take out an overdraft at the bank.

Raquel You mean you're borrowing money to pay off your loan?

Rodney *(Embarrassed and angry at the truth)* Yes!

Del And you wanna come back as my financial adviser?

Rodney I'll come back as anything! Look, I know your trading methods, I'm experienced in this line of business and working for you would be marginally better than being on the dole or in the barrel!

Raquel Something tells me this is not the best job interview you've ever given, Rodney.

Rodney I'm desperate, ain't I?

Del Alright then, you can have a job with Trotters Independent Traders – plc.

Rodney *(Immediately tries to regain his professional pride)* Fine… And what kind of wage structure can I expect?

Del Wage structure? The same as before.

Rodney Good! What was that, then?

Del How the hell should I know? Look, if I've got it on the hip I'll pay you.

Rodney And what title will I have?

Del We'll call you Lord Rodney.

Rodney I mean, company title! See, I thought I could be your new director of commercial development.

Del Yeah, sounds good to me. Now, as the Bible says, 'Clothes maketh the man'. The first thing I want you to do is whip round to your flat a bit lively.

Rodney And get my best suit?

Del No, get your car-cleaning gear.

EXT. THE GARAGE BLOCK OF THE TROTTERS' ESTATE. DAY

Del There y'are then, what d'you reckon?
Del's 'new' car is a 1977 Ford Capri. It was originally light green, but through years of neglect the paintwork has become totally matt in appearance. There is no shine to it whatsoever, the windows are dirty and a couple of hubcaps and the front bumper are missing.

The car is parked outside Del's garage, which has the doors up and open. Inside the garage we can see evidence of Del's trading stock – a chest-type deep freezer with an old washing machine on top of it, a couple of decent-looking hover-mowers, etc.

Rodney *(Referring to the car)* Is that it?
Del Yeah! How much d'you reckon I paid Boycie for it?
Rodney He charged you for it?
Del I stole it off him, Rodders. 400 nicker. It's a peach – handles better than Maradona. Only had one owner – Peckham Car Rentals.
Rodney laughs, believing this to be a change to the old Hertz van rental joke.
Del *(Del meant it and doesn't understand Rodney's laughter)* What?
Rodney I thought you were jo… Don't matter! Look at the paintwork! It's got no shine to it! I've never seen a car with a matt finish before!
Del That's just ground-in dirt. It's been a bit neglected over the years. A little bit of attention and elbow-grease and I'll have it gleaming.
Rodney Well, you've got more faith than me, Del.
Del That'll look brand new by the time I've finished with it. Now listen, Rodney. There's something I wanted to talk to you about.

It's a bit embarrassing, really. If you don't like the idea just say so, I'll understand.
Rodney I'm not cleaning it!
Del You bloody are!
Rodney Oh no! The days when you got me to do all your dirty work are long gone! I used to run my own computer section! I was an executive!
Del And now you're cleaning my Capri Ghia! Bear in mind, Rodney, you are now my employee!
Rodney Look, when I finally gave in to all your persuasion and accepted the job with Trotters Independent Traders, I assumed my role would be in a managerial capacity. Helping with buying and selling.
Del You will be helping us buy and sell! You see, it's all about image, Rodney. *(Indicates car)* And this is my image!
Rodney *(Studies car)* Yeah, can't argue with that one, Del!
Del And also remember, that since you walked out on Cassandra and your job, you have been sleeping and eating at my flat for nix! Now I'm perfectly willing to accept your resignation. I'll help you find a nice little bedsit. I'll even give you a paraffin heater and a mousetrap as a leaving present.
Rodney Alright, I'll clean it!
Del Now are you sure about that?
Rodney Yes!
Del Well, that's very nice of you. I'm grateful.
Del produces a cardboard box filled with car-cleaning material from the garage.
Del There you go. You'll find everything you need in there.
Rodney I'll never be able to get all this grime off it!
Del Of course you will! Giss it here.
Del takes a tin of compound and a couple of rags from the box. He rubs some compound on the rag.
Del You use compound to begin with.

He Ain't Heavy, He's My Uncle

He rubs the compound vigorously into the car's bodywork in a two to three-inch circle. Then he rubs it off with a clean rag.

Del Now a bit of T-cut.

He pours some T-cut on a rag and rubs that into the small circle. He rubs it off with a clean rag.

Del Cushty… Little bit of polish.

He pours some polish on to the rag and rubs that into the small circle. He rubs it off with a clean rag.

Del Lovely Jubbly… And last, but not least, a drop of sealer.

He pours some sealer on to the rag and rubs it into the circle. He rubs it off with a clean rag.

Del Voila!

We see, in among all the square metres of grime and dullness, a tiny oasis of shining paintwork.

Del Now just do that to the rest!

Rodney is left open-mouthed.

Del *(Checks watch)* Lunchtime already! Have fun.

Del moves towards the three-wheeled van, singing.

Del Ever since I was a young boy I've played the silver ball.

INT. THE NAG'S HEAD. NIGHT

The pub is crowded and noisy. Albert is seated at a table with a group from his over-sixties club, including Albert's friend Knock-Knock (about the same age as Albert) and a couple of other old boys, playing dominoes. Watching them play are three 68-year-old groupies, including Dora. She is smartly dressed and has blue-rinsed hair. She is also Marlene's mum. At another table, swilling pints and making a lot of noise, sit five scruffy bikers in their mid-twenties. The leader of this gang is Ollie. Standing around the jukebox are five skinheads, also in their mid-twenties. Del, Raquel, Boycie, Trigger and Marlene are standing at the bar.

Mike is behind the bar.

Del *(Referring to Albert and the over-sixties group)* Look at that lot, eh? It looks like the Tetley Tea folks' day out.

Marlene Albert's looking very smart. He must be after one of the ladies.

Mike I wonder if it's old Lil with the 'airy wart? Or is it the Widow Manky? Her with the disposable teeth.

Raquel You should have more respect,

Mike Those women went through a war for us.

Boycie Yeah, you can still see the bomb damage on some of 'em.

Marlene Ah, it'd be lovely if Albert could meet a nice old lady to keep him company. D'you know who he's after?

Raquel Yeah. Your mum.

Marlene My mum!

Del Yeah, him and his mate are both after sorting her out.

Marlene I'm not having this!

Mike No, but if your mum plays her cards right!

Del, Mike and Boycie laugh at this. Raquel tries to hide her laugh.

Marlene *(Calls)* Mum! I want a word with you!

Dora Yeah, alright, Marlene, talk to you in a minute.

Albert Can I get you a drink, Dora? You don't mind me calling you Dora, do you, Dora?

Dora Of course I don't mind – Albert.

Knock-Knock I just got Dora a drink.

Albert Why'd you let Knock-Knock buy you a drink? It was my turn.

Dora You can buy me a drink in a minute.

Albert Yeah, alright.

As Albert sits and takes up his dominoes, he and Knock-Knock look venomously.

Trigger How'd the kid's birthday party go?

Boycie It was a great success, Trigger. We had all the right people there, and Del and Albert turned up.

Del Right, what is it, same again? Mike! *(Referring to the skinheads)* Who're the morons from outer space?

Mike Dunno, Del. They've been using the pub for a couple of weeks now.

Del *(Suspicious of the group)* Yeah, I didn't think they were regulars.

Mike But, like I say, I don't know anything about them. They're most probably playmates of the mongrels.

(Indicates Ollie and co)

Del Yeah…*(Calls)* Ollie! Oi, Ollie! Over here, son.

Ollie joins him at the bar.

Ollie What you want, Del?

Del The little gang over by the jukebox. Know anything about 'em?

Ollie They started coming in here about a fortnight ago.

Del You ever seen 'em hanging round the estate at night?

Ollie Yeah, couple of times. D'you want me and the boys to beat 'em up?

Del No, no!

Mike Oi, I don't want no trouble in this pub!

Ollie And you ain't gonna get none, guv'nor, unless you wanna start it!

Del Oi, oi, pack it in, will you? Go 'n, Ollie, sit yerself down. I'll send you and the boys a drink over.

Marlene is at the domino table.

Marlene What you drinking, Albert?

Albert I'll have a large navy rum, dear. *(So the old ladies can hear)* Puts lead in yer pencil!

The old ladies squeal at his sauciness.

Marlene Well, there's a thing.

Albert Get old Knock-Knock a drink, will you, love?

Knock-Knock I'll have a pint of ordinary, dear.

Marlene *(Quietly to Albert)* Why'd they call him Knock-Knock?

Knock-Knock knocks his domino on the table twice, a sign that you cannot continue the play.

Albert It's because he's a very bad dominoes player!

Knock-Knock I'm a better player than you, Trotter!

Albert You've never beaten me at dominoes in all your life.

Knock-Knock I can beat you at anything. Even when we was at school I could beat you at anything!

Marlene Now, come on boys, start acting like grown-ups! D'you wanna drink, Mum?

Dora I'm alright, Marlene. Knock-Knock bought me one just now.

Trigger I had to laugh to myself tonight, Del.

Del Did you, Trig?

Trigger Yeah.

Pause.

Del Why, did something happen?

Trigger I was walking across the estate – past the garage block. It was half-past seven at night, pitch-black, and there's Dave polishing an old banger! *(Laughs)*

Del *(Laughs)* It takes all ki… *(Reacts. To Raquel)* Oh Gawd! I forgot about my director of commercial development!

Raquel You left him cleaning your car at night?

Del I forgot he was working for me!

Mike What's Albert and Knock-Knock playing at?

Marlene Dunno, looks like Ninja dominoes.

Mike What you having, Boyce?

He Ain't Heavy, He's My Uncle

Marlene Give him a large navy rum.

A seething Rodney enters, his clothes smeared with grease and polish.

Rodney Look at my clothes!

Del I told you to wear your car-cleaning gear.

Rodney A director of commercial development does not wear Doc Martens and stonewashed Wranglers!

Del When he's cleaning his guv'nor's Capri he does!

Rodney And I got Swarfega in me eye!

Raquel Your finger's bleeding, Rodney.

Rodney Yeah, that happened when me hand went straight through the bodywork! I'm bleeding, see! There's blood! Oh yeah. Mike, you got a plaster?

Del Oi, what d'you mean, your hand went straight through the bodywork?

Rodney There's a big rust hole in the wing. Boycie's blokes had stuffed it full of newspapers and body-filler and sprayed over it.

Boycie That is slanderous, Rodney. That must have happened before I took possession of the vehicle!

Rodney They were yesterday's newspapers!

Boycie Look, you took the car as seen! I don't owe you no favours.

Mike That's a bit unfair, innit, Boyce? Look at that 36-piece tea service he sold Marlene last month!

Boycie Yeah, that came in very handy. I gave it to the Boy Scouts' fete for their rifle range.

Mike That was genuine Dresden!

Del It was genuine antique Dresden!

Trigger And it was guaranteed dish-washer-proof!

Raquel *(Takes plaster from Mike)* I'll do it for you, Rodney.

She places the plaster on his finger.

Rodney I don't believe him sometimes!

I don't know how he can ask me – with my executive training – to go round to the garage block and clean the Pratmobile!

Raquel Don't let Del hear you call it that!

Boycie I remember a few years back when I had that important client coming over from Belgium and I was trying to get tickets to Wimbledon to impress him. You said, "Leave it to me Boycie, I gotta contact at Wimbledon".

Del I got you two tickets!

Boycie That's right! They drew nil–nil with Ipswich! That makes us even!

Del No way, Pedro!

Rodney I'll see you later. I'm going round Jevon's.

Raquel Del, my back's aching.

Del D'you wanna go home, sweetheart? I've had enough of this lot, anyway. You've got a choice of vehicles tonight, sweetheart. D'you wanna go in the van or the Capri?

Raquel Can we walk?

Del Of course. Well, bonjour to you all.

Del and Raquel exit.

Albert What would you like, Dora? How about a large snowball? Mike, a large snowball for Dora, please.

As Albert produces a wad of fivers we see a couple of the skinheads looking across at his money.

INT. TROTTERS' LOUNGE. NIGHT

Two hours later. Raquel, now wearing night attire, is seated on the settee watching TV.

Del enters from the bedroom wearing pyjamas and dressing gown.

Del *(Relieved at getting his suit and shoes off)* That's better. You alright, darling?

Raquel Yeah, I'm fine now.

Del Cushty. I'll pick my Capri Ghia up in the morning. My director of commercial development can drive the van back.

Raquel Del, I don't wanna nag.

Del Good. Shall I put a record on?

Raquel Can we afford to splash out £400 on another car? I mean, do we need another car?

Del Yes, we do! You see…

Raquel Look, just because the van gives me backache was no reason for you to buy another car!

Del But listen to me. The reason I'm…

Raquel *(Cuts in)* It's a waste of money. You do realise we've got a baby on the way, don't you?

Del Yes, little things remind me. Will you just shut up for a minute! It's becoming a dangerous cold world out there, Raquel. And I didn't want you walking down the shops or the launderette. I want you to drive there. So you'll be safe and sound. D'you see what I mean?

Raquel Is that why you bought it?

Del Yeah.

Raquel Ah, aren't you lovely?

Del Yeah.

Raquel Mmh! *(Kisses him)* I love you, Trotter.

Del Of course you do. You're only human.
They kiss jokingly.
Now they kiss again seriously.
Del is about to go in for the kill when he looks at her lump.

Del Fancy a cup of tea?
Rodney bursts through the front door.

Rodney Del! It's Albert!

Del Albert?? What about Albert?

Rodney There's no need to panic, OK?

Raquel What's happened to Albert?

Rodney He's been mugged!

Del He's been what?

Raquel Is he hurt?

Rodney No, not badly. He's got a bit of double vision, that's all.

Del Where's this happen, Rodney?

Rodney Well, in his eyes.

Del No, I mean…

Rodney Oh sorry! As he was walking home from the pub. I was just coming back from Jevon's and I saw this ambulance and a crowd of people standing round him.

Del Did he get a good look at 'em?

Rodney No. All he can remember is there were four of 'em. Look, they've taken him to the hospital. Come on, I've got the van downstairs.
Del and Rodney rush to the front door, closing the hall door as they go. Then the hall door opens again and Del rushes towards the bedroom.

Del Dipstick. Rodney!

Rodney *(To Raquel)* He's just gonna put some clothes on.

INT. TROTTERS' LOUNGE. THE FOLLOWING DAY

Albert, in pyjamas and dressing gown, is laid out on the settee. He has bruising round his eye and nose. He is now a very unhappy, almost frightened, man who has lost all confidence and is most probably suffering from shock. Del and Rodney, wearing identical suits, are standing over their stricken uncle. Rodney's shirt is unbuttoned at the neck to reveal he is wearing a single gold chain.

Rodney Look at him.

Del Looks bloody horrible, don't he?

Rodney They said he could be suffering from shock for a few days.

Del You wait 'til I get my hands on the bastards what done it. Then you'll see what a state of shock really looks like!

Raquel Now, you stay out of it! The police can handle this perfectly well on their own!

Del I don't need the Old Bill! The people round here have always sorted their own problems out. It's traditional. I remember years ago when I was about ten. Mum had some of her jewellery nicked by this good-

He Ain't Heavy, He's My Uncle

looking Italian bloke. He weren't good looking by the time Dad had finished with him!

Rodney But how could you be certain he was guilty?

Del Evidence, Rodney. Dad found one of Mum's earrings on the back seat of this bloke's car!

Rodney and Raquel look at each other. The doorbell rings. This alarms Albert.

Rodney It's alright, Unc. Just the door.

Rodney exits to the hall and opens the door to Cassandra.

Cassandra Hi.

Rodney Oh, hi.

Cassandra I just came round to see how Albert was.

Rodney He's not too good. Come in.

They enter the lounge.

Cassandra I heard what happened to Albert. How is he?

Del He looks 'orrible. They stole his pocket watch and all his money.

Cassandra Yeah, I know. How you feeling, Albert?

Albert A bit bruised, dear. I got jumped on by five of 'em.

Del Now don't go upsetting yourse... Five of 'em? Rodney, d'you wanna make Cassandra a cup of coffee in the kitchen?

Rodney Eh? Oh yeah. Shall we make a cup of coffee?

Rodney and Cassandra enter the kitchen.

Cassandra So you're working for Del again?

Rodney Yes. It wasn't an easy decision. I had quite a few offers from local companies – you know what these head-hunters are like.

Cassandra Well, not really.

Rodney Oh they won't take no for an answer. But in the end I plumped for Trotters Independent Traders. It was a mixture of family loyalty and a career move.

He asked me to be his director of commercial development. Seek out new openings, find gaps in the market.

Cassandra And if a gap doesn't exist, create one?

Rodney Yeah, that sorta thing. So I thought, that'll do me, lovely Jubbly! It's pressure all the way. I'm never off that phone.

Cassandra You've cut your finger!

Rodney Yeah, Del got me to clean his car yesterday and... I just did it as a favour. I don't know if you saw his new car parked downstairs. It's the green Pratmobile.

Cassandra *(Laughs)* Does he know you call it that?

Rodney No. I don't think he'd be too pleased.

Cassandra So things are going well?

Rodney Yeah. We're into property development, theatre...

Cassandra *(Indicates a box of toilet rolls)* Toilet rolls.

Rodney That's just... the retail sales division. We've got contacts in the City.

Cassandra What, White City?

(Laughs)

Rodney There's no need to laugh at us, Cass!

Cassandra I'm not laughing at you! I'm just trying to break the ice!

Rodney Oh... How's our flat?

Cassandra Much the same as when you left, Roddy. I wish I could say the same about you!

Rodney What's that mean?

Cassandra You've changed! You're getting more like Del. You're full of front and bullshit, Roddy! You're even wearing ths same clothes as Del.

Rodney These suits happen to be a new line we're selling. They're Romanian. We wear them to let the punter see what they look like.

Cassandra D'you think that's wise?

Rodney We know our market, Cassandra! And I am not getting like Del!

Cassandra You are, Rodney. *(Flicks his gold chain)* Look, you're even wearing a Del Boy starter kit!

Rodney Del told me to wear this because… Understand one thing, Cass! I am not getting like Del! No way, Pedro!

Cassandra No way, Pedro!

Rodney Look, I'm very busy, Cassandra.

Cassandra Yeah, see you, Rodney.

Rodney Look, I didn't mean it like that.

Cassandra Goodbye!

Cassandra exits.

Rodney I'll give you a bell during the week. *(Quietly)* Shit!

INT. TROTTERS' LOUNGE. NIGHT

One week later. Albert is seated in the armchair, looking through his old treasure chest of memories. He is wearing pyjamas and a woolly dressing gown. Raquel, in night attire, is asleep on the settee.

The door from the hall opens suddenly and Del enters in his dressing gown.

Albert jumps with fear at Del's entrance.

Del It's only me, Unc! I've put the security chain on. No one can get in. You alright now?

Albert Yeah, I'm alright, boy.

Raquel D'you fancy a coffee?

Del No, you stay where you are. Has he been out today?

Raquel No. He hasn't left the flat for the last week – well, ever since it happened.

Del Terrified, ain't he, poor old git… What you up to, Unc?

Albert Just looking through me old box. *(Shows Del a photo)* See that? That's where I was born. Tobacco Road, down by the docks. *(Another photo)* That's the front of Tobacco Road. There's yer nan – there's

your grandad. He'd just joined the army, doing his bit for king and country.

Del But he's wearing plimsolls and a jumper.

Albert Yeah, he'd just deserted.

Raquel Albert, Tomorrow, would you like us to take you back to where you were born?

Albert *(Sadly)* It's not there any more, dear. They knocked it down. That film you wanted to watch is on soon.

Raquel Oh thanks.

Del moves behind the bar and pours the drinks.

Del What film's that?

Raquel *Out Of Africa.*

Del Not another documentary about Aids?

Raquel No, it's a film with Robert Redford.

Albert Did I ever tell you about the time I was in Africa?

Del *(Under his breath)* About 3,000 times!

Raquel *(She gives Del a glance that tells him to shut up)* No. Why what happened, Unc?

Del *(Quietly)* During the war.

Albert During the war I was on this hospital ship. We'd picked up some of the wounded from Monty's North Africa campaign and then dropped 'em off in Durban. I helped carry some of them lads off the ship. It was tragic to see some of 'em, bloody tragic. I cried for em… Daft, eh?

Del There's nothing wrong with crying, Albert. I cried when me mum died.

Albert But you were only 16, Del. I was a full-grown man.

Del I shed a little tear when Rodney got married and left home… I cried even more when he come back!

Albert The most frightening thing in all my life happened while I was in Africa. While we were docked at Durban a couple of black blokes asked me and some of me

He Ain't Heavy, He's My Uncle

mates if we wanted to go out and see the jungle. We jumped at the chance. You're like that when you're young, ain't you?

Del *(Already getting bored)* Oh yeah, we've all done it.

Albert So off we all went on the back of this open lorry. Well, after a couple of hours the undergrowth started getting heavier and heavier. We were deep in the heart of the jungle. There was swamps and quicksand and everything.

Raquel *(Slightly sleepy through boredom)* Mmmh.

Albert In the end we had to get off the lorry and start walking. The lads were mucking about. You know, making Tarzan noises and all that.

Del *(Eyes closed and operating on auto)* Rascals.

Albert Anyway, somehow or another I got cut off from the rest of the party and found meself in this clearing. I was just about to retrace me steps when I heard a noise behind me. I turned round and standing there was the biggest lion I've ever seen.

Raquel is now asleep. Del's eyes are closed and he is just mumbling in his half-sleep.

Del Don't need all that, do you?

Albert I looked at him – and he looked at me. We just stood there – looking at each other. Then suddenly he went Raaaaggggghhhhhhrrrrrr!

(He lets out a massive and loud roar. He puts so much effort into it that his eyes are bulging.)

Del and Raquel wake with alarm.

Del Cor blimey, Albert! Leave it out, will you?

Albert I've never been so frightened... I did something very childish, Del. *(He is on the point of crying)* I wet meself! *(Holding back the tears)* A full-grown man – and I wet meself.

Del Hey, no, come on. That's nothing to get upset about, Unc. Any bloke would do the same if faced with a man-eating lion!

Albert I don't mean in the jungle. I mean just now when I went 'Raaaggghhhrrrr'.

Del Oh! Er... *(Looks to Raquel)*

Raquel Er...

A key is heard in the door. The door opens but is held by the chain of the security lock.

Rodney *(OOV)* I don't believe it!

The chain is long enough and loose enough for Rodney to put his hand round the door and unlock it. Rodney enters. Hangs his coat up and enters the lounge. Albert is exiting for the bedroom area, followed by Raquel.

Del *(To Raquel)* There's some of his stuff in the airing cupboard.

Raquel exits and closes the door.

Rodney Alright? How's Albert?

Del He's not his old self.

Rodney Oh good! Just a joke.

Del I bloody hope it was!

Rodney Alright, keep your hair on.

Rodney is about to sit in Albert's chair.

Del No!

Rodney *(Hasn't sat yet)* What?

Del *(Smiles)* Nothing.

Rodney sits in the chair.

Rodney So he's no better?

Del No, he ain't been out the door for ages. The doctor said he should get back to normal life.

Rodney That's right. I was there. You see, I think the problem is... *(He looks down at the chair as he suffers some mild and mysterious discomfort)* You are being very kind and considerate. You're being patient and understanding.

Del Yeah.

Rodney Well, that ain't normal, is it?

Del You looking for a doughboy round the ear, Rodney?

Rodney Ah, now that's normal! D'you see what I mean? This flat is all hurly-burly, shouting and arguing – nobody means any harm by it – it's just the way we are. But all of a sudden we're treating Albert with kid gloves. If it goes on much longer he'll start to accept that as normal. Then when we go back to real normality it'll put him back into shock!

Del So you reckon we oughta toughen up a bit?

Rodney The gently, gently approach hasn't worked.

Del I can't be hard on him, Rodney.

Rodney Nor can I! But… *(Looks down at the chair again and wonders what this feeling is)* We'd be doing it for him! Otherwise he'll take root in this flat.

Del Yeah… maybe.

Albert enters from his bedroom wearing fresh pyjamas and dressing gown.

Rodney *(Offering armchair)* Here you are, Unc.

Albert *(Emphatically)* No, you stay where you are, son. I'll sit over here. Alright if I have a drop of brandy, Del?

Del Yeah, of course, Unc. *(About to move to bar, then remembers Rodney's words)* You know where it is.

Albert Eh? Oh yeah.

Albert moves to the bar.

Rodney We've got a very busy day ahead of us tomorrow, Derek.

Del *(Hasn't caught on to Rodney's act)* Have we?

Rodney Yes!

Del Oh yeah, a very busy day. We won't have time to go down to get the shopping.

Rodney No. And we can't expect Raquel to do it, not in her condition.

Del That's true, Rodney!

Rodney So… *(Looks down at the chair again)* What are we going to do?

Del Albert, you'd better go 'n' get the shopping.

Albert Me? I can't go out there, Del.

Del Yes, you can!

Albert I don't really feel up to it yet, son.

Del You just pop down to the shop and get some fish fingers… Listen to me, Unc, we've got a busy time ahead of us, what with Trotter Independent Traders being in a phase of commercial augmentation and Raquel about to drop her chavy. We can't carry any lame ducks. You are starting to get under our feet. D'you understand what I'm saying? Get up and get out, 'cos you're no good to us the way you are.

Albert Yeah… I understand you, Del… I understand.

Albert moves to his bedroom.

Albert Goodnight, boys.

He exits to the bedroom.

Rodney That was a bit tough, weren't it?

Del What? You were the one who said…

Rodney *(Cuts in)* I'm not saying anything against you – just you were harder than I imagined.

Del Are you comfortable in that chair, Rodney?

Rodney Eh?

Del laughs. Rodney reacts. Del laughs louder

INT. TROTTERS' LOUNGE. DAY

The table is laid for breakfast. Albert's treasure chest is still in the room. Del and Rodney enter. Rodney is carrying a suitcase. Raquel, still in her dressing gown, appears at the kitchen door.

Raquel You're back early.

Del Yeah, it's parky out there this morning, sweetheart. I'm starving.

Raquel I'll do you a bowl of muesli.

Del Cushty.

Raquel exits to the kitchen.

Del Bloody muesli!

Rodney Albert's left his treasure chest out here. There's a photo of a ship going

He Ain't Heavy, He's My Uncle

down. *(Reads back)* 'June 27th, 1943. HMS *Lock* sinks'.

Del Look at all these telegrams the Admiralty sent Aunt Ada. 'Albert Trotter lost at sea presumed drowned.' Blimey, must have been rough on the old girl.

Raquel enters from the kitchen carrying a breakfast tray.

Raquel I'll just take this into Albert, then I'll do your muesli.

Del Lovely Jubbly.

Raquel moves to Albert's bedroom.

Rodney All the other telegrams say the same. 'Albert Trotter lost at sea presumed drowned.' She couldn't have taken 'em seriously in the end.

Del *(Reading another telegram)* No. Even the Admiralty didn't in the end. Look what this one says: 'Albert Trotter lost at sea presumed wet!'

Rodney Is that what it says?

Del 'Course not, you wally!

Raquel exits from Albert's bedroom carrying a note.

Raquel He's not there!

Del What d'you mean, he's not there?

Raquel He's gone! He left a note. 'I won't get under your feet any more. Your loving Uncle, Albert.'

Del and Rodney look at each other, both filled with guilt.

Rodney It must have been what you said last night.

Del What I said! I didn't wanna say anything 'til you come in and told me to say something!

Rodney Well, don't try an blame me!

Del And don't try and blame m...

Raquel *(Cuts in)* Will you two stop arguing? Go and find him!

Del Well, where's he gone?

Raquel I don't know! Go 'n' look!

Rodney She's right. Let's go. I'll take the van, you take the Pratmobile.

Rodney rushes to the hall and front door.

Del *(To Raquel)* What did he say?

EXT. NELSON MANDELA HOUSE. DAY

Rodney rushes from the doors towards the van. Del exits from the doors a couple of seconds later.

Del *(Shouts)* What do you mean, 'Pratmobile?'

Rodney *(Urgently)* Come on!

1. TOWER BRIDGE
We see the van and Capri pass each other on the bridge.

2. CHARING CROSS ARCHES
Tramps sitting round a fire. Rodney describes Albert to them. The tramps shake their heads. Rodney gives them a quid.

3. CHELSEA PENSIONERS
Del talks to them about Albert. They shake their heads.

4. PUB
Rodney approaches the pub and looks in through the door. He returns to the van. As he sits in the van we see rain falling on the windscreen.

5. IMPERIAL WAR MUSEUM
As Del exits the museum we hear a thunderclap. Del looks up at the skies and pulls his collar up.

6. RODNEY DRIVING THE VAN
Windscreen wipers going.

7. DEL DRIVING THE CAPRI
Windscreen wipers going.

8. HMS BELFAST
Rodney exits from the bridge. He feels the air to confirm it has stopped raining. Walks the deck.

 233

9. SEAMAN'S MISSION

Del, disappointed, exits from the mission.

10. STREET

Rodney punches out a number on his mobile phone.

11. MARKET CAFE

Del hears a ringing sound but doesn't know where it's coming from. He finally realises and produces his mobile phone.

Rodney Any luck?

Del No.

As Del answers we see Rodney wander into the background. Although they are only 25 yards apart, they cannot see each other because of an obstacle.

12. CARDBOARD CITY

Del moves a box to discover a young vagrant sleeping in it. Del describes Albert and asks, 'Have you seen him?' The kid holds his hand out for money. Del pays him, describes Albert again. The kid shakes his head and smiles.

13. LONDON BRIDGE

We see Rodney's head bobbing along with the rush-hour tide.

14. MARKET

We see Del among the market crowd.

15. LONDON BRIDGE

Rodney continues crossing the bridge with the crowd.

16. MARKET

Del chatting to a trader.

17. STREET/VAN

Rodney suddenly realises where Albert is.

18. WILD SHOTS

Wild shots of Del and Rodney realising where Albert is.

19. PORTOBELLO ROAD MARKET

Del walking through market.

20. FINAL SEQUENCE. EXT. YUPPY HOUSING DEVELOPMENT IN DOCKS AREA/RIVER. DAY.

We see a street sign which reads Tobacco Road.

The Capri screeches to a halt, Del alights, looks towards the river and smiles to himself. The van pulls up. Rodney alights. Del gestures towards the river. Albert is seated down near the river, looking out across the water.

Rodney *(Quietly, caringly)* Alright, Unc?

Albert What you two doing here?

Del We were worried about you, you silly old git. We've been looking all over London for you!

Rodney We found your note.

Albert How'd you know I'd be here?

Rodney Just a guess, I s'pose. This is where you was born, innit?

Albert Yeah. Tobacco Road. My house was… *(He looks around)* Well, somewhere round here.

Del What's it all about, eh? Running away from home at your age!

Albert A lot of things been going through my mind recently, Del. I didn't know if I was coming or going. I feel as if I let the family down *(Indicates the bruising)*. I let you two down.

Del Oh don't be so bloody daft!

Rodney You didn't let anyone down!

Albert I needed to be alone for a while.

Rodney But where were you gonna go?

Albert I hadn't given it much thought, Rodney. I didn't realise things had changed so much. The first time I left home, when I was about 15, I just came here and got a job on a tramp-steamer… Life seemed easier then.

Del It ain't all that difficult now, Albert. All you gotta do is come home – to your family.

He Ain't Heavy, He's My Uncle

Albert Thanks, son.

Rodney Come on, let's go.

Albert You know, once upon a time ships from all over the world used to sail in and out of here. The water used to be covered with a film of oil and when the sun shone it used to sparkle with all different colours. When I was a kid I used to think that rainbows lived in the river.

Del You were a bit divvy in them days as well?

Rodney *(A warning)* Oi!

Del Yeah, alright.

Albert There were tugs nudging freighters into position. Cranes lifting out timber from Canada and bananas from Jamaica. The pubs and the cafés were filled with sailors from a hundred countries. By the time I was seven I could swear in ten different languages. There used to be streets here as well. Loads of little two up, two down houses. 'Dockers' mansions' they used to call 'em. Ragamuffins kicking footballs against the walls. The women used to come out and chase us away with their brooms… They were rough people, but they were good people. During the Blitz some of the men painted a sign on the roof of a warehouse so that the Luftwaffe pilots could read it. It said 'Dear Adolf, you can break our windows – but not our hearts!' Look at what they've done to it now!

Del Yeah… It's triffic, innit?

Rodney Triffic?

Del You any idea how much these drums are worth, Rodney?

As Del speaks, so Albert looks appealingly to Rodney. Rodney tries to give Albert a reassuring look.

Del An arm and a leg, that's what they're worth. Lord Linley's got one of these. And Michael Caine. Makes you proud to be British! This is a bit of me, this is. I can see it now. Nice little black Porsche parked outside, me windsurfer tied to the roofrack.

Rodney and Albert walk back towards the van, leaving Del talking to himself.

Del A few friends from the City arriving for a little private party in yonder pub. A few glasses of Moët *(rhymes with 'poet')* and some pâté foie gras, 'cos I'm a champagne and liver sausage sort of person, and watch the old currant bun setting behind the Docklands arena. Paradise. Wait a couple of years for property prices to rocket, then knock it out to some Arab for twice the purchase price. Lovely Jubbly!

The van pulls away with Rodney and Albert inside, leaving Del staring dreamily across the waters.

TROTTERS' LOUNGE. NIGHT

Ten hours later. Albert is on the settee.

Raquel You alright, Unc?

Albert Yeah, I'm alright, dear.

Raquel You didn't have to go running off like that. Del didn't mean anything.

Albert I know, he's explained to me. It's just that I felt… well, I felt like a failure. I'm not a coward, Raquel. There was nothing I could do. There was six of 'em!

Raquel I know. Albert, nobody thinks you're… Six of them?

Del enters from the bedroom in his dressing gown.

Del Where's Rodney?

Raquel He went out for a drink. Again!

Del That explains it. I was talking to a couple of winos earlier and they said they were busy celebrating St Rodney's Day… *(Now a grave concern)* Wait a minute, I hope he ain't gone to the Nag's Head!

Raquel Why, what's happening at the Nag's Head tonight?

Del Eh? Oh nothing!

Raquel exits to the kitchen. Del sits and becomes deep in thought. There is a ring at the front-door bell. This alarms Albert.

Albert Is that the bell, Del?

Del Yeah, I think it was, Unc. *(He is about to stand when he changes his mind)* I'm a bit busy at the moment.

Albert Oh... *(Calls)* Raquel!

Del Raquel's busy as well. You answer it.

Albert Me?

Del Come on, Unc. You've got nothing to be worried about. I'm here.

Raquel You're gonna have to answer the door sometime or another, so it might as well be now...

The bell rings again.

Del See who it is, Albert.

Albert moves hesitantly towards the hall door. He opens the hall door and stares in fear at the front door.

Albert *(Calls)* Who's there?

Knock-Knock Knock-Knock.

Albert It's Knock-Knock!

Del Is it?

Albert I can't see him, Del!

Del Well, of course you can't. You ain't opened the door!

Albert I mean, I don't wanna see him! I can't face it, Del!

Del Alright, alright. Leave it to me.

Del exits to hall and closes the door behind him.

Raquel You can talk to Knock-Knock, Albert. He's your friend.

Albert I don't wanna talk to him, not at the moment.

Raquel But he's most probably come to see how you are. He might have bought a bunch of grapes.

Albert I'm not feeling all that well, love. I think I'll go to my room.

Raquel OK.

Albert moves to bedroom.

As he gets to the door, so Del enters from the hall. Del is now knowing and accusing.

Del Oi, stay right where you are! *(Produces Albert's gold watch)* Knock-Knock brought this back. There's a bit of luck, innit!

Raquel It's your pocket watch, Albert. Where's he get it from?

Del He found it in the bushes on that patch of grass near the swings.

Raquel What, where Albert was mugged last week?

Del No! Where Albert and Knock-Knock, while walking home from the pub, had a fight last week!

Raquel They had a fight?

Del Yeah, over Marlene's mum! And Knock-Knock knocked him out! He weren't mugged, the lying old git!

Raquel But what about his money that went missing?

Del He lost it all at dominoes to Knock-Knock!

Raquel Oh Albert!

Albert I didn't know what to say! I felt silly, losing to a man three years older than me. He kept saying he was better than me at everything. So I squared up to him and he hit me!

Del Have you any idea the problems you've caused? We've got a police investigation going on. I've been out looking for five muggers.

Raquel Six!

Del Oh it's gone up to six now, has it? Any more offers?

Albert I felt embarrassed! Once I'd said it I couldn't go back.

Rodney enters.

Rodney *(Excited)* Should have been down the Nag's Head. There was the punch–up to end all punch–ups!

Del closes his eyes and turns away.

Raquel What happened, then?

Rodney That mob of skinheads were in there, the ones Del said mugged Albert. Anyway, you know oily Ollie the greaser? Well, him and his gang have come and attacked the skinheads. There was blood up the wall, grease on the ceiling. Ollie and his

He Ain't Heavy, He's My Uncle

boys took a right hammering! It turns out them skinheads ain't skinheads at all. They're coppers!

Del They're what?

Rodney Undercover policemen. They were put on the estate a few weeks back when the muggings started.

Del Oh God!

Rodney What's up, Del?

Del Well, I... anyone would have done the same.

Raquel You didn't... you didn't... have anything to do with this, did you?

Del Well... I wanted revenge for what they'd done to that dozy old twonk! I sort of... kind of... gave Ollie 100 quid to sort it out.

Raquel Oh for God's sake! This baby will be born premature if I hang around you much longer!

Raquel storms to the bedroom and slams the door.

Del *(Appealing to her)* Be fair, sweetheart They looked like muggers!

Rodney When Oliver and his army get out of hospital I've got a fair idea where their first port of call will be!

Del Yeah, me too.

Albert Well, they better not try anything with me around! I used to be the Royal Navy boxing champion.

Del *(Fist clenched)* I'm gonna kill you!

Rodney grabs Del's raised hand.

Rodney Del!

EPISODE SIX

Three Men, a Woman and a Baby

INT. THE TROTTERS' LOUNGE. DAY

On the dining table is a plate covered by another plate.

Rodney, in pyjamas and dressing gown, enters from his bedroom looking depressed and slightly hungover. He flops down at the table.

Rodney Albert. *(Holds his head as this sends a sharp pain through his brain)*

Rodney lifts the top plate off. The plate under it contains the half-finished and congealed remains of last night's takeaway curry.

Rodney *(Revolted)* Oh – curry!

Albert enters from the hall carrying the Sunday papers.

Albert Oh you finally decided to get up, did you? You still a vegetarian?

Rodney Yes.

Albert Pity they didn't make booze out of animals – then maybe you wouldn't have a hangover!

Rodney Where is everyone?

Albert Raquel's still in bed, Del went a work about 6.00 this morning.

Rodney But it's Sunday! Don't he ever have a day off?

Albert He's a yuppy, ain't he? As he says, 'The business world never sleeps.' As the New York stock exchange closes, Tokyo opens. Del's gotta keep his finger on the pulse.

Rodney Triffic. Where's he gone?

Albert Petticoat Lane. He's got some gear to pick up off a mate. You feeling any happier? You looked very depressed when you come in last night.

Rodney That may have something to do with the fact that my marriage is in tatters and I've lost the best job I've ever had.

Albert But you're working for Del Boy now.

Rodney Exactly! Wouldn't you be depressed? If I'd stayed with Cassandra's dad, I'd have been running that firm within a couple of years.

Albert Well, one day Del will retire and Trotters Independent Traders will be all yours.

Rodney I know! Bloody hell! I wish there was something – anything – on the horizon that could raise my spirits.

Albert *(Can't think of anything at first)* Er… Del and Raquel's baby is gonna be born soon!

Rodney Oh God, I forgot about that.

Albert But that's a reason for celebration, innit?

Rodney For you and Del and Raquel, maybe. But how d'you think I feel? By the time I'm 45 Son of Del will be 16. What chance will I have? I can see it now. *(In adolescent voice)* "I've got a good idea, Uncle Rodney. I'll buy a load of old crap and you can go out and sell it for me. That way, Uncle Rodney, I'll have lots of money and wide-awake suits and you won't have a pot to piss in." And what worries me most is, I'll fall for it.

Albert That's stupid. It might not be a boy.

Rodney No, it's a boy alright. *Rosemary's Baby* was on telly the other night. It's Del and Raquel to a tee. In a couple of weeks' time we'll be awoken by the cries of our own little bonny, bouncing antichrist. It'll be sitting in its cot, head spinning round like a propeller, green gunge up the wall. They're bound to call it Damien.

Albert *(As if to cheer Rodney up)* They were thinking of calling him Rodney.

Rodney Rodney! Oh no, poor little sod.

Raquel, in her dressing gown, enters from the bedroom looking tired and fed up.

Raquel Morning.

Rodney Morning.

Albert Del's not back yet, love. Fancy a cup of tea?

Albert exits to kitchen.

Raquel Please, Albert. *(Yawns)* Sorry, I feel exhausted. He was moving around all night long.

Rodney He's always the same after a curry... Oh the baby!

Del enters from hall carrying a large cardboard box. The printing on the side reads: 'Crowning glory, wigs of distinction'.

Del Oh, the creature from the black lagoon has risen from its pit.

Rodney That's no way to talk to the mother of your child.

Del *(Kisses Raquel)* You alright, sweetheart?

Raquel Yeah, I'm OK.

Del *(Patting box)* Guess what I've got here.

Raquel No, go on.

Del Wigs! You know Mustapha from the Bangladeshi butcher's shop? Well, his nephew works for a top West End wig-maker. According to him they look after all the big stars: Jane Fonda, Sophia Loren, Anita Dobson, the lot. Now he gets these wigs for a quarter of the retail price.

Raquel A quarter of the retail price?

Del It's a concession to employees.

Rodney But a quarter of the price!

Del Alright, they're seconds. But with the kind of quality standards this company demands, one hair out of place and they're rejected. And that's where an opportunist like me steps in. And I've already sold 'em! All the old tarts down the Nag's Head have been waiting for these to come in for weeks. I can't move for advance orders. Lovely Jubbly.

Albert enters from the kitchen with teapot.

Albert Oh you're back, Del. Fancy a bit of breakfast?

Del *(Deliberately to annoy Rodney)* Yeah, do us a nice vegetarian bacon sandwich.

Rodeny is revolted.

Del So what are you up to today, Rodders? A Greenpeace rally, release a few nut cutlets?

Rodney Look, just because I have become concerned about what is happening on our planet is no reason to take the rise out of me.

Del No, but ever since you went vegetarian you've become a right miserable git.

Raquel There's nothing wrong with being vegetarian, Del.

Rodney That's right! One in five people in this country now refuse to eat meat. Mickey Pearce has become a vegetarian.

Del Yeah, but only since he got the sack from World of Leather. A man needs a bit of fat and stodge to solid things up. Any doctor'll tell you that. All that carrot and cabbage cobblers, no wonder you're depressed.

Rodney I am depressed because of the state of my life at the moment. I've got this horrible feeling that if there is such a thing as reincarnation, knowing my luck I'll come back as me!

Albert You've gotta pick yourself up and look around at all the things you've got in life.

Rodney I've done that, Unc! That's what got me in this state. Name me one thing I – not you – me, Rodney Trotter, has got to look forward to?

Raquel You're taking Cassandra to Hampton Court this afternoon.

Rodney Oh cos-mic! A castle and a maze. I just love looking at suits of armour and then getting lost.

Three Men, a Woman and a Baby

Del Cheer up, touchy tart. I'll tell you what, you can take my new second-hand Capri Ghia if you like.

Rodney No thank you.

Del Why don't you have a shower and put some decent clobber on?

Raquel Del's right, Rodney. It can make you feel a lot better.

Del Put a bit of joie de vivre back in yer life.

Albert Yeah. We wanna see the old Rodney Trotter back, don't we, Del?

Del *(Half-hearted)* Yeah.

Albert Snap out of all this doom and gloom.

Raquel Be optimistic, Rodney.

Del We all have a few dark clouds in our lives.

Albert It ain't such a bad old world, son.

Raquel You're young, you got your whole future ahead of you.

Rodney Yeah! You're right. I'm sorry.

Del Good boy. You know it makes sense.

Rodney Yeah. Well, I'm going back to bed for a while.

> *Rodney moves to his bedroom and exits as Del speaks.*

Del That's the spirit, Rodders. Onwards and upwards! Never say die, you lazy little plonker!

INT. THE NAG'S HEAD. DAY

> *A handwritten sign on the wall reads: 'Guess the baby Trotter's Name, £1 a try, winner takes the kitty. Ask at bar for entry form.' Next to it is a barrel with a slit in the top. One of the regulars is putting his entry form in the barrel and pays Mike a pound. Rodney, depressed, is alone at a table with an almost finished half of lager. He is dressed smartly, having just returned from his day out with Cassandra. Mike and Trigger are at bar.*

Mike *(Referring to Rodney)* Trigger. See if you can find out what they're naming the baby.

Trigger Why?

Mike Because I'm not allowed to go in for my own competition. But I'll let you enter and then we can share the winnings.

Trigger Leave it to me, Mike.

> *Trigger joins Rodney*

Trigger Alright, Dave?

Rodney Wotcher, Trig.

Trigger Have they thought of a name for the baby yet?

Rodney Well, if it's a girl Del wants to call her Sigourney, after the actress Sigourney Weaver.

Trigger And what if it's a boy?

Rodney He said he might call it Rodney.

Trigger Yeah? Who after?

Rodney Me.

Trigger Oh.

> *Del enters.*

Trigger All right, Del?

Del Hello, Trigger. I'll be with you in a minute.

> *Del approaches a couple of women.*

Del I've got those wigs I promised you, girls. Albert's just fetching 'em from the van.

Mike So?

Trigger What?

Mike What name have they decided on?

Trigger If it's a girl they're calling her Sigourney after an actress, and if it's a boy they're naming him Rodney after Dave.

Mike Brilliant!

Trigger Thank you, Michael.

> *Trigger writes on paper and hands it to Mike. Mike is about to fold paper when he studies it.*

Mike Why have you written Susan or Colin?

Trigger It's a sort of intuition.

Mike Jesus!

Del joins them at the bar as Albert enters with the box of wigs. Albert puts box on the floor close to Rodney and then sits at the table.

Del Put it down by the table, Albert.

Albert So how'd your day out with Cassandra go?

Rodney Don't ask, OK? Just don't ask.

Albert Why, what happened?

Rodney I'll tell you what happened. She told me it's all over between us. Me and Cassandra are no longer an item. Me and Cassandra are no more. She said we are finito – and right in the middle of the maze as well! God – you leave yer wife for a few months and… I just don't understand her any more.

Albert I know the feeling, son. When you and Cassandra first met, what was the big attraction?

Rodney Dunno. Lust, I suppose.

Albert Yeah, she struck me as that sort.

Rodney I'm talking about me.

Albert I know you are. I'm just having a joke with you.

Rodney Well, I ain't in a joking mood.

Mike So, you thought of a name, Del?

Del We haven't made up our mind, Michael. We're gonna go through our book of baby names. You'll soon know what we've decided on.

Mike When?

Del When I have a go in your competition.
Del, carrying drinks, joins them at the table.

Del So how was Hampton Court?

Rodney I don't wanna talk about it.

Del Why, what happened?

Albert Cassandra gave him the elbow in the maze.

Del Blimey, sounds painful. Look, you don't wanna worry about it, bruv. Plenty more fish in the sea.

Rodney It's not that simple, Del. That woman has left a mark on me.

Del So did your smallpox jab.

Mike Look, this is none of my business, Rodney, and you can tell me to keep my nose out if you like.

Rodney Keep yer nose out, Mike.

Mike I was married once and know exactly what you're going through.

Del You listen to the man, Rodney. His wife chucked him out years ago.

Mike You don't wanna take too much notice of things that are said in the heat of the argument.

Rodney She said that I'd always refused to adapt to married life. She said I wanted to carry on doing the same things that I'd always done.

Del What d'you say to that?

Rodney I said, "I'm not discussing it any more. I'm going down the Nag's Head." She said I lacked ambition! Me!

Del What a load of rubbish! How many times did Rodney take that computer exam?

Albert Must have been five times.

Del Exactly! How many of his fellow students could claim that, eh? They all went and passed first time.

Mike No staying power.

Del That could be your silver lining, Rodders. Most people come out of a broken marriage with a sense of failure. But you're used to it.

Albert Years of experience.

Mike I remember me and my missus. I had 18 blissfully happy years – then I met her.
Del, Albert and Mike laugh.

Trigger D'you find your way out of the maze alright, Dave?

Rodney No, I'm still in there, Trig.

Trigger I couldn't find me way out of there once.

Del You had trouble finding your way in once.

Trigger I had this bird with me. We had a right row. She wanted to go to the left and I

Three Men, a Woman and a Baby

wanted to go to the right... No, I tell a lie... She wanted to go to the right and I wanted to go to...

Rodney *(Cuts straight in)* Look, Trigger! Cassandra and I are intelligent people and we do not have rows about what is the quickest way out of a maze. God, I've never felt so depressed in all my life.

Del Come on, Rodney, pull yourself together.

Rodney *(Stands as if to leave)* I just wanna be alone.

Del *(Eases him back into his seat)* Listen to me. That is the worst thing you can do. It's times like this you need people round you.

Rodney But they just say stupid things about lust and mazes.

Del Never give up on people, Rodney. I know that most of the time they don't seem to understand. But when you're in trouble and you cry out for help, some will alway be there. Trigger's cousin Cyril's a perfect example. He owed 500 quid on his mortgage.

Trigger They were gonna be thrown out on the street the following day. He was very worried about it.

Mike So what happened, Trig?

Trigger He drove out to Beachy Head. Parked about five foot from the edge of the cliff.

Albert What, he was gonna drive off it?

Trigger Yeah! He just sat there for a couple of hours, his head resting on the steering wheel. People tried to talk him out of it, but he was too depressed to listen.

Del But then, and this is what I mean about people, Rodney, they had a whip-round and got him his 500 quid.

Rodney No! Who held the whip-round?

Del All the passengers on his bus. See, something will always come along to cheer you up. Just be patient, bruv. And in the meantime, try and sell a few of them wigs. Do us a chip sandwich, Mike.

Del, Mike and Albert move to the bar.
Rodney opens box and looks inside.

Rodney Del, these wigs. Did your contact say anything about the Jean Shrimpton style or the urchin look?

Del No. Just said they're wigs.

Rodney starts laughing.

Albert You were right, Del. He's cheered up already.

Now Trigger starts laughing with Rodney.

Del What you laughing at?

Trigger Dunno!

INT. THE TROTTERS' LOUNGE. DAY

Del, seething, is on the telephone. Albert is looking into the box of wigs. Rodney is trying to conceal his laughter.

Del *(Waiting for call to be answered)* Come on, Mustapha, hurry up!

Albert You'll still be able to sell 'em, Del.

Del How?

Albert I don't know. Just remember, Del, he who dares, wins.

Del Oh don't gimme that old pony, Unc. *(Now on phone)* Hello, is that the mosque?

Rodney I don't believe it. He's phoned a mosque.

Del I wanna speak to Mustapha about them syrups he flogged me... Is he? Well, tell him, when he's finished praying, to go back and have another one, 'cos when I get hold of him he's gonna need all the help he can get. *(Switches phone off)* I was gonna sell him all them hooky Cat Stevens' LPs, but he can forget it.

Raquel enters from the bedroom.

Raquel What's all the shouting?

Rodney *(Trying not to laugh)* There's a problem with them wigs Del bought.

Raquel What sort of problem?

Del *(Can hardly bear to say it)* They're blokes' wigs.

Rodney collapses with laughter.

Raquel *(Trying hard not to laugh)* Blokes?

Del Yes! Bloody men's syrups. This is not funny, Rodney.

Raquel Alright, Del, alright… Keep your hair on.

Del Oh don't you start, sweetheart. How are we supposed to sell these things?

Albert There's a lot of bald blokes come out of that building in Arnold Road.

Del That's a Hare Krishna temple. They like their heads looking like that. *(Searching through box)* Look at this! We've even got men's ponytails in here. *(Del begins punching out a number on his phone}* I'll handle the telephone sales campaign, Rodney. You see if you can flog a few in the pubs.

Rodney In the p…? How can I go up to a bald bloke in a pub and say d'you wanna wig? I'll get me face smashed in.

Del You'll have to work on your sales approach. Otherwise learn to duck. *(On phone)* Gordon? Del Boy. How you going, pal? Cushty. Listen to me, Gordon, are you still bald? Well, ain't you ever thought of doing something about it? Well, it's either a wig or a balaclava, innit? I mean, a bit of hair can make you look years younger… You've been thinking about a hair transplant. No way, Pedro. Well, I mean, it's gonna cost you at least 10 grand… Yes, of course you can get cheaper ones. Monkey Harris had one of them three quid hair transplants – have you seen him recently? Well, it's not a pretty sight, Gordon, not a pretty sight. I mean, you look at Frank Sinatra and Elton John and you can see they went to a top Harley Street clinic. Have a butcher's at Monkey Harris's bonce, looks like Bex Bissel did the job! Well, this is the reason I'm calling you. I've got a contact in a West End wig-makers. They've got every style, colour and size under the sun, and at very competitive prices. I'll send Rodney round with a selection. I'll leave 'em with you for a while. You ain't gotta feed 'em or nothing. Bonjour for now, Gordon.

Rodney produces a selection of sandy, auburn and one curly ginger wig.

Del They're no good.

Rodney I thought you meant ginger Gordon.

Del No, Jamaican Gordon. Blimey, put him in one of them he'll look like Ken Dodd's tickling stick! *(He flops into an armchair)* It's tough at the top!

INT. THE TROTTERS' LOUNGE.

A week later. Rodney and Albert are watching a documentary about the ecological disaster affecting the world. A sequence of the programme shows dead sea birds.

Rodney It's disgusting, innit?

Albert Yeah. They shouldn't put things on about dead animals when you're about to have your supper.

Rodney I'm not talking about the timing of the bloody programme. I mean, the damage that we have done to our planet.

Albert We ain't done nothing to the planet.

Rodney No, Unc. I don't mean that we, the Trotters, have damaged our planet – although there is one member of the family who could be described as an ecological time bomb. No, I'm talking about the human race in general. What are we gonna leave behind for the future generation? For the little kiddies in the infants schools, for the unborn millions?

Albert Yeah, like Del and Raquel's nipper.

Rodney I didn't actually mean him. Kids with three sixes on their heads don't count. I tell you, there'll be a few cathedrals go up in flames before that boy gets to his eleven-plus.

Del enters from the hall.

Three Men, a Woman and a Baby

Albert Alright, son? There's a fresh pot of tea on the table.

Del Cheers, Unc. I'll get a cup. I've just been to one of them antenatal classes with Raquel. Full of pregnant women it was. Everywhere you turned there was… lumps and… things.

Albert Why d'you have to go, then?

Del It's to get me ready for when we go into labour. They showed us films about how it all happens.

Albert You've already got some of them in the cupboard.

Del Not them sort of films. I mean films about the birth and that. I tell you, it's a miracle, a 42-carat miracle. Made a lot of the blokes feel ill. Didn't bother me though. I used to run a jellied eel stall.

Albert So what have you gotta do… you know… when it happens?

Del Well, basically, be on me toes. Make sure the old Capri Ghia is running well and whip Raquel down to maternity a bit lively. But the most important thing a father does is showing the woman consideration and understanding, patience and love. I mean, as luck has it, I'm like that anyway, but it don't hurt to be reminded.

Albert Where's Raquel then?

Del Oh the lifts ain't working again and she ain't as fast up them stairs as she used to be.

Rodney looks towards the open hall and front door and has this mental picture of Raquel, eight and three-quarter months pregnant, hauling herself up twelve flights of stairs.

Del How many of them wigs you sold in the last week, Rodney?

Rodney Well… er… roughly, none.

Del Well, I sold two tonight.

Rodney You're kidding!

Del No way, Pedro. It's the God's-honest. I met this woman I know from the market. Her and her old man both work at the hospital. She said he's been wearing a syrup for years, then last week their cat got hold of it. So she bought one off me as a surprise for him. Then on the way home I popped into the Nag's Head and sold Trigger one.

Albert But he's got hair.

Del I know. He said he wanted it for an emergency.

Raquel enters from the hall, exhausted.

Del Here you are, sweetheart, sit down here.

Raquel I'll go and change these clothes first.

Del I'll make us a cup of tea.

Del exits to the kitchen.

Albert So how was the antenatal class?

Raquel *(Referring to Del)* It's the last time I take him along. At the end of the class the doctor asked if there were any questions. Del put his hand up and said, "What time do the pubs close round here?"

Raquel exits to the bedroom.
Del enters from the kitchen.

Rodney That's typical Del. The world's dying and he's worried about last orders.

Del What's wrong with you, Rodney?

Albert He's been watching one of them green programmes. They were cutting a few trees down in South America.

Del Oh and Sting here's got the 'ump!

Rodney When are people gonna realise that we don't own this planet, we're merely leaseholders. It's our duty to maintain our world. But what are we doing? We're suffocating the forests with carbon monoxide! And that's causing the polar icecap to melt, which means the oceans will rise and the Thames will flood – like permanently.

Albert But we've got the Thames barrier now.

Rodney That won't do a lot of good when it's 15ft under water! *(Pointing out of the window to indicate the closeness of these*

areas) I mean, places like Deptford and Greenwich will be submerged for ever!

Del But think what it'll do for us.

Rodney Like what?

Del Well, when we come to sell this flat we'll be able to advertise it as having sea views!

Rodney What a ridiculous thing to say.

Del Alright, Rodney, what's really bothering you, eh? Is it just the destruction of the world?

Rodney I've got so many things worrying me. The polar cap is melting, the continental shelves are shifting, the rainforest is dying, the sea's being poisoned and I ain't had a bit in months.

Del So that's what's really worrying you? *(Indicating Albert)* How d'you think that poor old git feels? The last time he got his leg over, Nelson Mandela was in a borstal!

Rodney Can't you take anything seriously?

Raquel enters from the bedroom wearing her night attire.

Raquel *(Sensing the atmosphere)* What's wrong?

Albert Rodney ain't had a bit in months.

Raquel Oh.

Raquel exits to the bedroom.

INT. THE TROTTERS' LOUNGE

The following evening. Del is eating his dinner. Albert is reading one of Rodney's health and body magazines.

Albert Cor blimey. Things you learn. Do you realise if all my veins and arteries were stretched out in a line they would circle the world twice?

Del *(Trying to eat)* I'd like to try that one day. *(Del pushes his plate away)*

Albert Where's Raquel?

Del She had a bit of a twinge, so she's lying down.

Rodney enters from the hall

Rodney Alright?

Del Better than that, Rodders. I reckon we've had a right result with these syrups. Guess who I bumped into today.

Rodney Telly Savalas?

Del No. I bumped into that Stephen, the one who used to be Cassandra's boss at the bank. The one you smacked on the nose.

Rodney *(Still hates Stephen)* Oh him!

Del Yeah. Well, I bumped into him down the market today and you'll never guess: he's got one of 'em ponytails in his hair and I said to him, "What you doing with that Davy Crockett hat on?" just to break the ice. And apparently they're all the fashion up the City! All the yuppies are wearing them.

Albert But they look silly on men.

Del Yes, but today the sophisticated, intelligent young men don't mind making prats of themselves. Because it attracts the sophisticated, intelligent young ladies.

Rodney *(Examining one of the clip-on ponytails)* I can't see what the attraction is.

Del But you're a geezer! But if you were a young career woman you'd be getting the real hots for those things. And it don't need batteries. We'll make a fortune on them, Rodders.

Raquel enters from the bedroom carrying a baby's name book.

Del Hello darling, you alright?

Raquel Yeah, I'm OK now. What d'you think of Aaron?

Del Sorry?

Raquel I've been reading the baby's name book. Aaron Trotter.

Albert No, kids at school'll nickname him G-string. Aarona G-string. D'you get it?

Raquel Yeah, unfortunately.

Albert You gone off the name Rodney?

Del Yeah.

Rodney Thank God!

Del Troy.

Raquel Troy Trotter! I don't think so.

Three Men, a Woman and a Baby

Rodney Why don't you just call him Damien, eh?

Del Damien?

Raquel That's nice.

Rodney No, I was only joking!

Del I like that! Damien Trotter. That's got a sort of ring to it.

Rodney No, I was just having a wind-up, that's all. Why don't you call it Derek?

Del Yes. Damien Derek Trotter.

Albert You can't call him that! His initials'll be DDT.

Del Well, there'll be no flies on him, then, will there?

They all laugh at this.

Rodney No, when I said Damien, right, I was only…

The phone rings. Rodney answers the phone.

Rodney Trotters Independent Traders? *(Now fiercely proud)* Oh it's you, Cassandra! And what can I do for you? And what exactly do you want to see me about? Fine. Well, I'll pop round and see you sometime. Next week, next month – who knows? Thank you for calling. Bye. *(Switches phone off)*

Raquel Wasn't very friendly, was it?

Rodney Let people know where they stand, that's my motto. Cassandra seems to think that all she has to do is whistle and I'll come running.

Del Still, the least you could do was ask how she was.

Rodney I'll handle it my way, Derek, thank you… Well, I think I'll pop round and see how Cassandra is.

Del Yeah. That's the way, bruv. You've made her wait long enough.

As Rodney moves towards the hall and front door he pauses. Making sure no one sees, he takes a ponytail from the wig box.

INT. RODNEY'S AND CASSANDRA'S FLAT.

Music is playing. A pot of coffee and cups are on the coffee table. There is a ring at the front-door bell. Cassandra exits from bedroom and opens the front door to Rodney.

Rodney Hi.

Cassandra Why didn't you use your front-door key?

Rodney I dunno. It didn't seem right, somehow.

Cassandra Come in.

They kiss. As they do so we see that Rodney is wearing one of the tack-on ponytails. Rodney follows Cassandra into the living room.

At every opportunity Rodney tries to let Cassandra see his ponytail, believing this will impress her. But every time he attempts this she, for one reason or another, is looking in the opposite direction.

Cassandra Would you like a drink?

Rodney Nothing alcoholic. I've cleaned my act up.

Cassandra Good.

Rodney Coffee'll be fine.

Cassandra So how are things with the parents-to-be?

Rodney Oh, Nelson Mandela House is on amber alert. They're all just sitting there waiting for the second coming of the Prince of Darkness. I've said to Del you're gonna have trouble getting that kid shoes. Mothercare don't cater for cloven hooves.

Cassandra *(Laughs)* That poor baby!

Rodney Poor baby nothing. All the ancient prophesies are coming true. Satanic forces are gathering in the skies above Peckham, and Raquel's looking more like Mia Farrow by the day. You been up to anything exciting?

Cassandra Not really. I saw Stephen today.

Rodney Oh yeah!

Cassandra D'you remember Stephen? He used to work at my branch.

Rodney Yes.

Cassandra He's been moved up to head office.

Rodney Cosmic.

Cassandra You remember you used to call him a wally?

Rodney Yeah.

Cassandra I think you were right.

Rodney Was I?

Cassandra You'll never guess. He's only got one of those silly little ponytails *(Laughs)*

Rodney No? *(A weak little laugh)* What a wally!

From now on Rodney tries to stay in a position where Cassandra cannot see his ponytail.

Cassandra He looks like he's wearing a Davy Crockett hat! *(Laughs)*

Rodney laughs.

Rodney I thought they were all the fashion, though.

Cassandra Yeah, among lame-brains!

They laugh together. As Cassandra pours coffee, Rodney takes the opportunity and yanks the ponytail free, managing to pull a handful of real hair out in the process.

Rodney Aaugh!

Cassandra What's wrong?

Rodney Nothing!

Cassandra Are you OK?

Rodney Yeah, fine.

Cassandra turns to milk jug. Rodney throws the ponytail away.

Rodney It was a nice Sunday, wasn't it? Well, apart from the row we had in the maze.

Cassandra Yeah. I was right, though, wasn't I? My way was the quickest.

Rodney I don't think so. I looked at the map of the maze when I got home and I found… Yeah, I suppose it was. Sorry. Is that what you wanted to see me about? To discuss the quickest way out of Hampton Court maze?

Cassandra No. I wanted to discuss us and what's happening to us. Mummy and Daddy – well, Mummy really – insisted that I saw our solicitor for advice.

Rodney It's getting that heavy, is it?

Cassandra No, it's not getting heavy – it was just for advice, that's all.

Rodney And what did your solicitor advise? Take the git for every penny he's got, I suppose? Don't expect a cheque from me, Cassandra. If you want half my estate I could put it on a postal order.

Cassandra He didn't say anything like that. He advised us to talk.

Rodney Talk? But that's what causes the rows!

Cassandra That's what I said. But he advised us to try and find out why we argue every time we speak.

Rodney And what did you tell him? It was my fault?

Cassandra No, I didn't. I said we were both to blame. He asked whether we'd con-sidered adding to our numbers – something to concentrate both our attentions.

Rodney What – a baby?

Cassandra No, a dog. I don't think a baby would be a good career move.

Rodney Yeah, but I don't like dogs. Well, I don't mind 'em, it's just that when I was a kid I got bit by a Jack Russell. And a sausage dog, and this kind of half-poodle thing. Dogs just bite me – it's an instinct. A cat?

Cassandra No. I'm allergic to cats. They bring me out in a rash.

Rodney How about a parrot?

Cassandra No, they take so much looking after.

Rodney Yeah. A gerbil?

Cassandra No. I can't stand furry little

Three Men, a Woman and a Baby

things that run around. They make me go all funny.

Rodney So we're looking for something that don't take too much to look after, don't run around a lot and don't bring you out in a rash?

Cassandra Yes.

Rodney What about a tin of salmon?

Cassandra Oh don't get sarcastic, Roddy.

Rodney No, we could give it a name – Rex or something. Book it into the vets for its injection. Put a bit of string round it and take it for a walk every evening. Wouldn't take a lot of training, would it? We just threaten it with a tin-opener.

Cassandra You see what I mean? We tried to talk and you've just gone ridiculous again!

Rodney Because you put an obstacle in front of every good idea!

Cassandra I would have been perfectly happy with a dog but, just because you've been bitten three or four times, you dismissed my wishes.

Rodney Alright, we'll get a dog! Let's get a Doberman. Let the sod tear me limbs off and drink me blood! I don't care as long as it make you happy.

Cassandra At this moment in time that would make me ecstatic, Roddy!

Rodney Right, then…

Cassandra (*Under her breath*)… I'm going down the Nag's Head.

Rodney I'm going down the Nag's He…! Cass, we really should try harder to make this thing work. If not for us then for our tin of salmon.

Cassandra (*A tiny smile*) I'll phone you.

Rodney Yeah…

Rodney moves to the front door. As Cassandra is about to clear up some of the cups and things she spots the ponytail in a dark spot close to the skirting board. Cassandra screams. Rodney rushes back into room

Rodney What's wrong?

Cassandra Down there – by the chair. It's a mouse!

Rodney You sure? How'd a mouse get in here?

Cassandra How the hell should I know! Get rid of it!

Rodney Eh? Yeah, alright. Stay cool.
Rodney moves tentatively towards the creature then realises it is his ponytail.

Rodney No, that's not a mouse!

Cassandra What is it, then?

Rodney It's a… (*He senses what a great opportunity fate has presented him with*)… it's a rat!

Cassandra (*Screams*)

Rodney Sshush, sshush! You'll frighten it!…

Cassandra Get it out, Roddy, please!

Rodney OK. You don't wanna keep it as a pet?

Cassandra Get it out!
Rodney moves towards the 'rat'.

Cassandra Do you want a broom to hit it with?

Rodney No, it's OK, Cassandra. I've got my hand.
Rodney moves in for the kill. He stamps down hard on the rat and then goes into a Tarzan-type struggle.

Rodney He's a strong 'un. (*He now looks towards Cassandra with an 'is she still believing this rubbish' look*) He's struggling! Are you sure you don't want him as a pet? Cassandra screams.*

Rodney It's alright.
Holding the ponytail with both hands, Rodney moves to front door. He returns empty-handed.

Rodney I threw it out the landing window, I think I killed it.

Cassandra (*Throwing her arms around Rodney*) Oh Roddy!
Rodney embraces her.

Rodney It's alright, I'm here.

Rodney smiles to himself.

INT. THE TROTTERS' LOUNGE. NIGHT.

Del is seated at the table. He has one of the wigs on a large china dog and is brushing it. Raquel is stretched out on the settee watching TV. Albert is in an armchair, also watching TV. We now see Raquel hold her stomach as she feels a twinge. She checks her watch as if timing the contractions. We cut away to Del. As he brings the brush away from the wig we see a handful of hair stuck in the brush.

Del I don't believe it! Me wig's going bald! This is gonna call for a bit of creative sales-manship. I'll have to say it's the Bruce Willis look.

Albert During the war...

Raquel *(Another and stronger twinge)* Del, I think we better go.

Del Yeah, so do I. Goodnight, Unc.

Raquel Not to bed! To the hospital. It's started.

Del *(Calmly)* Are you sure?

Raquel Yes, I've been timing the contrac-tions. We'd better go.

Albert *(Horrified)* The baby's on its way? *(Starting to panic)* Well, do something, Del! Don't just sit there!

Del Oi, calm down!

Albert What are we gonna do? Phone someone! There's a baby on its way!

Del *(Grabs hold of him)* Listen to me! In my bedroom there's a leather-look flight bag containing Raquel's hospital things. Go and get it and take it downstairs to my Capri Ghia.

Albert Righto, Del. I'll go and get it. What's it look like?

Del It looks a bit like a fridge! It's a bag, innit, you old div!

Albert Aye, aye, Del. Leave it to me.
Albert exits to the bedroom.

Del *(To Raquel)* Nice and calm, that's what they showed us in the hospital. Albert, hurry up! *(He picks up the phone).*

INT. CASSANDRA'S BEDROOM. NIGHT

The room is in darkness, Cassandra in bed asleep. The bedside phone rings. Cassandra slowly wakes and answers phone.

Cassandra *(On phone)* Hello?

INTER CUT: TROTTERS' LOUNGE/CASSANDRA'S BEDROOM

Cassandra What d'you want, Del? It's 11.30!

Del I'm sorry to wake you, sweetheart, but I'm trying to find Rodney.

Cassandra He was here earlier, but he left about an hour ago. What's wrong?

Del Raquel's about to give birth to our baby.

Cassandra Have the labour pains started?
Rodney appears and signals emphatically 'I am not here'.

Del Yes.

Cassandra You'll phone me as soon as the baby's born, won't you?

Del Yes, 'course I will, sweetheart. I wanted Rodney to be there. Listen, I'll give you a bell as soon as I've got some news. Bonjour. *(To Raquel)* Here you are sweet-heart, take your coat.

Cassandra Give Raquel my love and tell her I'll be in to see her.

Del Yes, I will. And you give Rodney a nudge and tell him to get his arse down the hospital.

Cassandra Alright, Del.
She switches phone off.

Cassandra Del wants you with him!

Rodney That's ridiculous! I've never heard of the uncle being at the birth before!

Cassandra He doesn't want you in the delivery room! Just at the hospital with him!

Three Men, a Woman and a Baby

Rodney You don't know him like I do! He'll have me holding her leg up in the air or something.

Cassandra I'll get your clothes.

She climbs out of bed.

Rodney Oh Cass! I'm comfy here!

Cassandra Here's your trousers.

Rodney *(Looking from the window)* Oh God, it's a full moon! Son of Del is being born on a full moon! I knew it! I bloody knew it! A couple of hours from now you won't be able to sleep for the sound of howling.

Cassandra Oh don't be so silly! Where are the keys to the van?

Rodney Where's me crucifix? That's what I want to know.

Rodney turns the lamp on.
Cassandra feels in Rodney's jacket pockets for the keys and discovers the ponytail.

Cassandra Oh look, Roddy, it's that 'rat' you killed earlier! Doesn't it look like a clip-on ponytail when you get close up?

Rodney Ah no, listen, I never said it was a rat!

Cassandra You liar!

Rodney I said it looked like a rat! And it did, didn't it? I mean, you though it was a mouse!

Cassandra Where'd you get it from?

Rodney I was gonna wear it as a joke. It must have fallen out of me pocket.

Cassandra I could report you to the police. You took advantage of me – twice!

Rodney I know. If the case does to court, would you say three times?

Cassandra *(She picks up something to hit him with)* You're lucky you're on your way to hospital – it'll save the ambulance a journey.

Rodney Now, come on, Cass, pack it in. I've got a brother about to give birth!

HOSPITAL DELIVERY ROOM

Raquel is in labour. Del is bending over her.

Del Alright, sweetheart, the nurse has gone to get the delivery team. You've had your enema. Everything's going according to plan.

Raquel You're gonna stay here, aren't you, Del? Don't go running off and leave me.

Del I'm not going anywhere, sweetheart. I'm staying here with you.

HOSPITAL CORRIDOR

Rodney and Albert are sitting in the corridor outside the delivery room. A group of hospital staff enter the corridor.

Albert Are these the specialists?

Rodney No, they've just come back from a fancy-dress party. Of course they're the specialists.

DELIVERY ROOM

Del Are you alright?

Raquel Yes.

Del Good.

Knock at the door

Del Who is it – friend or enema? *(Tries to make Raquel laugh)* Friend or enema?

Raquel Shut up, Del.

Del Yeah, shut up, Del. It's alright, darling. I'll see who it is. You stay there, alright?

Opens the door to Albert.

Albert The specialists are on the way, Del Boy.

Del Thanks, Unc. You go and sit down, go on.

A sister and nurse enter, followed by a male midwife.

Excuse me, excuse me, John. We're having a baby in here.

Midwife I know, that's why I'm here.

Del What are you, a pervert or something?

Sister That's Mr McCullum. He's the midwife.

Del He's a bloke.

Midwife I'm a trained midwife. Now, please get out of my way.

Raquel Just let him do his job, Del.

Del No, he's a bloke.

Raquel I don't care if he's a trained chimp! Get out of his way.

Del Alright, alright, but you just watch it, OK? *(To Raquel)* Calm down, calm down. Remember your blood pressure.

Midwife How are you feeling, Raquel?

Raquel Not too bad at the moment.

Midwife Have you timed the contractions?

Sister Three minutes.

Del Is that good?

Midwife Yes, that's good.

Del Cushty.

Midwife Would you set the monitor up?

Sister Nurse, the gas and air.

Del *(Indicates foetal heart monitor)* What's that thing for?

Sister It monitors the baby's heartbeat.

Del Oh, Lovely Jubbly.

HOSPITAL CORRIDOR

Rodney It's going to be a boy. I know it is.

Albert Can't be sure of anything, son.

Rodney No, it's a boy. Mars and something else have come into conjunction and decided he would be born in Peckham.

Del enters the corridor from the delivery room.

Del They've got the baby's heartbeat. Half an hour's time we'll have the bestest knees-up our family's ever known.

Albert Is everything alright, Del?

Del Everything's absolutely fine. The baby's fine. Raquel's fine. In 48 hours' time we'll be going back to the flat with another addition to the Trotter family.

Rodney Oi, Del. Have they said anything about the sex?

Del Oh give her time, Rodney.

Rodney No, I mean…

DELIVERY ROOM

Raquel is now in advanced labour and in considerable pain.

Raquel How much longer is he going to take?

Del It's alright, sweetheart, alright. He'll take as long as he needs to take. He wants to make sure he gets everything just right, 'cos he's a perfectionist, like his dad.

Raquel I'm talking about the midwife.

Del Oh I see. Oi, you, pal, how much longer is this gonna take?

Midwife Nature will run its course, Mr Trotter. When baby's ready to put in an appearance, he'll let us know.

Raquel screams

Del Go on, give it everything you got, girl.

Raquel Don't you ever come near me again, Trotter.

Del There's no need to be like that, sweetheart. *(To the sister)* I suppose they're all like this, are they?

Sister No.

Del I'll get the gas and air.

Midwife bends down over Raquel and loses his wig.

Del looks down and sees the wig. He thinks it's the baby coming.

Raquel, Raquel, I can see his head. He's got a full head of hair.

Midwife reacts and grabs his wig. Attempts to replace it.

Midwife Some bloody spiv. *(Embarrassed, he removes the wig)* I'll scrub up.

The clock is showing 3.40am.

HOSPITAL CORRIDOR

Albert sits in the corridor while Rodney is pacing up and down. They react as they hear Raquel scream.

DELIVERY ROOM

Raquel is in the late stages of labour. Del is holding her leg.

Three Men, a Woman and a Baby

Raquel screams.

Del Come on, girl, give it some welly.

Sister Shouldn't be too long, Raquel. The contractions are becoming more frequent.

Raquel I know… I'm the one having the contractions. Would you let go of my leg, Del?!

Del Alright, sweetheart. Would you like some gas and air.

Raquel No thank you.

Del OK. *(Del takes a breath of the gas and air)* It's good stuff, this. Better not tell Rodney about it.

Raquel Oh no, here's another one.

Midwife Push hard, there's a good girl.

Raquel Del, can I hold your hand?

Del Yes, yes, of course you can, sweetheart, go on.

Sister Push.

Del OK, Raquel, steady on.

HOSPITAL CORRIDOR

Albert and Rodney listen worriedly to Raquel's screams and react surprised as they hear Del cry out.

DELIVERY ROOM

As Raquel continues to scream, she violently squeezes Del's hand.

Del Aaaaaargh!

The pain subsides and she releases his hand.

Raquel Oh, did that hurt, Del?

Del Yes, it did a bit, sweetheart.

Raquel Now you know what it's bloody well like!

Del This giving birth ain't all it's cracked up to be, is it?

Del takes more gas and air.

Midwife Breathe easily, Raquel.

Del Oh, it's his head, Raquel. I can see its head.

Midwife That's very good. The head's in position. It shouldn't be long.

Del I can see its head, Raquel, I can see…

Del exits to the corridor.

HOSPITAL CORRIDOR

Del Rodney, I can see its head!

Rodney Is it… you know, normal?

Del Normal? What do you mean, normal? Of course it's normal. I mean it's just a head.

Rodney There aren't any sort of numbers on it?

Del Numbers? What are you talking about, Rodney? What do you think this is, a bloody raffle?

Raquel screams. Del exits to the delivery room.

DELIVERY ROOM

Del That's it, Raquel.

Midwife There we are. The head's out. Relax now. Just relax for a minute.

Del Raquel, it's his face. He's got a little nose. He's got little ears.

Sister One more push.

HOSPITAL CORRIDOR

Albert and Rodney listen to Raquel's screams. They then react to a baby's cry.

Albert Well, that's it then. It's all over.

Rodney Well, that's me off then.

Albert Don't you want to see the baby?

Rodney No, I'm not fussed. I can see it tomorrow, can't I?

Albert Del won't like it if you go. It's important to him that you stay here, Rodney.

Rodney Yeah.

DELIVERY ROOM. RAQUEL IS HOLDING THE BABY.

Del It's a baby, Raquel.

Raquel I've been wondering what that swelling was.

Del We've got ourselves a lovely little baby.

Raquel I know. I love you.

Del I love you too, sweetheart.

Del exits to the corridor.

HOSPITAL CORRIDOR

Del We've done it! We've only bloody done it!

Albert Congratulations, son.

Del It's a little baby, Rodney.

Rodney Is it a boy or a girl?

Del Eh? Oh, hang on.

He exits to the delivery room.

DELIVERY ROOM

Del Is it a boy or a girl?

Raquel lowers babys blanket and shows Del.

Del It's a boy. I'll tell you what, he won't be frightened to get changed in the showers.

Del exits to the corridor.

HOSPITAL CORRIDOR

Del It's a boy.

Rodney reacts with a look of horror.

DELIVERY ROOM

Sister Well, Mr Trotter, if he keeps you awake at night, don't bring him back to us.

Del No thanks, sister. He can keep me awake as long as he likes. Thanks, doc.

Midwife My pleasure, and sorry about this. *(Indicates wig)*

Del That's alright. Here, listen. If you like I can get you a real good 'un. They normally retail at a hundred quid up West – to you, nothing.

Midwife No, really. I don't think I'll bother any more. Congratulations.

Del Thanks very much.

Raquel He's gorgeous. Look at that little face.

Del You want to look down there. He's got no worries.

Raquel If you say so, Del.

Sister enters from the corridor.

Sister I'll bet you wouldn't say no to a cup of tea?

Del Yeah, not half. Would you like one love?

Raquel Yes please.

Del Would you get Raquel one an' all? Alright, sweetheart?

Sister exits.

I'll get Rodney and Albert. *(Goes to the door)* Rodney, Albert, come on, come on. *(Looks to Raquel)* Here, cover yourself up, sweetheart. You might catch cold.

Rodney and Albert enter from the corridor

Here, give him to me, sweetheart. *(Takes the baby)* Come on, then. Rodney, Albert, let me introduce you to Damien.

Rodney is horrified.

Albert He's a little cracker, ain't he?

Del Yeah.

Rodney He's got your eyes, Del.

Del Yeah. You ought to see him down there. *(To baby)* Come on, you, come with me a minute.

Takes the baby to the window and opens the blind. He looks outside into the night sky.

There you are, Mum. I know you can see us. There he is, look, your first grandchild.

Raquel And last.

Del And last. Oh, you are such a lovely little boy, you really are. You've got a mummy and daddy who think you're the most precious thing in the whole wide world. You've got a lovely family around you. Yes, you have, look. You've got your Uncle Rodney to play with. Great-Uncle Albert. He'll tell you about all the places in the world he's been to – and sunk. And there's me. And you're gonna have all the things your daddy couldn't afford. 'Cos I've been a bit of a dreamer, you know. Yeah, I have. You know I wanted to do things, be someone, but I never had what it took. But you're different, you're gonna do all the things I always wanted to do and you're gonna come back and tell me about them. Tell me if they're as good as I thought they

Three Men, a Woman and a Baby

would be. You're gonna have such fun. You are, and when you get the hump, 'cos you're bound to get the hump sometimes, I'll muck about and make you laugh. 'Cos I've mucked about all my life, and I never knew the reason why until now. This is what it's all about. I was born for this moment. Yes. Oh we're gonna have such fun, we are, you mark my words. This time next year we'll be millionaires.

Cast List

Dora ★ Joan Geary

Knock Knock ★ Howard Goorney

Mechanic ★ Herb Johnson

Ollie ★ Tony London

Midwife ★ Ken Drury

Sister ★ Constance Lamb

Man in church ★ James Richardson

Tom the security officer ★ John Bardon

Mr Peterson ★ Max Harvey

Lennox ★ Vas Blackwood

Woman in kiosk ★ Jeanne Mockford

Checkout girl ★ Catherine Clarke

Lisa ★ Gerry Cowper

Andy ★ Mark Colleano

Pianist ★ Fred Tomlinson

Singer ★ Joan Baxter

Drummer ★ Derek Price

Stuntman/Double for Del ★ Ken Barker

Stuntman ★ Graham Walker

xvii

Cast List

Tony Driscoll ★ Christopher Ryan

Alan Parry ★ Denis Lill

Pamela Parry ★ Wanda Ventham

Jeff Stevenson ★ Himself

Registrar ★ Derek Benfield

Bronco ★ Ron Aldridge

Henry ★ Gordon Warnecke

Stewardess ★ Lucy Hancock

Newsreader ★ Richard Whitmore

Baby Tyler ★ Elliot Russell

Man in the pub ★ Ian Barritt

Trudy ★ Helen Blizard

Jules ★ Paul Opacic

Adrian ★ Ian Redford

First woman ★ Lyn Langridge

Eric ★ Trevor Byfield

Eugene ★ Roger Blake

Tony Angelino ★ Philip Pope

Roy Slater ★ Jim Broadbent

Cast List

Chinese takeaway owner ★ Takashi Kawahara

TV presenter ★ David Warwick

Clayton ★ Tommy Buson

Arnie ★ Phillip McGough

Otto ★ Mick Oliver

Grayson ★ Peter Rutherford

Mario ★ Frank Coda

Woman in crowd ★ Marie Lorraine

Steven ★ Sam Howard

Gary ★ Steve Fortune

Mr Perkins ★ Michael Fenton Stevens

Carmen ★ Gina Bellman

Trudy ★ Lusha Kellgren

Nerys ★ Andree Bernard

Elsie Partridge ★ Constance Chapman

Dr Shaheed ★ Josephine Welcome

Dr Meadows ★ Ewan Stuart

Nurse ★ Ann Bryson

Danny Driscoll ★ Roy Marsden

CAST LIST

Derek Trotter ★ David Jason

Rodney Trotter ★ Nicholas Lyndhurst

Uncle Albert ★ Buster Merryfield

Raquel Slater ★ Tessa Peake-Jones

Denzil ★ Paul Barber

Trigger ★ Roger Lloyd-Pack

Boycie ★ John Challis

Marlene ★ Sue Holderness

Cassandra Parry ★ Gwyneth Strong

Mickey Pearce ★ Patrick Murray

Jevon ★ Steven Woodcock

Mike Fisher ★ Kenneth McDonald

Emma ★ Francesca Brill

Marsha ★ Laura Jackson

Dale ★ Diana Katis

Snobby girl ★ Hazel McBride

Girl in Disco ★ Tracey Clarke

Barman ★ William Thomas

Adrian ★ Michael Shallard

One of my favourites -
all of us at Cassandra and Rodney's flat.

That's my boy!
The apple of my eye -
Damien.

The old sea dog imself —
Albert pictured on his Birthday in 1988.

Me, Raquel and Damie
(at 18 months).
Don't we make a
 happy family!

My dear old Grandad.
Pictured outside Nelson Mandela House.
Bless him.

My bruv—he may be
a plonker sometimes
but he's really a
diamond.

Rodney + Cassie's happyday . I'm not sure about that shirt of mine though!

Photo Album

attended the Arthur Murray School of Dance. *Qualifications:* 100 yards swimming certificate (later returned to its rightful owner). *Occupation:* Company director, MD of Trotter's Independent Traders (TITCO) plc, chairman of Trotter Watch (Security) Ltd (defunct), Trotter's Ethnic Tours Ltd (dissolved), chief executive of Trotter's International Stairs Agency (under investigation). *Significant other:* Rachel (Raquel) Turner. *Dependents:* Damian Derek. *Clubs:* The One-Eleven Club, The Down By The Riverside Club, The Shamrock Club (membership lapsed). *Country address:* Trotter Towers, Minstead, Surrey. *Town address:* 368 Nelson Mandela House, Nyerere Estate, Peckham.

TROTTER, Edward Kitchener (Grandad) (dec.) *Born:* 9.7.1909 at 10 Peabody Buildings, Peckham Rye. *Died:* 23.2.85. *Education:* Home tutelage. *Qualifications:* None. *Occupations:* Formerly lamplighter, trainee chef at south London Nose and Throat Hospital, part-time painter and decorator, self-employed gun-runner during the Spanish Civil War (deported from Spain 1936), gave up career to become veteran unemployed. *Military Service:* Served in 1st Battalion Pioneer Regiment (1940-1941) (deserted). *Clubs:* The Lamplight Club, Greek Street (expelled 1937).

TROTTER, Joan Mavis Trotter (née Hollins) (dec.) *Born:* 10.4.1920 at The Duke of Wellington public house, Old Kent Road, London. *Died:* 12.3.1964. *Education:* Peckham Junior School, The Emma Hamilton Senior School for Girls, Deptford. *Qualifications:* Diplomas in home economics, needlecraft and metalwork. *Married:* Reginald Arthur Trotter at The Lady of The Divine Rosary on 15.5.1948. *Dependents:* Two sons, Derek and Rodney. *Hobbies:* Big Band Music. *Clubs:* Charlton Athletic Fan Club.

TROTTER, Reginald Arthur *Born:* 12.5.1920 at Duke of Essex Maternity Hospital, Romford. *Education:* Unknown. *Qualifications:* Unknown. *Occupation:* Itinerant labourer, later brief spell as hospital porter at Newcastle Infirmary. *Married:* Widower, Joan Mavis (dec.) *Dependents:* Two sons, Derek and Rodney. *Home address:* Unknown.

TROTTER, Rodney Charlton *Born:* 26.2.1960 at 368 Anthony Eden House (Now Nelson Mandela House), The Bevin Estate (now Nyerere Estate) Peckham. *Education:* Peckham Primary, Martin Luther King Comprehensive, Peckham, Basingstoke College of Art and Design (expelled after one year for marijuana offence). The Peckham Adult Education Centre - Business and Commercial Studies department. *Qualifications:* GCEs in Maths and Art, DIC (Diploma in Computerisation). *Occupation:* Financial director of Trotters Independent Traders (TITCO) plc. *Previous occupation:* Nocturnal security officer with Trotter Watch Ltd, computer section manager at Parry Print Ltd. Winner of the MegaFlakes art competition (under 15 section). *Married:* Cassandra Parry on 12.2.1989. *Dependents:* None (but watch this space!) *Clubs:* The Groovy Gang (lapsed). *Home Address:* 7 George's Court, Bridge View, London E1.

Hobbies: Interest in uniforms!

TULSER, Denzil *Born:* 8.8.1948 at Princess Margaret Maternity Unit, Liverpool. *Education:* The Penny Lane Infants School, Liverpool, Dockside Secondary Modern, Peckham. *Qualifications:* 3 GCEs. *Occupation:* Self-employed driver. Runs Peckham Parcels (formerly Transworld Express). *Married:* Corinne Jameson at Peckham Register Office 5.5.1982. *Divorced:* 1991. *Clubs:* The One-Eleven Club. *Home address:* 107 Hillrise Road, Balham.

TURNER, James *Born:* 12.6.1933 at Winifred Turner Hospital, Plymouth. *Education:* Nelson Primary, Plymouth, Hardiman Grammar, Plymouth. *Qualifications:* 1 School Certificate, 1 Higher Certificate. *Occupation:* Lt-Cdr in Royal Navy 1953-1965. Now runs Turner Antiques. *Married:* Audrey Rose on 7.6.1955 at St Mary's Church, Chipping Norton, Gloucestershire. *Dependents:* 1 daughter, Rachel. *Home address:* 10 Queen's Terrace, Chipping Norton.

TURNER, Rachel (Raquel) *Born:* 4.6.1957 at Hammersmith Maternity Hospital, London. *Education:* Chiswick Primary School, the West London Grammar School. *Qualifications:* 5 O Levels, 1 A Level (Drama). *Occupation:* Actress/Entertainer. Member of singing duo 'Double Cream', flower seller in *My Fair Lady* (US tour), lizard in *Doctor Who* (BBC TV), exotic entertainer for the Peckham Strip-o-Gram Co, Raquel in 'Raquel and Tony' (singing duo). *Married:* Roy Slater (divorced). *Significant other:* Derek Trotter. *Dependents:* Damian. *Home address:* Trotter Towers, Minstead, Surrey. *Town address:* 368 Nelson Mandela House, Nyerere Estate, Peckham.

Hospital, Croydon, Surrey. *Education:* City of Birmingham Boys School, Cardiff College of Technology. *Qualifications:* 6 O levels, 1 A level (Geography), diploma in Travel and Tourism. *Occupation:* Travel agent. Proprietor: Alex Travel, 31B High Street, Peckham. *Married:* Claire. *Dependents:* Anne and Emma. *Clubs:* Union Jack Club, Marbella, Association of Independent Travel Agents, RAC. *Home address:* 8 Sunview Rise, Battersea. *Other address:* Los Harrando, nr. Marbella, Spain.

SLATER, Roy William *Born:* 15.5.1948 at St George Hospital, Fulham, London. *Education:* Arthur Murray School, Lewisham, Dockside Secondary Modern. *Qualifications:* 10 CSEs. *Occupation:* Unemployed. *Former occupation:* Detective chief inspector with the Metropolitan Police. Former undertaker's assistant in Colchester. Arrested own father for having a defective rear light. Sacked by Metropolitan Police following his jailing for fraud and corruption in 1986. *Criminal Record:* 12 cases of Fraud, 17 cases of corruption. *Sentence:* Five years in jail. Loss of police pension. *Married:* Rachel Turner in 1977 (divorced). *Dependents:* None. *Clubs:* None. *Home address:* I'd rather not.

SNELL, June May *Born:* 3.7.1950 at St Mary's Hospital, Wapping, London. *Education:* Wapping Pier Junior School for Girls, Dockside Secondary Modern. *Qualifications:* 'I would have received many passes and degrees but I was taken suddenly and unexpectedly pregnant at a young age.' *Occupation:* Mother and home-builder. *Married:* Separated. 'He was very unreliable and don't think he was the father of one of my children.' *Dependents:* 1 daughter Debby, 1 son, Jason. *Clubs:* 'Only the pudding club! No, I shouldn't laugh.' *Home address:* 265 Zimbabwe House, Nyerere Estate, Peckham.

STOCK, Sandra Ann *Born:* 17.12.1960 at St Mary's Hospital, Portsmouth. *Education:* Manor Court Primary School, Portsmouth, Headley School for Girls, Northwood. *Qualifications:* 8 O levels, 3 A levels. *Occupation:* Police officer. Formerly beat officer in south London, now attached to south London Area Drugs Squad. Rank: Detective inspector. *Married:* Detective Sergeant Ross Lewis on 17.3.1986. *Clubs:* Battersea Badminton Club. *Home address:* Not disclosed.

TROTTER, Albert Gladstone (aka Boomerang Trotter) *Born:* 19.11.1920 at 77 Tobacco Road,

Wapping. *Education:* Thomas Pound School, Peckham. *Occupation:* Seaman. Joined SS Princetown as junior stoker 1936. Transfer to Royal Navy in 1937. Posted to HMS Orange (sunk 1940), HMS Finch (sunk 1941), HMS Angel (sunk 1942), HMS Jerome (sunk 1942), HMS Flash (sunk 1943), HMS Lock (sunk 1943), HMS Devon (sunk 1944). Joined elite Marine parachute unit and transferred to HMS Shepherd (shore base – bombed 1944). Post-war joined merchant navy. *Medals:* King's Bravery Medal, World War Two medal, 7 good conduct medals. Nicknamed 'the ferret' after falling down pub cellars – Victory Inn, Portsmouth (1946), Coach and Horses, Crossed Keys Off-Licence, Gravesend (1949), Peckham Rye (1951), Thatched Inn, Canning Town (1953), Brunswick Club, New Cross (1955). *Married:* Ada (deceased) *Clubs:* British Legion, Peckham Over 60s. *Hobbies:* Piano. *Country address:* Trotter Towers, Minstead, Surrey. *Town address:* 368 Nelson Mandela House, Nyerere Estate, Peckham.

TROTTER, Cassandra Louise *Born:* 16.6.1966 at St George's Maternity Hospital, Blackheath. *Education:* Nelsmith School for Girls, London and West London College of Further Education, Peckham Adult Education Centre - Business and Commercial Studies department. *Qualifications:* 8 O levels, 3 A levels. Joined UK National Bank plc in 1985 as trainee. Selected for fast-track promotion scheme in 1987. Seconded to Overseas Investment Division in 1989. Transferred to Peckham Branch as Head of Small Business Section in 1992. *Clubs:* UK National Bank plc Sports and Social, Peckham Badminton. *Married:* Rodney Trotter on 12.2.1989. *Dependents:* None. *Home address:* 7 George's Court, Bridge View, London E1.

TROTTER, Damian Derek *Born:* 3.2.1991 at Whittingham Hospital, Peckham, London. *Education:* The Bernie Grant Memorial Primary, Peckham. *Occupation:* Student. *Qualifications:* Head prefect (Relieved of post after incident with dinner-lady's bike.) *Country address:* Trotter Towers, Minstead, Surrey. *Town address:* 368 Nelson Mandela House, Nyerere Estate, Peckham.

TROTTER, Derek Edward (Del) *Born:* 12.7.1948 at St Mary's Hospital, Deptford, London. *Education:* The Terminus Infant School, New Cross, London, The Peckham Primary, Peckham, London, Dockside Secondary Modern. Later

School for Boys, Newbury, Warwick University Business School. *Qualifications:* 12 O levels, 4 A levels, BA (Hons) in Financial Management. *Occupation:* Banker. Assistant Head of Overseas Investment Bureau with UK National Bank plc. *Married:* Joanne. *Dependents:* None. *Clubs:* Wapping Gym and Spa, Central London Baseball. *Home address:* Top Floor Flat, Ridley House, Jameson Street, Wapping E1.

exactly!

PHILLIPS, Beverley Joanne *Born:* 3.5.1955 at 14 Curlew Road, Chipping Ongar, London. *Education:* Mountbatten Primary School, Pinner, Murrayvale Comprehensive, Pinner, Highlands Technical College, Northwood. *Qualifications:* 4 O levels, Teeline shorthand, Pitman typing, City and Guilds in Medical Administration (Credit). *Occupation:* Formerly dental receptionist at Peckham Health Centre, Now retired. Divorced (1984). *Dependents:* 1 son, Peter. *Home address:* Presently residing at The Long Meadows High Security Rest Home, Esher, Surrey.

RIDGEMERE, Lord Peter CBE *Born:* 10.10.1915 at Ridgemere House, Ridgemere, Berkshire. *Education:* Maidenhead Preparatory School For Boys, Eton College, Sandhurst Military Academy. *Qualifications:* 1 School Certificate, 1 Higher Certificate. Commissioned 1st Berkshire Light Infantry in 1933. Promoted to Captain, Royal Engineers in 1938, Promoted to Major, Royal Engineers in 1942. Mentioned in Dispatches for action in France 1940. Awarded King's Medal for Gallantry, 1944. Attached to GCHQ in 1944. Director: National Northminster Bank (1950 onwards). Chairman: Foundation for Anglo-Dutch Friendship. Deputy Lord Lieutenant of Berkshire (1964). *Married:* Alice Northam, now Lady Ridgemere. *Dependents:* Charles, Erica. *Clubs:* Army and Navy. *Home address:* Ridgemere House, Ridgemere, Berkshire.

ROBERTSON, Sidney Eric *Born:* 12.4.1933 at Westminster General Hospital, Westminster, London. *School:* Woolwich Primary, Woolwich Secondary. *Qualifications:* Woodwork Certificate. *Occupation:* Chef. Proprietor: Sid's Café, 101 South Street, Peckham – burgers, bacon and tea: a house speciality. *Criminal record:* Unintentional attempted poisoning (1965), running an unhygienic eating house (1976) running an unhygienic eating house (1979), running an unhygienic eating house (1982). *Married:* Freda. *Dependents:* 1 daughter, Sally. *Clubs:* The Bar-B-Q Line Dancing Club, Sydenham, London. *Home address:* Above the café, 101 South Street, Peckham.

RUTTER, Arnold (Arnie) *Born:* 10.3.1939 at John Goodwin Hospital, Crawley. *Education:* Fryatt Preparatory School for Boys, Crawley Grammar School. *Qualifications:* 6 O levels, 2 A levels. *Occupation:* Jeweller. *Criminal record:* Fraud 1975, 1982. *Married:* Patsy. *Dependents:* Two sons, Gary and Steven. *Clubs:* Master Jewellers' Federation. *Home address:* Casa Petit Fleur, Nueva Andulucia, Costa Del Sol, Espana.

ST JAMES, Jevon. *Born:* 4.1.1966 at Jean Hutchings Hospital, Bracknell, Berkshire. *Education:* Binfield Primary School, Bracknell Comprehensive School. *Qualifications:* 8 O levels. *Occupation:* Property developer/businessman. Owner: St James' Properties. *Married:* 'I'm married to my ambition, my mistress is the dream. I suppose mere mortals like you wouldn't understand that.' *Dependents:* 'To most of the women I have met I am their reason for living. Sometimes it weighs heavy, but, hey, what's a boy to do?' *Clubs:* Zoom, Ritzy, Hammersmith Palais and the WH Smith Book Club 'coz I'm not just beautiful.' *Home address:* 12 Garden Mansions, Streatham.

SALE, Heather Mary *Born:* 13.4.1955 at Chiswick Maternity Home, Chiswick. *Education:* Chiswick Primary School, Egham Girl's School. *Qualifications:* 3 O Levels. *Occupation:* Housewife. *Married:* Victor Graham Sale on 5.5.1977. *Dependents:* 1 son, Darren. *Home address:* 13 Goven Way, Bitterne, Southampton.

SCHUTZ, Anna Eva *Born:* 18.7.1965 in Dusseldorf, Germany. *Education:* Reinhard School for Girls, Dusseldorf. *Qualifications:* 7 Higher Grades. *Occupation:* Au Pair. *Married:* Klaus Eichlemann. *Dependents:* 1 son, Eric (from previous relationship with Spencer Wainwright). *Home address:* 129 Bitte Strasse, Dusseldorf, Germany.

O'SHAUGHNESSY, Brendan Patrick *Born:* 12.7.1950 at Shamrock Terrace, Cork, Ireland. *Education:* St Mary's School for Boys, Cork. *Qualifications:* None. *Occupation:* Painter and decorator. *Clubs:* The Shamrock, London Hurling. *Home address:* 123 Gatcombe House, Kensal Road, White City.

Phil the floot

SIM, Alex John *Born:* 4.5.1952 at Croydon District

MARSHAM-HAYLE, Lady Victoria *Born:* 6.6.1962 at Covington House, Upper Stansmere, Berkshire. *Education:* Roedean, Gstaad Ladies College, Switzerland, Milan School of Art, Sorbonne. *Qualifications:* 10 O levels, 3 A levels, degree in Fine Art. *Occupation:* Art dealer. Proprietor: Gallery Claude, 198 King Street, Chelsea. *Married:* Hon. Charles Pigdon on July 8th 1988. *Dependents:* 1 son, William, 2 daughters Hannah and Isabella. *Home address:* Glover House, 12 Queen's Terrace, Kensington.

MEADOWS, Dr Robbie *Born:* 3.4.1955 at King George Hospital, Edinburgh. *Education:* William Grey School for Boys, Edinburgh, Queen's College Medical School, London. *Qualifications:* 11 O levels, 4 A levels, degree in Medicine, PhD in Medicine. *Occupation:* Doctor. *Current Job:* Consultant at Peckham General Hospital. *Clubs:* Peckham General Sports and Social Club. *Partner:* Dr Cathy Cook. *Dependents:* 1 son, David. *Home address:* 12 The Mews, Bakerstone Street, Clapham.

MILLS, Kenneth (Jumbo) *Born:* 2.5.1946 at St Mary's Hospital, Peckham, London. *Education:* Summers Primary, Lewisham, Dockside Secondary Modern. *Qualifications:* Two CSEs. Ran Eels on Wheels with Del Boy. Emigrated to Australia in 1967. Now runs Mills and Co Office Cleaners Pty. Ltd. and Mills Automotivation Pty. Ltd. *Married:* Patricia. *Dependents:* Rochelle and Mike. *Home address:* Penthouse Flat, 12 Ashton Street, The Rocks, Sydney, NSW, Australia.

O'KEITH, Father Patrick *Born:* 12.5.1920 at the Sacred Heart Convent for Fallen Women, Castletown, Co. Wicklow, Ireland. *Education:* Castletown School For Boys, Trinity College, Dublin. *Qualifications:* 7 grade passes, degree in Theology. *Occupation:* Formerly priest at The Lady of The Divine Rosary, Peckham Rye, London. At present serving 6 years imprisonment for possessing 10 Kalashnikov night-scopes and 16 Armalite shells. *Clubs:* The C Wing and Prayer Club, HMP Pentonville. *Home address:* HMP Pentonville.

PARRY, Alan Peter *Born:* 17.3.1948 at St Mary's Hospital, Peckham. *Education:* Battersea Primary School, Thameside Secondary Modern School. *Qualifications:* 7 CSEs. *Occupation:* Company director. Began career as apprentice machine operator at Clark's Printing Works, Balham. Left to form own company in 1976. Now runs Parry Print Limited. *Married:* Pamela. *Dependents:* 1 daughter. Cassandra. *Clubs:* Blackheath Tennis. *Home address:* 10 Grove Road, Blackheath.

PARTRIDGE, Elsie (nee Fodgen) *Born:* 19.3.1918 at St Jude's Hospital, Clerkenwell. *Education:* Clerkenwell Junior School, Peckham Senior School for Girls. *Qualifications:* None. *Occupation:* Former housewife, now retired but maintains her interest in communicating with the afterworld and holds regular séances. *Widow:* Formerly married to William Partridge (deceased). *Present significant other:* Albert Trotter. *Dependents:* Arthur, Cedric, Bernard, Ann, Phyllis, John-John, Maria, Barry, Julia, Richard, Averil. *Clubs:* The British Association of Mediums, The Peckham Senior Citizens Fun Club. *Home address:* 12 Nelson Mandela House, Nyerere Estate, Peckham.

PEARCE, Michael (Mickey) *Born:* 4.5.1961 at 12 Golden Lane, Peckham. *Education:* Peckham Junior School, Balham, The Martin Luther King Comprehensive School, Peckham (formerly The Dockside Secondary Modern). *Qualifications:* None. Disqualified form sitting GCE exams after stealing the answers from the headmaster's desk. *Occupation:* Formerly managing director – Pearce and Trotter Enterprises (defunct). Erstwhile film director; projects include 'Night Nurse' and 'Patsy Does Peckham' for which he received much acclaim and a twelve month suspended sentence. *Current occupation:* Sales executive for Sun Sola Windows. 'I am a lone wolf.' *Dependents:* 'I wouldn't be surprised.' *Clubs:* The Down By The Riverside Club, Deptford, The Peek-A-Boo Club, Kings Cross. *Home address:* Flat 57, Mahattma Gandhi House, Nyerere Estate, Peckham.

PETERSON, Nigel Harold *Born:* 12.6.1950 at The Beeches, Little Chalfont, Buckinghamshire. *Education:* Chalfont St Giles Primary School, Adrian Hodge School, Watford. *Qualifications:* 9 O levels, 4 A levels. *Occupation:* Supermarket manager with Topbuy Superstore, High Street, Peckham. *Married:* Valerie (separated). *Clubs:* Kingston Golf Club, Peckham Bridge Society, The National Trust, London Ornithological Society. *Home address:* The Oakhouse, Common Road, Esher, Surrey.

POUND, Stephen Christopher *Born:* 10.10.1964 at Broad Oak Farm, Hungerford, Berkshire. *Education:* Hungerford Primary School, Kings

Infants School, Dockside Secondary Modern, Peckham, London (expelled). *Qualifications:* O level Biology, City and Guilds in Synthetics. *Occupation:* Dealer in adult exotic materials and publications. Owner of Climax adult shop, Brecon Street, Peckham (licence revoked – now defunct). *Married:* Maureen – now divorced. *Dependents:* None (at least none that will own up). *Home address:* Not known, emigrated recently to Bangkok

LANE, Brian (Bronco) *Born:* 17.6.1952 at Francis Hospital, Dartford, Kent. *Education:* John Sherwin Memorial School, Dartford. *Qualifications:* Lost in post. *Occupation:* Painter and decorator. *Hobbies:* Stealing stupid things. *Married:* Sandra. *Dependents:* 1 daughter, Kylie. *Home address:* Suite 5, Hotel Schubert, Runway Lane, Gatwick, Sussex.

LOMBARDI, Louis *Born:* 16.4.1921 in Milan, Italy. *School:* Manotti School, Milan. *Qualifications:* None. Prisoner of war in Britain (1943-1945). Moved to London 1946. Proprietor of Lombardi Pers, 45 High Street, Peckham. *Married:* Mary. *Dependents:* Boncetti; Giuseppe and Giovanni. *Clubs:* Peckham Working Men's Club, Peckham Bowls Club. *Home address:* 45 High Street, Peckham.

MACKAY, Irene Mary *Born:* 6.8.1945 at Braintree Maternity Hospital, Essex. *Education:* Ditton Primary School, Braintree, Chamberlain Secondary Modern, Braintree. *Qualifications:* None. *Occupation:* Housewife. *Married:* Tommy Mackay. *Dependents:* Marcus. *Home address:* 16 Biko House, Nyerere Estate, Peckham.

MACKAY, Thomas William (Tommy) *Born:* 5.12.1940 at St Phillip's Hospital, Birmingham. *Education:* Sheridan Primary School, Edgebaston. The Waverley Detention Centre, West Yorkshire. *Qualifications:* 5 A Levels, Degree in Economics, Doctorate in ᵃent Roman History (all later discovered to have been stolen from Bamber Gascoigne's flat). *Criminal record:* Wounding with intent (6 months suspended), GBH (9 months), attempted murder (12 months), armed robbery (12 months), refusing to pay Poll Tax (3 years). *Married:* Irene (separated). *Dependents:* 1 son, Marcus. *Clubs:* 'Yes, and baseball bats and pick-axe handles.' *Home address:* HMP Parkhurst, Isle of Wight.

MACKENZIE, Margaret *Born:* 4.3.1953 at Hammersmith Infirmary, London. *Education:* Chelsea School for Girls, Kingston Polytechnic. London School of Dance, Knightsbridge. *Qualifications:* 10 O levels, 3 A levels, degree in Public Administration. *Occupation:* Housing and welfare officer, Peckham Borough Council. *Clubs:* Chiswick Ladies Badminton Team, Hammersmith Salsa. *Home address:* 1a Beak Street, Streatham.

MAGUIRE, Michael (Mental Mickey) *Born:* 31.12.1960 behind the changing rooms at the Tooting Bec outdoor swimming lido. *Education:* The Peckham Junior School, transferred to The Herbert Lom Primary School for the Severely Disturbed, Bodmin, Cornwall. *Qualifications:* Awarded 'The Boy Most Likely to Succeed' Diploma at the Rampton Hospital for the Criminally Insane (1977). *Hobbies:* Leading member of the Trotskyite Anarchist Party (now defunct). Lead singer with A Bunch of Wallies (popular band) who had a hit record in 1985 with 'Boys Will Be Boys'. Arrested for Breach of the Peace 1978, 1979, 1982 (twice), 1983, 1984. Charged with common assault for throwing an egg at prime minster Margaret Thatcher – charge dropped. Sent for psychiatric reports in 1990 after being found naked in Selfridges' Christmas grotto. *Occupation:* (From 1992) freelance advertising copywriter. From 1995, chairman and chief executive: Maguire, Maggarity, Perkins and Jackson Advertising Agency. *Clients include:* The BBC, The International Tobacco Corporation, Australian Airlines and The Liberal Party. *Clubs:* Soho House, Tramp, The Royal and Ancient. *Married:* Hon. Sophie Walker-Parkinson. *Dependents:* Camilla and Che. *Home address:* c/o MMPJ plc, 18 Gordon Square, London W1.

MARSHAM-HAYLE, Sir Henry (14th Duke of Malebury) *Born:* 12.7.1935 at Covington House, Upper Stansmere, Berkshire. *Education:* Eton College, Cambridge University. *Qualifications:* 8 CSEs, 3 A levels, degree in Politics, Philosophy and Economics. Served in 1st Battalion Berkshire Regiment from 1956 to 1973. Rank on leaving: Colonel. *Married:* Jane William-Smythe (dec.) on May 4th 1960. She died in a skiing accident on October 13th 1974. *Dependents:* 1 daughter, Victoria Anne (Lady Victoria). *Clubs:* Army and Navy, Berkshire Hunt. *Home address:* Covington House, Upper Stansmere, Berkshire.

Stallard Road, Chelsea. (Ceased trading January 1984 after woodworm infestation.) *Clubs:* Valerie's, All England Lawn Tennis, Confederation of British Antique Dealers. *Home address:* 166 Kings Terrace, Chelsea. *Country Residence:* Monet House, Henley-on-Thames, Buckinghamshire.

DRISCOLL, Anthony Gary *Born:* 7.2.1953 at Kennington Underground Station. *Education:* Peckham Primary, The Clement Attlee Secondary Modern, Woolwich, Ashford Juvenile Remand Prison. *Qualifications:* None: 'The school burnt down the night before I took me eleven-plus.' *Criminal record:* 'Are you into life support machines?' *Occupation:* 'I sell insurance.' *Married:* Candy – 'She disappeared some years back.' *Dependents:* 'Me brother.' *Clubs:* 'Who's bin talking?' *Home address:* Kray Hall, Kingswood Lane, Purley.

DRISCOLL, Daniel Erroll *Born:* 6.4.1948 at HMP Holloway, London. *Education:* Peckham Primary, The Clement Attlee Secondary Modern, Woolwich, Ashford Juvenile Remand Prison, Sydenham Borstal for Boys, Reigate Detention Centre. *Qualifications:* Middleweight Boxing Champion (1963) Maidstone Young Offenders Home. *Occupation:* 'I sell insurance.' Single. *Dependents:* 'Me brother.' *Criminal Record:* Six months for burning down the Clement Attlee Secondary Modern School, Woolwich, June 1964. *Clubs:* 'I have interests in quite a few.' *Home address:* Kray Hall, Kingswood Lane, Purley.

FISHER, Michael David *Born:* 12.12.1950 at 106 Kitchener Road, Acton, London. *Education:* The Austin Green Junior School, Acton, The Appleton Grammar School, Acton. *Qualifications:* Five GCEs, City and Guilds in Public House Management (Pass), City and Guilds in Catering (Fail). Occupation: Landlord, The Nag's Head Public House, Peckham High Road. *Married:* Susan (separated). *Clubs:* 'I've got a pub to run! I've only got one pair of hands!' *Home address:* The Nag's Head, Peckham High Road, London.

GILBEY, Lennox *Born:* 17.1.1966 at St Mary's Catholic Hospital, Peckham. *Education:* Thameside Primary, Battersea, The Martin Luther King Comprehensive (formerly Dockside Secondary Modern). *Qualifications:* 1 O Level in Business Studies and Organisation ('I couldn't fit the rest in'). *Occupation:* Head of Security at Topbuy Superstore, 32 High Street, Peckham Rye. 'Too busy.' *Clubs:* 'Yeah, every weekend.' *Home Address:* 17 Cutler Road, Peckham.

GRIFFITHS, RAYMOND (The Great Raymondo) *Born:* 11.2.1949 at Davies Goode Hospital, Bristol. *Education:* The Arthur Weeks School for Boys, Bath, Shelagh Laughton Drama Academy, Swindon. *Qualifications:* 6 O levels, 1 A Level, Diploma in Stage Management. *Occupation:* Professional Magician. Runner-Up in Act of the Month, Butlins, Rhyl (1976), Bronze medal for Effort, Whitstable Magic Festival (1982). *Agency:* 'A close friend, Jason, looks after my career.' *Dependents:* Mother, Ida, and cat, Tiggy Moo. *Home address:* c/o Jason Paris, 'Hair Today Salon', Paradise Street, Bradford.

HABIBI, Abdul *Born:* 12.4.1951, Cairo, Egypt. *Education:* Alahram School, Cairo. *Occupation:* Jeweller. Owner of 'Forever Diamonds', Hatton Garden, London. *Married:* Fatima, Nishma and Cheryl. *Dependents:* Vashti, Mohammed, Hossny, Iman, Ghazi, Hussein, Ikbar, Ahmed, Ali, Sayed, Bimal, Chentelle and Marty. *Clubs:* Stringfellows, Annabelles and Pussy Galore. *Home address:* 15 Colligan Avenue, Southfields, London.

HARRIS, Pauline *Born:* 19.11.1954 at Grange Hospital, Ruislip, Middlesex. *Education:* Ruislip Primary School, Gordon Hayes Memorial School. *Qualifications:* Six CSEs. *Occupation:* Former air stewardess. *Married:* 1. Bobby Finch of Peckham (dec.) 2. Mervyn Baker of San Francisco (dec.) 3. William Jones of Texas (dec.) Once engaged to Del Trotter. *Clubs:* British Airways Executive Gold; Easyjet Frequent Flyers; The Spa, Chelsea; Paradise, New York. *Home address:* 12 Tower View, 17 East 33rd Street, Chelsea, New York.

HOSKINS, Terrance Winston *Born:* 30.9.1958 at St Albans Maternity Home, St Albans, Hertfordshire. *Education:* Chorleywood Primary School, Rickmansworth Comprehensive. *Qualifications:* 6 O levels. *Occupation:* Police officer. Began career with Metropolitan Police in 1978. PC attached to Peckham Police station. Promoted to detective sergeant in 1985. Promoted to inspector 1990. *Married:* Jenny. *Dependents:* Robert, Geoffrey and Martin. *Clubs:* West Ham Supporters Club. *Home address:* Not disclosed.

JOHNSON, Barry *Born:* 15.3.1950 at Gravesend Maternity Hospital, Kent. *Education:* Dover

(handwritten margin note, left:) ...s ...tuy is ...it ...tered ...wn – ...st like ...ke's ...eer!

(handwritten margin note, right:) she'll get caught one day

ANGELINO, Anthony *Born:* 1.4.1956 at Eden Hospital, Essex. *Education:* Hornchurch Primary, McMillan Comprehensive. *Qualifications:* O Level music. Single. *Hobbies:* Singing. Formerly Tony in 'Raquel and Tony' (singing duo). *Occupation:* Dustcart operative, charity work for 'The Peckham Senior Citizens Fun Club'. singer/compere on the 'Those Were The Days' Roadshow. *Clubs:* The Englebert Humperdink Fan Club. *Home address:* 56 Wilson Road, Catford, London.

ATTWELL, Solomon (Solly) *Born:* 16.4.1935 at 152 Elisha Street, Bethnal Green, London. *Education:* Bethnal Green Junior School, The Shepherds Bush School For Boys, University of Essex. *Qualifications:* 8 CSEs, 4 A levels, BA in Law. *Occupation:* Solicitor. *Business address:* Attwell, Attwell and Attwell, 67 High Street, Peckham (above Gino's Fish Bar). Investigated by the Law Society in 1976, 1980, 1981, 1992. (Nothing proven.) *Married:* Ruth. *Dependents:* Rebecca, Nat and Lionel. *Clubs:* Kingston Golf Club, Esher Grand Lodge. *Home address:* Ivy House, Windle Lane, Kingston-upon-Thames, Surrey.

BALL, Colin (Trigger) *Born:* 22.4.1948 in the back seat of a burnt out Vauxhall Wyvern abandoned on Figgs Marsh, Mitcham, Surrey. *Education:* The Ernest Bevin Junior School, Deptford (May 1953), the LCC Home for Children with Learning Difficulties (June 1953), Dockside Secondary Modern. *Qualifications:* Cycling Proficiency Diploma (Grade 3) February 10th 1960. *Criminal Record:* Three months detention for being found in possession of a stolen bicycle, February 10th 1960. Found guilty of theft of 3000 Green Shield stamps, August 1964. Received one year correctional training and an electric blanket. Extremely single. *Clubs:* The Nag's Head Christmas Club. *Home Address:* Flat B, 16 Mugabe Road, Peckham (next to Blockbusters).

BOYCE, Aubrey Terrance *Born:* 31.1.1948 at Queen Victoria Hospital, Woolwich. *Education:* London Bridge Infants School, Woolwich Junior School, Dockside Secondary Modern, Peckham Technical College (expelled). *Qualifications:* Six CSE (two grade 1), 1 A level (Maths). *Hobbies:* Breeding tropical fish. *Occupation:* Company Director. *Owner:* Boyce Automobiles and Car Hire (Peckham) Ltd, Boyce Luxi Cars plc, Boyce Bargain Basement Motors Ltd, The Happy Punter Car Corner, Tulse Hill. *Married:* Marlene. *Dependents:* One son, Tyler. *Clubs:* The One-Eleven Club, Peckham Rye, St Martin's Lodge, Hammersmith, RAC Club. *Home address:* Dundeling, 12 Kings Avenue, Streatham. *Country Residence:* Maraub Cottage, Tregower, Cornwall.

CHAMBERS, Edward (Ready Eddie) *Born:* 19.7.1952 at St Margaret's Hospital, Blackheath. *Education:* Churchill Primary School, Blackheath, Wilmslow Secondary Modern School, Blackheath. *Qualifications:* 3 O levels. *Current occupation:* Club owner. Formerly landlord: The Golden Lion, Croydon. *Owner:* The Mardi Gras Club, Margate, The Scream, Clacton. *Married:* Tracey. *Dependants:* Luke, Hans and Leia. *Clubs:* Margate Golf and Squash Club, Mercedes Owners Club. *Home address:* Tower View, Margate, Kent.

CHINN, Benny *Born:* 12.6.1929 at King George Hospital, Hong Kong (Now Mao Tse Tung People's Health Centre). *Education:* The Princess Alice School, Kowloon (Now the Ho Chi Min Education Facility) *Qualifications:* CSE in Cookery (Grade 3) *Occupation:* Restaurateur. *Owner:* The Golden Lotus Chinese Restaurant, 11 High Street, Peckham. *Married:* Su Lin. *Dependents:* Alexander, Gregory, Xiao Ping. *Clubs:* Peckham and Deptford Anglo-Chinese Club. *Home address:* 11 High Street, Peckham.

CLARKE, Thomas *Born:* 1.5.1922 at St Thomas' Hospital, London. *Education:* Clapham Primary School, Arthur Ruttle Secondary School, Battersea. *Qualifications:* City and Guilds in Woodwork and Metalwork. Joined Royal Logistics Corps 1938. Saw action in France, North Africa and Italy. Left Army 1961. Joined Wilson Engineers Ltd in 1962. Made redundant 1973. Security guard at Topbuy Superstore, 32 High Street, Peckham in 1975. Made head of security in 1980. *Retired:* November 1986. *Married:* Joan. *Dependents:* Peter, Angela and Daphne. *Clubs:* RLC Old Comrades Association, Bude Sea Anglers Club. *Home address:* 10 Seaview Road, Bude, Cornwall.

DAVENPORT, Miranda Sophia Jane *Born:* 17.4.1955 at Nicholson Maternity Home, Esher. *Education:* St Winifred's School for Girls, Kingston, Lycée de Sacre Bleu, Switzerland. *Qualifications:* 12 O levels, 3 A levels, Pitman typing and shorthand (Distinction). *Occupation:* Company director. *Owner:* Davenport Antiques.

[handwritten note:] Watch 'er, she'll try to Stitch you up like a turkey

[handwritten note:] Not much more than a shed!

PECKHAM'S
WHO'S WHO
2000

Published Annually since 1849